COPY 26

AMERICAN
Small Sailing Craft

AMERICAN
Small Sailing Craft

Their Design, Development, and Construction

By HOWARD I. CHAPELLE

W · W · NORTON & COMPANY

New York · London

W. W. Norton & Company, Inc., 500 Fifth Avenue, New York, N.Y. 10110
W. W. Norton & Company Ltd., 37 Great Russell Street, London WC1B 3NU

ISBN 0 393 03143 8

PRINTED IN THE UNITED STATES OF AMERICA
FOR THE PUBLISHERS BY THE VAIL-BALLOU PRESS
4567890

Contents

Foreword   xi

Introduction   3

1.   Colonial and Early American Boats   8

       The Sloop   18
       The Periagua   18
       The Shallop   20
       The Pinnace   22
       The Whaleboat   22
       The Cutter   24
       The Wherry   25
       The Yawl   27
       The Moses Boat   29
       The Punt and Flat   29
       The Bateau   33
       The Canoe   36
       The Centerboard   38
       Rigs   41

2.   The Scow and Bateau   45

       The Garvey   53
       The Pound-Net Scow   67
       The Scow Sloops   70
       Beach Punt   78
       The Bateaux   80

Dories 85
New Jersey Beach Skiff or Seabright Skiff 94
The River Yawl-Boats 97
The Flat-bottomed or "Flatiron" Skiff 100
The Sharpies 104
Shooting Punts or Skiffs 133

3.   The Shallops   136

The Hampton Boat 137
New England Boat and Isle of Shoals Boat 141
The Crotch Island Boat 145
The Square-sterned Hampton Boat 152
The Tancook Whaler 162
No Man's Land Boat 168
The Block Island Cowhorn 172
The Erie Boat 178
The Mackinaw Boat 180
The Huron Boat 184
The Delaware Sturgeon Skiff 185
Columbia River Salmon Boat 186

4.   The Skiff and Yawl-Boat   193

The Whitehall Boat 195
The Connecticut River Shad Boat or Drag Boat 200
The Delaware Gill-Net Skiff 203
Oars, Tholes, and Rowing 203
The South Jersey Beach Skiff 206
The Melon Seed 208
The Barnegat Sneak Box 209
The Delaware Ducker 216
The Peapod 217
The Yawl-Boat 222
Newfoundland Boats 223
The Bahama Dinghy 226

5.   Sloops and Catboats   232

The Bermuda Sloop 233
The Newport Boat 240
Providence River Boat 242

The Waterboats 244
The New York Sloop 244
The Noank Sloop 249
Eastern Catboat 252
Albemarle Sound Boat 257
The Eastport Pinkies 261
Muscongus Bay or Friendship Sloops 266

6. Foreigners and a Native   277

The Boston Hooker 278
The New Orleans Lugger 282
The San Francisco Dago Boat 286
Greek Sponging Boat 291
The Chesapeake Bay Log Canoes 291

7. The Newcomer, the V-bottom   305

The Flattie 309
Bay Skiffs 318
The Skipjack 323
Gulf Scow Schooners 332
Port Isabel Scow Sloops 334
The V-bottomed Garvey 336

8. On Building Boats   341

Tuning Up 343
Seaworthiness 345

Appendix   349

Index   357

Illustrations

(*Between pages 174 and 175*)

Port Isabel scow sloop
Tancook whaler
Scow sloop *Target*
New Haven oyster sharpies
Seine boats
Sailing dories and two-masted lobster boats
Eastport "pinky"
Cowhorn *Island Belle*
New Hampshire Hampton whaler
Albemarle Sound seine boat
San Francisco feluccas
Monhegan fishing boat

Plans and Perspectives

1.	System of the "whole molding"	12
2.	Ship of the line's longboat	19
3.	"Two-masted boat" type	21
4.	Man-of-war's pinnace	23
5.	Deal cutter	24
6.	Two wherries	26
7.	Ship's stern boat	27
8.	Skeg-built longboat	28
9.	Single moses boat	30
10.	Double moses boat	31
11.	Colonial punt	32

12.	Rowing punt	33
	Colonial bateau (perspective)	34
13.	Colonial bateau	35
14.	Birch canoe	37
15.	Whaleboat, first half of 19th century	42
16.	Whaleboat, 1850–70 type	43
	New Jersey sailing garvey (perspective)	58
17.	Old-style New Jersey garvey	61
18.	Small working garvey	62
19.	Single-sail garvey	63
20.	Garvey box	65
21.	Two-masted garvey	66
22.	Pound-net scow	69
23.	Small scow sloop	71
24.	Casco Bay fyke-net scow sloop	77
25.	West Indian beach punt	79
26.	Modern lumberman's bateau	82
27.	Small double-ended bateau	83
28.	Wisconsin lumberman's bateau	84
29.	Banks dory of the 1880's and 90's	88
30.	Modern Banks dory	89
31.	Cape Ann sailing dory	91
32.	Two-masted sailing dory	93
33.	New York Bay skiff	95
34.	Ohio River yawl	98
35.	Mississippi yawl	99
36.	Cape Cod oystering skiff	101
37.	Maryland double-ended skiff	103
38.	One-man tonging sharpie of 1870's	106
39.	One-man New Haven sharpie	109
40.	New Haven sharpie, 35-foot class	111
41.	New Haven sharpie, 1900	115
	Old-type one-man sharpie (perspective)	117
42.	New Haven racing sharpie of 1880's	119
43.	Last type of racing sharpie	120
44.	North Carolina sharpie	123
45.	Florida sharpie, 1894	125
46.	Sharpie schooner, Juan de Fuca Straits	127
47.	Ohio pound-net boat	129
48.	Rig of Ohio pound-net boat	130
49.	Piscataqua River gunning skiff	134

50.	Hampton whaler	143
51.	Isle of Shoals boat, *Alice*	144
52.	Isle of Shoals boat, 1890's	146–147
53.	Crotch Island pinky	148
54.	Extreme Crotch Island pinky	151
55.	Matinicus Island boat	153
56.	Lines of half-model, New England boat	154
57.	Casco Bay Hampton boat	156–157
58.	Kingston lobster boat, 1885	159
59.	Kingston lobster boat, 1893	161
	Tancook whaler (perspective)	163
60.	Tancook whaler	164–165
61.	Sail plan, Tancook whaler	167
62.	Vineyard Sound boat	169
63.	No Man's Land boat	171
64.	Block Island boat	175
	Mackinaw boat (perspective)	177
65.	Erie boat	179
66.	Lake Huron Mackinaw boat	181
67.	Mackinaw boat, Lake Michigan	183
68.	Lap-strake Huron boat	184
69.	Delaware River sturgeon skiff	187
70.	Columbia River gill-net boat	189
71.	Rig of Columbia River boat	190
72.	New York Whitehall boat	197
73.	Sailing Whitehall boat	199
74.	Connecticut River drag boat	201
75.	Long Island Sound drag boat	202
76.	Delaware River gill-net boat	205
77.	South Jersey beach skiff	207
78.	New Jersey "melon seed"	209
	Sneak box (perspective)	210
79.	Barnegat sneak box, 1880	213
80.	Arc-bottom sneak box	215
81.	Delaware ducker	216
82.	Peapod, 1911	218
83.	Sailing peapod	219
84.	Old sailing peapod	220
85.	Large sailing peapod	221
86.	Yawl-boat	223
87.	Newfoundland skiff	224

88. Newfoundland boat 225
89. Bahama dinghy 227
90. Bermuda sloop 235
91. Bermuda sloop of 1885 239
92. Newport boat 241
93. Providence River boat 243
94. New York Bay sloop 247
95. Noank sloop 251
96. Eastern catboat 253
    Albemarle Sound boat (perspective) 257
97. Albemarle Sound boat 259
98. Quoddy sloop 263
99. Muscongus Bay sloop 267
    Centerboard Muscongus Bay sloop (perspective) 268
100. Friendship sloop—lines 271
101. Friendship sloop—scantlings 273
102. Friendship sloop—rig 275
103. Boston Irish cutter 279
104. New Orleans lugger 283
105. San Francisco Dago boat 287
106. San Francisco felucca 289
    Frisco felucca (perspective) 290
107. Poquoson log canoe 299
108. Nanticoke log canoe 301
109. Chesapeake Bay racing log canoe *Jay Dee* 303
110. Long Island skipjack 307
111. Martha's Vineyard skipjack 308
112. Chesapeake flattie 311
113. Eastern Shore stick-up skiff 314
114. Chesapeake Bay skiff 319
115. Modified sharpie skiff 320
    Bateau *Messenger* (perspective) 323
116. Skipjack *Messenger* 325
117. Sail plan, *Messenger* 327
118. Sinepuxent skiff 330
119. Chincoteague skiff 331
120. Gulf Coast scow schooner 333
121. Texas scow sloop 335
122. V-bottomed garvey sloop 337

Foreword

MY RESEARCH into the field of American commercial sailing boats has been carried on intermittently over a period of nearly twenty-five years. It began, about 1924, as a self-educational project to explore the "art" of small-boat design, on which there had been little published. As time passed and more and more material was found, the beauty, distinction, and practical good qualities of many types became apparent, and the matter became one of greater personal interest. A number of persons were found who had similar interests, sometimes confined to a single type of boat, who were generous enough to aid in the search for material. Many made direct contributions in time, notes, and even plans which were often of very great value, since boat types were even then disappearing so rapidly that it would have been impossible to obtain information alone and unaided. Any value that this study may have must be credited to a very great degree to those who have contributed to the material presented here. Among the most active contributors were

Mr. Charles Baltzer	Commander George Cunha, U.S.N.
Mr. George Stadel, Jr.	Mr. Wilbur Morse
Mr. Paule Loring	Mr. J. P. Shaw
Mr. Randolph Stevens	Mr. Vernon D. Tate
Mr. Frank A. Taylor	Mr. Paul J. Barry
Mr. Wayne B. Yarnall	Mr. Henry Rusk
Mr. F. L. Petch	Mr. D. F. Taylor
Mr. Alfred S. Brownell	Mr. Frederic Fenger

Mr. Herbert L. Stone   The late Ralph M. Munroe
Mr. Carl C. Cutler   The late W. P. Stephens
Mr. Earle Geohagen   The late Charleton Smith
The late Larry Huntington   The late Lincoln Colcord
                 The late Lewis H. Story

Some material on particular types of American commercial small craft has been published, particularly in yachting and sporting papers and books. A little material has also appeared in marine research journals in recent years, but the bulk of the historical information on small-boat types must be sifted from publications dealing with the fisheries and yachting. The piecing together of technical information, particularly on rigging details, has required use of contemporary photographs and models: the former have come from the collection of the old Fish Commission or from private individuals; the models from the Watercraft Collection in the United States National Museum.

The following publications and books have been of particular value:

Yachting, New York City.

Rudder, New York City.

Forest & Stream, New York City.

Maine Coast Fisherman, Portland, Me.

The American Neptune, Salem, Mass.

Le Yacht, Paris, France.

The Field, London, England.

The Mariners' Mirror, London, England.

Small Yachts, C. P. Kunhardt (new and enlarged edition, 1891), Forest and Stream Publishing Company, New York City.

A Manual of Yacht and Boat Sailing, Dixon Kemp (4th edition, 1884; 8th edition, 1895), Horace Cox, "Field" Office, London, England.

Architectura Navalis, F. R. Chapman, Stockholm, 1768.

Naval Expositor, T. R. Blanckley, 1750.

Of Plimmoth Plantation, William Bradford, Massachusetts Historical Society, Boston, Mass., 1912.

The Catalog of the Watercraft Collection, Carl W. Mitman, United States National Museum, Washington, D.C., 1923.

The History of New England, John Winthrop, 1853.

Skeps Byggerij eller Adelig Öfnings Tionde Tom, Äke Classon Rålamb, Stockholm, 1691.

Report on the Shipbuilding Industry of the United States, Henry Hall, Special Agent, 10th Census, Washington, D.C., 1883.

The Fishing Industries of the United States, G. Brown Goode & Associates, Washington, D.C., 1887.

Report upon the Participation of the United States in the International Fisheries Exhibition, Bergen, Norway, 1898, Joseph W. Collins, Washington, D.C., 1899.

The Fore and Aft Rig in America, E. P. Morris, New Haven, Connecticut, 1927.

Schepen Die Verdwijnen, P.J.V.M. Sopers, Amsterdam, Holland (1942?).

These books are referred to in the text by the author's names, as are a few others not listed here.

Public and private institutions in the United States and abroad have been highly valuable sources of information and their staffs have been of the greatest assistance. Material of great value has been obtained from the following:

United States National Museum, Smithsonian Institution, Division of Engineering & Industry, Washington, D.C.

The Mariners' Museum, Newport News, Va.

Peabody Museum, Salem, Mass.

Mystic Marine Museum, Mystic, Conn.

Congressional Library, Washington, D.C.

National Archives, Washington, D.C.

The Franklin Institute, Philadelphia, Pa.

New York Public Library, New York City.

Newburyport Historical Society, Newburyport, Mass.

Searsport Marine Museum, Searsport, Me.

Portsmouth Athenaeum, Portsmouth, N.H.

Maryland Historical Society, Baltimore, Md.

New York Yacht Club, New York City.

The National Maritime Museum, Greenwich, London, England.

The Science Museum, London, England.

Ministry of Marine, Paris, France.

Nederlandsch Historisch Scheepvaart Museum, Amsterdam, Netherlands.

The published work of the late Martin C. Erismann, an American naval architect who began a study of American small craft early in this century (which was brought to an end by his untimely death), has served as a useful guide, not only to material but also to the standards of research that should be followed in the study of old sailing craft.

Valuable material, in the form of boat plans and drawings made in the eighteenth and nineteenth centuries, was obtained from the "Hillhouse Collection" in the possession of the Hill Shipyard in Bristol, England, through the courtesy of Mr. John Hill. Some plan material was obtained from the Fish Commission papers, now in private hands and in the National Archives.

The chapter on early American small craft of the colonial period was made possible by the generosity of the Simon Guggenheim Memorial Foundation, which permitted study of the small-craft plans in the Admiralty Collection of Draughts, now in the National Maritime Museum, London. With respect to this, the unstinted aid of the museum staff should also be particularly acknowledged.

The staff of the Division of Engineering and Industry, Smithsonian Institution, United States National Museum, Washington, D.C., also deserve special acknowledgment, for they have been patient and helpful over a very long period and have furnished extremely valuable material.

Mention should also be made of the work of Mr. Allen Beechel, who made the interesting perspective drawings for this book.

Howard I. Chapelle

AMERICAN
Small Sailing Craft

Introduction

IN THE present-day search for small sailing craft, low in cost and easily maintained, the once numerous types of small working boats formerly employed in the longshore fisheries should be considered. In the days of sail, particularly in the last half of the nineteenth century, about two hundred distinct types and subtypes of small boats were in use in North America. Each had been developed to work in its home waters and weather conditions and to meet the physical requirements of its employment. Most of these small sailing craft are now gone: their value in commercial work was destroyed when sail was replaced by low-cost gasoline engines in work-boats. A few types became extinct earlier, owing to exhaustion of local fishing grounds, changes in fishing gear, or construction of harbor facilities (as at Block Island, where the building of an artificial harbor caused the beach boats to go out of use). In any case, types once numerous are now represented by a few rotting and abandoned hulks, by dusty half-models lying forgotten in a boatshop loft, or by a few sketches in a sailmaker's plan book. Some types, indeed, have left no record behind them other than a few casual references in newspapers and correspondence that show only that they once existed.

The small sailing work-boat did not disappear because it was impractical, slow, or leewardly, or because it was not strong, lasting, or seaworthy. The work-boats were developed by trial and error over a rather long period to meet the requirements of their

3

use, within the limitations of low cost and the available materials. It must be remembered that a work-boat is not left on her moorings when it blows, rains, or snows, but must get out and help the owner earn his living. These considerations are what make the sailing work-boat worth examination by all boat sailors at a time when the standardization of our yachts has produced so many misfits for the conditions of local use and when "yachting standards" in construction, finish, rig, and fittings are rapidly becoming too expensive for the majority of small-boat sailormen.

The usual solution of the small-boat sailor's problems has been to offer him mass-produced craft, but this has resulted in even narrower standardization in hull and rig and more misfits for local conditions and individual needs. Even this means has not accomplished as low a cost as might be expected, because the expense of distribution, sales, and advertising often exceeds the cost of manufacture.

As opposed to the mass-production boat, the idea of employing the cheap work-boat appears both practical and attractive: by use of work-boat types the owner can obtain a boat suited to his home waters and weather; he can have a distinctive boat, built in many cases by himself or with local aid and with available materials; and he can avoid the appearance of sameness that now afflicts our yachting fleets. But these advantages pale beside the economic one, for the work-boat types are not only relatively cheap to build, they are cheap to maintain. In spite of this, most of the work-boats were good sailers and as lasting as the average yacht—longer-lasting, in fact, than many stock boats. The acceptance of the work-boat type implies that you can get only what you pay for in a boat and that to "sail cheap" you must give up varnish for paint, mahogany for pine, bronze for galvanized iron, gadgets for simplicity, and luxury for plain living. What is left? A boat that is individualistic, that sails and performs well, and that does her job, costing no more than one can reasonably afford; that is all.

Owing to the limitations of the space available, all types of American small work-boats in the sail period cannot be shown and described. Some are omitted because of a lack of suitable technical information, some because they were too limited in their features, and others because they were too large. The size of the boat seemed an important consideration in view of the primary purpose of this book; the types presented here were selected with a view to possible amateur construction, and experience indicates that the largest hull an amateur should attempt is about 40 feet on deck. With this element of amateur construction to be considered, it is necessary to place emphasis on the easily built types.

The plans given here are attempts to reproduce accurately the original boat in all respects by scale drawings. Where the spars, sails, and rig were not available for measurements, they were drawn, as far as was possible, from information obtained from sailmakers, builders, and owners and, in some cases, from scaled photographs and models. Particular attention is given to construction and fittings, especially those that might be useful today. The drawings are usually sufficient to allow building, perhaps with the aid of some of the existing textbooks on boatbuilding. Construction details of at least one example of each type are given, and these can be utilized for other examples of the same type. The original rigs are shown in the same manner, and it is hoped that these will receive attention and will be tried out, for they are usually very simple and efficient. The highest achievement in design, construction, and fitting is to obtain efficient operation and retain simplicity; this is being forgotten in the construction of many boats today.

Modern standardization has had one unfortunate result that has not received much attention. Each section of the country has had its own boatbuilding methods and fancies. With the concentration of boatbuilding in a few areas, the methods of building once used elsewhere have been forgotten. Hence, many fallacies have arisen as to what really constitutes good boatbuilding practices, and have led to much unnecessary cost in construction. The truth is that "good boatbuilding" is no more than "good enough to do the job and last the required time," and has no particular relation to rabbeting, notching, or boxing in the framework. Just as practical methods of construction have been forgotten, so have some practical hull-forms been overlooked. The modern trend toward very limited hull-form selection is wholly unnecessary, and the over-emphasis on the "fair line by batten" that seems to afflict many modern designers is producing far too many spindle-shaped hulls. One of the important technical aspects of a study of the small sailing work-boats is that they show the wide range of hull-form that is possible and advantageous.

This book, it can be seen, is primarily a book of designs for the use of the amateur and professional boatbuilder, and is a reference book, perhaps, for the student designer. It is proper, therefore, to give a word of warning. The work-boat types shown are unities in hull and rig. They were thoroughly tested in the field of their operation by critical and competitive means. Therefore, the inexperienced designer, builder, or owner should hesitate to "improve" upon them until he has had actual experience with the original. The cure of an imaginary ill in one of these boats may be as unfortunate as taking a strong medicine before being sick—either may make you ill indeed. Attempts at improving local types by an inexperienced person may destroy any advantage they might have. Be sure you know what you are doing when you begin to improve the design of a boat.

The reports on the qualities of the types are based on personal experience in many cases; in others, the testimony of a number of owners has been obtained. The purpose is, of course, to explore the advantages of hulls and rigs that are now practically forgotten, and to discover the dangers too. Obviously, this is important, and it is to be regretted that facilities for the study of boat types in these respects are so limited at present. It is hoped that enough information is given to allow "tuning up" and adjustment for any type built.

If the reader becomes interested in any type of work-boat, he will undoubtedly desire to know something about its history and development. Unfortunately, the histories of American small-boat types are obscure: competent contemporary observers were not much interested in the "poor fishermen's boats" and there has been a great deal of distortion of facts in so-called local tradition. It is a characteristic of this field of maritime history that an apparently rational account can be made by use of local claims and traditions regarding an individual type or class of boat. But when a neighboring area is examined it becomes apparent that something is wrong. The two accounts plainly imply that each section had no relation with its neighbors so far as boatbuilding and design were concerned. This is so unreasonable that suspicion cannot be avoided, and the histories of many of the individual boat types must be accepted with skepticism.

The available information indicates that most of the small-boat types in North America were of comparatively recent origin, in spite of local claims to the contrary. This raises the questions of what boats were used in early times in America and what the backgrounds were for the later hulls and rigs. The following chapter is an attempt to describe the early boats, the state of progress in boat construction and design, and the classes used, from the early colonial period to, say, the first half of the nineteenth century when the distinctive types of local craft came into existence. The spread of rigs in early years requires attention, as there has been much speculation on this; final conclusions cannot yet be reached, but the apparent weakness of many theories can be suggested. If the representation is not as complete as can be desired, it must be remembered that a history of small craft is not the objective here; rather the emphasis is on the more practical matter of the usefulness of the small sailing work-boat of the past.

CHAPTER 1

Colonial AND Early American Boats

THE ENGLISH colonists, upon reaching the American shores early in the seventeenth century, found themselves without water transport in a wilderness where the only practical roads were the waterways. There were no boatbuilders among them and there were few who had any acquaintance with handling small boats. Their need for boats was immediate, however, and was met in some instances by retaining some of the boats of the ships that had brought them out. But the individual settler usually had to obtain a canoe from the nearby Indians by barter; and in time and with practice, he acquired enough skill to use the canoe alongshore and for travel on protected waters. Even with the retention of boats from the ships that entered the colonies, there were too few craft to meet the needs of the colonists, and the canoes were not suited for the transport of heavy goods that was rapidly becoming necessary. Almost every colony sent home to England for skilled boatbuilders and shipwrights within a year after the first arrivals had reached the new land.

With the arrival of boatbuilders from England, the construction of small boats for fishing and transportation began, to be followed by larger craft for alongshore voyaging, for exploring, or for off-shore fishing. A few still-larger vessels that were suitable for oversea communication were built when the need arose. In the early fishing settlements, as at Newfoundland and Monhegan Island, the boats had been brought over by the ships that brought the fishermen. There is no reason to believe that boats of a special or local design were as yet required; the early colonial records refer only to small craft of the ship's boat class—the shallop, pinnace, and skiff. The only local type mentioned was the "cannow."

The question of what these boats were, in hull and rig, has for a number of reasons been the despair of historians. The names of these boat types were never precise in meaning, and the name of one type was often applied to craft of widely varying characteristics. Many of the colonial writers were not at home in maritime nomenclature and they wrongly applied the names of types. When the name of a boat type was employed, the context seldom allowed a picture of the boat to be drawn. The records show that a "shallop" in one case might be a ship's boat, but in another a decked craft was obviously referred to; a "pinnace" might also be a boat in one reference, but elsewhere the name would be applied to a seagoing vessel. The late Professor E. P. Morris, in his well-known book, *The Fore and Aft Rig in America*, made a full report on the names of boat types in colonial records, so there is no need to re-examine these records for additional information.

It is possible, at least, to establish grounds for reasonable assumptions regarding these boats, in spite of the unsatisfactory colonial records. It should first be noted that the lack of preciseness in such names as "shallop" and "pinnace" is not confined to these isolated cases in maritime nomenclature. "Barge," as an example, may be a lighter, a long, narrow rowing boat, a ship's boat, a galley, or even a galley-ship—depending wholly upon the date of its usage and the context in which it stands. Similarly, "cutter" may be a ship's boat, a sailing vessel of specific rig, a revenue vessel, or a hull-form once used in racing yachts. "Sloop" may be a vessel of specific rig, a ship's boat, a sailing man-of-war of a specific rate, or a small modern war vessel. "Galley" could be a rowing and sailing craft, which might range in size from a ship's boat upward to a full-rigged ship. Unfortunately, the old marine dictionaries were not contemporary with the colonial records; their definitions of boat types are often obscure and unapplicable to early seventeenth-century usages.

Since all authorities are in agreement that a large part of the names of boat types in colonial records applies to craft of the ship's boat class, an effort must be made to find out what these probably were in hull and in rig. It is apparent that the colonial records offer little information and are at best no more than a catalogue of the names used in early American nautical language. Shipping is represented in many seventeenth-century pictures, but the types of boats and vessels shown are never identified. There are a few textbooks on naval architecture, beginning late in the seventeenth century, and a few boat plans, dated from 1690 on, exist in European museums. These establish the fact that the shallop, a large open boat for shipboard use, was called "chaloup" by the French, "sloep" by the Dutch, and "slup" by the Swedes. It is also readily established that "shallop," as a name for this style of boat, was gradually replaced by the names "longboat" and "launch" in the eighteenth century. But diligent search has not yet produced a small-boat plan or an identified small-boat picture of a date earlier than 1688.

This may not be so great a handicap in visualizing what a shallop was, say in 1630, as it may seem. A Swedish shipbuilding book, *Skeps Byggerij eller Adelig Öfnings Tionde Tom*, written by Åke Classon Rålamb and published at Stockholm in 1691, was reprinted in facsimile by the Sjohistoriska Museet in 1943. This book shows plans not only of an English wherry and barge, but also of a "slup" and of three double-ended ships' boats, one of which is also called a "slup." But of even greater importance, the book contains plates showing the hand tools used then by boat and ship carpenters, sailmakers, draftsmen, and gunners. There is, in addition, a plate showing shipyard methods.

This last plate is very important, for it shows that boats were then built on stocks, on which the keel was erected, with stem and stern or transom in place. In addition, five complete molds are shown. This style of setup is just what is used today, some two hundred and sixty years later than Rålamb's book! The tools and equipment shown in the plates are not far different from the hand tools of today; though cruder in design, the old tools would nevertheless be effective. The plate showing Rålamb's tools was recently inspected by a 64-year-old New England boatbuilder, who readily identified all but one of the tools and remarked that he had seen or used some tools just like a few of those shown.

The inference that might be drawn from this evidence is that, tools and boatbuilding methods having changed so little in more than two and a half centuries since 1691, it is probable that these tools and methods existed before 1600. Thus, Rålamb's boats might well represent those used by the early colonists in America between 1610 and 1690. Rålamb's boats were not innovations in his time, of course. Chapman, in his *Architectura Navalis*, published in 1768, shows vessels and boats that are known to have been built over twenty years earlier; so it is possible that the actual date of Rålamb's boats is not 1691 but 1671.

Whole molding was used in ships' boats, both in design and in lofting, from sometime before 1600 to about 1780; in ships, the British Navy used the same system until as late as 1730. The principle involved will be understood from Figure 1, which shows the molds for a longboat of about 1715. The characteristic of whole molding was the similarity of the molds formed at bow and stern and the great hollow made in the lower water lines, close to the keel near the stem and post. This method was related to those of ship design as expressed in Mathew Baker's manuscript, *Fragments of English Shipwrightry*, of about 1584.

With reference to Chapman, his drawings show that the ships' boats of his time were practically alike in all the great maritime powers of northern Europe. Taking his plans, Rålamb's, and those in the Admiralty Collection of Draughts (now in the National Maritime Museum at Greenwich, England), it is possible to add to the circumstantial evidence. The Admiralty plans begin with a drawing, dated 1706, showing nine boats. These show that ship's boat design was quite static from Rålamb's time to about 1760; it is probable that it had been equally so for at least fifty years before Rålamb's book, when there had been less interest in the design of boats, apparently, than in 1691.

"Pinnace" is an old name in English marine nomenclature and, together with "barge," was used in the fifteenth century to name a galleylike vessel. In 1550 the pinnace was a galley-ship and was the same as the rambargo, or ram-barge, a long narrow vessel for rowing and sailing. A rambargo is among the designs prepared by Sir Robert Dudley about 1612–20 and shown in Charnock's *History of Naval Architecture*. This, then, is a ship pinnace, and a picture of one of these, the *Black Pinnesse*, exists in T. Lant's *Celebritas et Pompa Funeris*, 1587. These ship pinnaces were undoubtedly the forerunners of the galley-frigates and galley-ships of the late seventeenth and early eighteenth centuries. The plans of boat pinnaces in the early eighteenth century show a long, nar-

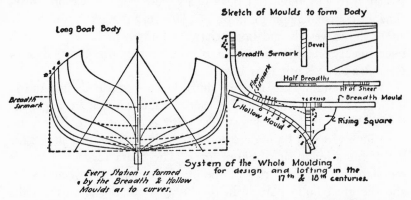

Fig. 1. System of the "whole molding" for design and lofting in the seventeenth and eighteenth centuries.

row pulling-boat, fitted with from one to three masts; occasionally these boats are shown lateen-rigged. There was no direct relationship between the square-rigged ship pinnace and the boat—except, perhaps, that both were built to row or sail fast.

Little can be said about the colonial "skiff"; the name appears to be loosely used in colonial records to mean "dinghy" in the modern sense. There is no reason to suppose that in the seventeenth century it meant a flat-bottomed rowboat. The cannow, or canoe, was a dugout in the colonies, except in eastern New England, in what is now Maine, where birchbark and elm bark canoes were in use on the coast and inland. The dugouts appear to have been as long as thirty or forty feet in some instances, and rather narrow. The dugout was easily built by an unskilled white man out of the large and easily worked timber available, and this produced the boat canoe of the eighteenth century in New England, and probably on the Chesapeake as well.

It has been noted that a "shallop" might be a decked and masted boat in the seventeenth century. In the light of evidence from the next century, it seems reasonable to suppose that the earlier boats were also no more than enlarged ships' boats, wholly or partly decked, and with a two-masted rig. Such craft were probably the ones used in the early New England fisheries. Two other craft—the great shallop and the double shallop—are referred to in colonial papers. It is the consensus that these were merely shallops of great size. This may be true of the great shallop, but the double shallop might be a double-ender like Rålamb's double-ended "slup"; the use of "double" in this sense will be mentioned later. There are a few instances where it would appear that a lengthened shallop became a pinnace. This has been accepted to mean that a pinnace might be an enlarged shallop, but it is more probable that the pinnace thus formed was given its name because it became long and narrow and better suited to row and sail fast. While there is no evidence to support the claim, it is possible that the name "pinnace" had become a connotative term similar to the later term "cutter-model," and implied beam-to-length ratio without regard to rig or size of hull.

"Sloop," in the earliest colonial references, is obviously a vessel large enough for coastwise voyages. Late in the seventeenth century boats of this name were in use in some colonies, but nothing has been found regarding the small sailing sloop until early in the eighteenth century. Lighters are rarely mentioned, and it is impossible to be sure whether these were scows or round-bottomed vessels of the hoy class. Both types were in use in England in the seventeenth century, at any rate, and were used in lighterage. It should be emphasized, perhaps, that the great increase in colonial maritime activities did not take place until the English civil war in 1641 cut off trade overseas and the colonies had to shift for themselves. This brought about the intercolonial trade with the West Indies and an overseas trade as well. To support these, there was an increase in fishing and coastal trade, both of which caused a great deal of small-craft construction.

The rigs used in colonial craft need not be traced back to their possible origins on the continent. This is a matter of European, not American, maritime interest. There can be no question where the rigs used in the colonies came from—they came from England. The early seventeenth century found many rigs in use in the British Isles; in the *Fragments of English Shipwrightry* is shown a sketch of a small boat or vessel rigged with a spritsail mainsail and with a jib tacked to the stemhead. One- and two-masted square-sail rigs were in use as well and are shown in many English pictures. The lateen sail was in use as a spanker on all square-riggers and was undoubtedly used on small boats like the pinnace; it was certainly well known to English seamen all through the sixteenth and seventeenth centuries. It has been the custom to state that the lateen rig was used in the seventeenth century by New England fishermen, but no authority for this has been found; the lateen sail was better fitted for use in small craft in protected waters. The earliest evidence of a lateen-rigged boat in American waters is in a painting of the Spencer shipyard, now in the Maryland Historical Society; the date of the painting is uncertain but is probably between 1725 and 1755. In the foreground is a two-masted lateener, apparently too large to be a ship's boat and too small to be a vessel; it may well be a local coastal type.

The leg-of-mutton rig does not seem to have been used very much in the colonies or in England, in the seventeenth century; its place was taken by the shoulder-of-mutton, which did not have a jib-head but, rather, a very short gaff (or club) at its head. The jib-headed sail existed on the continent, however, and it is probable that it was occasionally used in colonial America. Careless draftsmanship in the early pictures makes it uncertain whether all the boats with this rig had clubs. At any rate, a two-masted rig having shoulder-of-mutton sails—the foremast the shorter and in the eyes of the hull, and the longer main placed slightly forward of amidships—was the popular rig in English and American ships' boats and small craft. This rig remained popular until late in the eighteenth century. A boom was sometimes carried on the main; the fore often overlapped and was "lug-fashion," in being boomless.

A similar rig is shown in Dutch paintings and drawings as early as 1629. A variation of this rig is to be seen in some pictures of about 1700 which show two spritsails instead of the shoulder-of-mutton. About this time short-gaff sails appear in English pictures. The addition of a bowsprit and jib to these rigs took place sometime before 1708, on pictorial evidence. The long-gaff or standing-gaff sail of the hoy was, of course, unsuited for small craft. The hoisting-gaff of some length may have evolved from the old short-gaff rather than from the hoy sail; it is noticeable that the early sloops had short gaffs, but that these gradually lengthened in the eighteenth century. The earliest date of a rig can hardly be established by the earliest date it is found in a picture, of course, and it may be assumed that in nearly every case the rig was in use at least twenty years prior to its earliest portrait. Some early records speak of the "masts and yards" of a boat, and from this the inference has been drawn that the boat was rigged with yards—square, lateen, or lug. However, the heading "Masts and Yards" is used on many old plans in lieu of "Spars," and the dimensions of the booms and gaffs are listed under "Yards."

The history of the lugsail is not yet known. No pictorial evidence of the use of this rig in America appears until after the Revolution. Yet it is apparent that two-masted boats rigged with square sails were in use in both England and America in the seventeenth century, and it is very difficult to believe that the weather tack was not brought inboard to a point close to the mast, to cant the yard and thus tauten the luff on the wind. This simple step would do away with the bowlines or the spritlike "vargord" usually required to steady the luff of square sails when close-hauled. It is possible that this was done and that the modified square sail thus formed had, as yet, no rig name in English.

It will be seen that the boats of the seventeenth-century colonies must have been on European models, except for the canoes. There is little record of flat-bottomed craft, except with regard to the "plat" used by French fishermen near the mouth of the St. Lawrence; this seems to have been the ancestor of the dory. The plank canoe, formed of three wide planks, was probably built as soon as wide plank could be made. This type and the scow were the plank boats most easily built by men of small skill, so there is reason to think these craft were numerous by 1670. The colonial boats of this century must be reconstructed, but at least there are grounds that would assure some accuracy.

Foreign influence on the design and rig of colonial craft has long been a matter of speculation. The effect of New Amsterdam while in Dutch hands has been particularly a subject for discussion, and some authorities believe that the sloop rig, the leeboards, and the flat-bottomed hull in New England were directly imported from this colony. This supposition is hardly reasonable. In the first place the Dutch colony was not only very small, but its activities afloat were limited. Twenty-six years after its founding, New Amsterdam had only about a thousand inhabitants. It was a Dutch East India Company's colony, and was rigidly controlled—only the company's representatives could trade and explore alongshore. There was little boatbuilding, and the company's employees spent most of their time on repairs. The oversea trade was the important operation, and the company had no more interest in local boatbuilding and development than did the Hudson's Bay Company. There is, indeed, little to support a belief that this colony could have had any influence on its neighbors in maritime affairs.

A similar story has grown up about the influence a Dutch boatbuilder had on the introduction of the leg-of-mutton sail into America. The story goes that he ran away from his ship or was wrecked at Bermuda and went into the employ of the governor. His boats had leg-of-muttons and this sail spread to the Chesapeake by means of the trade between the Bermudas and Virginia, and so the leg-of-mutton is in use on the Bay. The only difficulty with this interesting story is that it does not appear possible to show that the leg-of-mutton has had a continuous existence on the Chesapeake since colonial times; in truth it is very difficult to prove that the leg-of-mutton existed on the Bay throughout the nineteenth century.

The lack of continuity in the history of American small-boat types and rigs shows quite plainly that rigs were introduced at widely separated places simultaneously, or at different periods. The important rig forms—the gaff sail, the leg-of-mutton, the lateen, the square sail and the sprit—were standard before the colonies were far advanced, and so there has been the possibility of selection from the early colonial years to the end of the sail period. This is as true on the Chesapeake as at New Haven, or at Portland, Maine, and is the reason why there was no single type or rig used exclusively in an area where a local type existed. Thus, there were gaff sloops in use in the New Haven oyster fleet and in the Chesapeake fleet, though in both the leg-of-mutton form is said to be typical.

The colonial craft of the eighteenth century are far better represented in surviving records than are those of the earlier century. Beginning with 1717, there are a few pictures of American ports which often give valuable information on small craft. From this century there also remain governmental records (including military and naval accounts of colonial operations), some private correspondence and legal papers, and, from about 1746 to the end of the Revolution, some useful newspaper advertisements, all of which give some information about small-boat types. An increasingly great quantity of small-boat plans in England serve to show what American small craft were like—in fact, a few plans of American-built boats are also to be found there.

There is no need, nor is there space, to examine all of this material in detail; it will be sufficient to use much of it as a catalogue of the types of craft, ships' boats, and coastal small craft that were used in America during the eighteenth century. Pictorial sources show that small sloops, as well as small boats rigged with two-masted leg-of-mutton or shoulder-of-mutton sails, were very common. There are also drawings that show the two-masted, lateen-rigged boat on the Chesapeake, and what appear to be square-rigged boats at Boston. Governmental records refer to such types as "bateau" in military operations, and "cutter" in naval activities just before and during the Revolution, and also mention "pinnace," "barge," and "launch." Private papers speak of "wherry," "cutter," "whaleboat," and "barge." The newspapers are prolific of the names of types; "longboat," "yawl" and "yawl-built," "boat-canoe" and "canoe," "moses," "periagua," "shallop," "barge," and "flats"; small sloops and schooners are also mentioned. The "doree" is referred to in a report as being at the Isle of Shoals as early as 1726; "galley," as a small boat, is mentioned on Narragansett Bay in 1750; and French records refer to "bateau" and to the large birch "maître" or "grand canots" of the fur traders.

Except for the bateau and the various canoes, none of these boats are other than ships' boats of a type then common. The only exception to this among the ships' boats is the moses, which was the boat of the West Indian traders only. One type—the two-masted boat—appears often in Boston papers in the years between 1740 and the end of the Revolution. Fortunately, there is enough description of this type to permit its classification.

The Sloop

The small sloop of the eighteenth century was a well-developed hull and rig combination. The sloop rig was used not only in coastal boats but also in some of the larger ships' boats of the shallop-long-boat-launch class. The sloop shown in the 1717 picture of New York is perhaps fairly typical: the hull has a strong, fair sheer without any breaks in it; the bow is slightly curved and without a cutwater or decoration of any kind; the transom is flat and of moderate rake, with the rudder hung outside. The hull in the example was at least partially decked and, as a guess, it was about 28 feet in length. The mast is stepped rather well forward and has much rake; its head is very short and there is no topmast. The gaff is rather short and the boom overhangs the transom considerably. The bowsprit steeves up a good deal and is not on top of the stemhead, but to starboard of it, much as in the later cutter-rigged craft. There are two shrouds on a side and two stays to which headsails are hanked.

A boat of this rig, shown in Figure 2, is a longboat of the Royal Navy of between 1725 and 1740; the original plan is undated and is in the National Maritime Museum. The rig is much like the one shown in the small sloop in the 1717 New York picture, except that the mast is farther aft and with less rake. The bowsprit is shown to port of the stemhead here. The rig suggests a trend toward the later cutter rig. The reeving of the main halyards is not clear; either there is a single halyard for peak and throat, or the two halyards reeve through a large, single, multiple-sheave masthead-block. Judging by pictorial evidence, the single halyard seems most likely. The plan is apparently an excellent representation of the early sloops.

The Periagua

Large dugout canoes fitted to sail were often called "periaguas" in eighteenth-century accounts. In one case a Boston vessel sighted a "schooner-rigged periagua filled with men" in the West Indies. Chapman, however, uses the name to identify a rowing punt, but this application has not been found in American records and papers. At the end of this century, the name was in use at New York for a shallop type of boat having a foremast in the eyes of the hull, raked forward strongly, carrying a short-gaff foresail having a loose

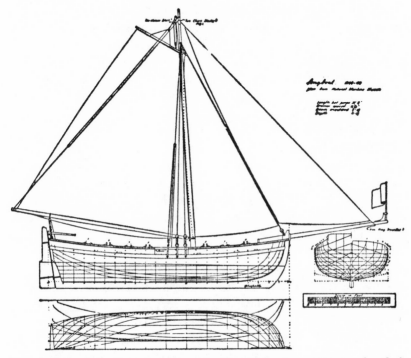

Fig. 2. Ship of the line's longboat, showing early sloop-cutter style of rig for small craft.

foot and overlapping the main. The mainmast raked strongly aft and had also a short-gaff sail but with a boom at its foot. There was no jib. This rig had probably grown out of the dugouts in early years but was now applied to hulls of varying description: scows, shallops, and ferries. The application of "periagua" to this specific rig existed at New York at least as early as 1785. The name seems to have been particularly used to indicate some kind of large West Indian dugout, perhaps a log-hull with plank raising strakes, that was long popular with freebooters there.

The Shallop

This type-name was going out of fashion in the eighteenth century; for ships' boats it was being replaced by "longboat," and then by "launch," which seems to have derived from the Spanish "launcha," used for this class and for small, open gunboats. "Launcha" seems to have appeared during the war with Spain in the 1740's. We have seen that the two-masted rig had become popular in these ships' boats, and from a comparison of longboat plans in the Admiralty Collection of Draughts, and drawings by Chapman and others, it appears that the "two-mast boat" described in Boston newspaper advertisements between 1746 and 1784 is the old "shallop" under a new name.

A two-masted sailing boat is preserved among the plans in the Anderson collection of the unpublished Charnock plans now in the National Maritime Museum, and this is shown in Figure 3, with the sail plan reconstructed from a list of spar dimensions dated 1761. The date of the Charnock plan is unknown, but the style of workmanship and the paper used suggest it was made between 1750 and 1768. The boat is shown without boom on the main, as she was an open boat and it is probable that such boats would be thus rigged. Decked boats had boomed mainsails in this rig in Dutch pictures in the previous century. The boat of Figure 3, enlarged and with a deck and cuddy added, is very much like the surviving pictures of the New England Chebacco boat of the end of the eighteenth and the first decade of the nineteenth century. The drawing particularly resembles the "dogbody." This apparently disposes of the traditional story that the Chebacco boat was invented at Essex, Massachusetts, after the Revolution and that the first one was built in an attic in that town. The truth is that the Chebacco, whether square or pink-sterned, was no more than the old shallop and was used as far back as the middle of the seventeenth century.

That Figure 3 is a fair example of the colonial two-masted boat can be seen by newspaper descriptions of the type. One of the most complete is in the Boston *Gazette* of January 21, 1782:

"Stolen and carried off last Wednesday night, from Rainsford Island by a number of British prisoners, the State Hospital Two Mast Boat. She is 23 feet keel, a long cuddy with a fireplace and cabins [bed-places or bunks in modern language] in it, one anchor and cable, a new foresail, her mainsail old, a new boom not tarred and her sides painted yellow." The stolen boat evidently had a boomed mainsail and a lug-footed foresail.

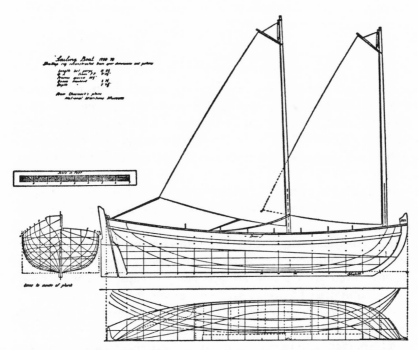

Fig. 3. "Two-Masted Boat" type. This craft was not a ship's boat but was designed as a dockyard service boat.

Another advertisement in the same paper, Sept. 8, 1777, adds somewhat to the foregoing:

"Taken away from the end of Tilestone's Wharf, on Wednesday night last, a lap streak Two mast Boat, painted black and yellow, the lower streak Chocolate color, the masts yellow, the top of the foremast Black, the top of the Main-mast not Black, a graplin on board instead of an anchor."

From other sources, boats of this class are found to have ranged from about 18 feet to 28 feet in keel length. A Virginia source of 1738 speaks of a two-masted shallop 19 feet on the keel and having a cuddy or cabin. The two-masted boat, open or decked, appears to have been a widely popular type in America throughout the century. The "two-mast" rig, for the lack of a better name, might be called the "shallop rig." It is worthy of comment that no evidence of a ketch variation of this rig, with the main shorter than the fore, seems to have been in use in the eighteenth century, in spite of its popularity in the last half of the nineteenth.

The Pinnace

The ships' boats of the pinnace class in the eighteenth century seem to have followed a very standardized design, judging by English plans and those shown in Charnock's unpublished lot, or in Chapman's book. The boats are long, narrow, and sharp-ended, with much dead rise, and have rounded stem profiles and narrow, square sterns. This type of boat was now primarily a naval ship's boat. The rig shown by Chapman is shallop-fashion, but with spritsails; it is known that two- and three-masted lateen rigs were also used.

The American barges used during the Revolution appear to have been of the pinnace type: long, narrow craft from 30 to 45 feet in length, fitted with a gun at each end, perhaps, and with waistcloths supported by iron stanchions along the sides, to mask the oarsmen. These craft were also rigged to sail; leg-of-mutton, spritsail, and lateen rigs were in use, apparently.

The pinnace and its sister, the barge, were also used as ceremonial craft, to carry officials and private citizens from place to place, or to engage in water-parades of state. Chapman shows many such craft, and they are usually characterized by a pink-sterned projection of the gunwales, to carry a coat of arms or some other decoration, above and aft of the narrow transom. It is known that a few boats of this class existed in the colonies, and that Penn had one at his estate on the Delaware. A typical ship's pinnace of about 1745 is shown in Figure 4, which serves to show the sharpness of the lines of this class.

The Whaleboat

This type of boat appears to have been quite popular with Americans in the eighteenth century, not only as a working boat in whaling for which it had been developed, but also as a boat for coastal transportation and to carry mail and goods express along the coasts. Long whaleboats were also built to serve as barges, armed and fitted in much the same manner as the barges previously described, and are mentioned in American privateering records before and during the Revolution. Long whaleboats were also employed in the numerous military operations on the American lakes in the eighteenth century.

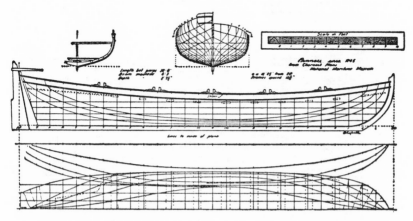

Fig. 4. Typical man-of-war's pinnace, 1700–1750, showing fine lines that could be produced by whole molding.

Chapman shows the lines of a Greenland whaleboat of the middle of the eighteenth century; she is not greatly different from the later American whaleboats employed on shipboard but has more rocker in her keel than was later the fashion in such boats; and she is also smaller, being only about 24 feet long. The early American whaleboats were often straight, or nearly so, on the keel. Some whaleboats were built as gentlemen's barges; these seem to have been sharp-ended with much dead rise, built for speed, and handsomely finished. The widespread activity in shore-whaling in the northern colonies before the Revolution undoubtedly caused the wide use of the whaleboat and encouraged boats of abnormal length. No plan of a boat in the eighteenth century of the whaleboat type has been found, except Chapman's drawing; the later whaleboats will receive attention when the nineteenth century is reached.

The Cutter

Beginning about 1760, the cutter is often mentioned in naval records of activities on the American coasts. The type is particularly referred to with regard to revenue work and law enforcement, in seizing illegal goods, or in pressing men for naval service. The cutter, as a ship's boat, seems to have come into use in the

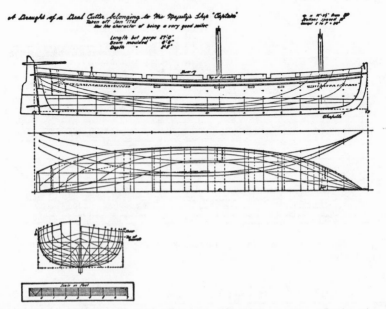

Fig. 5. Cutter of a type used by Customhouse officers in the colonies, showing the excellence of model possible before the Revolution.

Royal Navy about the middle of the eighteenth century, and plans of the type are common from 1757 on. The majority of the early plans show boats ranging in length from 20 to 28 feet. The early plans and references in England indicate the possibility that the boat was an adaptation of a purely local type used at Deal—a forerunner of the later Deal galley and Deal galley-punt. Chapman shows a sail plan of a "Deal cutter," rigged with three masts having sprit-sails (the aftermost a jigger), a bowsprit, and small jib.

Figure 5 shows a good example of a cutter such as was used on the American coasts prior to the Revolution. Lap-strake construction was almost universal in this class, and the boats were modeled and rigged to row and sail very fast. "Gig," as a name for this class of boat, came into being almost as soon as the cutter came into use in the Royal Navy.

The chief characteristics of the cutter, aside from her speedy model, were the use of rocker in the keel for quick turning and the use of notched oar ports in the wash strake, following what may have been an earlier practice on the Mediterranean, as shown by the French felougue figured by Chapman. Another feature was the peculiar setback of the transom abaft the sternpost rabbet and the reverse chine formed in the tuck; this also appears in 1760–70 in the larger sailing cutters with lap-strake construction.

What the true relation was between the boat cutter and the larger vessel cutter, has yet to be established—both seem originally to have been local types popular in smuggling and other illegal activities. The two-masted boat described in the 1777 Boston *Gazette* might have been a cutter. Some of the cutters had lug rigs as early as 1768, a dipping lug forward, and a small standing-lug jigger.

The Wherry

This form of fast rowboat was an English development, originally employed on the Thames as a waterman's boat for river transportation to carry passengers and light goods. The date of the introduction of the type is uncertain, but it may have been in the early seventeenth century. The boat seems to have been a development of an early small galley type, and the early wherries had a grabbow faintly resembling the bow of the old Mediterranean galley. The boat was so well known that both Rålamb and Chapman show the type.

Figure 6 shows a wherry of about 1697, very much like Rålamb's earlier example, also a working boat of the type of 1760. These boats are characterized by very sharp lines and flaring sides; the later models of the eighteenth century had the sheer raised and flared sharply outward at the oar ports, to "outrig" them for more efficient rowing. The boats somewhat resembled the Turkish caïque, once common on the Bosporus, or some of the India-built small boats, in profile at least.

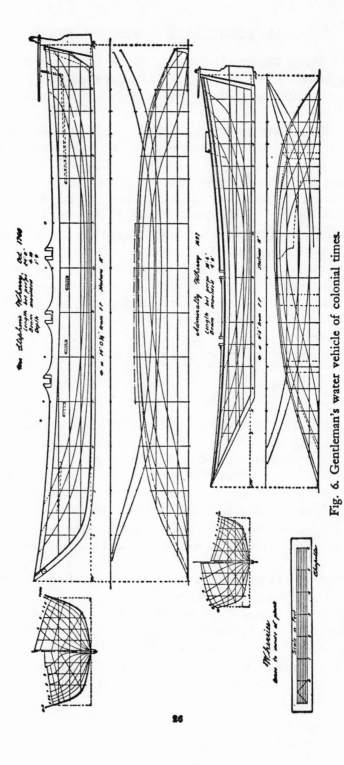

Fig. 6. Gentleman's water vehicle of colonial times.

Wherries were built both with the sharp stern shown in the 1697 boat and by Chapman, and with a narrow square transom as shown in the 1760 boat, which may still be seen on many Thames rowing skiffs today. The wherry was the "fashionable" gentlemen's boat of the eighteenth century and so was introduced into the colonies as soon as planters and merchants were able to afford such luxuries. A variant of the wherry was a barge on the same general model, much longer and more ornate than the usual working wherry. This name was also applied to certain classes of sailing craft in the British Islands, but such an application of the name appears unknown in America.

The Yawl

The yawl seems to have been merely a small boat for shipboard use, and the evidence of any special build or model is confusing. The type first appears in 1706 in the Admiralty plan of nine boats

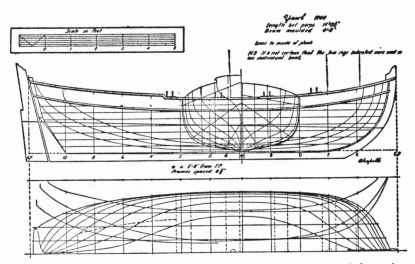

Fig. 7. Ship's stern boat of the eighteenth century; often used for other purposes.

mentioned earlier; this shows two "yawles," one about 22 feet long and the other 23 feet. The larger is called a "Westindia Yawle" and is a full—and rather burdensome—boat, and both "yawles" have

narrow transom sterns above a strongly curved sternpost and rabbet. Other yawls, shown in plans dated from 1740, are relatively
short, wide boats, some with one and others with two masts.

The type is much mentioned in American records in the last half
of the century, and the yawl-boat seems to have been built in almost every shipbuilding village or town. A variant of the type,
shown by Chapman, was the yawl-longboat, which appears to have
been longer than the usual run of the class. The yawls seem to

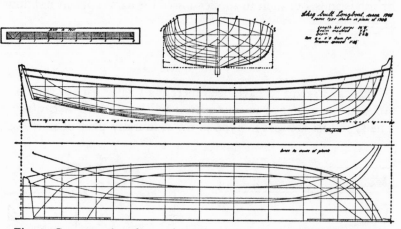

Fig. 8. Common skeg form of hull used for small craft in America.

range from about 18 feet to 24 feet in length and were variously
rigged—Chapman shows a yawl with a sprit mainsail and jib. It
seems probable that "yawl" was the name applied to a ship's stern-
boat. Figure 7, a rather typical example from the eighteenth century, shows a yawl with two masts. Old Boston newspapers mention such boats with "two gaffsails"—the shallop rig.

An apparently popular variant of the yawl was a boat built with
a skeg instead of a planked-up deadwood, as shown in Figure 7.
The skeg-hull seems to have been particularly popular in merchant
ships that needed a burdensome yawl, or longboat, to work off
beaches or in shoal water. Figure 8 shows the lines of a skeg-built
longboat of about 1745. This style of boat can be traced back to
the 1706 drawing of nine boats, one of which is a large longboat
with a skeg and called "A Boat for Landing Men in 1706." The

skeg-construction appears to have been quite common because of its cheapness.

The Moses Boat

In American newspapers, between 1748 and 1800, there are often references to "moses boats," particularly at Boston. This name is still used in the West Indies as a name for a heavy beach-boat used to lighter casks. The modern boats are heavy craft, having a rather wide, square stern over which the casks are loaded from the beach, using skids. The moses of the eighteenth century, shown in Figure 9, is a single moses, taken off in 1806 in the noted Hillhouse shipyard at Bristol, England. The boat is a short, heavily built beach lighter; the type ranged from 14 to 16 or 17 feet over all. The boats had a heavy-timbered cradle amidships to carry the huge hogsheads of molasses then in use.

Figure 10 shows a double moses, which is no more than a double-ended single moses, as can be seen. This plan is from the same source as the plan in Figure 9. The importance of the double moses is that it apparently gives the key to what the double shallop of the seventeenth century may have been—a double-ended longboat. It seems very likely that the double shallop was the ancestor of the pink-sterned type of Chebacco, or Jebacco, boat already discussed.

The Punt and Flat

This was a common type of boat in America during the eighteenth century and took many forms according to its employment. A flat is shown in the picture of New York in 1717; the boat is apparently a ferry and is a rectangular scow, with curving "rakes" at the ends and with platforms at bow and stern; the rest of the hull appears to be open. The single mast stands right forward, on which there is a boomless spritsail shown furled on the mast. No leeboards are indicated, and it is probable that the boat had an outside keel to allow it to sail on the wind. This is a very old form of boat, simple to build and very efficient where shoal draft was required. The type had been used in England and on the Continent

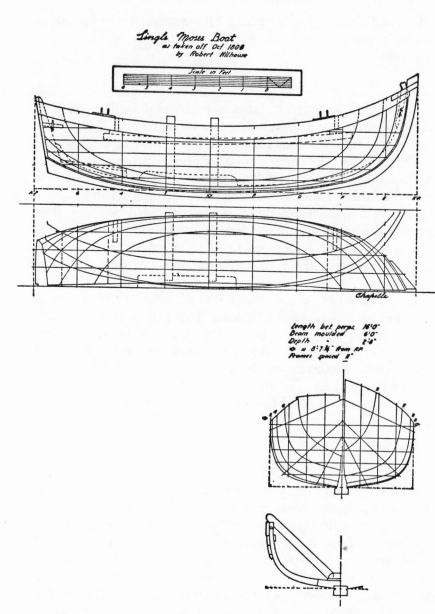

Fig. 9. Type of boat used in the West Indian sugar trade, 1740–1820.

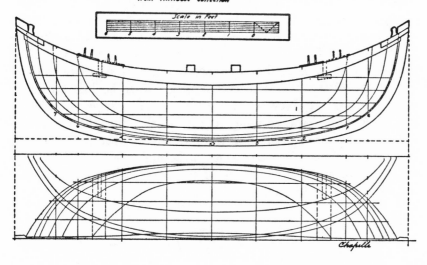

Double Moses Boat
1806
from Hilhouse Collection

Scale in Feet

Chapelle

Length bet perps   16:0"
Beam moulded   6:0"
Depth   1:8"
O is 6:0" from F.P.
Frames spaced 11"

Lines to inside of plank.

Fig. 10. "Double," as shown here, meant double-ended rather than "double standard size."

before there had been American colonies and was very well known. In American accounts, the scow appears under various names such as the "flat," "radeau," and "gondalow" or "gondolo"; the latter name was more commonly used to indicate a flat-bottomed, chine-built, double-ended boat of the pram class.

The great need in America for shoal-draft boats for use on the bays, rivers, and lakes, its low cost, and its scow construction, quickly and easily built, made the type very popular, both in late colonial times and afterwards. The rectangular, rather boxlike ferry-flat shown in the 1717 New York picture was the most primitive type; the "punt-form" was an improvement. In the latter the sides were not straight fore-and-aft but were sprung so that the bow and stern were somewhat narrower than the hull at amidships. This is supposed to improve the sailing of the scow hull; at any rate, the practice improved its appearance.

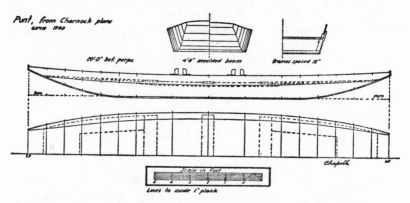

Fig. 11. Punt type in the colonial period, used for river navigation.

Figure 11 shows a typical rowing punt used in England at the middle of the eighteenth century, which well represents the type (but not the bottom construction) still in use in America, and the hull-form once common in many American sailing scows.

Chapman's periagua is a more developed scow and is shown in Figure 12; this is a style suited to more open waters than the first example and was also designed for rowing. The upsweep at the oar ports suggests that this boat may be of English origin, as it is like that of the wherries. Boats similar to Chapman's example are still used in America; the "John boat" used on the Ohio and Mississippi is one example, and the longer and narrower sister used in the Ozarks is another.

During the Revolution, scows rigged as sloops, schooners, and square-riggers appear to have been built in America; sloop-rigged scows may have been common as early as 1725. It has not been established when the name "scow" became popular in America. The name was probably derived from the Dutch "schouw" and has

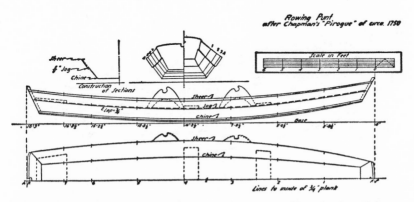

Fig. 12. Old form of rowing punt, from Chapman, still to be found in use in America.

been used to indicate a square-ended hull having a flat, or nearly flat, bottom. The application of "scow" to such craft does not appear in the seventeenth century; in fact the word has not been found until well into the eighteenth century. It should be noted that "punt" was often used in England in the eighteenth century to designate a short round-bottomed boat, or dinghy.

The Bateau

The French word "bateau" meant no more than "boat" in the first years of the French settlement in Canada, but early in the eighteenth century this word had become accepted as a type-name for a double-ended, flat-bottomed, chine-built small boat much used along the St. Lawrence and on the American lakes. The hull type is a very old one—it was apparently common in medieval craft, as is shown by an archeological find in England in 1822–23. In the old bed of the River Rother, in Romney Marsh, extensive remains of a pram-built vessel about 64 feet long, believed to have been sunk there about 1287, were discovered and excavated. The hull-form of this vessel was little different from that of some of the Dutch and Baltic prams of more recent times, and the construction was basically the same. This construction probably developed from a plank canoe, such as some American Indians built once they had obtained tools from the white men to make the plank.

Colonial Bateau

The bateau of French Canada may have been a direct adaptation of one of the many French flat-bottomed small craft. Their use of "plats" in fishing, at the mouth of the St. Lawrence in the seventeenth century, is an indication of this. The English colonists probably had knowledge of such craft, or of similarly built small boats, prior to their coming in contact with the French bateau, but it is most probable that the French name and the boat itself were taken over by colonial frontiersmen.

"Bateau" has come to be accepted, in America, as a specific type of boat and as a method of construction as well; in one locality, the Chesapeake Bay, the name is now applied to the chine-built hull and is particularly used to designate a V-bottomed hull. It should be explained, perhaps, that "chine-built" is used here to indicate construction in which a definite angle is formed between the bottom and the sides in a hull.

The colonial bateau was built in lengths up to 40 or 45 feet and was primarily a rowing and poling boat for use on rivers and lakes. A few craft of the frontier class are said to have been as long as

84 feet and as short as 18 feet in the nineteenth century, which indicates the range of length possible in such a type. Some of the eighteenth-century bateaux apparently were also fitted to sail and had outside keels to allow sailing close-hauled. Such hulls, in lengths up to about 75 feet and with more beam in proportion than employed in the frontier boats, were also called "gondolos," with variations in spelling, and were rigged as sloops, cutters, and, perhaps, schooners; some—for example, Arnold's gunboats on Lake Champlain, in 1776—had a one-masted square-sail rig.

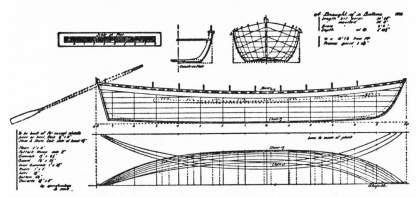

Fig. 13. Design of a colonial bateau, probably for use on Lake Champlain in Burgoyne's campaign of 1776, from an Admiralty draught.

The regular river and lake bateau was much employed in military operations on the American lakes in the French and Indian Wars and in the American Revolution. The type was in use in Maine and northern New York before 1740. Luckily, we know just what such craft were like; Figure 13 is a drawing of one of the bateaux designed for the American lakes in 1776; the plan is one found in the Admiralty Collection of Draughts and the date is penciled on the original plan; the boat was probably intended for the Lake Champlain campaign. The drawing shows a well-developed hull differing but little from later craft of the same type used by North American lumbermen and fur traders.

The relation of the dory to the bateau is a speculative matter. The use of the plat by the early French fishermen in the Bay St. Lawrence allows the suggestion that the New England fishermen adapted the bateau in this form through their contact with these boats in their cod fisheries in this area, which were very active by 1700. No explanation of the name "doree" or "dory" can be given. The hull of the dory is constructed in the same manner as the bateau and the French flat-bottomed boats. It seems highly probable, therefore, that there was some connection or relationship between them.

The problem of the flat-bottomed skiff, cross-planked on the bottom, and its relation to the bateau requires attention. The sharpie, or flatiron skiff, differs so much in constructional methods that it is impossible to be certain that it ever had any relation to the bateau, and it may have been a development, local in nature, out of the scow or punt. The cross-planked bottom has not been found in any eighteenth-century craft in the plans and descriptions inspected in America and England. None of the old Dutch small craft, in fact none on the continent, seem to have employed this mode of building. As a generality, the bateau was built right side up with a complete system of transverse frames; the bottom was formed first. In the cross-planked-bottom skiff, the sides were first made and sprung over molds, and the bottom was planked with the hull upside down; there were no complete transverse frames as a rule. The slight available evidence suggests that cross-planking was an American invention in flat-bottomed boat construction, though it hardly seems reasonable that so practical a method of building could have been overlooked in Europe.

The Canoe

The canoe had firmly established itself for white men's use throughout the eighteenth century and is often mentioned in American records of the 1700's. Besides the periagua there were smaller dugout craft, such as boat canoes, which were square-sterned dugouts of chestnut or white pine, about 15 feet in length and a little over 4 feet in the beam. Longer canoes of this type were used in Maryland and in other southern colonies. The most common model was a rather trough-shaped one, having ends somewhat like the lip of a spoon. This style of boat has often been found in excavations, and one of the last examples of the model was the canoe once used at New Haven for oyster-tonging; a number of these canoes are preserved at the Mystic Marine Museum, Mystic, Connecticut. The model was marked by a rather flat bottom and slightly rounded sides having moderate sheer. The canoe looked much like a Thames punt, and, indeed, in the southern colonies such canoes were sometimes called "punts." The addition of a raising strake, or a sheer strake to raise the sides, was common in the West Indies early in the eighteenth century, and the practice was probably followed on the Chesapeake and elsewhere on the main.

The birchbark canoe was, to Europeans, a curiosity, and early travelers gave much attention to these craft. A few plans were made; the earliest found is presented in Figure 14. This drawing

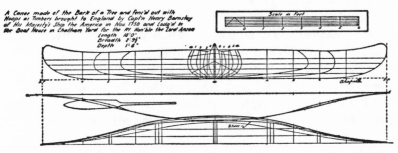

Fig. 14. A drawing of a birch canoe prior to the American Revolution.

was made about 1715 by Admiralty draftsmen, from a canoe brought over by the Royal Navy ship *America* (built at Portsmouth, N.H., 1748–49), on her maiden voyage. This circumstance indicates that the canoe had come from Maine or the upper Piscataqua. This class of canoe was used by the eastern Indians for hunting and for carrying messengers. Such craft are mentioned in accounts of the Indian raids on Maine coast settlements in the French and Indian wars, but are more commonly referred to as being used inland.

Most authorities believe that the Indians rarely built large birchbark canoes until they came under the influence of the French, when the "grand canots" about 36 feet in length appear. Available information points to the probability that nearly all the Indian canoes had low, or moderately low, ends and that the high, up-curved, and oddly shaped bow and stern were very rare.

If there were any local types of small boats developed in America in the eighteenth century, no reference or description has been found as yet. The bateau is no more than a borderline case and may, with the canoe, be classed as an American type. The Chebacco boats have usually been considered a local type produced late in this century, but, as we have seen, it appears to have been, at most, no more than a variant, and perhaps an enlargement, of the earlier shallops in hull and rig. It is possible that some type may have existed without being recorded, but until evidence is found this is no more than a speculation. It is highly possible that some local types were in their earliest stages of development, such as the Chesapeake log canoe and the New Jersey scow or garvey, but this too is mere speculation.

The fact must not be overlooked that, as in rigs, the eighteenth-century American had ample opportunity to select any style or model of hull suitable to his pocketbook and use and was not confined to a laborious development of some primitive class of boat. The various round-bottomed craft that have been mentioned were in use all along the coast, and, in nearly every community, the scow and some other form of flat-bottomed boat was in use.

In discussing the background of American small-boat types it is necessary to carry the matter into the first half of the nineteenth century, as it is at present, at least, quite impossible to establish a claim that many of the distinctive small-boat types began development before 1850; a few may have started development as early as 1825. Local tradition makes such claims at least. The rise of certain improvements in boat rigs and fittings in the early years of the nineteenth century also requires attention, to indicate what knowledge must have been available at the time the various small-boat types began to be employed.

The Centerboard

One of the very important fittings in American small boats is the centerboard, which was employed very extensively throughout the country after 1850. It would be risky indeed to assume that the centerboard was really an American invention, though the Americans can at least claim the greatest interest in the device. Two types of centerboard have been used in this country: the rectangular board pivoted at the fore end and controlled by a lanyard or lift handle, and the dagger board. The latter is a blade-shaped board in a short case and is lifted out of its case when raised. The dagger board is suitable only for very small boats, of course.

The idea of preventing leeway in shoal-draft hulls had plagued boat and ship designers for generations. The European maritime nations had arrived at two solutions: one solution was to employ an outside keel of some depth to act as a fin, but this, to be very effective in rough water, required much depth in the keel and thus destroyed the shoal-draft qualities; the other solution was the employment of leeboards, of which the Dutch were perhaps the leading exponents. These leeboards were leaf-shaped and were pivoted at the gunwale on each side, a little abaft the mast in a sloop, or a little forward of amidships in a two-master. By dropping the one on the lee side, the boat could be sailed close-hauled without sliding away to leeward. Leeboards had become known in England before the American colonies were well established.

Certain primitive people and the Chinese had also solved the problem. The latter had not only used leeboards, but also a form of dagger board placed in the eyes of the hull in some of their small craft. It is not known when these improvements were adopted by the Chinese; it is commonly supposed to have been long before Europeans had developed the leeboard.

The dagger board is known to have been used in sailing rafts by the Formosans, who inserted a number of such boards between the large bamboos forming the rafts. A similar scheme was used by South American Indians in their balsa-wood rafts, a highly developed type of which was used by Brazilian Indians. This style of sailing raft, the jangada, is thought to have first been seen by white men prior to 1526, and is still in use. The jangada usually has a number of dagger boards, which are inserted in slots cut between the logs along the centerline of the raft, and by raising or lowering one or more of these, the rafts can be balanced under sail; the boards can also be raised when beaching, so that they and the raft are not damaged by grounding.

The idea of the dagger board seems to have occurred to white men in the eighteenth century, without there being, apparently, any knowledge on their part of the primitive dagger boards just mentioned. In 1774, a British naval lieutenant, Schank, produced a long, shallow, rectangular dagger board, or, as he called it, a "drop-keel." This was not wholly satisfactory, and later, in 1789, he developed a multiple-board system in which three narrow boards in short cases were distributed along the centerline of the hull, the middle one being the largest. These were raised and lowered by tackles. The experiment, almost reproducing the general plan used in the jangada, was so successful that Schank, now a captain in the Royal Navy, succeeded in getting the Admiralty to use drop keels, first in a large cutter, and then in schooners, brigs, and ship-sloops. There was some opposition to the idea, growing out of leakage in the improperly constructed cases, and the fitting never became popular in men-of-war. The improvement of pivoting a single long board is claimed as the invention of another British naval officer, Shuldham, in 1809, but it does not appear that much notice of it was taken in England.

The drop keels were publicized in the textbooks on naval architecture published in England at the end of the eighteenth century and in the early years of the nineteenth. These books reached America, and Mr. John R. Stevens, the Canadian marine historian, has found indications that drop keels may have been considered in the design of small schooners for use on the American lakes early in the 1800's. In 1811, the first American patent for a pivoted centerboard was granted to Joshua, Henry, and Jacocks Swain, the grant being dated April 10. This received a good deal of attention, apparently, and by 1825 the pivoted centerboard was in use in America in quite large craft, sloops, and schooners. The Swain patent was followed by a large number of others for "improvements," but the fundamental principles of the Swain board have been popular since 1811.

The leeboard has been in use in America but has never been very popular and has been confined to the scow types. It is doubtful, however, that the fitting was employed continuously in any locality since colonial days, and it seems probable that this universally known device had been employed, discarded, and re-employed along the coast, as the situation warranted.

Rigs

The early years of the nineteenth century appear to have been a period of experimentation with boat rigs in America. This is shown by the sail plans appearing in many drawings of naval boats. One plan, dated 1819, not only shows the schooner and sloop, complete to topmasts, but also such un-American rigs as the settee and dipping lug. The sliding gunter rig is also shown. This rig seems to have been introduced in some gunboats built under the supervision of Edward Preble, Captain, U.S.N., in 1804.

The gunter rig had been suggested by James L. Cathcart, an American diplomat, and was taken from a then well-known Mediterranean rig, the houari, which was used on rather large craft. In this there were short lower masts on which was hoisted a yard that stood vertically, forming an extension of the lower masts. On these were loose-footed leg-of-muttons. The houari was really a schooner, having a headsail, and seems to have been a French development of the shallop rig. Though the houari rig, with the addition of booms, became popular in ships' boats because the short spars could be stowed withinboard, the rig required rather complicated fittings to hold the yard, and this prevented the gunter from ever being widely employed in commercial small craft, where the sprit would do as well. Since stowage of the spars was no requirement in the latter craft, the usual long-masted leg-of-mutton could be used if that sail were wanted. The variety of sail and rig forms that might be seen along the coast, in ships' boats alone, offered a catalogue for the selection of rigs for commercial small boats. In hulls, this same source offered a variety of form, from the yawl-boat to the whaler, fast or burdensome, as desired.

The same urge that had led to the improvement in sailing vessels in America must have affected the design of ships' boats; the evidence of this is in the plans of United States naval boats, which show tremendous improvement between 1812 and 1840. It is shown also in the whaleboat. Figure 15 shows a typical whaleboat of about 1820–30, a rather full and burdensome boat. Compare this with Figure 16, an improved boat of about 1852, such as is shown in many contemporary pictures of American whaling. Improved sailing qualities have been guaranteed by the addition of a centerboard and the finer lines, which also improved rowing qualities. This boat is very similar to the gig-whaler, which became popular in Arctic exploration, and also as a naval ship's boat.

In the American whaling industry, there were a variety of whaleboat models until the business had so declined that the boats were all built in one port, and finally by one or two builders. Then the "standard" boat came into existence. The rig of the boats also became standardized to a sprit-mainsail, with occasionally a jib set to the stemhead. Earlier pictures show a variety of rigs in use:

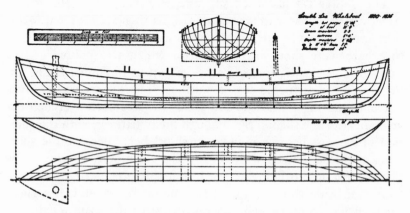

Fig. 15. Whaleboat of the first half of the nineteenth century.

dipping lug, settee, and even a gaff main with a topsail set above it.

The general knowledge of rigs and hull-forms in America, during the first half of the nineteenth century, was undoubtedly great, for there is evidence in almost every large port that builders were working to produce faster small craft and more weatherly rigs and better gear. A steady rise in the employment of ironwork seems to have taken place in small craft, and the use of the centerboard was spreading. But the use of the latter remained spotty. For example, the Chesapeake log canoes do not appear to have adopted the centerboard until after the Civil War, in spite of the fact that Bay vessels were using it extensively in the 1840's. The fitting was not taken up by the New England small-boat builders, except along the Sound, until after 1870. The reason may have been that builders in New England thought the centerboard and its case too expensive and did not employ it until competition forced them to. Improvements in fishing boats are subject to economic considerations, and until a fishery became highly profitable there was a tendency to resist the addition of fittings and to confine improvement to modification of hull-lines and rig-form.

The time when distinctively American small-boat types begin to appear is now reached, and the supposed "invention" of each is best left to discussion when the individual types are examined. It will now be apparent, at least, that there is no reason to suppose the

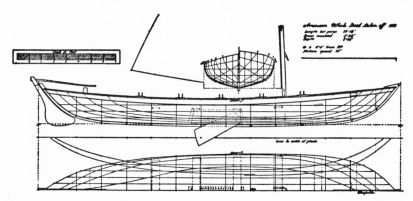

Fig. 16. American whaleboat of 1850–70 of a type built for sailing and used extensively in the Arctic.

owners and builders of the local types of American small craft could have been ignorant of more than one rig or hull-form or that each type *must* have been the result of continuous local evolution since colonial times. There were a few such types, the lumberman's bateau for example, but these were rarely confined to a single building locality. In the majority of types, the evolution took place in a period of perhaps twenty-five years, when the small-boat fisheries became highly profitable and competition forced owners and builders to constantly seek improvement. This produced pride in ownership and a favorable attitude toward improvement, within practical limitations of use and cost. When this reached an extreme, as it did in some instances, the results were unnecessary refinements, excessive cost, and, finally, more or less decadence, which was sometimes corrected by a depression in the fisheries. Instances of this will be left for later indication; the point to be made is that progress in commercial small-boat design in the days of sail was not one of steady and continuous improvement, where the latest would necessarily imply the best.

CHAPTER 2

THE SCOW AND Bateau

FLAT-BOTTOMED craft in a great variety of model, rig, and size were used in the fisheries, as well as in coastal and inland water transportation, during the last half of the nineteenth century and well into the twentieth, in both the United States and Canada. Craft of this type were used wherever there was shoal-water navigation or a necessity for low-cost boats.

The most primitive of the flat-bottomed hull-forms, the scow, was employed in great numbers and had an extraordinary spread throughout North America. Not only were there examples of the type in use along the entire Atlantic Coast, from the Maritime Provinces to Mexico, but also on the Great Lakes, on Champlain, and on any of the rivers large enough to be used for small-craft navigation. Flat-bottomed boats and vessels of scow construction were used on the Pacific Coast and in the Canadian northwest as well. Often, the scow was of elementary form, rectangular on deck, and rough, simple, and undistinguished in character and appearance. But some types of sailing scow had highly developed rigs and were excellent sailing craft within the conditions of their work.

The bateau model, comprising the dory, the lumberman's bateau, and the flat-bottomed skiff or sharpie, was almost as popular as the scow form. This model was usually looked upon as an improved scow, more seaworthy and somewhat more costly. The bateau model is divided into two classes or subtypes. The first class includes the lumberman's bateau, the fisherman's dory, and the Jersey beachman's skiff. The bottoms of these are planked lengthwise the hull, over floor timbers which are part of the side frames. The second class takes in most of the large sailing sharpies and nearly all of the flat-bottomed skiffs, except some river boats. In these the bottom is planked athwartships, and the frames are confined entirely to the sides of the hull and often are no more than cleats to hold together the strakes that make up the sides.

The name "sharpie" has come to be applied to most boats in the second class. The origin of this name is uncertain. In two cases the name has been given to boats not of the skiff type—on the Chesapeake to a double-ended, V-bottomed sailing boat, and on the Jersey beaches to a double-ended beach skiff, or small surfboat. "Sharpie" came into use at least as early as 1857 in America. It appears probable that the name was created to distinguish between the sharp-bowed flat-bottomed skiff and the scow; so "sharpie" meant "sharp-bowed." This would readily lead to a corruption of meaning to include "double-ended." Before "sharpie" became popular, the name "flatiron skiff" appears to have been rather widely used as a name for the rowing-sailing, flat-bottomed, and sharp-bowed skiff. The "flatiron skiff," as a name, was in use as late as 1884 in some areas. The term was very popular, apparently, at New Haven and on the Connecticut shore, and it was so descriptive of the small skiffs that it was readily understood and thus retained its popularity for a long time.

The two classes of bateau model really represented two fundamentally different construction methods in other respects than in the bottoms alone. The first class, which included the dory and the Jersey beach skiff, and at least part of the lumberman's bateaux, were lap-strake construction so far as the sides were concerned and were built right side up as a general rule. The bottom was first formed and sprung to fore-and-aft camber, then the frames were set up on this as though it were a keel, after which the sides were planked. This is the style of building that appears to have been universal in English flat-bottomed boats.

In the better-built craft, the bottom plank of the sides was nailed continuously to the thicker bottom, along the seam formed by the junction of the bottom and the side—the chine. But some craft, notably the lumbermen's bateaux, depended upon fastenings in close-spaced frames to hold the chine seam tight. It appears probable that the right-side-up method of building came into use because of the ease of planking lap-strake sides in this position and, once established, this system was applied to boats caravel-planked, or smooth-sided.

In this form of building it is usual to omit the chine log, a longitudinal stringer or batten that is sometimes used to back up the chine seam. Sometimes, boats built in this manner are called "dory-built," since the construction is typical of the fisherman's dory. The existence of a complete transverse frame system in this class has led to the use of rounded sides, between bottom and gunwale, in many craft; the beach skiff is a good example. The obvious trend resulted; the sides got more and more round, and the bottom got narrower until it became no more than a wide, plank keel.

The skiff-build, as represented in the second class, invariably has straight flaring sides, caravel-planked in American commercial small craft. The cross-planked bottom is commonly nailed alternately, at each strake end, to the lower side-strake and to a chine log. The side frames rarely extend to the bottom and are often mere cleats between the top of the chine log and the gunwale, or sheer.

These boats are commonly built upside-down; the sides are first sprung to shape over molds and bow and transom pieces, with the chine logs either let into the molds previously, or formed and nailed to the sides before springing. The bottom is then nailed on, and the boat is righted for finishing.

Normally, there is a limit to the size of a boat that can be built in this manner in the small commercial boatshop—the limit being a size and weight of hull that would be difficult or dangerous to right with the readily available gear. But this is overcome in some sections by springing only the lower one or two strakes of the sides and the chine logs and then nailing on the bottom, after which the hull is righted and the sides raised to the desired height. This reduces the weight and height of the hull at the time it is righted and allows the upside-down setup to be employed in boats as long as 55 feet at least. With any form of cross-planking, this setup is a great saver of labor and time; hence its wide use in America.

It appears that this style of build is practically unknown in Europe in flat-bottomed boat construction. Perhaps the skiff-build is an American innovation, but so far no sound proof of this has been found, other than lack of evidence abroad.

In most of the sharpies and skiffs, as well as in some of the dory-type boats, the stem is not rabbeted; instead, it is formed of an inner V-shaped piece, or stem liner, which is used in shaping the sides. When this is done, an outside piece of cutwater is added that covers the raw ends of the side planks. In this manner, a "built-up" rabbet is formed and the fitting of the side plank at the rabbet of a stem is avoided, since the sides may be merely sawn off just before the cutwater is fitted. There are a number of variations in this construction that had best be left until shown in a type of boat. The stem may be built in two pieces even when curved, as in the dory. In these the cutwater is small in section and is steamed and then bent into place over the stem liner and side plank.

The sailing boat with the flat bottom, whether scow- or skiff-built, requires some fitting that will permit her to sail on the wind without excessive leeway. In early times, as we have noted, the attempt was often made to accomplish this by the use of an external keel. But this was hardly a satisfactory method in boats where shoal draft was desired, since the keel, to be really effective, had to be quite deep. In American small craft this external keel did not long survive, except in isolated cases. In the scows the leeboard became common, and its use continued as late as the opening years of the twentieth century.

It seems quite apparent, however, that the Americans had come to view leeboards as a rather crude and primitive device that was only suited to very low-cost hulls. Hence, the use of leeboards seems to have been almost entirely confined to scows and to certain log-built craft. But the use of two leeboards and their attendant gear, European fashion, does not seem to have ever been very popular in America. Here the single leeboard, which need not be shifted from side to side, was by far the most common; the double leeboards seem to have been confined to a few sloop-rigged scows.

The single leeboard, as fitted in America, may possibly be an American adaptation. In this, the leeboard was located on one side of the hull, usually pivoted in some manner to the rail or sheer-strake; sometimes a bolt was used, and in other cases a rope or chain grommet over a pin or cleat was employed. This mounting would be wholly inadequate to meet the stresses formed when the board was to weather, as the board was never shifted in tacking, so the blade of the leeboard had to be secured lower on the hull in some manner. This was usually accomplished by the use of a rod or bar of iron passing outboard of the leeboard, like a huge staple. In many scows there was also a short wooden guard inside the lee-board and the staple, or rack, which forced the board to stand nearly vertical and not follow the flare of the sides. The guard and rack were long enough fore and aft to allow the leeboard to rise or pivot toward the stern, if the board touched bottom while under-way.

The rack was often very heavy and was of very long, shallow U-form, the ends of which either passed through the hull and were wedged inside, or formed pads which could be through-bolted to the hull. The rack and guard were usually placed as close to the load water line as was possible, or close to the chine in small craft. The result, it can be seen, was a very cheap and simple off-side centerboard, in effect, which not only required no case but also was out of the way of cargo placed in the hold or on deck. Since these scows were not sailed at great angles of heel, the off-side posi-tion of the board had no adverse effect on windward ability. The advantages of the single leeboard were so great, particularly in scows carrying deckloads, that the centerboard never entirely replaced it before the end of sail.

The American sailing skiff, and the sharpies that followed her, rarely used leeboards, as far as has been discovered. The few in-stances known are individual and isolated cases. The reasons for this neglect of the leeboard in sharpies are speculative. It seems proba-ble that the skiffs and sharpies did not become popular in the fisheries and among small-boat users until the centerboard had become well known. Since these craft were apparently considered as improved scows and were somewhat more expensive, the additional cost of the centerboard, as compared with leeboards, would perhaps not be objectionable.

The little that can be found about sailing skiffs before 1857 indicates that the craft were small and were, in addition, open or half-decked craft with no pretensions as cargo carriers. It should be noticed here that there is no pictorial evidence of the existence of the New Haven sharpie type before 1857, yet the earlier existence of this and similar hull-forms is vouched for by other evidence— Dixon Kemp, in his *Manual of Yacht and Boat Sailing* states the sharpie could be traced as far back as 1835. If this is true, the use of leeboards may have been common in this type at such an early date. The log canoe used at New Haven as late as the 1880's employed leeboards, and there is no technical reason why the sharpie could not also have had such fittings in early stages of development. The use of leeboards and centerboards in a single locality was not uncommon in America and was to be seen wherever the sailing scow existed for any length of time.

The appearance and details of the sailing scows and bateau models varied a great deal as each subtype was particularly suited in some manner for its employment and economic limitations. But, in general, all of these flat-bottomed craft had certain qualities in common: they were light in draft, low in construction cost, and quickly built even when the carpenters were without great skill. Some of the boats were very fast sailers and some were surprisingly seaworthy. The low cost and shallow draft were the prime arguments in favor of these craft, of course. Dollar for dollar, and hour for hour of building labor, the scows produced the most boat, then came the various bateau models.

The sailing scows were very often quite remarkable for their surprising weatherliness and turn of speed under sail; in spite of their clumsy appearance the scows often had the elements of great speed in their hull design. Many of them, due to their beam and flat bottom, were very powerful craft that could carry a large spread of sail in proportion to their displacement. Some had long, sweeping lines in sides and bottom that also produced speed and steadiness on the helm as well. The large sloop- and schooner-rigged scows were often smart sailers when light, and there are numerous instances recorded when these big scows showed their sterns to fast commercial sailing craft and yachts. When the bottom profile was correctly designed, the small sailing scows were very fast indeed and in strong winds were able to plane in spite of their weight. Some of these small scows must be considered as among the forerunners of the very fast yacht-racing scows and the more recent planing boats that are now engaging the sailing yachtsmen's attention.

The scow-form is not usually considered as unduly seaworthy; yet craft of this form have been used in very rough water. Some of the military landing craft of World War II were no more than slight modifications of the scow-form, and, as many yachtsmen found out, such craft could take a great deal of rough going. The small sailing scows, such as the New Jersey garvey or the small Maine scow sloops, were not craft suitable for deepwater sailing, but were fully capable of long coastal voyages in summer weather. The greatest danger in most of the small sailing scows would be that of capsizing when in unskilled hands. Primarily, the sailing scows should be viewed as craft suitable for protected waters.

The low building cost of the scow, while basically inherent in the type, is really produced by a combination of design and construction. This combination is necessary in all sizes of sailing scows and consists in the use of flat sides, flaring outward, a flat bottom in transverse section, and straight or slightly sprung sides longitudinally. The springing of the sides helps to produce, with little waste of material, the sheer at the gunwale and camber in the bottom. There is little difference in cost in the shaping of the bow as long as it is a design that can be easily planked. The construction requires cross-planking on the bottom; longitudinal planking almost invariably adds greatly to the cost and labor of construction.

With the usual construction of the scow, the sides are very important longitudinal-strength members, and so they are usually quite thick, and the strakes forming them may be edge-bolted or doweled together. In addition, the sides are usually given additional strength by the use of cleats, or short frames. Practice varies somewhat in the manner of fitting these; some builders notch the side frames over the chine logs, and this necessitates standing the frames on edge. Other builders cut off the side frames at the top of the chine logs, which permits the frames to stand on the flat. The choice should depend upon the profile of the chine, theoretically, for if the chine profile is so straight that it would closely parallel the grain in the side plank there would be great danger of the sides splitting, if the side frames do not lap the chine logs. But if the chine profile crosses the grain in the side planks, then the log itself will prevent splitting, and the side frames may well stop on top of the chine logs.

The manner in which the sheer is finished and the deck beams are secured is of relatively little importance, except that strength in the securing of the deck beams to the sides is very necessary. Common practice is to employ a sheer stringer either inside the frames, or outside the frames and notched into them; to the sheer stringer are nailed or spiked the ends of the deck beams, which are cut in length to fit snug to the inside of the side of the boat at the sheer strake.

There are two schools of thought among builders as to the best mode of fitting the chine log in scows. One is to use long lengths, usually cut to profile from plank. In some cases the design permits straight stock of the desired section to be bent directly over the molds for most of the length of the bottom, and the ends are then pieced up with wide plank; this is occasionally seen in the New Jersey garveys. In both methods, the side frames can either notch over the chines or be cut off at their tops. The second school runs the frames from the inside of the bottom plank to the sheer, either on the flat or on edge. Between these frames, the chine logs are formed of short blocks running from frame to frame. In this construction it is obvious that the chine logs add nothing to the longitudinal strength of the hull and are mere supplementary nailing pieces for securing the bottom. For this reason the method is used only when the side-plank is thick enough to allow edge-bolting.

The keel structures used in scow construction vary a great deal, but the most common is the use of a flat plank as a keelson, thickened and widened in way of the centerboard case. Large sailing scows often have heavy plank keelson structures, formed by one or more planks set on edge to give depth. The rabbeted keel appears to be unknown in American scow construction and would, of course, serve no useful purpose except in V-bottomed hulls. In addition to the keelson, some scows have a longitudinal batten nailed to the bottom plank, about halfway between the keelson and the chine logs on each side of the boat. This batten is usually a plank and serves to prevent the bottom plank from warping or "cupping."

It will be seen from this general description of the construction of the scow that the aim is always utmost simplicity combined with great strength. The structure is designed as a whole to comply with this objective, and not in accordance with any theory of "good construction" or finish. Functionally, of course, there is no real excuse for designing or building a scow unless very low cost is the aim, for there are other types that are cheap and of shallow draft. But, as will be seen, this course was not held to in small sailing scows, and rather expensive V-bottomed and round-bottomed hulls of the scow type occurred in some localities.

The Garvey

The way to examine scow design, build, and rig is to discuss some examples of small American sailing scows that show details and that had typical qualities of the type. Among the small boats of this form, the New Jersey garveys were perhaps the best developed. This scow, unlike some types of local small boats, was built with some variety in appearance, model, proportion, and rig. This was due to the numerous uses of garveys and to the fact that these craft were built by a large number of builders throughout the eastern part of southern New Jersey. The range of the type extended along the coast, from the southern portion of Barnegat Bay to the Delaware, an area that included the counties of Ocean, Burlington, Atlantic, and Cape May. The center of this building, however, was at Tuckerton and its immediate vicinity. The garvey was also built inland, on the numerous creeks and streams running to the eastern bays.

The garvey varied a good deal in size, owing to the needs of the boat's employment. On inland waters the garveys were often large scows or pontoons, which could be used in the transport of farm produce and freight on narrow streams. Another class was used in fishing in the creeks and for tonging oysters close to home, or in clamming. These boats were commonly unrigged and form the class locally known as "rowing garveys." The most common size of these craft was between 18 and 20 feet in length, about 4 feet beam at chines and 6 to 8 inches more beam at gunwale. The rowing garveys ordinarily had ends only 6 to 8 inches less in width than at amidships. The depth was usually small, 14 to 16 inches. The profile was often that of a river punt, with a nearly flat bottom fore and aft until close to the ends, where the bottom was brought up rather sharply to the "end-logs" or bow and stern transoms. There was much variation in the depth of the ends, 4 to 12 inches perhaps.

A few builders preferred a form that was not greatly unlike the hull shown by Chapman, but usually with less flare, sheer, and rocker. These rowing garveys were commonly fitted with a short deck at bow and stern and a rather wide covering board along each side, with a low coaming around the cockpit thus formed. This was not required by any desire for seaworthiness but to form working platforms for poling the boat in the shallows and when tonging or loading. The boats were usually fitted for two pairs of sweeps, using wooden tholes set on blocks on the covering boards. The boats usually had two or three thwarts as well. There were garveys both greater and shorter in length than the limits given as most common, and some of the river garveys are said to have been as long as 35 feet.

The second class of garvey was the "sailing garvey"; this covered a greater range in size than the first class. The smallest of these craft was the gunning skiff, from 12 to 14 feet in length, decked and usually fitted for rowing and sailing. These boats were commonly used in the marshes and narrow creeks, as the flat bottom could be easily poled or towed over the mud flats. For such work, the garvey skiff was often preferred to the famous Barnegat sneak box. Both boats were rather lightly built for this service, but the garvey skiff was the cheaper to build of the two.

The next class of sailing garveys was the bay fishing boats, used in tonging, clamming, and fishing. These were well-developed sailing scows, from about 16 to 17 feet long and one-masted, to 24 to 28 feet long and two-masted. There was still another, the boats from 28 to 32 feet in length, which were sometimes used in oyster dredging and for transportation. These large garveys were commonly gaff-mainsail sloops, having a single large jib and a short bowsprit. Some of these large garveys were built with V-bottoms at the end of the last century.

The smaller sailing garveys, one- and two-masted, were fitted with spritsails; the masts were rather short and the sprits quite long, so the heads of the sails were usually cut with some peak. Since the sails were not very large, the spars were light. The single-masted boats often had no boom, and the leech of the sail stood nearly upright. The two-masters seem to have employed booms almost entirely, and in their sails the heads were often short enough to rake the leech a good deal.

Since it was often desirable to row these garveys, before cheap gasoline engines appeared, the proportion of beam to length in garvey hulls was usually small; the beam on the bottom was usually about one-fifth the over-all length. Such hulls had a limited range of stability under sail and the low spritsail rig was well suited for these narrow boats in waters subject to occasional violent squalls and gales. The jib was not particularly useful in these craft; it would be merely an additional sail located in an unhandy position and its gear would be much in the way in a working boat of the common sailing garvey size. About the beginning of the twentieth century, a few garveys were fitted with leg-of-muttons having sprit-booms, but these did not become popular. A few small garveys were also fitted with gaff sails; however, in the small working boats, this sail was not a real improvement over the spritsail, unless the boats were of such size that the sprit was heavy to handle. Hence, the large dredging garveys were commonly gaff sloops.

The spritsail has never been very popular with yachtsmen, for it is rarely a handsome sail. It is, however, a very efficient and safe sail for small craft. It requires such short, light spars that they may usually be struck and stowed in the boat. When loose-footed (without a boom), letting the sheet fly will instantly relieve the sail in a sudden squall. The sail may be quickly reduced by unshipping the sprit and letting the peak fly out to leeward. The peak may then be caught and secured to the luff, thus creating a crude triangular sail, about half the area of the original. The spritsail has been considered a better windward sail than the gaff sail, but on this point of sailing its set depends upon having the sprit well peaked, and the foot, if loose-footed, very carefully sheeted. A spritsail cut square and long at the head, so that the sprit does not peak up much over 45 degrees to the mast, is a poor form of the sail when close-hauled.

The sail and rig used in the small garveys show that the Jersey-men understood the spritsail very well indeed. The one-masted, loose-footed sail usually had its leech almost vertical and the head was cut with much peak. There were one or two reefs in some sails. The sprit stood at a small angle to the mast; if there were reefs, the heel of the sprit was above the uppermost reef band when in place. The heel was supported by a rope formed into a figure eight, the large eye around the mast and the small eye over the shouldered heel of the sprit. To peak the sprit, the figure eight, or snotter, was shoved up on the mast, where it jammed. Some-times, the snotter was served with marline to increase its life. Some fishermen had, in addition, a light single-part halyard, the standing end knotted to the crossing of the figure eight and the fall rove through a small block at the masthead and thence to deck; the belay usually was around the boom or the tack eyebolt if loose-footed. This halyard was used to raise the snotter and to hold it up—on the larger sails it really peaked the sprit and made it easy to slack off when caught in a squall. The usual jammed-snotter was sometimes impossible to slack down with the sail full of wind, particularly when the sail was fairly large. The head of the sprit, in any case, was shouldered or cleated so that it could engage a rope eye turned into the peak of the sail. The upper end of the sprit then stood a few inches, 4 to 6, above this eye when the sprit was peaked up.

The reason for the nearly vertical leech of the loose-footed sprit-sail was said to have been that this overcame the objection, in all such sails, of the clew coming forward in tacking. If there were a block on the clew of a loose-footed sail, cut with a raking leech as in, say, a leg-of-mutton, the block might strike the helmsman or crew in tacking, when the sail was flogging about in a fresh breeze. However, in a small spritsail garvey the clew block for the sheet was rarely used, the sheet being rove through a brass or wooden cringle there, to form a dumb sheave. The standing end of the sheet was usually an eye put over a pin in a thwart or in the sternsheets; the fall held in the hand or passed over another pin. The whole sheet was usually shifted from side to side in tacking so that the foot of the sail stood at the right angle to the wind; such sails cannot be pinned down amidships, as the sail then takes a twist which is not at all desirable in windward sailing. Very few boats with the loose-footed spritsail used the traveler and mainsheet horse, it is claimed; pins that could be shifted in a thwart were thought better in sheeting the loose-footed spritsail correctly. This form of sail undoubtedly required as much care in sheeting as a jib does.

The boomed spritsail was easier to sheet, of course, and the small sails of most garveys required only a thimble on the boom, or, at most, a small block. The garvey sailor rarely used more than one block on the sheet; only on large boats were two employed as a rule. The spritsail was commonly laced to the mast; this was the usual spiral lacing, which passed through small metal rings or thimbles seized square to the luff-roping at each grommet in the sail. The eye of the rings or thimbles was thus up-and-down, and this is said to have prevented the lacing from jamming in hoisting or lowering the sail. When a boom was used it was commonly laced to the foot of the sail with spiral lacing; in rare cases the boom was a sprit to which the sail was not laced, but this may have been an attempt to adapt the leg-of-mutton's sprit-boom to the spritsail. Old fishermen claim that the garvey spritsail was heavily reinforced with patching, particularly at tack, throat, and peak. Loose-footed sails had, in addition, a large patch, with reinforcing carried up a few feet on the leech, at the clew. The sails are reported to have been of rather light material, drill being much used.

The construction of the garveys was rather typical of all scows: the sides were first formed and sprung over molds and transom and end-block in an upside-down position, and then the bottom was put in place. A local practice was to use marline along the chines instead of the more usual wicking, placed before the bottom boards were secured. The marline was considered more certain and lasting in obtaining a tight chine. Great care was taken to make the inside of the bottom seams tight, and so no caulking was used between bottom boards. There are indications in some old boats that the inside seam was driven up until the wood crushed slightly, which insured continual tightness after swelling once took place. This practice was possible with the white cedar used in these hulls. The sides, of the same lumber, were quite thick, and the edge-bolts were usually not much over 12 inches apart on centers.

The chines were usually in long lengths pieced up at the bow, but the block style, set in between frames, seems to be increasingly common in power-garveys and is now the popular construction in the Maryland power-garveys. The bottom planks are nailed both to the side planks and to the chine logs. Boat nails are used throughout the boat; the heads are well set and puttied. The keelson is no more than a batten in most boats; in the way of the centerboard

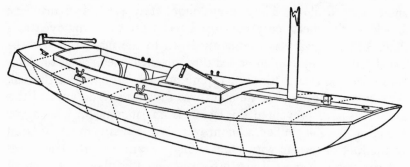

New Jersey Sailing Garvey, Small Type

case it is thicker and wider than elsewhere. This is sometimes accomplished by shaping the keelson out of thick stock but more commonly by piecing the timber out of two or more pieces of stock of varying scantlings. Side battens, between keelson and chine logs, are not employed owing to the properties of the white cedar.

The decking is rather heavy and in many garveys is quite conventional and is laid over a few deck beams of very moderate camber, which may be carried to the extreme ends of the hull. At Tuckerton, however, an unusual plan is very common: the covering board is set at a crown or bevel for the full length of the cockpit coamings. The ends of the coamings and the covering boards are supported by end-coamings formed like a deck beam, reaching across the hull, and shaped to fit these longitudinal members. Afore and abaft the ends of the cockpit, the deck is not only flat but the deck planks are laid athwartships. This feature may be seen in some of the plans and is used in modern power-garveys as well as in the old sailing craft. The framing and general construction employed in the garvey require strong thwarts to hold the flare of the sides, for the covering boards are not heavy enough to do this unaided. The latter are usually supported by side frames on edge, forming brackets or gussets.

In a few old boats having frames on the flat, a few small knees support the covering boards. Hence, before the molds were removed from the hull to allow decking, two or three heavy thwarts were put in, according to the length of the hull, resting on short riser pieces nailed to the inside of the side planks between the frames at the required height. The thwarts held the sides apart and helped the hull retain both sheer and fore-and-aft camber in the bottom.

When some sailing garveys were converted to power, the thwarts were removed and then the sides fell in, losing the flare, sheer, and the rocker in the bottom. Power-garveys have followed this change in model and trend toward wall-sided and straight-sheered hulls. The lack of thwarts or bulkheads amidships would make it very difficult to obtain much flare in the power-garveys without some change or addition in structure, such as the incorporation of the heavy transverse frame, or strongback, used on the Chesapeake in dead-rise construction. In recent years the V-bottom has appeared in garveys, and the resulting changes in construction methods have restored some of the flare once used in the sailing craft, with a corresponding improvement in appearance.

The centerboard of the garveys was quite large and, when raised, stood well above the gunwale. The shape was rather standardized when pivoted: the forward end of the board was about the case height; the after end stood about twice as high with a strong rake to the trailing edge of the board and the after case log. The dagger board, used only in gunning skiffs, was the curved pattern that brought the lower portion abaft the slot when lowered. The centerboard case was supported by at least one thwart, placed at either the fore or after end of the case, as the builder fancied. The pivot pin, in pivoted boards, was often made of hardwood, and either a lanyard or a metal lifting handle was used to work the board. The metal lifting handle, when used, could be lowered to rest on top of the raised board, as it was pivoted close to the top of the centerboard.

The handle was V-shaped to jamb in the case when the board was all the way down; this kept the board from rising unless grounding occurred. The lanyard appears to have been more common. The metal lifting handle was, however, a rather standardized fitting in small working centerboarders, from about 1880 to 1905, all along the Atlantic Coast.

The single leeboard was also used and lasted to within memory of living fishermen and builders, say into the 1890's. This was the simple board slung by a small rope grommet or lanyard over a pair of thole pins. The board was held to the side by the common iron rack placed horizontally, low on the side of the hull and long enough to permit the leeboard to cant upward and aft when it struck bottom. To make the board stand upright and not cant with the flare, it often had a narrow wooden bar nailed on its inboard side, deep enough to keep the board at the desired perpendicular. The leeboard was usually to starboard, and no lifting lanyard was used.

The rudder was hung outboard on small sailing garveys and inboard on larger craft (a length of 20 feet was the usual division point). In the old boats the rudderpost was of wood, and, with the inboard installation, there was a wooden rudder trunk between bottom and deck. The rudder was then also secured by a set of pintles and gudgeons to a strong skeg, which usually reached as far forward as the after end of the centerboard slot. Later, the rudderstock was made of iron and the rudder trunk became an iron pipe threaded into the bottom plank and wedged at the deck. The heel of the rudderstock was then supported by a simple iron heelstrap low on the skeg. The rudder blade was angular in profile, and the "balance" type does not appear to have been used. The boats steered with a short tiller, having a fitting to take the head of the rudderstock.

Traditionally, the garvey is said to be the oldest form of boat used in South Jersey and, indeed, its physical characteristics give some support to the claim. However, no pictorial or documentary evidence is apparently available to support the tradition, so it must be accepted with reservations. Even the development of the type cannot be traced; only the form and variations existing in the last seventy years at most are known.

Figure 17 shows a one-masted garvey of the old type, with inboard rudder and wooden rudder case. The age of the boat cannot be determined; she was either a very old boat reaching back into the 1880's or one built in some isolated community at a later date. The hull-form shows a pontoonlike shape and is not unlike the form used in large scow sloops. The run is rather long, however, and the lines indicate a good sailer and (for its length, 19′ 3″, and beam, 5′ 4″) a good carrier. This appears to have been a type of garvey, once popular south of Barnegat, that has now been replaced by a hull that is sledlike in profile, rather than scowlike.

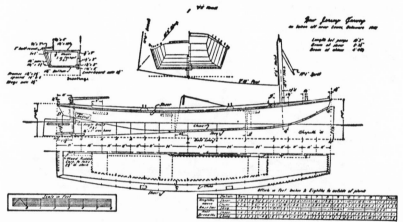

Fig. 17. Old style of New Jersey garvey.

Figure 18 represents the more modern hull and shows a small fishing garvey whose hulk was measured in the fall of 1950. This is a rather narrow boat, 18′ 4¾″ in length and only 4′ 9″ beam at the gunwale. Narrow garveys of this class were handy craft for working alongshore and in the marsh streams where it was necessary to row, pole, paddle, and sail. The narrow beam did not permit a large sail area, and so the rig is proportionately smaller than in the garvey shown previously. Small beam was popular with fishermen, before the days of the cheap gasoline engine, because in many localities it was necessary to row the boats long distances when calms occurred. On much of the Atlantic Coast the summer mornings are calm, then a southwest wind may come up and last until late afternoon, when another calm period usually occurs. The exact time the calms would begin and end could not be gauged accurately, and so it was not unusual for a fisherman to row his sailboat out and home again. The stiffness of the flat-bottomed hull

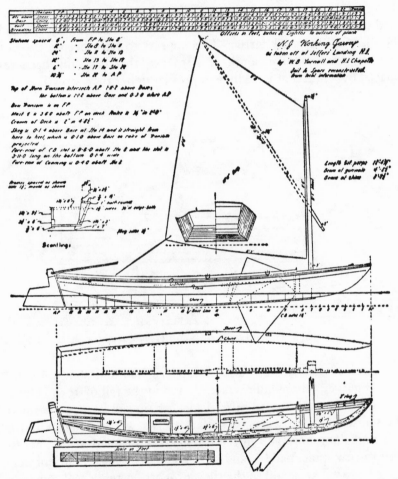

Fig. 18. Small working garvey showing construction and the one-sail rig once very popular.

was sufficient in the narrow models to give much stability, and there is evidence that the narrow-beamed boats were better sailers than wide hulls of this model.

Figure 19 is the plan of a somewhat better-finished sailing garvey,

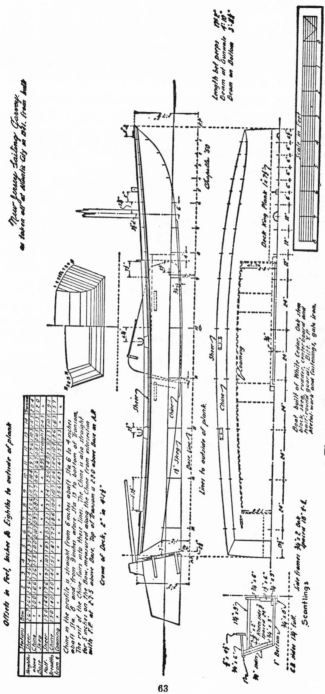

Fig. 19. Single-sail garvey of about 1906.

63

17′ 2″ long and 4′ 10½″ beam on deck. This boat was one of a class of sailing garveys that were sufficiently developed to attract the attention of some yachtsmen. Early in this century, an attempt was made to introduce this type into the pleasure fleet. It failed, however, because of prejudice against the flat-bottomed, square-ended hull, and only a few of the yacht type were ever built. The boat shown is apparently a working boat, but her design and relatively light construction indicate she was built on the yacht model, if not for yachting purposes.

Pleasure boats of this form had leg-of-mutton sails and sprit-booms. Garveys on this model were very fast sailers and under right conditions would plane, as would many flat-bottomed, working sailboats. The elements of design in this garvey model are sound for a low-cost, fast-sailing boat.

Figure 20 shows the lines of a gunning garvey built near Tucker-ton. This is the smallest of the sailing garveys and was a competitor to the famed sneak box and served somewhat the same purposes. The gunning garvey, however, was not as seaworthy as the sneak box and was less well known. This form of garvey was well suited for gunning in the marshes and could be poled or hauled over the mud more easily than the sneak box. The garvey type is therefore still in use (and many retain sail and dagger board), for the boat is cheaply and easily built. The peculiar deck construction of the Tuckerton garveys is shown in this boat; the flat decks must have been convenient for stowing decoys. The chief objection to this boat as a gunning skiff would be her noisiness in open water, and she was therefore less suited to open waters than the sneak box. The example shown was reputed to be a boat of superior qualities under sail.

The most common garvey in the fishing business on the South Jersey shore was the two-master, and the most popular size was from 24 to 26 feet in length. Figure 21 shows the plans of one of these boats, made from measurements of an old sailing garvey at Tuckerton and from additional information obtained from builders still alive there and from fishermen who had owned such craft. The boat measured was 26′ 0″ long, 6′ 5″ beam on deck, and 5′ 3″ on the bottom. The profile of the hull, as can be seen, is much like the smaller sled-type shown earlier, and the boat is an easily driven scow that would sail fast. The rig, which was popular among American fishermen all along the northern half of the Atlantic Coast, is the two-masted spritsail type, in which the foremast was taller and

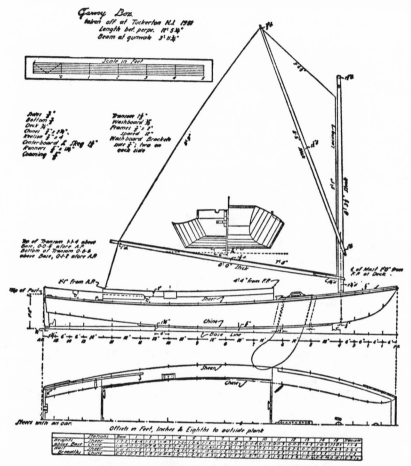

Fig. 20. Old garvey box, substitute for a sneak box.

the foresail larger than the main; a rig and spar plan that might be described, for the lack of a better name, as a "cat-ketch." The rig was particularly popular in half-decked boats, as we shall see.

Lacking a jib, this sail plan was handy and flexible in balance and so could be worked single-handed. The rig was well in the boat, and the small spars and masts could be readily unshipped even in rough water. The drawing also shows the flat fore and after decks of the Tuckerton build that has been described. There is no need of a lengthy description of this boat, since the plan is quite complete.

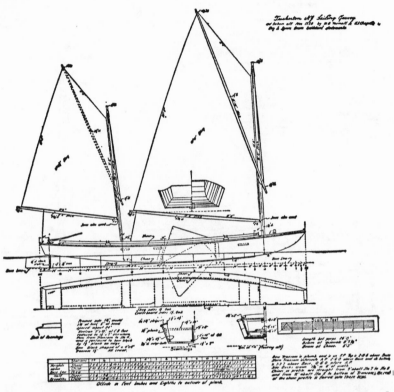

Fig. 21. Typical New Jersey sailing garvey, two-masted rig, showing flat decks afore and abaft cockpit, as built at Tuckerton, New Jersey.

Such boats were usually built by rule of thumb, without models or plans. This example could be reproduced, as could the others, by the usual projection and expansion of the sides to obtain their shape, since the sections show parallel lines in the body plans. This would allow the usual garvey setup and building practices to be followed, without stocks being required. Incidentally, a boat of this approximate size and model cost $50 in 1900, complete except for sails.

There was apparently no standard scheme of painting the gar-veys; most of them had white topsides and gray or brown decks; the interior was gray and the bottom copper red. One practice is still followed in some power-garveys: the top of the copper, under the bow overhang, is not straight across but is swept up from each chine in circular arcs to the centerline of the hull so that at this point the copper is 3 or 4 inches higher than at the chines. This seems to have no practical advantage and is probably just decoration.

With the introduction of power, the garvey type of hull has spread southward across the Delaware and is now the local type as far south as Chincoteague Bay, Accomac County, Virginia, a little to the northward of the entrance to the Chesapeake. In addition to the V-bottom, these garveys often have shallow tunnel sterns. Fishermen in these garveys seem to have no hesitation in working outside the bay in the open Atlantic, and the boats are said to get into trouble rarely. There are numerous attempts to "beautify" the power-garvey by carrying up the V-bottom all the way to the foredeck and by making the bow narrow, but on the whole the low-cost construction methods are closely adhered to wherever the garvey is built. Except for gunning skiffs, there appear to be no sailing garveys alive in New Jersey.

The Pound-Net Scow

There were other small sailing scows less "boatlike" than the garvey. One of the scows most numerous in the fisheries was employed in driving poles for pound nets and in the construction of fish weirs. The boats of this type were usually sailing scows, sometimes sloop-rigged and sometimes cat-rigged, with a boomed gaff sail. The pound-net scow was used on the Great Lakes, on the Chesapeake, at Cape Cod, along the Maine coast, and elsewhere. It was used to carry the poles out to the location of the fish traps, and the poles were driven into place from it. For this it usually carried a small manually operated pile-driving rig that could be set up after it came to anchor; the crew set up a pole and then, with the rig, drove it into place. These scows were usually decked and were without cabins or cuddies, since they did not stay out overnight. The traps were commonly located close enough to port so that the scows went to and from their work in a working day, or thereabouts. On the Great Lakes, particularly on Lake Erie, the pound-net scows were called "stake boats" and were vertical-sided, rectangular hulls with rather short curved rakes at bow and stern. The boats were from 25 feet upward to 50 feet in length and from 6 to 8 feet beam—some of the larger, as much as 10 feet— and were usually cat-rigged with a boomed gaff sail.

Another rig, the peculiar two-masted rig of this area (used in the sharpies there), was also used in the larger boats. The chief peculiarity of these scows was a deep slot or notch in the stern, used to pull the stakes or poles at the end of the season, which required the rudder to be hung off center. A hand winch for pulling the poles was located over the slot. At the bow, two projecting timbers were secured, on which the driving rig was shipped; these timbers also steadied the stake when ready to drive. The driving rig was made of two upright timbers and a crosspiece, the driving hammer rode on the uprights, and a block on the crosspiece took the hammer line. The heels of the two timbers socketed into the projecting timbers at the bow, a foot or so forward of the hull, and the uprights were supported by two light timber stays leading aft to the deck. When driving stakes, the boat was moored with four anchors whose lines were belayed to timberheads or cleats on each quarter. Poles were carried fore and aft on deck on both sides of the hull. The stake boat had a large centerboard amidships. In lines, these scows were primitive, having neither sheer, flare, nor rocker.

On the coast, the stake boats were somewhat more developed, particularly the craft used on Cape Cod, at or near Provincetown, Massachusetts. Figure 22 shows one of these boats, sloop-rigged, having the characteristic hull and arrangement of this class of boat. While many of these craft were sloop-rigged, old photographs show that the cat-rigged boat was the most common. The Cape Cod boats usually had some flare to the sides, as shown in the drawing, as well as some sheer, but the bottom rarely had any fore-and-aft camber. The hull was completely decked; a small hatch aft allowed part of the hold to be used to stow gear. There were two pump boxes, one at each rail, and in old days these had the common wooden plunger, but in the twentieth century the sheet-iron "fisherman's pump" was used, by inserting the barrel in the old pump boxes. There was a large centerboard, of course, and a skeg aft supporting a rudder, made up much like a centerboard case and centerboard. Thus, the rudder was an auxiliary center-

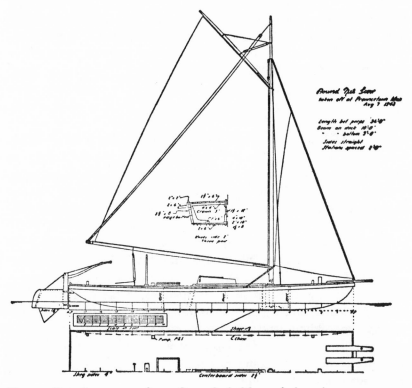

Fig. 22. Pound-net scow from Cape Cod. Most of these boats were cat-rigged.

board and the additional draft acquired by the dropped blade made steering safe when there was a roll to the sea, as there often is on the Cape shore. The rig was small and the mainboom-end was well inboard.

These boats are reported to have been quite fast under sail and weatherly but were never employed in rough weather. The driving rig was the same as used on Lake Erie, but it was usually placed off-side in the sloop-rigged boats. The eastern scows did not have the stern slot, for pulling stakes, used on Erie. The stake boats at Provincetown were 30 to 38 feet long; the boat shown is 36 feet long and 9 feet 8 inches beam over the sheer strakes, 10 feet over the guards. The boat shown in Figure 22 represents a large number of the small sailing scows used all along the coast and has a rectangular deck outline, straight, flaring sides, and rounded rake-ends fore and aft; the after rake was sometimes the longer, but it was not unusual to make the fore rake the greater. In the stake boats the fore rake was always the shorter to carry the weight forward when driving stakes.

The Scow Sloops

Small, decked scow sloops, having a cuddy and a cargo hatch, were very popular in the last half of the nineteenth century all along the coast and on the large lakes and rivers. The small scows usually were jib-and-mainsail rigged, but the larger ones, 45 feet and upward in length, were very often fitted with topmasts and gaff-topsails, as well as a jib-topsail in some sloops.

These scow sloops were sometimes rectangular in deck plan, but the better-built hulls usually had sprung sides. There was usually some flare in the sides and sheer at the gunwale. The small scow sloops were employed in such occupations as carrying farm produce, firewood, and ice; in the fisheries, they carried supplies and engaged in tending fish traps; and in rare instances they were used to house fishing gangs. The large scows were in the brick, stone, and firewood trades; some ran ice to Boston from Maine, and many made coastal voyages.

This wide variety of occupations resulted in scows built to a wide range in dimensions and in the details of construction and fittings, to suit their employment. Yet the hull-form and some fittings remained rather standardized. One almost universal fitting in the large scows was the stockless rudder; this appears on the majority of scow sloops and schooners on the East Coast and also in the San Francisco scow schooners on the West Coast. The stocked rudder, usually hung outboard, had much popularity only in the small scows. The large scows sometimes had bulwarks, but these were rarely used in the small sloops, being replaced with a low log

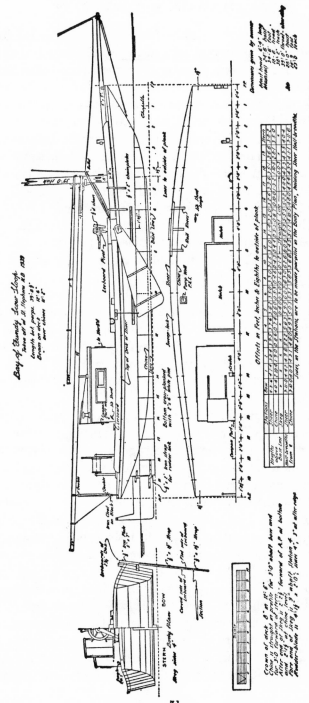

71

Fig. 23. Small scow sloop of the Maine type but more refined in model than many of the type. Most of this size were employed in carrying cord wood and farm produce on rivers and bays on the coasts of Maine and New Brunswick.

rail. Leeboards were much used in Maine waters and in the lower Bay of Fundy; elsewhere, centerboards were common. The double leeboard was rather more popular than the single board in the scow sloops.

Figure 23 represents a rather typical small scow sloop, possibly a little better designed and finished than many of her class. This boat was employed in carrying supplies to a cannery on Quoddy Bay and had been built at or near Back Bay, New Brunswick, about 1901, by a carpenter from Bath, Maine. When measured in 1939 at St. Stephens, N.B., she was fully loaded with canned goods, and though left high and dry by the tide, her construction could not be completely studied. The boat was observed under sail afterwards, and she appeared a very fast sailer, considering her heavy load. She was heavily canvased, was well handled by the crew of two, and seemed to be very quick in tacking.

This boat measured 39′ 8″ on deck and 12′ 4″ beam at the gunwale; her flare of side was moderate and her ends, compared with the beam, were rather narrower than was generally the case. On the whole, the boat had a strong resemblance to the small scow sloops once popular on the Kennebec and nearby rivers in Maine —as would be expected, since her builder was from this section of the state.

Particular notice should be taken of her stockless rudder, which has been spoken of earlier as a rather typical fitting of New England scows as well as of others. This type of rudder was hung on the skeg in the usual manner, with pintles and gudgeons, but instead of a stock and tiller, a horn projected upward at the after end of the blade, to just above deck level. From the upper end of this horn, the wheel ropes led to quarter blocks and thence to the drum of a steering wheel mounted in the old fashion on A-frames. The customary reeving of the wheel ropes was as follows. At the quarters and on the outside of the transom or stern log there were heavy eye bolts; to these the standing parts of the wheel ropes were made fast, not with a splice but seized. The wheel ropes then passed through single blocks bolted on each side of the horn and from there back to the quarters and either through pivoted lead-blocks on deck, or through a sheave in each quarter in the taffrail, if the wheel were well aft. From here the ropes were usually carried direct to the wooden drum, where the bitter ends were stapled in the old fashion. Some scows had an additional set of lead-blocks on each side of the wheel, to keep the wheel ropes out of the way of men working on the quarters. This arrangement gave a safe and powerful control of the large "barn-door" rudders, hauling them around instead of twisting them with a stock and tiller. If the wheel ropes became slack, adjustment was made at the eyebolts without any unreeving. Hemp line was used, lanyard stuff, which did not stretch too much. In large craft, the use of a gun-tackle purchase between quarters and horn gave the necessary power. This inexpensive and powerful steering gear has much to recommend it; it can be quickly built and readily repaired, without resort to a blacksmith or machine shop.

The eastern scows, if fitted with leeboards, often had them pivoted on bolts through the sides, in the plank-sheer, or through the log rails. This had the disadvantage that if the weatherboard was not hoisted promptly in tacking in a fresh breeze it would be torn from the side, possibly doing serious damage to the hull. As a result, some scows had racks fitted on both sides as in the single-leeboard arrangement. But the most satisfactory alternate was to pivot the boards on a length of chain toggled to the inside of the log rails and to the outboard face of the leeboards. This, if of proper length, would allow the weather leeboard to trail outward and rise, if not raised in time, without breaking away, after which the board could be housed when convenient. The "broken-wing" effect of the leeboard to weather would thus be no danger to hull or leeboard. The chain pivot is shown in the figure. The hoisting of the board in this example was a single-part lanyard belayed to cleats on the rails abreast the wheelman. The jib sheets also belayed aft on the sides of the cabin trunk, so the boat could be tacked by the man at the wheel, unaided.

In large scows, there was often a purchase on the fall of the leeboard lanyards, inside the rail, to give power to raise the heavy boards. The leeboards were usually flat-sided, apparently, but in a few cases, and in the example here, the inside face of the board was slightly convex from edge to edge while the outboard face was flat. The boards, when down, did not parallel the centerline in the example. Due to the shape of the side of the hull at the position of the boards and to the side chocks, the boards had a slight cant so that the leading edge of the leeboard would point very slightly to windward. This was supposed to make the scows more weatherly, and in recent years it has been noticed that a similar practice existed in some Dutch leeboard craft, though they have wing-section boards of a more developed shape.

The rig of the example requires no comment, for it is the usual American sloop in all respects: the jib-and-mainsail combination employing a large jib with a very slight overlap set up on a bowsprit. A generous number of reef bands marked the sloop-rigged scow, for, like most very shallow hulls, her range of stability was not great. By the time the lee rail went under, a wise captain began to reef. The master of the New Brunswick scow claimed that he could weather deep sloops if he kept the scow sailing hard, and did not pinch her, for his speed and the leeboards would set him to weather of his apparent course in smooth or moderate sea. He stated the boat was best in a fresh breeze and smooth water and that she was a rather poor drifter. A couple of sweep-locks in the rail enabled the crew to move her in a calm, but when seen an outboard-engined skiff was used for towing under such conditions. However, a pair of 16-foot sweeps were still carried on end in the rigging for emergency, thus showing a regrettable lack of trust in modern engines.

For some years after the introduction of the gasoline engine into the yachting fleet, a few of these small scow sloops afloat were converted to yachts, particularly on the Maine coast. A rare individual had been built for this purpose, usually with a longer and even more unsightly house than in the working scow. These latter craft were, in fact, sailing houseboats. Similar scow sloops were sometimes used by gunning clubs. In spite of their cumbersome appearance, they were very useful boats with a reasonable turn of speed, well suited to working in narrow and shoal waters. But the type has never become popular in the pleasure fleet, even in those areas where it was well known and most useful, for it was not a thing of beauty and only appealed to the most practical sailor.

In Maine, the center of scow-building in the days of sail was at Woolwich, across from Bath on the lower Kennebec River. Local tradition claims that the first settlers in this section used "flats" or "gundelows," and it is therefore supposed that the scows are lineal descendants of the colonial craft. The continuous existence of the type since colonial times has not been established, and the appearance of the scow at various places on the Maine coast is probably the result of need and of a widespread knowledge of the type, rather than an example of long-term local development. It should be observed also that the Kennebec scows showed no individualism in design, as compared with other classes of scows on the coast.

One of the most attractive of the working scow sloops was the Casco Bay type used in the fyke fishery in the 1880's and early 90's. These were centerboard scows, 35 to 45 feet long, low-sided, and with a rounded fore rake and a shallow transom stern. The run was unusually long, and due to the trim of the boat the bottom came up to the fore rake in a long straight line, making a fast sailing boat. The flare of the sides was small but in spite of this the boat did not look clumsy.

There are a number of pictures of this type, and one hulk was found in 1938. This craft, though slightly above the length limit established for this study of fishing boats, is shown in Figure 24. It is the only detailed drawing possible because only one hull has been found.

The construction is an unusual one for a scow, as it was built with a rabbeted chine log the full length of the boat, sprung to shape apparently, except forward, where it appears to have been shaped from natural crooks. The sides of the hull, edge-bolted, stand in the upper rabbets of the chine logs; the bottom, planked fore and aft, in the lower rabbets. There is a complete framing system in addition, and the floors and side frames are of sufficient depth to allow two fastenings in the laps at the chines without the use of knee timber.

A heavy inside keelson runs the length of the hull, scarphed in four places so it could be shaped out of slightly crooked stock. The skeg is continued forward past the centerboard slot and faired into a rounded external cutwater. The extension of the skeg, in way of the centerboard slot, is not increased in siding, since the skeg and the whole outside shoe are quite wide and are beveled off to a thin face only along the cutwater from a point where the fore rake begins. The rig was a rather lofty jib-and-mainsail, without any peculiarities.

These scows were usually built at South Portland by ship carpenters during the dull summer months. The fyke net was a hooped fishing net, forming a trap, and the large deck space of the scow was necessary in setting or taking up this fishing gear. This style of fish trap had only a short period of popularity on the Maine coast, as the gear was expensive and readily damaged by a gale.

Among the scows used in New England were those on the Piscataqua River, New Hampshire; these were single-leeboard, open or half-decked scows fitted with the lateen-like sail and rig of the gundalow in this area. This rig has a very short mast, to which is slung an almost vertical yard carrying a triangular loose-footed sail. It is usual to call this sail a lateen, but it really is the old loose-footed leg-of-mutton, for the yard stands so upright and is slung so low that there is practically no sail forward of the mast. The heel of the yard is counterweighted, and the whole purpose of the peculiar rig, now extinct, was to allow the spar and sail to be easily dipped to pass under a low bridge at the entrance of Great Bay, just above Portsmouth, N.H., and other bridges upriver.

Small barges or scows of the rectangular model were used in carrying hay and brick clay in Massachusetts. A well-developed scow sloop, about 40 feet in length, was commonly employed on the Connecticut River. It was a leeboard scow much like the example in Figure 23, but with a stocked rudder. The wheel was mounted on a heavy, low tiller and moved from side to side with it—the old "shin-cracker" gear also employed in many whaleships in New England. The Connecticut River sloop usually had no bowsprit but did carry a topmast and gaff-topsail, and a jib-topsail as well, to enable it to work under the high shores of the river when the lower sails might be becalmed. These scows had an oak rack outside of their leeboards (they carried a pair) instead of the usual iron-rod type. They were built with low bulwarks or log rails and had a trunk cabin well aft.

Scows of much the same appearance were to be found on the Great Lakes, on Lake Champlain, on the Pacific Coast, and on the St. Lawrence. Large scow sloops, about 60 feet in length, were em-

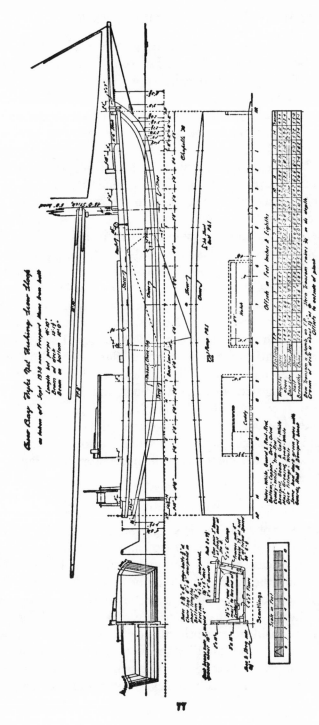

Fig. 24. Highly developed type of Maine fishing scow used extensively on Casco Bay in the 1890's. Jib-and-mainsail rig.

ployed in the Quincy, Massachusetts, granite trade, and similar sloops, even larger, were used in the Hudson River brick trade. As late as 1932, a large scow sloop hailed from Havre de Grace, Maryland, operating on the Chesapeake; smaller sloop and schooner scows were once numerous there. Scow sloops were also used on the rice plantations in the Carolinas, and small sloop-rigged and schooner-rigged scows have been used all along the Gulf Coast, to the Mexican border. Many of the southern scows had V-bottoms, and these will be examined later when that form of hull is discussed. Even the round-bottomed hull was adapted to the scow form, but this also must be left to later examination.

It is rather rare to find a scow in America planked fore-and-aft on the bottom, though many had fore-and-aft sheathing placed over cross-planked bottoms. The fore-and-aft planking was confined almost entirely to the Casco Bay scows and the V-bottomed scows in southern waters, to river boats, such as the "sturgeonhead" and the other river scows in the Canadian Northwest, and the western river John boat. The sturgeonhead was a round-bottomed scow, sometimes built with a marked chine along the bilge, but with rounded transverse frames, and the Canadian scows were regularly framed boats having sprung sides, often clench-built, and flat bottoms. The John boat was very much like Chapman's punt drawing. The fore-and-aft planked bottom on these craft was employed because, when running rapids or beaching on a stony shore, it withstood the blows of driftwood and stones much better than the cross-planking.

Beach Punt

Few scows, except some garveys, have been used as beach boats. An example of such craft—one that employed the fore-and-aft planked bottom once used in the Bermuda Islands and in some West Indian areas—and the only example found, was a Bermudian boat preserved in the Mariners' Museum, at Newport News, Virginia. This boat is shown in Figure 25 and is catalogued as a "Bermuda dory," but I am unable to trace this name elsewhere. The boat was sometimes called a "beach punt" in the West Indies; the name was also applied to any small beach boat, so it cannot be accepted as the correct type-name. The boat was never sailed and was simply a rowing scow, fitted to land on the beach. The construction is very similar to that of the English Thames punt, but the boat is of far different proportions. Steering and sculling was accomplished by an oar which passed through the stern overhang, in a shallow water-tight well. The shelter amidships protected goods and was mounted on a sort of outrigger on each side, which was also used to mount oarlocks. The plan shows the peculiarities of this boat in other respects; the boat obviously was well suited to working off shoal

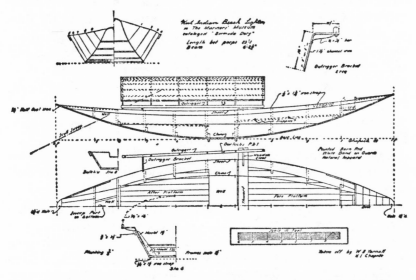

Fig. 25. West Indian beach punt for carrying passengers and freight, about 1910.

beaches where the surf was not excessively dangerous. It is possible this type is a survival of a much older "flat" or beach lighter from colonial times. The boat has a faint resemblance to the ancient Egyptian ships, but, of course, is on a different hull-form.

The types of scows discussed here are but a small part of those used in American waters, even in the small class. But enough of them have been shown to allow examination of the most-developed local models and rigs and the most common methods of construction in the flat-bottomed category. The varying degrees of refinement in design, construction, and rig can be more fully realized later, when the other forms of scow, round-bottomed and V-bottomed, are presented. The rather primitive form of the working scows has prevented the type from becoming well known in marine literature, yet the sailing scow was unquestionably one of the most efficient working boats produced in America, before motors appeared in the commercial fleet.

The Bateaux

The skiff and its successors or relatives, the various sharpies, comprise a large proportion of the flat-bottomed craft in the days of sail in America. Less numerous, but probably the oldest form, were the bateau and its relatives, the dory and river skiff. Since the available evidence indicates the bateau form of construction to have been the oldest, the types in this category should be considered first. It will be remembered that the bateau category of types is based upon the arbitrary distinction of fore-and-aft bottom planking combined with a transverse frame-system.

The lumberman's bateau is the lineal descendant of the colonial bateau shown in Chapter 1, and it is possible to trace the continuous existence of this boat in the northern states and in Canada from about 1755 right down to the present, in the records of military campaigns, travelers' accounts of the northern wilderness, and reports of the fur trade, throughout the nineteenth century, and in lumbering publications in the twentieth century. The hull-form of this type has changed little, judging by the one plan of 1776 and the plans of modern lumbermen's bateaux. The boat was a double-ended, flat-bottomed type, with straight, or curved, flaring sides between bottom and gunwale, raking bow and stern, and with rather marked sheer and fore-and-aft camber to the bottom. Some boats, particularly those with curved side frames, were lapstrake, but on the whole the smooth-planked or caravel-built sides were popular.

The range in size was very great—from about 12 feet over-all for the smallest boats mentioned in available records up to the recorded maximum length of 84 feet. At one time, about the middle of the last century, the bateaux used in the fur trade and in lumbering were usually 30 to 36, 40 to 45, and 50 to 52 feet over-all. The proportions of the boats varied somewhat; thus, an 18-foot bateau was 3 feet wide over the gunwales, 12 inches deep amidships, and in this depth the sides flared about 3½ inches. The stem and stern raked 24 inches and from bottom to gunwale; at the ends of the bottom, the hull was 15 inches deep. The length of stem and post along the rake was 30 inches, and the rocker of the bottom was 3½ inches at each end.

Such a boat was usually propelled by paddles, and, upstream, it was poled with setting poles. A rowing bateau 24 feet long was about 5½ feet beam at the gunwale, 3½ feet beam on the bottom, and about 22 inches deep amidships with about 3 inches rocker at bow and stern. The bow and stern were not alike in this boat; the bow raked about 3 feet and the stern 2, the stem being 4 feet 8 inches along its rake and the stern 2 feet 11 inches. The greatest beam was usually just before amidships, so the bow was fuller on bottom and gunwale than the stern. The boat sheered up a good deal forward and there were two thwarts, one just forward of amidships and another about 4½ feet farther aft. The boat rowed with two pair of oars on double tholes. A 36-foot boat was 7 feet wide over the gunwales, 5 feet on the bottom, and about 22 inches deep amidships; such a boat would have four thwarts. The larger boats, from 36 feet upward, rarely exceeded 9 feet beam over the gunwales; even in the 84-foot length, according to a description, the maximum beam was but 10 feet 2 inches.

Figure 26 is the plan of a modern lumberman's bateau of a type much used in Quebec Province. She is 31′ 11″ long, 5′ 3″ beam, and the model is considered a very good one for fast-running streams. The amount of rocker in the bottom appears to be somewhat greater than in most boats of this class. The construction is shown in the plan and requires no explanation. The seams in the bottom plank are sometimes made tongue and groove, or fitted with a spline, but this practice is by no means universal.

On the St. Lawrence River, from Montreal to the Gaspé Peninsula, the common rowing skiff is a small bateau, double-ended, and somewhat on the lumbermen's model with one marked departure—the bottom is cross-planked skiff-fashion. Figure 27 is a good example of these boats, which pull well and are surprisingly seaworthy. They are used for both pleasure and commercial fishing. The sides are commonly of one very wide plank; the few side-frames seem to be employed largely for the purpose of supporting short risers in the way of the thwarts. Apparently sail is not used in these boats, but information on early boats of this type has not been obtained and it is therefore possible that these craft were once fitted for sail. This boat may be said to represent a transition between the true bateau and the flat-bottomed skiff in which the form of the bateau is combined with the construction of the skiff. The question of how early the cross-planking was used in such

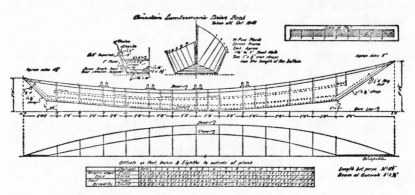

Fig. 26. Modern lumberman's bateau, Province of Quebec, for use on rivers having rapids.

boats as this cannot now be answered, and this example illustrates the difficulty in discussing the history of the bateau-skiff methods of construction.

A round-sided and clenched lumberman's bateau is shown in Figure 28. This was a type of boat popular in northern Michigan and Wisconsin. The construction of the sides is the standard clench method, but, instead of notching the frames to fit the laps on the inside of the planking, shims are used to give the same support to each plank or strake. This boat was 31′ 6″ molded length and had a beam inside the sheer strakes of 5′ 6″, while the molded beam of the bottom was but 2′ 0″ amidships. The laps die out near the bow and stern, becoming "dory" lap, so as to come flush at the posts. This example of the lumbermen's bateaux is most refined in model and construction.

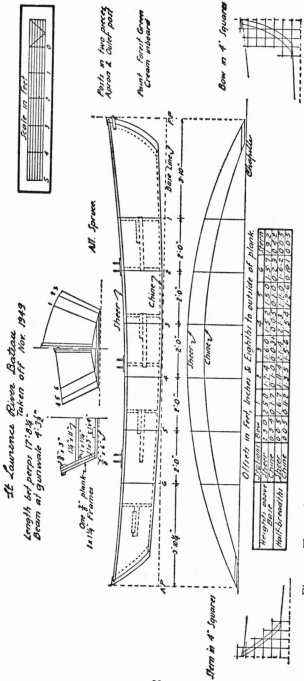

Fig. 27. Type of small double-ended bateau used below Quebec on the St. Lawrence River.

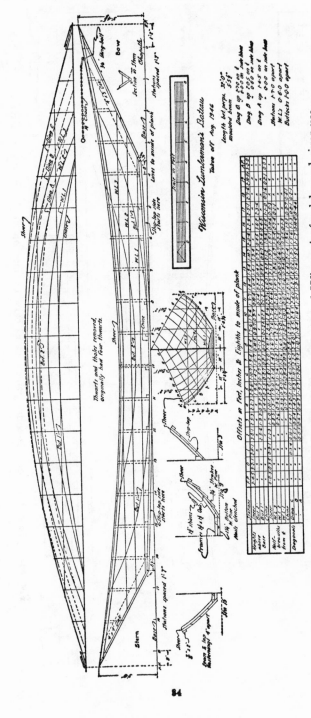

Fig. 28. Type of bateau developed in Michigan and Wisconsin for lake and river use.

Dories

The fisherman's dory seems to be closely related to the bateau in both construction and history. Whether or not both are descendants of the various flat-bottomed double-enders of Europe, such as the "bêtes" of the coast of Provence, is an unsolved puzzle, though certainly there is a physical resemblance in many cases. There is the record of flat-bottomed boats used on the Gulf of St. Lawrence in fishing in early days, and the early appearance of the New England fishermen in these waters suggests a connection between the New England dory and the early French boats. However, the physical likeness would, in this discussion, permit the dory to be classed as a bateau type of hull on this ground alone.

It cannot be determined with certainty when the New England style of dory came into being. A set of models in the Peabody Marine Museum at Salem, Massachusetts, purports to show the development of the dory from a rather wide-sterned skiff to the modern narrow-sterned boat. The reliability of these models as evidence appears open to some question, as the ones representing the "first" models may not be contemporary.

The assumption that the modern dory may have descended from the wide-sterned skiff would be a natural one until the construction was taken into consideration. Furthermore, the wide-sterned dory cannot be accepted as an indication of an early type on this ground alone, since such craft were built on the Pacific Northwest Coast well into the 1880's and are now in fashion in boats built for outboard motors. At any rate, some kind of dory-type boat was in use on the Massachusetts coast as early as 1726. It was not until the introduction of dory fishing in the Gloucester fishing schooners about 1850 (many authorities place it at 1856–1858) that the so-called "bank dory" began to be developed. It is highly probable that the dory had previously been used only in longshore fisheries, as all bank fishing was then done with hand lines from the decks of the schooners.

The bank dory was developed specifically as a ship's boat, but it became so well known and so common a type that it not only was used alongshore but influenced the design of some local fishing boats. The bank dory was also very important in that it was the first type of American small boat to be mass-produced on a large scale. This class of dory originally became popular because it could be lightly, but strongly, built, which made hoisting it in and out of a vessel an easy matter. Also, the dory was so formed that, by the simple removal of the thwarts, a number of these boats could be nested and thus carried in a small space. The dory, although a flat-bottomed boat, was seaworthy, particularly when loaded, and rowed rather easily. Light, it was a tender boat that required skill to use without capsizing. But in its proper employment the bank dory had the weight of its fishing gear and bait aboard, which was sufficient to give stability. When caught far from the mother ship by a sudden gale, the doryman usually threw over his fish and much of his gear and then, by placing himself in the extreme bow or stern, scudded to leeward.

The bank dory by 1870 had gradually evolved into five standard lengths: 12, 13, 14, 15, and 16 feet. These lengths were on the bottom, from the heel of the stempost to the bottom of the transom; thus, due to the rake of the ends, the boats were actually nearly 4 feet longer. By experiment, the form of the bank dory, in suitability for its employment, reached as near perfection as is possible in any boat. By 1880 it was being mass-produced in the Massachusetts towns of Gloucester, Beverly, Essex, Newburyport, and Salisbury. The last-named town was then the center of the industry, with seven shops producing from 200 to 650 boats a year, according to Hall, in *The Tenth Census of the United States*, 1880.

The dory was also built in large numbers at Seabrook, New Hampshire, and at Portland, Cundy's Harbor, and Bremen, Maine, with Cundy's Harbor leading in Maine. By 1888, the famous Gloucester firm of Higgins and Gifford was leading in the mass production of boats, and was building dories, seine boats, and other small craft in great numbers.

The firm of Higgins and Gifford, established in 1873, advertised in 1886 that it had built over 3,000 boats in the preceding thirteen years—small yachts, rowboats, yawls, lifeboats, seine boats, and dories. Its most numerous lines in production thereafter were seine boats and dories, which had great reputations for excellence in design and build. In fact, the model and construction of the Hig-

gins and Gifford bank dory became the standard in the type by
1886 and was much copied.

Another noted dory builder in this period was the firm of Hiram
Lowell, at nearby Amesbury, which succeeded Higgins and Gifford.
In the present century, Amesbury became the center of dory production, and the Amesbury dory was the standard of the fishing
fleet.

Figure 29 is an example of a Higgins and Gifford dory originally
taken off for *Forest & Stream*, in 1887. Though the magazine published the lines, the details were not given. The drawings not
only show the lines and scantlings but also the patent clip used to
join the floor futtocks to those of the sides, which did away with
the necessity of using natural crook frames, or knees. The peculiar
half-lap used instead of the usual clench-lap is also shown; the
slight projection in the "dory lap" disappeared at the extreme bow
and stern. This construction is still employed in dories.

It will be noted that the stem is not rabbeted and is made of
a stem liner, or apron, cut out of a natural crook to the required
curve with the small outside piece or cutwater bent on and nailed
after the sides had been fitted and the ends of the strakes sawn off
flush with the forward face of the stem liner. The typical transom,
called by some the "tombstone" because of its suggestive shape, is
shown. For all practical purposes, the extreme narrowness of its
bottom makes the dory double-ended.

In the construction the bottom is set up after being shaped, the
seams grooved and splined, and the two or three planks forming
the bottom are secured to one another by cleats, which come between the frames. The bottom is then sprung between special
horses to the mold of the fore-and-aft rocker, 3 to 6 inches forward and 2 to 5 inches aft, depending upon length and on the
fancy of the builder. The frames are then set up and the stem
liner and transom secured, to fit rakes formed on the stocks. The
hull is then planked, the gunwale and guard put in place, the inboard work is finished off, and, finally, the cutwater is added and
the boat painted.

Every piece of the dory's structure was made from a master
pattern and only the lengths of the side plank and such pieces as the

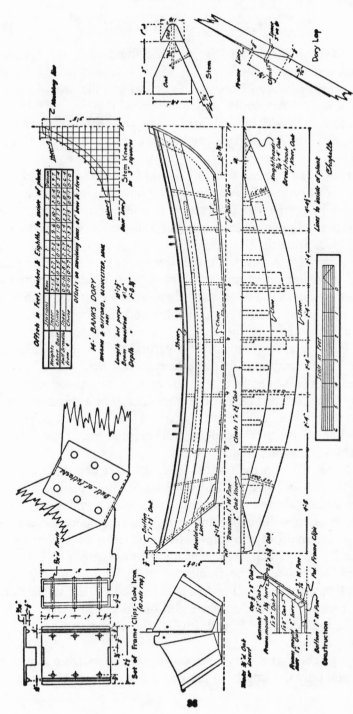

Fig. 29. Drawings of an old "stock boat" Banks dory of the style carried by Gloucestermen in the 1880's and 90's.

86

gunwales and guards required being sawn to length when the boat was being erected. All metalwork and fastenings were of iron. The patent frame clips were first galvanized wrought iron, but in later years steel clips were used in some dories instead. The clench nails were the standard galvanized wrought-iron tack. Double wooden thole pins were always used. There was usually a mast hole in the forward thwart and a light step under it for a short mast that carried a small loose-footed spritsail; sometimes a jib was set. Since the dory had neither keel nor centerboard, the sails were only effective running free, and the use of the jib seems to have been an affectation.

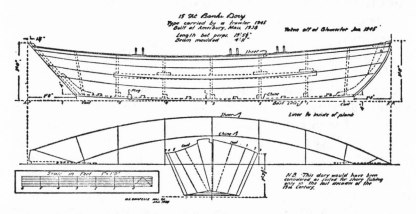

Fig. 30. Modern Banks dory, scantlings approximately those of the older dory of 1880.

When sailing, the dory was steered with one of her oars. The hand-liners used the smaller dories, 12- and 13-footers; the others were for haddock and halibut fishing. The boats were built of white pine and cedar plank, with the frames and stem work of white oak. The transom was of white pine, and thwarts, risers, and cleats on the bottom were of oak.

The amount of rocker and sheer was originally determined by the use to which the dory was to be put. A boat built for use inshore in smooth water was usually given a little rocker and sheer. In more recent times the bank dory has been built with very little sheer and rocker and with a good deal less flare to the side, as is shown in Figure 30. This boat is somewhat stiffer than the old dory but harder to row and far more clumsy in appearance. With the decline in the use of the dory in hand-lining, the boat, sadly enough, has gradually become somewhat decadent in model.

The weight of the dories varied with the size, of course, and there was also some variation in the weights of models by the various builders. The 12-foot dory usually weighed about 160–170 pounds, the 13-footer about 180–190 pounds, the 14-footer about 190–195 pounds, the 15-footer about 240–260 pounds, and the 16-footer about 300 pounds. Shore-fishing dories were often lighter owing to the omission of parting boards under two or three thwarts, which kept fish from sliding all over the bottom, and to the use of fewer thwarts. Dories usually had four to six sets of frames, with two sets of side cant frames, but the latter were sometimes left out of the shore boats.

The two smallest dories rowed but one pair of oars, as a rule, but the larger ones had two pairs. In each case, however, there was one additional rowing thwart with tholes, to allow the oarsman to trim a loaded dory by using the extra thwart. In 1887, a few bank dories were fitted with centerboards as an experiment, but the idea does not seem to have proven useful enough to set a fashion. The purpose of the scheme was to reduce the labor of rowing a loaded boat back to the schooner. To allow nesting, these dories were fitted with a patented metal folding board that required a case only 4 inches high.

Shore dories were often fitted with centerboard and sail, and some types developed into full-fledged sailing craft. There were three localities in particular where the sailing dory was popular with lobstermen and other inshore fishermen. Cape Ann, from Gloucester around to Essex, was one such place. Here a rather wide, open dory, fitted with centerboard, rudder, and a spritsail and jib rig, came into use sometime about 1873. The type was gradually improved, by the addition of washboards extending the full length of the hull, to reduce the danger of swamping when heeled under sail in a fresh breeze. These boats were straight-sided, had moderately wide bottoms and great flare of the sides.

Figure 31 shows one of the last of these dories; it was said to have been built by Higgins and Gifford. The boats were said to have all been much like the one shown except there were many with less overhang in the bow. The characteristic rig of the Cape Ann boats is shown, and worthy of notice is the retention of the curious lifting straps which were used forward to hook in the jib tack and aft as a substitute for a mainsheet horse. These straps were large hemp grommets, passing through the hull from side to side. The construction of these dories was the same as in the bank dory, except for the addition of a series of deep, short deck beams to support the light wash or covering boards along the sides. Most boats were said to have four small knees, in addition, supporting each covering board. The cen-

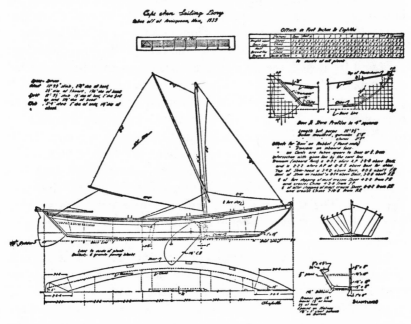

Fig. 31. Dory designed for sailing, with the old form of sprit-mainsail once popular in many types of boats in New England.

terboard case had a distinctive rounded top used in sailing dories, and the board was worked by the usual folding rod.

Swampscott, to the south, was another center of building. Here the popular sailing dory was an open boat, usually with slightly rounded side frames and rigged with a low leg-of-mutton having a long, high-cocked boom and a jib tacked to the stem. The boat was lighter than the Cape Ann dory and was more of a beach boat. The round-top centerboard case was used here also. In the 1890's the Swampscott dories attracted much attention because of their speed, and a racing sailing dory appeared that was known as the "clipper dory." The boat was much like the working boat, usually about 21 feet long, but with a rather narrow bottom and very rounded sides. The Swampscott dories were, like all of their class, rather tender in strong winds, and eventually the racing dories were constructed with half-decks and cockpit coamings.

In both the Swampscott and Cape Ann working dories, the main-sheet was never belayed but was held by a turn over a pin and by the helmsman. This allowed the mainsail to be let fly when the boat was overpressed. The spritsail, with its loose foot, was the safest because it split the wind more quickly than the boomed leg-of-mutton. As the wind freshened, the jib was usually taken in and the boat sailed under mainsail alone. When two men were in the boat, however, it was possible to carry the jib, as one man could hold the sheet. The boats were not luffed in a squall but were kept moving by slacking the sheets. Being light craft, a luff and the resultant loss of head-way made them unmanageable, and when they fell off they might readily capsize. As in all small open or half-decked light-displace-ment boats, the dory required skillful handling in strong winds and heavy sea. The tiller was often replaced by a yoke and steering lines so that the helmsman could keep his weight to windward at all times.

Two-masted dories were used, both at Swampscott and at Boston. These were rather large half-decked boats, 20 to 24 feet long on the bottom, sometimes fitted with a small cuddy. This class is said to have originated at Swampscott in the 1880's, and as these large dories became popular, their building extended to Rockport, Gloucester, and East Boston. At Boston the Italian fishermen adopted these boats for the inshore fisheries, and the height of their popularity there was in the 1890's. Figure 32 represents a typical dory of this class, the largest type of dory-model sailing boat em-ployed in the fisheries. These dories did not carry a jib but were, in effect, sharpie-rigged except that booms were laced to the foot of the sails. These boats required ballast and, with experienced handling, were safe and able small craft in heavy weather.

Some of the more expensive boats of this class, built late in the 1890's, aped the clipper dory in having the rounded side, and at least two were built with iron ballast keels through which their centerboards dropped. Generally speaking, however, these large sailing dories were lightly and cheaply built and were not long-lived; when heavily loaded, they are reported to have strained markedly when pressed with sail. Nevertheless, the large dory represents a seaworthy flat-bottomed type that deserves more attention than it has yet had from boat sailors.

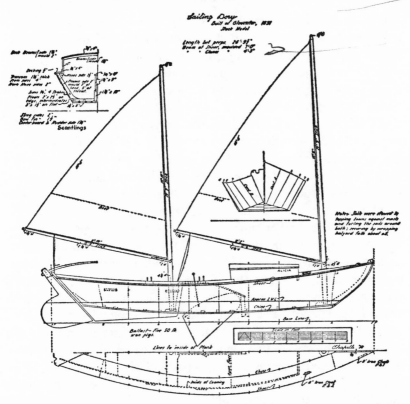

Fig. 32. Two-masted sailing dory popular with Italian fishermen at Boston, in the 1890's. (See Appendix for offsets and dimensions.)

There were many variations in the dory model. In Nova Scotia a double-ended dory, having both ends curved in profile and with rounded sides between bottom and gunwale, has been popular, and similar boats have been used in New England. In some round-sided dories caravel-planking has been used, and in some the sides have been rounded so much that the flat bottom is now no more than a wide, flat keel. These departures from the true dory model, flat-bottomed and flat-sided, are usually no more than attempts to "improve" the dory, at the expense of its low-cost construction, or to convert it into something it was not originally intended to be.

New Jersey Beach Skiff or Seabright Skiff

Closely related in structure to the round-sided dory was the northern New Jersey beach skiff, a forerunner of the noted Seabright skiff. These boats ranged from about 18 feet in length upward to 36, and their rig varied with the length. The smaller boats were single-masted, with a loose-footed spritsail and a jib tacked to the stemhead, while large skiffs were two-masted, sometimes with the spritsail rig of the garvey, and sometimes with the leg-of-mutton rig, usually without a jib. These boats were originally beach boats, launched and landed on open beaches exposed to the surf. Therefore, they were clench-built to allow the lightest possible construction consonant with strength, for the clench-build permits a very flexible skin, supported by extremely light framing. In the smaller skiffs, however, full advantage of the very light framing was not always taken, for the light cedar hulls, because of their small size, could be easily handled on the beach. Hence, the small skiffs sometimes had fifteen to twenty-five sawn frames, while the large skiffs would have double that number of very light steam-bent frames. The small boats were somewhat more rigid than the large skiffs, but the smaller boats' lighter loads made this no serious objection. The clench-build, because of the continuous fastening along the seams or laps, is particularly well fitted to withstand the great shocks of beaching, which would loosen the caulking of the ordinary caravel-build.

The beach skiff of northern New Jersey had one peculiarity of model that does not appear in the round-sided dories of northern waters. In the Jersey boat the after end of the garboard or lower strake of the side is brought up and in, to come vertical at the sternpost, and the bottom of the square transom is at the top of this strake on the post. As a result there is a reverse chine formed in the run between the lowest side-strake and the next above, somewhat as was noticed in the cutter of 1762. This form of run makes for a steadier-steering boat and permits deeper loading without drag; also, it aids pumping or bailing by the steersman when running the surf singlehanded.

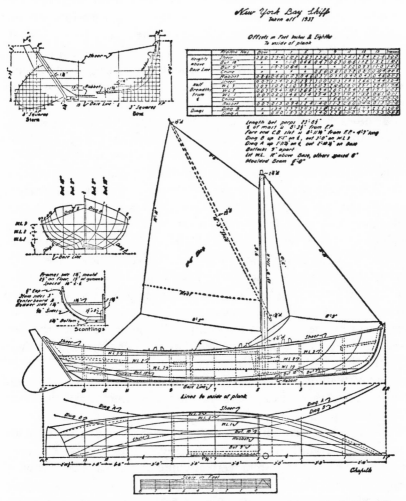

Fig. 33. Old beach skiff, northern New Jersey and New York Bay "Seabright" model.

The mode of construction is that of the common dory in principle and requires no explanation here.

It will be noted that the flat bottom is quite narrow in these skiffs, as may be seen in the drawings of a small skiff, Figure 33. This is an old sailing skiff and shows the characteristic appearance and proportions of the Jersey beach skiffs north of Barnegat Bay. To the southward, the beach skiffs have such round sides that the flat bottom becomes a wide flat keel. The Jersey skiffs, therefore, are examples of a transition from a flat-bottomed model to a round-bottomed one, within a relatively small area. The beach skiffs of northern New Jersey, before the introduction of the gasoline engine, were always open boats; those in the south had covering boards and a short foredeck.

The beach skiffs of northern New Jersey, when fitted with sail, had rather small wooden centerboards and employed a rudder, though in the surf they would have to use a sweep, of course, for which there was a deep notch in the transom. Skiffs built on New York Bay were used in oystering and were ceiled up over the frames, usually for their entire length. The true beach skiff was not ceiled, however. The north Jersey skiffs were able boats, rowing easily and sailing well; they were not racing boats and far more emphasis was placed on their being able to get home in bad weather than upon speed alone. Anyone who has witnessed the tremendous surf built up on the Jersey beaches in a heavy easterly gale, realizes that this is no place for a play boat in heavy weather. Before motors were introduced and before there were any harbor improvements, the Jersey beachmen were noted for skill and courage in handling their boats in heavy surf; they had some reputation as wreckers as well. There were but two sections of the United States where much beach work was necessary in sailing days, the Jersey beaches and the south shore of Cape Cod.

The beach skiffs built in New Jersey were always planked with cedar; sawn frames, if used, were usually of cedar roots. The bent frames, if used, and the stem were of white oak, as were the gunwale cap, thwarts, and sternpost. The working boats were usually fastened with galvanized wrought iron but the use of copper became common toward the end of the nineteenth century.

The history of the beach skiff is very difficult to trace; a square-sterned sailing skiff is mentioned in 1836 and seems to have been developed at first as a wrecking and lifesaving boat, rather than as a commercial fisherman. With slight modifications and an increase in size, the related Seabright skiff became a highly satisfactory motor-boat—one whose combination of speed and seaworthiness brought it a great reputation in the period of liquor smuggling during the late Prohibition Era.

The River Yawl-Boats

Of the bateau-dory class, the river skiff, or yawl, of the Ohio and Mississippi Rivers, is the remaining member to be described. This boat was in use as early as 1845 and appears to have been developed in its present form as a river steamer's service and lifeboat. This led to the development of a wide stern, to permit carrying heavy line ashore without depressing the stern so much that the boat would be in a dangerous or unhandy trim. This was accomplished by twisting the side planking sharply, as the stern is approached, so that here the boat is quite wide at gunwale, but narrow on the bottom. The result was a burdensome, easily rowed boat of very good qualities, and so the river yawl has survived with little change, until very recent years at least.

Figure 34 is an excellent modern example built by J. W. Weaver, Sr., at Racine, Ohio, early in this century. Similar skiffs were built by Fred Bell and by George Smith at Racine. The model cannot be said to be a local one, however, as similar skiffs were built at towns along the whole length of the Ohio and Mississippi—in fact, wherever there was steamboat navigation.

The model has been a standard one with the U. S. Army Engineers, and a drawing of one of these skiffs was in the *Engineer's Field Manual* (Part 2), of 1909, used in 1914–19. This boat could be built 18 to 24 feet in length with a beam at gunwale of 5' 2". The 18-foot skiff was the most popular size of yawl, and such a boat is shown in Figure 35. The boat was planked with white pine, but cedar and cypress were also used; the frames, stem, transom, skeg, and guards were of oak or yellow pine. Fastenings were of iron throughout. The stem was usually shaped to an arc of a circle in profile and was rabbeted. Building appears to have been done on a special stock which held the frames, transom, and stem, while the sides were bent. The bottom (always planked fore and aft) was then laid and the skeg placed, before the hull was righted to finish it inboard. The chine edges of the bottom plank were rarely beveled with the side in any of the river skiffs, but stood square to the plank here and sometimes at the transom as well.

The river yawl was primarily a rowboat until recent years; now

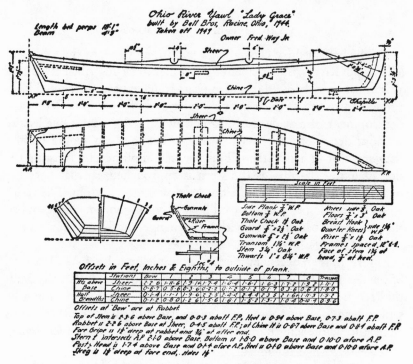

Fig. 34. River skiff or yawl.

the outboard motor often replaces the "white-ash breeze" of earlier times. In the nineteenth century there were skiffs fitted with centerboards and sails, for use on the lower Mississippi in particular. These boats were used by fishermen, trappers, and rivermen in their work. They were little different from the modern yawl in hull and were variously rigged, some with a boomed leg-of-mutton and some with the ubiquitous loose-footed spritsail.

Figure 34 is an example of one of the early sailing river skiffs and is probably rather typical of these boats. One noticeable detail in the river skiffs is that the gunwale top is never beveled and always stands square to the flare of the sides. The boats are heavy and very

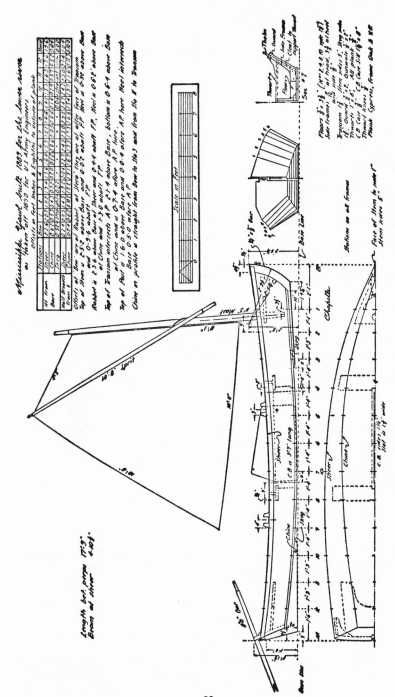

Fig. 35. River skiff fitted to sail, for use on lower Mississippi, 1889.

strong, and last extremely well. In very recent years, skiff-building has died out on the Ohio.

The Flat-bottomed or "Flatiron" Skiff

The flat-bottomed skiff, or "flatiron skiff," will be taken as the starting point for a discussion of the cross-planked flat-bottomed craft that include the sharpies once widely used in the United States. The flatiron skiff is an almost universal type of low-cost rowing boat, sometimes fitted with sail and, nowadays, built to carry an outboard motor. This class of boat has been built by both amateur and professional builders since early times in the United States, but the origin of the model and construction is unknown. It first drew the attention of marine writers on the Connecticut shore of Long Island Sound, but there is no reason to suppose it had originated there.

This skiff has been so widely built and by such a variety of builders that it appears in countless models, ranging all the way from very poor to excellent. The sailing skiffs were often somewhat better in model and build than the rowing boats. The preferred model for both skiffs, however, required a rather fixed chine-profile; this came aft from the stem in a straight line, usually sloping downward slightly and then, abaft amidships, the chines curved up and ran from there to the transom, either in a very gentle curve or straight in the finished hull. In some boats there was actually a slight angle in the bottom, at the beginning of the run, though this would be considered very crude work by the professional builders. To crown or camber the forebody along the bottom was also looked upon with scorn by professionals of experience, for this seems to make the flat-bottomed skiff hard to row and slow under sail. Usually, there was a good flare to the sides amidships, and very often the side planks were twisted from the stem aft, but not to such an extent as in the western river skiffs. The boats are often, and rightly, said to be easy to build but hard to design.

As an example of a well-designed flatiron skiff, Figure 36 will serve. This individual skiff happens to be one of a type once used on Cape Cod, but she is in no way different from the skiffs used as sailing work-boats along the shores of Long Island Sound in the last four decades of the nineteenth century. The usual sprit leg-of-mutton rig was used in most of these skiffs, though a few had sprit-sails or short-gaff sails instead. The scantlings in the example are rather typical: a 15-foot skiff would have ⅝″ sides, but the bottom, chine logs and frames would be of 1″ stock. The favorite timber for these skiffs in southern New England was white pine, with oak

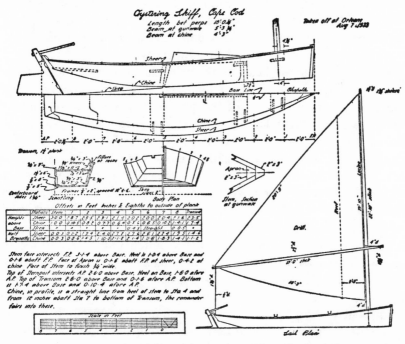

Fig. 36. Typical sharpie skiff used in southern New England for oystering, clamming, and for general purposes.

for stem, skeg, rudder, and centerboard. Cedar was sometimes used for sides. On the whole, these skiffs were rather heavy. The very high-tucked stern, giving a shallow much-raked transom, was popular in working skiffs because it allowed heavy loads to be carried without forming a drag by immersing the transom. This style of stern also allowed proper trim, without ballast being required, in spite of the weight of the mast forward. New England skiff and sharpie sailors appear to have looked with disfavor on trimming these boats so that the heel of the stem was submerged; at most they trimmed so that the heel of the stem just touched the surface, and even when loaded they kept the stem nearly clear of the water.

Generally speaking, the beam of the whole range of flat-bottomed American types was small in proportion to length, and the skiffs usually had a beam not much exceeding one-third the total length, and, due to flare, the bottom width was only about one-fourth the length. The small beam was the result of the widespread belief that a wide, shallow boat would lose way in tacking in a sea, and when paying off on a new tack would fall off so much that it would be in danger of an upset if the mainsheet were not slacked away a great deal. A narrow boat, on the other hand, was less inclined to this fault and held her way in tacking far better, particularly with a little weight in her. Most of the small sailing skiffs were entirely open, as in the example, but some, used where rougher water was to be expected, were fitted with washboards and sometimes were half-decked. A few flatiron skiffs carried the sloop rig, gaff-main, and a big jib set on a bowsprit; these were rather popular on western Long Island and in New York Bay in the 1870's and 80's. Clench planking in the sides was very rarely used in the flat-bottomed working-boat skiffs in America.

The flatiron skiff often looked too much like its namesake to allow Figure 36 to be taken as representing all such skiffs. Some, such as the Cedar Keys gaff-rigged boats, had full bows and a tumble-home stem that made this Florida skiff extremely ugly. Wall-sided and poorly proportioned skiffs undoubtedly outnumbered the graceful boats found in southern New England and on the Chesapeake.

The double-ended skiff, much like the St. Lawrence bateau in model, was rather more popular as a gunning skiff than as a fishing boat. However, the double-ended flat-bottomed skiff was in use in the crabbing industry on the Chesapeake in the 1880's, as is shown by the government fishery reports and by a few photographs. The flat-bottomed boat cannot yet be traced on the Chesapeake; it was in use in some portions of the Bay as early as 1862, and photographs of two-masted flat-bottomed skiffs, leg-of-mutton rigged, exist that show the skiff was popular in 1879.

The square-sterned skiff did not survive far into the twentieth century, except in a small one-masted boat, 14 to 18 feet in length.

It was replaced in popularity by the V-bottomed skiffs in the late 80's and early 90's of the last century. But the double-ended flat-bottomed skiff has retained its popularity on the southern part of Maryland's Eastern Shore. There are slight variations in the boats: one is rigged with a small leg-of-mutton and has short decks at each

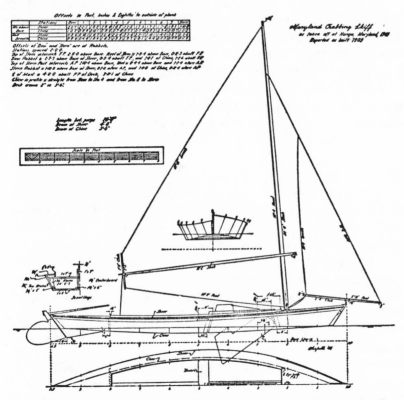

Fig. 37. Double-ended skiff from Maryland, once widely used on the Eastern Shore in crabbing, showing the "balance jib."

end of the hull with a very narrow washboard along each gunwale. This class of boat has been long in use at Smith Island, Chrisfield, and Deal Island. A very similar type, but with a jib and mainsail rig and half-decked, was used both in these waters and to the northward at Hooper's Island. Figure 37 shows one of the latter type.

Some boats had the jib set on a stay, and the so-called "balance jib" appears to have become popular after 1898. The boats show no distinctive construction features and are of very simple design and build, but are good sailers in smooth water. They are rarely over 24 feet in length and most of them are 17 to 20 feet. The boats are built entirely of local pine and juniper, iron-fastened. The type shown in Figure 38 used to engage in work-boat racing at regattas. With the decline of the sailing skiffs on the Bay, this racing has ceased and the sloop-rigged type is practically extinct while the less developed double-enders are becoming fewer in number with each passing year. The hull characteristics of the double-enders of both classes are the same: straight raking ends and a good deal of flare. Only the square-sterned Chesapeake flat-bottomed skiffs attempted the curved stem, and the lines of these are rather like the western river skiffs, but with less width at the gunwale aft.

The Sharpies

The larger boats, over 20 feet in length, on the flat-bottomed skiff model and construction, are usually called "sharpies," without much regard to rig. These boats were built, in the last quarter of the nineteeth century, in lengths up to 65 feet or more and had one- and two-masted rigs including the two-masted leg-of-mutton, a gaff, and a gaff-mainsail-and-jib-headed-topsail-in-one rig on the Great Lakes. The cat, sloop, and schooner rigs were used on the sharpies; a few rigged as ketches or yawls were employed in commercial work, but these rigs were more common among yacht sharpies.

The sharpie seems to have begun its climb to popularity in the fisheries at New Haven, Connecticut, in the 1870's. The origin of the New Haven sharpie is unknown, though many attempts have been made to explore the matter. One tale is that the type came into use when timber for the log-canoe dugouts was no longer available, and that the sharpie was merely an enlargement of the flatiron skiff. A correspondent signing himself "B" wrote the editor of *Forest & Stream* magazine in 1879 that the first sharpie was built at New Haven by a Mr. Taylor, who came there from Vermont, but no date is given.

In the model room of the New York Yacht Club there is a half-model of a sharpie-sloop named *Lucky* which was built in the early

1850's. Pictorial evidence exists of the sharpie hull and rig from 1857 on. Kemp, as has been said, states that the sharpie "could be traced back to 1835," but nothing in the way of direct evidence is mentioned. In view of the fact that men writing to *Forest & Stream* between 1878 and 1885 appear unable to state the date of origin, it seems very likely that it was earlier than 1840 anyway.

The New Haven sharpie was primarily an oyster-tonging boat developed in hull and rig for this work. Steadiness, reasonable carrying capacity, low building cost, and good sailing qualities were desired—and the boat had to row well. The ability of the early builders, it seems, imparted to the boat a particularly graceful appearance, and this, with her speed, led yachtsmen to take an interest in the type.

Thomas Clapham, who did much to encourage the adoption of the type in yachting, was a well-educated man and a prolific writer. Having suffered financial reverses in the 70's, he turned to sharpie building, and, taking the New Haven boat as a point of departure, he added dead rise fore and aft and finally amidships, turning out what eventually was a V-bottomed hull on sharpie proportions, which he called a "nonpareil sharpie"; it was also called a "Roslyn sharpie," after the town where Clapham first developed the modified model. Clapham also introduced the yawl rig which was, in effect, a sliding gunter forward with a leg-of-mutton jigger. He built one or two working sharpies, but really was engaged in yacht-building. His importance to us is that his attempts to convert yachtsmen to the type by correspondence, which included challenges and lengthy arguments in favor of the sharpie, have led to the present rather complete record of the development of the type from 1878 on. Not only is there much published information, but the letters, articles, and published plans led others to measure boats and to make plans, some of which have survived.

The earliest model of the New Haven sharpie is shown in Figure 38. This is redrawn from a rough plan originally preserved by the late W. P. Stephens, once yachting editor of *Forest & Stream* magazine. The plan had been received by the magazine with a letter, in 1879, describing the sharpies. This information (except for the plan) appeared later in Kunhardt's *Small Yachts, Their Design and Construction* without acknowledgment. The letter was signed

"B," and it was this correspondent who told the name of the supposed inventor, "Mr. Taylor." It is probable that the very poor drawing of the sharpie that appeared in *Forest & Stream*, and then in *A Manual of Yacht and Boat Sailing*, by Dixon Kemp, in England, and

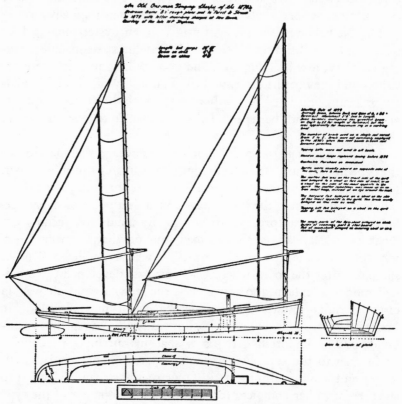

Fig. 38. Plan of an old sharpie showing typical working rig of the two-masted New Haven boats. The brails shown here disappeared in the last sharpies used. The drawing shows the usual proportions of the rig employed at New Haven, 1870–1900. (See Appendix for offsets and dimensions.)

also in the French magazine *Le Yacht*, is based on this plan. Kunhardt, the then yachting editor of *Forest & Stream*, was much opposed to boats of the sharpie type; if he made the published drawing he obviously had not attempted to follow the original closely, for the published plan was no more than a caricature of a sharpie.

Figure 38 shows a boat very little different in fundamentals from the sharpies of twenty-five years later, except that the 1879 boat is much smaller and has somewhat more rake and flare to the sides than was common in the later craft. The boat was only 26′ 10″ long; in later times such a small sharpie usually had but one mast and was a "one-man boat." The 1879 sharpie has two masts, and so must have been worked by two men. The fitting of the thwarts is also different from the practice in later sharpies, and the secondary mast position is in the fore thwart, a custom that died out afterwards. Due to the flare, no doubt, the 1879 boat has rather more rocker and sheer than was the practice later.

The two-masted rig of the sharpie at New Haven consisted of the two leg-of-muttons, each with a sprit boom, as shown in Figure 38. The outer ends of the sprits were shouldered to enter rope grommets at the clews of the sails; the fore ends reached forward of the masts. Here they were supported by a snotter rove as follows. An eye was formed in the standing end large enough to pass loosely over the sprit. From here the tail is passed around the mast and seized to form a close-fitting eye; the end of the tail is spliced into a single-sheaved block, as shown in the drawings of the New Haven sharpies. Where it passed around the mast, it was a sliding fit. A simple tackle was formed, the standing part turned into the becket of the block and then passed around a sheave in the fore end of the sprit, then rove through the snotter block and the fall belayed to a wooden cleat on the fore side of the mast. This tackle was powerful enough to set the sprit hard aft and thus flatten the sail. The foresail sheet was two single parts, like single jib sheets, while the mainsheet was usually a gun-tackle purchase, the lower block being mounted on an eyebolt or short horse close to the stern of the boat.

The sails appear to have been laced to the masts in early boats, but by 1880, at least, mast hoops were in use. The sails were hoisted by a single-part halyard, a sheave being usually placed in the masthead within 8 inches of the truck. The reef band was parallel to the hoist. In early boats the reef was made by a series of brails leading through thimbles on the luff-rope and spliced into a single fall, which permitted reefing without lowering the sails. In later boats there were usually two reef bands fitted with reef points and the sails had to be lowered to reef, the points being turned in as the sail was again hoisted. In either plan the sprit tackle was slacked off until the reef was made and then again set up; as the reefs were made, the heels of the sprits projected farther forward of the masts. The tack of the sharpie sail was seized to an eyebolt or cleat low on the mast. In setting up the sprits in the New Haven sharpies, the purpose was to set the sails very flat. This tended to bind the sprit-snotters on the masts; hence the heel tenons of the masts were made round and often had brass bearing-plates on both step and at top of heel tenon, so that the mast could revolve easily. The partners were lined with greased rawhide to aid this. No shrouds or stays were ever used, nor did working boats employ jibs and bowsprits.

Some boats had vertical clubs at the clews, which permitted more sail area, but this was not popular in working boats at New Haven. The two-masted sharpies were always built with three mast steps. One was well forward for the foremast, and the main was in a thwart a little abaft the after end of the centerboard case, or, in later boats, was held in an iron clamp secured to the top of the after end of the case. There was a mast step either in a thwart at the fore end of the case, as in the old boats, or in the foredeck just forward of the fore coaming. In summer weather the two masts were carried; in fall, winter, and spring, one mast was carried in this last step; some boats carried the foremast there and some the main. In the old and small boats it was possible for a strong and active man to shift the masts from one step to another afloat, but this could not be done in the later sharpies. When one man worked a sharpie she usually was fitted with one mast, even in summer.

The boats were handled, when two-masted, very much like a sloop, the foresail being tended like a jib. In strong winds the helm was never put down without slacking the fore sheet, as the stern might go under and trip the boat, causing her to capsize. Due to the lack of skeg, and the powerful turning effect of the balanced rudder used in these boats, they would turn in a very short radius, in fact under certain conditions in their own length. The working sharpie, with two sails, was fast, handy, and surprisingly seaworthy, but required a skillful hand at the helm.

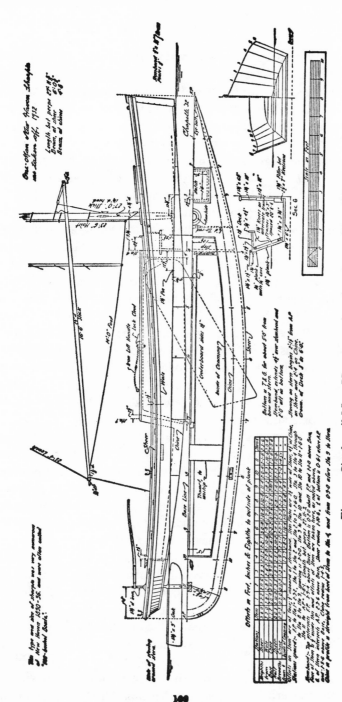

Fig. 39. Single-sail New Haven tonging sharpie, small model.

In the early sharpies it is apparent that the centerboard was deeper and somewhat shorter than in later boats. The 1879 sharpie shows the old style with the board coming above the case-top. This was eventually discontinued, as it was in the way of the rather low-cut foresail and the open case was easily jammed by shell being accidentally thrown into it, when culling oysters.

In the 80's the sharpies had become standardized in two lengths: one about 35 feet, capable of carrying between 150 and 175 bushels of oysters and worked by two men; the other between 26 and 28 feet, carrying about 75 to 100 bushels and usually worked by one man. The larger boats retained the two-masted rig in summer, but the smaller boats rarely used the two-masted rig at any time and so were usually built with a single mast step only. The small sharpies were very useful where it was necessary to pass under low bridges, as the spruce mast could easily be unstepped and then raised again if necessary. These boats were fitted for rowing, of course, as were all the New Haven sharpies. Figure 39 shows a one-man sharpie of the small class, as taken off an abandoned hull at New Haven in 1932. In structure and general model she differed little from the larger boats; the example was one of the last of the small type built at New Haven. The stern is somewhat deeper than was usual in the larger boats and more like that of the special sharpies built to race in the oystermen's races at regattas. The type of boat shown here was very popular in the late 80's and early 90's, and large numbers are to be seen in the photographs made by the Fish Commission at New Haven in this period.

The large class is the better known of the two, and a number of plans exist, two of which were taken by the writer from surviving boats in this century. The sharpie is now extinct at New Haven, and one of the measured boats is in a museum. Figure 40 is supposedly the oldest of the surviving boats, and the drawing was made from careful measurements taken in the Mariners' Museum, where the boat is preserved. The boat is claimed to have been built in the 1880's, and this is supported by the fact that the boat had been built with a mainmast thwart which was not employed in the 90's. The model used in this boat is typical of the New Haven sharpie. She is a long, low, and rather narrow skiff hull, having the favorite round stern of the tonging sharpies. The typical stem con-

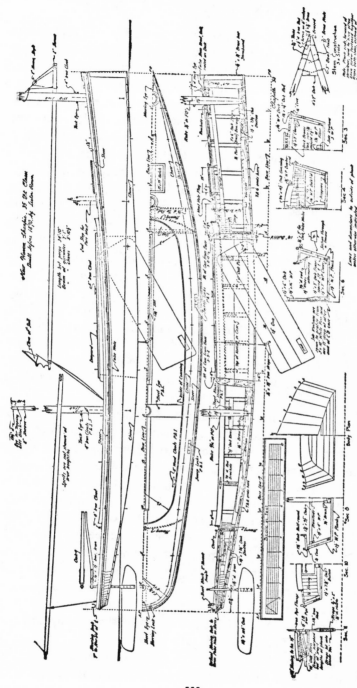

Fig. 40. Two-man tonging sharpie of the 1880's, showing typical construction of the 35-foot boats. (See Appendix for off-sets and dimensions.)

111

struction is also shown, as is the step-bulkhead which replaced the thwart-and-bulkhead seen in the early sharpie of 1879.

The sharpies required a great deal of longitudinal strength, and this was obtained by the use of a built-up keelson structure which was made of three planks on edge. The middle one was a filler that stopped short at each end of the centerboard slot. The keelson did not run to the ends of the hull; a couple of feet abaft the foremast it was scarphed to a flat keelson plank and on this was placed the mast-step block. The flat plank usually extended under the large V-shaped stem liner. Aft, a similar flat-plank keelson was scarphed in, the scarph usually being about at the after end of the load water line, and through this plank passed the iron pipe rudder-tube, the plank forming a reinforcement to the bottom at this point. The other longitudinals were the chine logs and the sides. The sheer clamp was not continuous and only served to support the deck beams at bow and stern. Due to the long, open cockpit, the sharpie would "pant" (the gunwales moving in and out as in a folded sheet of paper when it is held boat-shape and subjected to longitudinal bending), and so there was not only the fore bulkhead and its thwart-like step but also a mainmast thwart in the older boats. These served as compression members. The tension member was forward where the tall foremast caused the greatest strain; here there was a heavy tie rod (set up with a turnbuckle-link) which ran athwartships, and its ends were upset over clench-rings on the outside of the plank, usually on the face of the oak false wale or deep guard that ran along the sheer. The after bulkhead was rarely used as a strength member and was merely a vertical-staved partition to hold things stowed under the after deck. The lower portion of the fore bulkhead, under the step, was the strength member there, the upper portion being mere staving, as can be seen in the plan.

The construction of the round stern was quite simple: stern frames, built up of short lengths, were scarphed together and set at sheer and chine to form the desired rake of the stern; around these was nailed thick, narrow staving which was dressed off smooth. The rake required the staving to be slightly tapered from sheer to chine. The light oak false-wale was usually formed of short vertical staving or was bent around the stern staving (this required shaping out of very wide stock to allow for rake) at the

THE SCOW AND BATEAU

sheer, to which was added a small half-round of the same material to form a rubbing piece; these were then carried in long lengths the whole length of the gunwale. The entire hull was usually one color, gray or white, except for the bottom.

The long balance rudder is another typical feature of these boats; it was often as long as 6 feet and sometimes as wide as 15 inches, but 12 inches would be the more common width. The rudder blade was "balanced" by having it extended 12 to 18 inches forward of the centerline of the rudderstock; the fore end of the blade was usually rounded up from below, sled-fashion, and the top edge, ahead of the stock, was cut down to parallel the bottom of the boat. In surviving boats the length of the blade has invariably been reduced from its original length, owing to the fact that in their last years of activity the boats had been used with one mast and with the small mainsail at that. Even in the smallest sharpies, the blade originally was 4 feet or more in length.

The rudderstock was made by a blacksmith of wrought-iron rod and was formed with a clevis to fit over the rudder blade. Above this it was round to a couple of inches below the head, where it was shouldered and squared. The stock was made 36 to 40 inches long, to permit the stock to be moved up and down to alter the depth of the rudder blade. To hold the stock in any desired position, holes were drilled through the round of the stock where it came above deck; an iron pin placed in any hole rode upon an iron pipe flange screwed over the rudder tube at deck and kept the stock from dropping. The upper hole, close to the head, often had a small bolt that served as a stop, to prevent the rudder from dropping entirely out of the boat. The tiller was of oak and had an iron strap fitted to take the head of the rudderstock. The ability to drop the rudder made steering possible in a sea. The rudder was always placed as far aft as possible, as shown in the drawing, to obtain maximum turning power; but in this position it might lift out when the stern came up on a sea or the boat heeled much if the blade could not be lowered. When in shallow water, or in beaching to haul out, the blade could be raised out of harm's way.

The centerboard had become very long and rather shallow, as had the case, which was now topped with a cap. Both lanyards and lifting handles were in use; the pivot bolt was an oak pin. The board was sometimes weighted with lead but usually depended upon the weight of its edge-bolting and on being of water-soaked oak to sink when lowered. When the lifting handle was used, the board need not be counterweighted, as the lifting handle was shoved under a special cleat that held the handle down when the board was lowered. Normally, the board was not lowered quite as much as shown in the illustration. It should be added that some details shown do not exist on the boat at the Mariners' Museum and are reconstructed from other information to show typical details in sailing days.

Figure 41 shows another sharpie of this class, built about 1900, and measured in 1925. A slightly older boat is preserved in the Mystic Marine Museum, Mystic, Connecticut. The drawing shows the slight changes that had occurred since 1890. The most important change was the omission of the mainmast thwart, which had been in the way when shoveling oysters or shell in unloading. The omission, it must be said, was scarcely an improvement, as time has shown that this change seriously weakened the hull, permitting the sides to fall in at the gunwale and the sheer aft to be decreased. The working of the long, open hull, when loaded and under sail, was much increased, and leakage is said to have resulted. In the new plan the mainmast was supported by a heavy iron strap around the mast and secured to the upper portion of the centerboard case. This arrangement usually moved the mast a little forward of its old position. This caused the foot of both foresails and mainsails to be slightly altered in length, along with the sprits. The centerboard had been slightly increased in depth, and the case too.

Both boats shown here were built by Lester Rowe, who had become prominent in sharpie building as early as 1880; previously, a man named Graves had been the leading builder. Of course, many sharpies were built by their owners, and among these there was much variety in appearance and finish, but, in the main, the proportion of length to beam remained quite constant. Some boats were built square-sterned, with sharply raked transom, and there was variation in the rake of the stem, flare of the sides, and the amount of sheer at the gunwales. There was also a wide difference in finish in such boats, ranging all the way from crude to excellent. The boats were built of white pine and oak, iron-fastened.

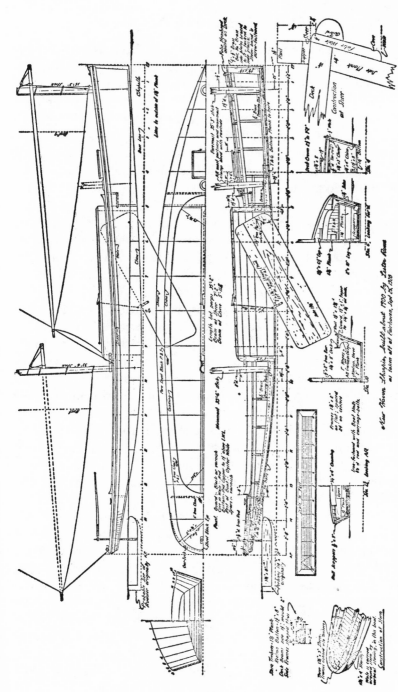

Fig. 41. New Haven sharpie, final model and fittings. (See Appendix for offsets and dimensions.)

The standard proportions appear to have been as follows: the beam at the chines amidships was roughly one-sixth the total length of the hull, or slightly less; and the flare of the sides was about 3½ inches to 4 inches per foot of depth amidships, although in practice each side flared about 7¼″ in 22 to 24 inches of depth at mid-length (the depth of the hull was arbitrarily taken here, as the hull actually became much shallower from this point aft). The amount of rocker fore and aft was usually about 12 inches forward and about 18 or 19 inches aft with the round stern, and an inch or two less with the square stern in boats 35 to 36 feet long. The heel of the stem was usually about 2 inches out of water.

The New Haven sharpie was a surprisingly handsome and graceful boat in spite of her straight sides, for the sheer was usually well proportioned and the appearance of the sharpies was much helped by the rather low freeboard. The rig was also graceful and rather lofty: the foremast of a 35-foot boat was between 28 and 36 feet in length; the main was between 26 and 34 feet; the fore sprit was 19 to 20 feet; the main sprit averaged a foot shorter. The masts in the 1880's were about 4½ inches in diameter at the partners, but later this became 5½ inches, and the head was between 1½ and 2 inches in diameter. The smaller diameter of the masts in the older boats was due to the then extensive practice of unshipping masts at some of the low bridges, but in time either the low bridges had disappeared or the waters above such bridges were no longer used, and so the practice gradually died out. The sprits were about 3 inches at the middle and 2½ inches at the fore end; the after end was about 2 inches at shoulder.

The one-man sharpies usually had single masts somewhere between 24 and 28 feet long, 4 to 4½ inches in diameter at partners and 1½ inches in diameter at head. The sprit was usually between 15 and 17 feet long and about 2½ inches in its greatest diameter. Some two-masted boats had vertical clubs 2 to 4 feet long at the clew of the foresail, but these were not popular in working boats and were rarely used except in yachts or in the special racing sharpies, where the vertical clubs were used on both sails and were often very long.

The sharpies were almost invariably half-decked, as they were narrow boats that were inclined to sail on their sides in strong winds. Therefore, the washboards were wide and there was always a coaming in addition. A few sharpies were rigged as sloops, some with leg-of-mutton and some with gaff mains, but local opinion was that the rig was not a successful one in a sharpie. One three-masted sharpie-rigged boat is known to have been built, 60 feet over all and 9' 10" beam, but the general run of working sharpies at New Haven did not much exceed 36 feet, with a rare individual as long as 40. When yachtsmen became interested in the type, a number of large sharpies of various rigs were built, some over 60 feet over all. The Coast and Geodetic Survey long employed two

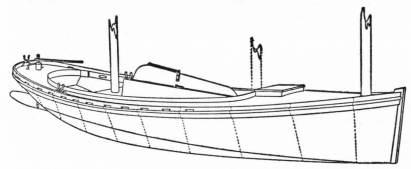

Old-Type One-Man Sharpie

large sailing sharpies, the *Spy* and *Transit*, on the Florida coast.

The racing sharpies were built on working-boat lines and construction and were, by common consent, of the same approximate dimensions. There were minor departures: the run was usually flatter, giving a deeper stern than in the working sharpies, and the beam was often greater amidships, particularly in the last of the type. The hulls were usually better finished and black walnut bulkheads and seats were common. The coamings were usually varnished, and some attempt was made to approach yachting standards in paint work.

The racing rig was much greater than in any working sharpie, as the racers used "springboards" to outrig the weight of their crew to increase sail-carrying power. Kunhardt gives part of the spar dimensions of the racing sharpie *Carrie V*, a 35-foot boat, with

8-foot beam. She had a 45-foot foremast, 6 inches in diameter at partners, and a 40-foot mainmast, 5½ inches at the thwart. Both masts tapered to 1½ inches diameter at the head. A plank bowsprit 17 feet long was fitted. The fore sprits when set up overlapped the mainmast, and the heel tackles therefore had to be slacked in tacking, and jibing was fatal. Eight-foot and 10-foot clubs stood vertically at the clews of the fore and main sails; the fore club was the longer. The crew was made up of twelve men, of whom nine would use the springboards to hold her on her feet. The weather bilge was kept just touching the surface of the water if possible, as the boats went faster and held on better at this heel.

Two plans of racing hulls and one sail plan are available. The older boat is a square-sterned racing sharpie supposedly built about 1884; the plans and measurements were preserved by the late Larry Huntington, but the original source of the measurements and drawings is unknown. Kunhardt gives dimensions of a yacht sharpie that is quite close to this racer, and it is possible that these boats raced as a class separate from the professionally manned sharpies of the *Carrie V* type. The Huntington drawings show a longer and narrower hull than that of the *Carrie V*, with much shorter spars and less heavily canvased.

Figure 42 shows the plan and illustrates the extremes in rig reached in this class of sharpie. The iron outrigger, the huge centerboard, and the belaying cavils forward, near the foremast, are typical features of the racing craft. The outrigger was obviously copied from the old "sandbagger" racing sloops to allow the mainsheet to be properly located on the long overhanging main sprit, and the cavils forward were required to belay the additional sails—the jib, square sail, and, in a few boats, a square topsail as well—carried on the foremast of these boats.

A somewhat later example is shown in Figure 43. This boat existed until 1932, when she was accidentally burned in her storage shed near New Haven. I came across her in 1928 and obtained permission to measure her hull, but her spars, except the bowsprit, were not available, and so no spar or sail plan can be shown. This boat had been built sometime between 1888 and 1894 for racing on Lake Champlain, but owing to the owner's death the sharpie remained at New Haven and was raced there three or four times.

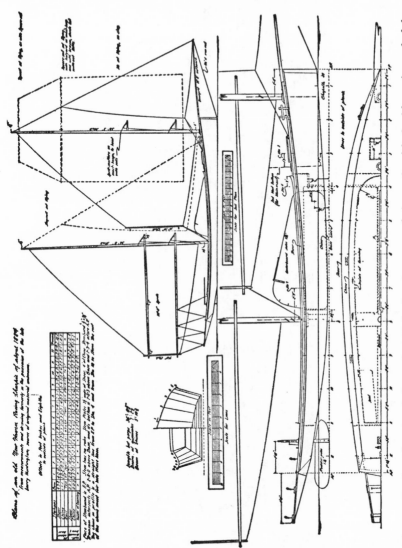

Fig. 42. Racing sharpie of the early 1880's showing type of rig used, with double sprits and clubs.

119

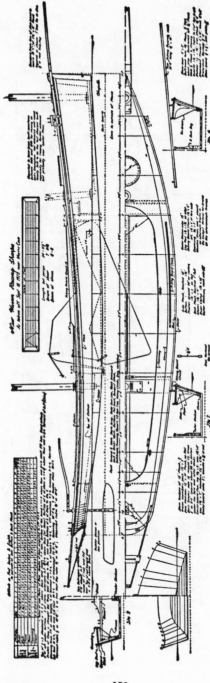

Fig. 43. Last type of racing sharpie, showing details and fittings used in these sailing machines.

She was then placed in a small shed and remained there until her destruction. This sharpie was a powerful boat and very much like the *Carrie V* in proportions, so the latter's spar dimensions would probably approximate the ones used in this boat. A few refinements in details can be seen, over the first example, but it is apparent that the main thwart had been so low that the bury of the mainmast was inadequate; hence it was increased by the addition of a heavy block to the top of the thwart. The extremely shallow bury of the mainmast must have been a source of trouble in the racing sharpies, but a similar condition existed in the racing log canoes of the Chesapeake, and in both it is surprising how the mainmasts stood so well, without shrouds and with their small bury.

The New Haven sharpie began to attract the attention of tonging oystermen and others as early as 1870. It carried a large load on a shoal draft, and with its decking and covering boards it had a good platform on which to work. The round stern was a particular advantage as the tonger standing there could work long-handled tongs without their being interfered with by the quarters. The rig also had real advantages, as tonging is usually done in smooth waters and preferably in light winds or calms. The sharpie was usually brought to windward of the tonging bed, and then, with her foresail set and her helm lashed, she was sailed slowly to leeward, and tonging began. The speed of the boat was readily controlled in light to moderate breezes by slacking off the sheet, and it was not uncommon for the sheet to be slacked all the way so that the foresail flapped over the bows, with its sprit projecting directly ahead.

In calms the boat either drifted with the tide or was anchored and then shifted with sweeps; the sharpies rowed very easily. Underway, tonging was done from the side decks, of course. When anchored, the boat was moored, at times, by the stern, as she rode easiest this way; and the round stern was considered drier than the square. When tonging from the stern, the rudder was often dropped and reversed so that the blade was not in the way.

There was another advantage: the hull was quickly and cheaply built and so represented a small investment. In spite of this, the boat was acknowledged, by all acquainted with her, to be a good sailer in the average conditions of weather in which tongers worked.

The speed of the sharpies has ample testimony, and some of the large boats were found to have sailed at remarkable rates: one sharpie covered eleven nautical miles in thirty-four minutes, and another averaged 16 knots for three consecutive hours. These high speeds were obviously with started sheets and with the hull in a planing attitude. The accepted New Haven model planed at very low speeds, considering its weight—a 35-foot sharpie weighed about 2,000 to 2,800 pounds stripped of rig and gear—and its bottom was so shaped that the boat was practically in the early stages of planing when it began to move fast. Unfortunately, this matter was not pursued very far in print, as the editor of the then leading yachting magazine (*Forest & Stream*) was C. P. Kunhardt, who was opposed to such hulls and was a fanatical supporter of the deep keel and heavily ballasted hull used in the English cutter yachts in this period. "It would be opposed to the lessons of practice should such small bodies and rigs on a (given) length be accepted as equal in general ability of yachts of more power"—a statement of his that indicates his approach to the sharpie, and to the principles of light-displacement design incorporated in its model. At the end of the nineteenth century, a few designer-builders were working on the sharpie: Clapham, Huntington, and the Canadian amateur, Duggan. From these men came the racing scows and the high-speed sailing classes that existed in the 1890's and in the early 1900's on the western lakes and on the Atlantic Coast. In the latter area the scow finally died out and her qualities were forgotten until the recent revival of "planing boats" in the small racing classes. It has been forgotten, of course, that planing sailboats owe their existence to the lessons taught by the garvey and the New Haven sharpies in the 80's and early 90's.

The qualities of the sharpie led to the introduction of the type into the Carolina Sounds in 1874. In this year the late George C. Ives had Graves build a 34-foot sharpie at New Haven, which was delivered in 1875. This boat, used in fishing at Beaufort, North Carolina, outsailed local boats and proved able enough to work in the fierce gales that sweep the Carolina Sounds in the fall and spring. As a result, the sharpie gradually replaced the local types there.

The Carolina sharpie was built locally, soon after the Ives' boat became known. Gradually, local departures in rig and model ap-

peared. Figure 44 shows the appearance of one of the Carolina
sharpies; the drawing was made in 1927 by Huntington from
measurements of an old boat he found near Beaufort. This boat,
which fishermen said had been built about 1890, is almost a counter-

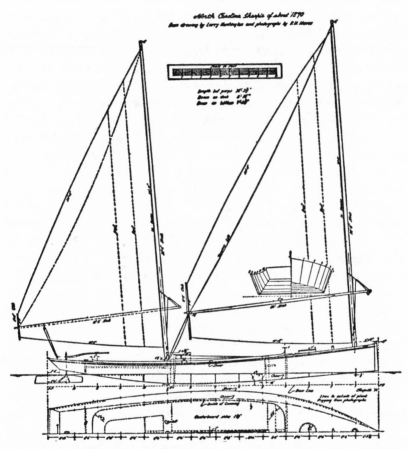

Fig. 44. Sharpie rig with club and single sprit on square-sterned North
Carolina hull. (See Appendix for offsets and dimensions.)

part of the rigged model of an "Atlantic Coast sharpie" in the
Watercraft collection of models in the Smithsonian Institution.
Morris took this model to be an attempt to show the New Haven
sharpie and judged it adversely. Though the model is indeed rather
crude, the Huntington evidence shows that it is generally accurate.

This applies to a great number of the fishing-boat models in the Smithsonian; they may be rather crudely built as examples of the modeler's art, but they are usually quite accurate representations of the parent types, at the time the model was made. It is therefore rash to criticize them on modern evidence, and a type must be studied fully to find out whether or not a model represents some early stage of development now extinct.

The Carolina sharpies gradually increased in size, and by 1890 many boats were 40 or 45 feet in length, and cabins were often added. Soon the boats were rigged as schooners, and these became numerous in the oyster-dredging on the Carolina Sounds. In this work large sail area was required, and so the schooner rig replaced the old New Haven sharpie sail plan. The older boats had used the leg-of-mutton with sprit-booms, but the vertical clubs at the clews of both fore and main soon became popular there and continued until the rig was replaced with a bald-headed gaff-schooner rig, which seems to have occurred during the 90's. The Carolina schooner-sharpies were usually between 42 and 50 feet long and 10 to 12 feet beam. In general, the Carolina sharpies were wider than the ones at New Haven, in proportion to length, and were not as fast as the latter but were safer and more powerful working boats.

In 1876, the late R. M. Munroe took a sharpie, built by Brown of Staten Island, to Biscayne Bay, Florida, and this boat led to the introduction of the sharpie there. Munroe devised a small double-ender with narrow bottom and very flaring sides amidships, which became known as the "Egret" model, after the original boat of the type, and was very seaworthy for use along the coast. The original *Egret* was employed in carrying mail in all weathers from Palm Beach to what is now Miami.

Boats were built by others with square and round sterns and often on very crude designs. Figure 45 shows an old sharpie built at Cedar Keys, in 1894, and illustrates a style of rig that once had some popularity in Florida. The plan was made by Huntington at my request, while he was staying at Cedar Keys, in 1928. Schooner-rigged sharpies up to about 60 feet in length became common, and many of these looked like small coasting schooners above water, having strong sheer and fiddleheads. Most of these schooners

were gaff-rigged; a few with leg-of-mutton fore and main sails and
with a large jib were usually rather narrow.

The sharpie was introduced into France, about 1880, by L. More,

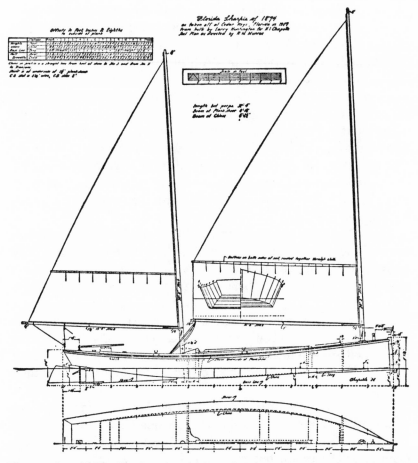

Fig. 45. An old Florida sharpie with a style of rig once popular in Florida
and on Lake Champlain. The Cedar Keys sharpies were often smaller than
this boat, 18 to 22 feet, and rigged as gaff-mainsail cats.

a French yachtsman and writer. In 1883, the French government had some armed two-masted sharpies built. These were about
49' 2½" long and had the relatively great beam for a sharpie of 13'
1½" for the stated length. Each of these boats carried a Hotchkiss

revolving cannon mounted on top of the cabin trunk and were intended for the use of colonial police. The rig was the old sharpie style with the standing reefing lines of the 1879 sharpie shown in Figure 39. The plan of the armed sharpies appeared in the January 14, 1883, number of the French magazine *Le Yacht*.

Sharpies appeared on Lake Champlain in the late 70's, sponsored by the Reverend W. H. H. Murray, who wrote for *Forest & Stream* under the sobriquet of "Adirondak Murray." These were mostly pleasure boats; however, a few were used for commercial work on the lake. The boats were chiefly remarkable for their variety of experimental rigs, which included two-masted, boomed leg-of-muttons and a combination of boom and batten, such as was used at Cedar Keys. Square topsails on this rig and the addition of a large jib were also tried. Gaff sloops were built, but the two-masted sharpies were more common. Racing sharpies were popular, and Burlington, Vermont, was the center of sharpie-building on the lake.

The sharpie also appeared on the West Coast and an example is shown in Figure 46. This was a type of boat once used at San Juan Island, working in the halibut fishery in Juan de Fuca Strait and neighboring waters. The boat was a double-ended gaff-schooner sharpie of rather good model, but heavily built and ballasted and not intended for great speed. These boats were used during the 80's and into the 90's and are shown in a few photographs of the period and are also mentioned in Fish Commission papers. Nothing has been found concerning their origin; the type has been extinct for a generation at least.

A distinctive type of sharpie existed on Lake Erie and on some of the other Great Lakes during the last quarter of the nineteenth century. This boat probably had some distant relationship to the Connecticut sharpies, but it cannot be readily traced. The Erie sharpie seems to have originated in Ohio, which had been settled to a great extent by people from Connecticut and Massachusetts. In 1881, at Sandusky, Ohio, Hall noted the local builder to be a man from Virginia named George Littleton. One of Hall's notebooks containing data on these sharpies is in the possession of the Searsport Marine Museum, and there is a great deal of material on the boats in Fish Commission publications and in field reports.

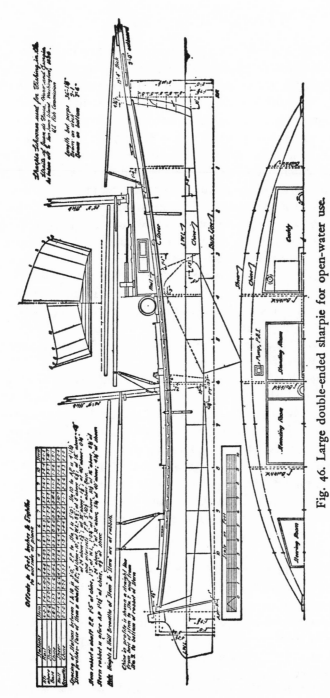

Fig. 46. Large double-ended sharpie for open-water use.

127

A good example of the Ohio sharpie is shown in Figures 47 and 48, drawn from detailed measurements and sketches contained in a field report to the Fish Commission. The drawing is supported by a number of other rough plans apparently intended to be used in Fish Commission publications. There are excellent models of these Lake sharpies in the Watercraft Collection, but, unfortunately, one model is identified in the published catalogue as a "North Carolina sharpie," which has led to much confusion on the part of Morris.

The boats ranged from 20 to about 42 feet in length, with much variation in the proportion of beam to length. Many of the boats were entirely open; most had narrow covering boards along the sides. These sharpies were all square-sterned, with a balance rudder hung outboard. The stem was rabbeted and the bottom cross-planked. All of the boats were used in tending pound nets and were very burdensome compared with the New Haven craft. Like the New Haven boats, they were built almost entirely of white pine, with some oak where necessary. The most popular lengths were between 28 and 36 feet in length, but, in general, the length varied with the place of employment.

At Sandusky, Hall found the boats to range from 24 to 42 feet in length, with the average boat 36′ x 10′ x 3′, two-masted. (These are the approximate dimensions of the boat shown in Figures 47 and 48). At Huron, Ohio, the average boat was 32′ x 9′ x 3′. At Green Bay, the boats were about 28′ x 9′ 6″ x 3′. At Dover Bay, the boats were 20′ to 26′ x 7′ 9″ to 9′ 6″ x 28″ to 36″. The amount of sheer, the rake of the stem, the flare of the sides, and the quantity of fore-and-aft camber in the bottom seem to have varied a great deal, and this could be traced, in the reports by Hall and others, to the fact that the boats were built by both boat-builders and fishermen, without plans or models.

In spite of their variations in proportions, the pound-net sharpies showed a basic model: raking bow and transom, rather strong sheer and rocker, and the rather wide stern, with its outboard rudder. In one respect there was some difference of opinion among Ohio builders as to the location of the greatest beam; many placed it slightly abaft amidships, as in the example shown, but others placed it a little forward of amidships.

Hall and other observers agree that the boats were very stiff and

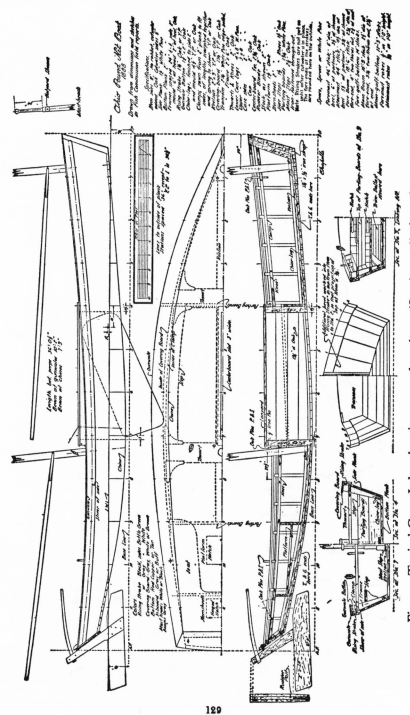

Fig. 47. Typical Great Lakes sharpie or pound-net boat. (See Appendix for offsets and dimensions.)

129

able, and, with their very large rigs, were very fast sailers in spite of their beam. It is probable that the adverse effects of the great beam in these sharpies were counteracted by the very heavy loads they habitually carried in their business. They appear to have em-

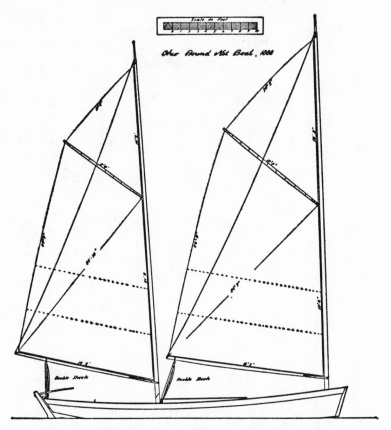

Fig. 48. Rig of pound-net boat shown in Figure 47.

ployed some stone ballast as did most of the sharpies, which usually had a small tier of stone paving block or sandbags as ballast to give momentum in tacking. The weight carried by the lake sharpies was probably great enough to overcome the drag of the balanced rudder, set at so sharp a rake. In a light sharpie, such a rudder put over hard would make an ideal brake, rather than a steering fin. The balance rudder must be put over slowly, in any case, but when the post is on a rake the greatest caution is required in handling it in light weather or the boat will go into irons.

The rig of the lake sharpies is an interesting one, combining the advantages of the gaff with those of the true leg-of-mutton. Like the gaff sail, the sail area can be made large in the lake rig without excessively tall masting, and, with a two-masted rig, the space between fore and main masts can be well filled. With the sharp-head, a simple single halyard serves and the gaff becomes no more than a light batten, requiring no bands, jaws, or other hardware. The drawing shows the sail and the rigging details; the gaff is replaced by a double batten, screw-bolted through the sail. Few boats had a set of jaws on this double batten; the heel was usually seized to a mast hoop. Thus, the sail shape became, in appearance, a gaff sail with topsail above it, yet the gear required was that of the true leg-of-mutton. Rigs much like this, in shape of sail, have been tried on the Atlantic Coast, but only on Lake Erie did they become widely accepted. Many of the Erie sharpies had lug-footed foresails, without any overlap on the main. The large sharpies almost invariably had boomed foresails.

This type of sharpie is now wholly extinct. It shows, in parts of its design and construction, some possible relation to the New Haven sharpies, yet not enough to permit the conclusion that it is a mere adaptation of the eastern model. Any attempt to discuss its probable history therefore becomes merely a speculative exercise and of no practical value. The rig was a most unusual one and is well worth study. It should not be supposed that the rig of the example in Figure 49 was the only one used in the pound-net sharpies, for there are references showing that some were sloop-rigged. It might be well to call attention to the fact that the two-masted rig of the lake sharpies was also applied to a round-bottomed hull, with a profile much like the sharpies, at Erie, Pennsylvania, in the 1870's and 80's. All of the pound-net boats on Lake Erie were not sharpies, any more than all the oyster boats at New Haven were of this build.

The sailing sharpie had become so well known by the 80's that it appeared in some form wherever such a boat would be of use, on Western rivers and on the Canadian lakes. Almost every known rig seems to have been tried out in these craft, for many of them were pleasure boats suitable for experimentation. Just as the oystermen thought improvements might be made in the rather lofty leg-of-mutton of the New Haven type, so yachtsmen in the 1880's attempted a safer and equally simple rig.

In these days, when the leg-of-mutton-style sail, in a narrow, lofty jib-headed form, is so popular and so universally considered *the* sail, it may be well to show just what the real objection to the sail was, in the eyes of oystermen and yachtsmen of the last century. It was not alone the high regard for the gaff sail that then was widespread, but rather the knowledge that the leg-of-mutton was fundamentally a sail that limited area, with due reference to hoist and length of foot. So, to make a large leg-of-mutton sail, you had either to lengthen the foot or increase the hoist. There were usually very practical limitations on the length of foot, for too long a boom was not only impossible to reef but would drag in the water when it was slacked off, and the boat heeled, with very dangerous results. So the trend was toward moderate boom, or foot, length, and increased hoist, as in the sharpie; for it was noted that if a boat with such a sail was sharply heeled, the sail spilled the wind and thus reduced heeling-power at extreme range. Yet another difficulty arose: the higher the head of the sail was carried, the higher became the center of effort—or center of wind pressure in the sail—and the more readily the boat heeled to the extreme range. In sharpies and other shoal craft, this high center of effort can be a source of danger, and it was this that created interest in lower sails, such as that used on Lake Erie, which allowed much area yet preserved a low center of effort. Even the light spars of the sharpie (and the modern hollow masting) do not overcome the objection, for the pressure of the high center has far more effect on initial heeling than the relatively few pounds saved in light masts. Taking all points of sailing into consideration, the high, narrow leg-of-mutton, or jib-header, rarely has enough area; hence the present fashion for numerous and large additional light sails, which would have been wholly undesirable in working boats. Such considerations prevented the old leg-of-mutton from ever being widely popular in working boats in this country and explained why, when the leg-of-mutton was used, it usually had masts entirely unsupported by rigging in small hulls, so that the bending of the masts and the resultant spilling of the wind relieved the boat before the danger point of capsize was reached. Once the maximum height of hoist had been reached in the sharpies, it is very noticeable that additional increase in sail, by means of leg-of-muttons, took place low, using such dodges as vertical clubs and double sprits, or boom-and-batten.

Shooting Punts or Skiffs

The flat-bottomed boat, in skiff-form either with square or sharp stern, was long popular as a shooting boat. There were many more varieties than in the scow model, and many were no more than very small, decked, square-sterned sailing and rowing boats, of the "flatiron" model. Others were really decked double-ended bateaux, such as the type long popular on the Chesapeake. There were a few, however, that were distinctive craft—one of which is shown in Figure 49. It is a form of ducker once popular on Great Bay, upstream on the Piscataqua River a little above Portsmouth, New Hampshire. The boat is heavily built, to stand the abuse and neglect such boats get, and is propelled by a sculling oar through the stern, as well as by poling or paddling on suitable occasion. The gunner lies flat when sculling in approaching wildfowl, handling his oar with one hand. The boat is built of white pine, except for stem and transom, which are oak. A leather apron, made up in a truncated cone, is nailed to the scull port in the after bulkhead, and the scull is forced through this from outboard so that leakage through the low port is avoided; this was often neglected in smooth-water shooting, however. The long, thin bow was designed to permit the boat to work well in floating ice. This gunning skiff, or punt, is probably descended from the English gunning punts, directly or indirectly, but nothing has come to light that proves the Piscataqua skiff is a descendant of a colonial type.

The building of flat-bottomed boats has been so common in America, from early times to the present day, that one would think we have learned and retained all there is to know on the construction methods to be used in such craft. Yet one of the common complaints about cross-planked bottoms today is that there is often leakage in the overhangs, where the bottom may be alternately wet and dry owing to wave action or variation in loading. The old boatbuilders knew of this difficulty and, in the New Haven sharpies and similar craft, solved the problem very simply by employing tongue-and-groove or splined seams in the bottom of the overhangs. Curiously enough, it is rare to find this done today.

The cross-planked bottom is sometimes objected to, on the grounds that the cross-seams cause "skin friction" and slow sailing. This is rather academic, as the flat-bottomed cross-planked hull is hardly a construction one would choose for an open racing class; and in a one-design class or a cruiser, this theoretical objection certainly could not be considered important. But, whether or

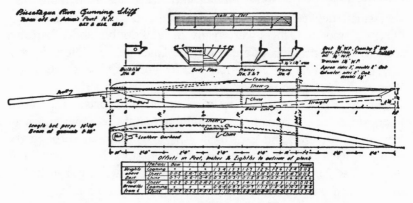

Fig. 49. New Hampshire ducking skiff built about 1920.

not skin friction is entirely a matter controlled by smooth surfaces in a hull, the cross-planked bottom is really a matter of economics, and if there should be a slight loss of speed resulting, it can be excused on the grounds that "money makes the mare go" and that there is not enough money in hand to make her go the maximum possible speed. The use of a fore-and-aft planked bottom in the sharpie entails the addition of a complete transverse framing system, which adds to both cost and labor; that is one of the reasons why cross-planked bottoms have always been preferred in sailing sharpies. This construction is also the strongest, for the connection between sides and bottom is the weakness of the framed and longitudinally planked bottom in sharpies.

It should be quite apparent that there is no justification for the contempt often expressed toward flat-bottomed craft; this is due to insufficient experience or to mere prejudice. In sailing, the flat-bottomed hull is usually heeled, and, because the boat is sailing more or less on its chine, giving V-sections, there is less pounding than one would suppose. Past experience has shown that flat-bottomed hulls may be very fast and even have such respectable qualities of seaworthiness that they may venture to sea in the summer as safely as most yachts of their length. There need be no great concessions in beauty, speed, strength, longevity, and summer-seaworthiness, if economic factors suggest the employment of flat-bottomed hulls for sailing.

CHAPTER 3

THE Shallops

THE SUCCESSORS to the colonial shallops, among the small boats, were half-decked craft, except for a few beach boats. Although they could be rowed in calms, they were primarily designed to sail and had some ballast. The majority were two-masted, and a few retained the old shallop masting. The hulls were round-bilged with some rise in floor. Both clench and caravel construction were used, according to the type and location of build. These boats were usually double-ended, as were the old "double shallops" perhaps, but square-sterned craft were not uncommon in this class. Most of the boats carried a two-man crew, but nearly all were to be sailed by a one-man watch. As most shallops were out only in daylight when working, only a few of the larger ones had cuddies. The counter stern was rarely employed —when it was, it was usually a sign of decadence because it served no practical use in these small boats and added unnecessarily to building costs.

Low cost in construction was not inherent in most of the models used and was obtained only through simple building methods, cheap hardware and fittings, simple rigs, and the use of local building material. The cost also controlled the size of the boats, and they were built as small as their services would permit, usually from 18 to 28 feet in length. In any case, they could not approach the low cost of the flat-bottomed types, but the additional expense was justified by the severe sea and weather conditions the boats were required to meet. This was particularly the case in the boats that had to work in open waters in the fall and winter months, when safety and handiness in a small boat are vitally important to the crew.

The Hampton Boat

One of the once numerous types of small boat in New England was the Hampton boat. Under this type name there were really two distinct types of boats of very doubtful relationship, each type having two variations or subtypes. The older of the two distinct types was the New Hampshire Hampton boat; the Maine type may be accepted as a more recent and perhaps an independent design. This has led to confusion in the attempts to trace the development of the type, and its history has become clouded by conflicting local claims and other evidence. The various accounts of the rise of the Hampton boat may be summarized as follows. The type was invented by Enoch Chase in 1805, in the Seabrook-Hampton townships of New Hampshire, near Newburyport, Massachusetts. The model had a long, sharp bow and a "pinky" stern; the boat was two-masted and ketch-rigged, with a shifting bowsprit and jib for light-weather work. The first boat was very successful, and it was copied at first locally and then by Maine builders in Casco Bay, who, according to one historian, were at the time acquainted only with whaleboats and their small counterpart, the Reach boat. Other historians have recorded that David Doughty, a Maine builder at Great Island, introduced the centerboard in 1868, that David Perry Sennet, a builder at Bailey's Island, introduced the square stern as an improvement over the "pinky" stern, and that he also was the first to use strip planking, in 1877. Another claim is that the first square-sterned boat was built in 1860 by P. A. Durgan at Harpswell. Thus, the boat is traced from an early "invention" through a gradual local development from sharp stern to square, and with a centerboard added, the inference being that each step was a complete innovation in Maine.

The various descriptions of the original New Hampshire boats in the fishery reports are from the 1880's. Two examples of the boats, which survived until 1936–38, do not show the long, sharp bow mentioned. In fact, this part of the Enoch Chase story may be a mere invention of a historian, just as the reasons for the spread of the type into Maine are pure inventions by the same authority. In the first place, customhouse records and other sources show that the Maine builders and boatmen had other small craft besides whaleboats in 1805. In the second place, the Reach boat did not come into use in Maine until about 1870, when it began to be built at North Haven, Maine. This was the double-ender which is obviously referred to as a counterpart of the whaleboat—which it was not. So far, about all that can be accepted is that a double-ended boat called the "Hampton boat," "Hampton whaler," and other names, as will be seen, came into use early in the nineteenth century in the Hampton Beach district. The name "whaler" does not necessarily prove the boat was a descendant of a whaleboat, though it is possible in this case.

The spread of the type eastward was due not to the ignorance of Maine builders and fishermen of types other than whaleboats but to the fact that the New Hampshire boat was found very useful in the codfishery around Newfoundland and in the Gulf of St. Lawrence. For many years, from at least as early as 1833 to as late as 1888, the New Hampshire boats were taken to these waters by Maine and Massachusetts schooners, each carrying from two to four boats on deck and one in the stern davits. The boats were used in cod fishing, and, when the schooners were loaded, the boats were often disposed of by sale to Newfoundland, Labrador, and New Brunswick fishermen for use as shore boats. Hence the New Hampshire boat became known as the "Newfoundland boat" and the "Labrador boat" and was really a stock boat. The demand for the double-ender led builders in New England, from New Bedford to Casco Bay in Maine, to build to the same general model, and so the boat was also known by the 1880's as the "New England boat."

The addition of the centerboard to the Maine-built boats in 1868 is probably a local tradition of doubtful value—the centerboard was in use in the small Muscongus Bay sloops, practically next door so to speak, as early as 1857. By the date of the alleged introduction of the centerboard, the building of the double-ender in Casco Bay had become very active at Crotch Island, now Cliff Island. Hence the Maine double-enders were often called "Crotch Island pinkies," though they did not have pink-sterns. It should be noted, perhaps, that in Maine the name "pinky" has often been applied to any sharp-sterned sailing boat, even though the pink-stern was not used. This modification or variant of the New Hampshire boat is recorded in numerous half-models and by a few hulks that existed until about 1940.

The introduction of the square stern into the Maine boats is considered a step in evolution by Sennet. The claim is not supported by a date, unlike the case of the introduction of the centerboard. But from the manner in which the claim has been made it appears that the square-sterned boats are considered as innovations on Casco Bay shortly after 1868. This can hardly be, however, as Cundy's Harbor on Casco Bay was by then a noted building place of the square-sterned yawl-boat. The Durgan claim was supported by a half-model alleged to have been used to build the square-sterned boat of 1860, and it obviously was very similar to a yawl-boat in model.

The most prominent feature of the square-sterned, Maine-built Hampton boats has been the extremely long, sharp, and wedge-shaped bow. It seems that this feature was employed in the original story of the invention of the New Hampshire boat, because the author of the claim knew the Hampton boat of his time (1906). All available evidence shows that the New Hampshire Hampton boat did not have such a bow; at least, it did not have this bow in its last years, when the Maine boats can be shown to have had the characteristic forebody. Where did this bow come from? It might be claimed that it was developed in the boats built at Crotch Island, since models of these now existing show both the New Hampshire bow, slightly modified, and also the bow of the square-sterned boats. The difficulty here is that it is yet to be proved that the wedge-shaped bow in the Crotch Island boats appeared before the square-sterned boats had it.

It has been natural to assume that once the square-sterned boats appeared, the building and development of the sharp-sterned boats on Casco Bay ceased, but this is a mere assumption that is not realistic. In fact, the double-ender continued to be built as late as 1890, long after the square-sterned boats appear in the records; it is said by one builder's family that he built both the sharp- and square-sterned boats as late as 1896. It is also apparent, from the Durgan half-model, that the claim in his behalf does not explain the wedge bow.

In 1883, *Forest & Stream* published a letter from a yachting summer visitor at Matinicus Island, at the western mouth of Penobscot Bay, in which a very full description of the boat then in use there is given. The correspondent not only speaks of the sharp, long bow but states that the boats were all alike and very numerous and that there were none like them elsewhere. His description of the boats and their rig is verified by a later reference by Goode, 1887, in which the Matinicus Island boats are described. Both descriptions agree with the rigged model of a Matinicus Island boat acquired by the Watercraft Collection in 1883; the model departs from the two descriptions only in having a short, heavy counter. Since it can hardly be thought that these boats sprang into existence and became numerous in a very short period, it must be supposed the boats had been developed at least a decade earlier. It would, then, be wholly unlikely to have originated either at Harpswell or Bailey's Island. It should be noted that Goode and his co-workers were very careful to mention any distinctive types of fishing boat used in American waters, yet do not speak of the Casco Bay boats as a distinctive type. However, a detailed description is given of the New Hampshire boat.

It is probable that the square-sterned boat was not a development out of the New Hampshire boat by way of Casco Bay, but rather that the former developed to the eastward independently and invaded Casco Bay in the 1880's, where it first influenced the Crotch Island model and then gradually replaced it in general popularity. However, in the process, the name "Hampton boat" was retained, since this name was already applied to boats being built in Casco Bay. Hence, it may well be that two distinct types finally had a single type-name. In any case, the involved evidence regarding the boats illustrates the difficulties facing the historian of many of the small boat types.

New England Boat and Isle of Shoals Boat

The New Hampshire Hampton boats may be divided into two subtypes or forms. One is the original form—the small fishing boat, which commonly ranged between 17 and 25 feet in length; boats from 17 to 23 feet were usually carried by fishing schooners for cod fishing. The boats were all rather lightly built, clench fashion, over bent frames; those over 20 feet in length were commonly partly decked. According to descriptions that have survived, they were two-masted and carried schooner or ketch rigs with or without a bowsprit and jib. In the 1880's many of these boats carried spritsails, but the gaff rig appears to have been quite common, and Goode mentions that the leg-of-mutton was also used. The boats were without centerboards in the late 80's, at least, and had only moderate draft.

The other form of the New Hampshire boat was known as the "Isle of Shoals boat"; it apparently was also called the "shay" in Newburyport. This boat undoubtedly had originated as a shore boat of the standard New Hampshire Hampton-boat model used for fishing around the Isles of Shoals, hence its name. But when a summer hotel was built on the Isles after the Civil War, the boats became party boats to take tourists to and from the islands, on picnics, and on fishing trips. This brought the boats into prominence, and references to the boats appear in the 1880's; by this time they had grown in size, and ranged from 25 to 30 feet in length. They were really enlarged copies of the New Hampshire model and were lap-strake, keel boats of very moderate draft. They were all shallop- or schooner-rigged, with gaff sails in most cases. Some boats retained the old spritsail, however, and a few had a full schooner rig, topmasts and all, with a cuddy. Most of the boats carried a lug-foresail and had little or no decking.

Two examples of the old New Hampshire model existed late enough to be studied; one of them was sailing as late as 1937–38, and the other was a boat found rotting in a marsh near York, Maine, in 1936. It was possible to take off the lines of the latter, which appears to have been a very old boat. Figure 50 shows the hull lines; the rig was reconstructed from the statements of fishermen who recalled the boat, and from sketches in the fishery reports. It was not considered worth while to attempt to record her structure, because it was conventional and had been repaired so often as to make identification of all original parts very difficult. The drawing shows the features of the boat; they compare well with the available descriptions of the type. The deck arrangement appeared original in layout—at least the deck framing showed no evidence of alteration. The peculiar outrigger allowed the sheet horse for the main to be abaft the rudderhead, which is an arrangement seen in sketches of the boats in 1888. The boat was clench-planked of cedar and white pine over bent frames and was lightly ceiled inside in way of the standing rooms and fish hold. The lines indicate an easily rowed boat, of small power, that would sail well with a small rig. These boats, with their relatively shallow draft, would go to windward quite well if sailed nearly upright. If heeled sharply they sagged to leeward and made little headway. The New Hampshire model shows indications of being designed for beaching, which may be one of the explanations of the popularity of the boat for shore fishing in Canada.

The boat that was observed under sail was somewhat fuller-ended than the example shown in Figure 50; she was schooner-rigged with a short bowsprit. She appeared to sail quite well, and once, when seen in squally weather, showed great speed reaching. In rough water the boat was not very close-winded. She was only decked at the fore end and was at the time (1937–38) used as a pleasure boat. I had the opportunity of seeing her under sail a number of times and of inspecting her out of water in the winter of 1937–38, when she was showing signs of age. The boat required handling in much the same manner as a large schooner and was dry and easy in her motions in rough water. No other examples of the type have been discovered.

The Isle of Shoals boat survived, in at least one example, as late as 1932. This was the *Alice*, built at Kittery, Maine, in 1875; she was originally rigged with spritsails, but sometime later in her life she was fitted with the gaff rig. This boat was lap-strake planked over bent frames in the conventional manner. The lines are shown in Figure 51; the boat was reputed a good sailer and very seaworthy. Her catboat bow seems unusual—it appears in none of the photo-

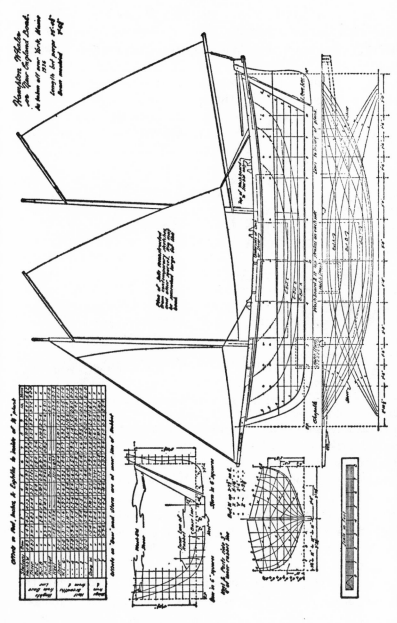

Fig. 50. Drawing of the hulk of a Hampton whaler, Labrador, or New England boat, probably built about 1880–85.

graphs of Isle of Shoal boats—and was probably a fancy of her builder. Her lines are sharp and she has somewhat the appearance of having been built on the molds intended for a somewhat longer boat.

A somewhat more typical example is shown in Figure 52; this drawing is composite and is made from a half-model from which nine boats were built at Newburyport sometime between 1883 and 1894. The construction details in the drawing are based upon the

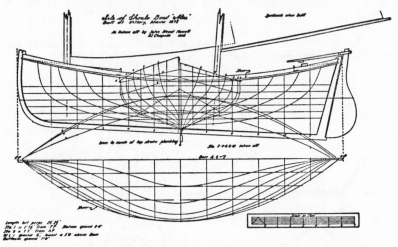

Fig. 51. Lines of the last Isle of Shoals boat known to exist.

Alice and a portion of the wreckage of one of the Isle of Shoals boats. The rig is drawn from a sailmaker's plan and from photographs of one of the boats in 1896. The details shown of the rig appear to have become characteristic. The sails hoisted with single halyards in which the masthead block was slung from an iron rod or crane fixed in the masthead. This was not mere tradition, as Morris and others have thought, but a mode of preventing the halyards from chafing at the masthead block through not leading fair with it when the gaff was off. The iron crane revolved in a socket in many boats. The lofty position of the masthead block made the peak part of the halyards lead well aloft, which prevented the gaff from sagging to leeward. The idea that the gaff always sags is incorrect; this is not an inherent fault of the gaff rig, as many suppose, but rather the result of faulty design in the rig.

The Isle of Shoals boat was built with plank of cedar or white pine, with frames, keel, and posts of oak, and with spars of spruce or white pine. The fastenings were commonly wrought iron, but copper was used in some of the last boats built. Boats of the type shown in Figure 52 were built all along the coast from Gloucester to Kittery, and at Amesbury. The boats went out of fashion about 1906, when the gasoline engine became common; the end of the Isle of Shoals type was hastened by the capsizing, with loss of life, of an overloaded boat during a thunderstorm in the 1890's.

The Crotch Island Boat

The Crotch Island pinkies must be judged by the many half-models that have survived and by a few hulks whose lines have been taken off. It is apparent, however, that the development of this type cannot be traced in detail, since determination of the stages in evolution is impossible. None of the available material appears earlier than 1880. The Casco Bay type had become a powerful sailing boat by this time, fitted with the centerboard, ranging from 20 to 24 feet in length, and not suited for use by the fishing schooners, as the original type had been. Rowing was a required ability in any small boat in this period, and this necessitated easy lines and rather small displacement. This explains the relatively shallow draft of the boats, which was also a factor in maintenance. The boats were operated from small coves on the mainland and from island villages which had no marine railways or maintenance facilities. Each owner had to take care of his own boat, and the Crotch Island boat or Hampton boat could be easily hauled up on skids, with a block and tackle, for repairs and painting. The open waters in which the boats worked made seaworthiness a prime requirement; hence the double-ender retained some popularity right up to the end of sail in commercial fishing.

Figure 53 shows an example of the type; the drawing was made at Yarmouth, Maine, in 1937. The boat illustrated had been used as a yacht, and a cuddy had been added. However, the original decking had not been disturbed, and it was possible to measure the original arrangement. No information as to the builder or date of construction could be obtained, though it was agreed that the boat had

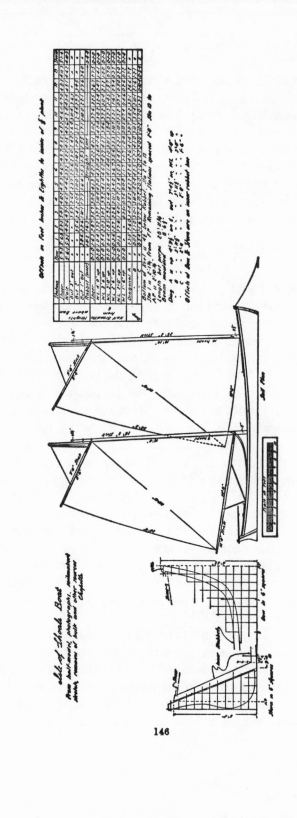

Lines of Lloyds Boat
from half-model, photographs, unhauled
sketch, remains of hulls and other sources
Chapelle

146

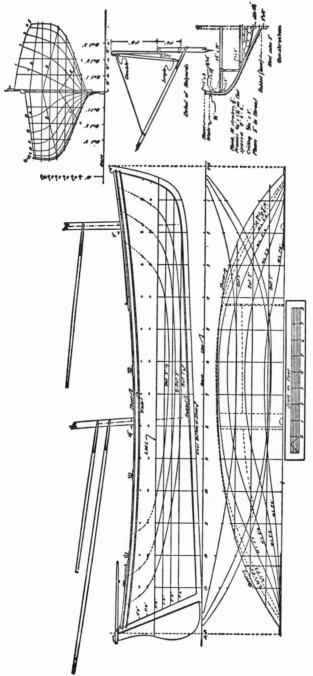

Fig. 52. Plan of a late Isle of Shoals boat, built in the 1890's, showing rig and construction.

been built about 1895 and that she came from one of the islands in Casco Bay. The model of this boat shows a somewhat longer run than in the New Hampshire boats but is not as extreme as some of

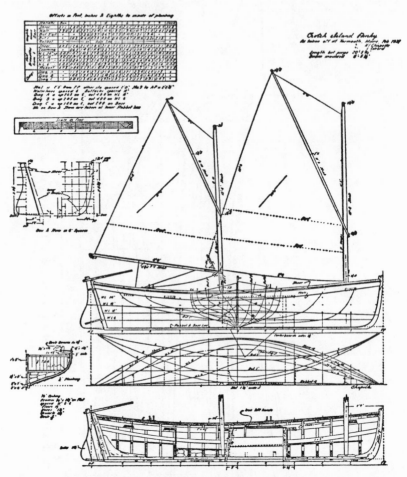

Fig. 53. Casco Bay double-ender or Crotch Island pinky.

the Casco Bay double-enders. The run is somewhat exaggerated in the drawing, owing to the use of level lines, parallel to the keel rabbet, in fairing. The level lines were used in order to compare the hulk with the lines of half-models of the type. Most of the latter are made with lifts parallel to the rabbet, which allows the mold sec-

tions to stand perpendicular to the keel, thus making the boats easy
to set up in building and insuring greater accuracy in following the
design. There was no real disadvantage to this method unless displacement calculations were to be made—and these were not necessary in the eyes of the boats' builders.

The construction is the conventional lap-strake, except that a
wide plank keel was used; this was molded in width so that amidships it was wide enough to bed the centerboard case securely. The
Casco Bay boats rarely took the fullest advantage of the plank
keel construction, as these boats commonly had a rabbet along their
keels. The plank keel was a very popular mode of construction for
American centerboard boats from about 1850 to 1898. The requirements for a lightweight boat with very narrow side decks for hauling lobster pots and fishing gear produced the minimum decking in
the Casco Bay boats. The boats were built of local timber—northeastern cedar or white pine for plank; red oak, white oak, and
hackmatack for frame structure. The boat measured had cedar
which was quite knotty, though all knots were very small. The
northeastern cedar could rarely be had in clear stock in any great
length, and it was found that small knots did no harm. Butts in the
lap-strakes were used—a butt block was placed clear of the lap to
secure them.

The rig of these boats was a two-masted ketch sail plan, but
usually lacking the jib and bowsprit. The foresail was lug-fashion
with some overlap of the main. A small diagonal club was always
used at the clew to make the sail stand smoothly. A temporary boom
was used on this sail when running; this was a sweep or other convenient pole and not a regular spar. The mainsail was boomed and
the foot of the sail laced. To avoid fouling the leech of the foresail
by the heel of the main sprit, the latter was placed either quite low
or high on the mast, clear of the overlap. Some boats had the sprit
so rigged that its projection forward of the mast was very slight.
This was done by using a very short snotter. Some fishermen used
a mast hoop, with a small rope eye turned into it, as a snotter; no
heel tackle appears to have been used. The sails were held to the
masts by wooden hoops and hoisted with a single halyard.

The usual small-boat practice with the spritsail—of first hoisting the sail and then shipping the sprit, by inserting its head into a

loop at the peak of the sail and, finally, resting its heel in the snotter
—would have been very difficult in these boats in rough water. For
this reason, the Maine fishermen did not lower the sails and unship
the sprit except when unrigging. They furled the foresail by slacking the heel through lowering the snotter on the mast; then they
peaked up the sprit against the mast and furled the sail around
both. The main required the boom to be topped, as well as the
sprit. This practice made furling and setting sail easy, in spite of
the rather heavy spars used, and allowed the sails to be kept out
of the way while fishing. The jib was not popular, old fishermen
said, because the sail was merely additional gear to be handled and
a jib was thought to add little to the speed of these boats. The working rig was handled as in the sharpie, the foresail being worked in
the same manner as a jib. The sheets were single parts, as the fishermen preferred simplicity and quick handling to an easy-working
rig. The easily driven hulls of these boats made a relatively small
sail area sufficient, and this made the rig easy to handle by one or
two men.

Figure 54 shows a more exaggerated boat of this type. The drawing was made from a half-model, with the aid of a photograph of
a similar boat. The model was the design of John Walker, who began building on Crotch Island but removed to Yarmouth, where
he built both the double-ender and square-sterned Hamptons well
into the late 1890's. A number of half-models made by Walker exist, and all are characterized by the peculiar cockup at the stern,
evidently under "pinky" influence. Some models showed this to a
very marked degree, and this must have made the boats rather
difficult to plank. The wall-sided bow and very flat run are carried
to an extreme in this example and follow the trend in design that
marks the Casco Bay square-sterned Hampton boats.

The builders and fishermen considered the long run very important both for speed under sail and for safety. In a heavy following
sea this style of run created little wake disturbance, which would
have caused the sea approaching from astern to break. Should this
happen the boat might broach and capsize or swamp; either would
be fatal in a winter gale. The wall-sided bow with its deep and
marked forefoot threw very little spray, as it did not "tramp" or
pound; this prevented icing up when the boats were bucking into

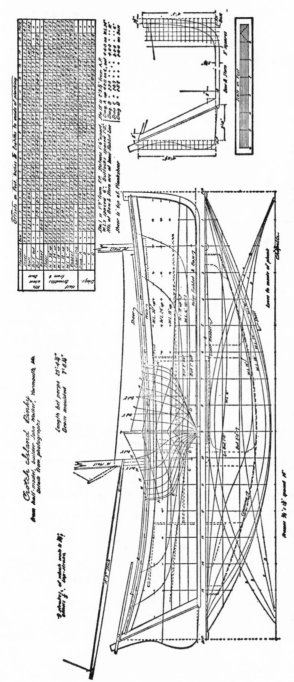

Fig. 54 Design of an extreme Crotch Island pinky, one of four models by this builder that have been found.

a head sea to windward in very cold weather. These Casco Bay double-enders were very fine small craft, fast and able, and had a striking appearance under sail.

The Square-sterned Hampton Boat

The Matinicus Island boat is represented by a couple of half-models, by a rigged model in the Watercraft Collection, and by the descriptions already mentioned. One of the old half-models, obtained from the island, is shown in Figure 55. The rig and arrangement are reconstructed from the Watercraft model and from the descriptions. The date of the model is in the late 1880's, according to its original owner, and it is claimed to have come from a builder on Muscongus Bay, where boats for both Matinicus and Monhegan islands were then built. In the 1870's and 80's, the town of Bremen was noted for its boatshops, which turned out lobster boats, shore boats, sloops, and smacks—both keel and centerboard. Fish Commission reports and Hall indicate the Matinicus Island type of boat was used along the shore of the main, from Boothbay to Rockland, to a limited extent.

The hull is marked by an extremely long, sharp, and rather straight-sided bow and a very flat run, which, combined, produce what is known as the "double-wedge" model. This became very popular in later years in fast motorboats having relatively small power. The sailing model appears to have originated in the New York half-decked sloops of the 1840's and 50's. The Matinicus boat has a very strong sheer with a hint of reverse forward to give a "powder-horn sheer"; this is apparent in many Maine small-boat half-models. The transom is raking and rather narrow; the Watercraft model shows a short and rather heavy counter stern, with rudderpost inboard. This seems to have been introduced into Muscongus Bay built small-craft in the 1870's, when the boatbuilders there were beginning in their small craft to copy, to some extent, the models of fishing schooners.

The rig used at Matinicus, in 1883–87, was the sloop with a sprit mainsail. No boom was used, and the sheet lead was made more flexible by the use of a light club at the foot against the clew, as in the Cape Ann sailing dories. The drawing shows a very hollow

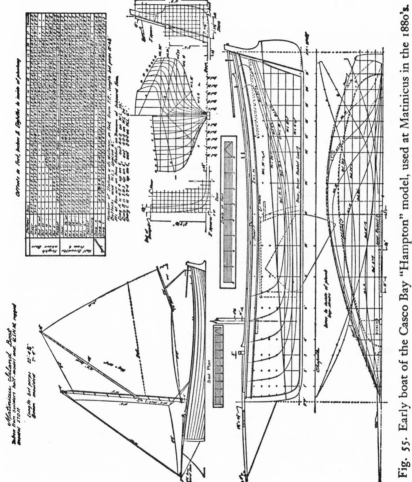

Fig. 55. Early boat of the Casco Bay "Hampton" model, used at Matinicus in the 1880's.

foot, following that of the rigged model, but I think the sail would be cut as in the dories and the hollow would then appear gradually as the sail stretched. The sprit appears to have had a mast-hoop snotter and was hoisted with the sail, perhaps. The boats are consistently described as lap-strake centerboarders about 22 feet long, and very fast sailers. Another rigged model in the Watercraft Collection shows that a very similar hull was used at Monhegan; this model is rigged ketch-fashion, with two spritsails and a jib tacked to a short bowsprit. The Monhegan Island boat thus represented had a short counter.

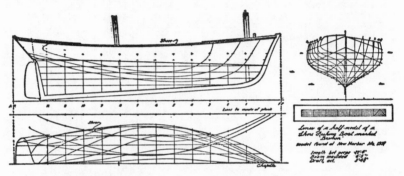

Fig. 56. Half-model believed to be a New England fishing boat of the 1880's related to the Casco Bay type.

Fish Commission field reports and Hall make many references to keel boats of somewhat similar size and rig in use along the shore of the mainland. They were called the "New England fishing boats," but this does not appear to have been strictly a type-name; rather, it was a loose classification. A rigged model of such a boat, acquired in 1876, is in the Watercraft Collection. The boat shows the influence of the then popular schooner-model, but the rig was either the common gaff or spritsail, masted as in the Crotch Island type. The model in the Watercraft Collection is sprit-rigged. The boats of this class are referred to in a manner that suggests they were in widespread use along the whole New England coast from Massachusetts Bay eastward.

Figure 56 shows the lines of a very nicely finished half-model obtained at Bremen, Maine, in 1937, which was first thought to be of a pleasure boat, but its very close resemblance to the Watercraft model indicates it may be one of the same type. The mounted half-model showed a two-masted boat, the lines faintly resembling the characteristic form of the Friendship sloop. No information about the half-model could be obtained, and the only marking was "Bremen" on top of the sixth lift. The top of the half-model indicates narrow washboards or side decks only, but the Watercraft model shows a long foredeck and an oval cockpit coaming, the rudder-head coming through the after deck. The type shown in both models seems to have been the result of a fad—which has occurred in both Maine and Nova Scotia in more recent times—of copying large schooners in small fishing boats. The New England fishing boat, it is said, often resembled the Providence River catboat in hull, and these were keel too, with straight stems. The boats all appear to have been replaced by centerboarders and must have been transitional types between older keel boats and the newer light-displacement centerboarders on the New England coast. Just what influence, if any, this class may have had on the Maine Hampton boat is problematic; the resemblance shows only that there may have been two-masted, square-sterned boats on the keel-sloop model in use close to the area where the square-sterned Hamptons may have originated.

One of the latter is shown in Figure 57; this is a 23-foot boat built at Orrs Island, Maine, about 1900. The boat shows the characteristics of the Maine Hampton boat to a marked degree. The drawing was made from the half-model, which the owner said was employed to build a strip-planked boat. The effects of this style of building can be seen; the very sharp hollow in the tuck and the hard turn in the bilge approaching the transom would have been very difficult to plank by any other method. The outside sternpost is used in strip-planked boats, as a rule, because this avoids the use of a rabbet on the sternpost. There is no rabbet cut along the plank keel; the top edge is beveled for the garboard strips and is backed in many boats by an inside plank or keel batten. The construction section shows this practice and is copied from a smaller strip-built Hampton, seen at Orrs Island in 1937, which had been built in 1910 and was still serviceable. She was 22 feet long, 7 feet beam. The rig is reconstructed from numerous descriptions and a sailmaker's sketch of 1901. A shifting bowsprit and a small jib were some-

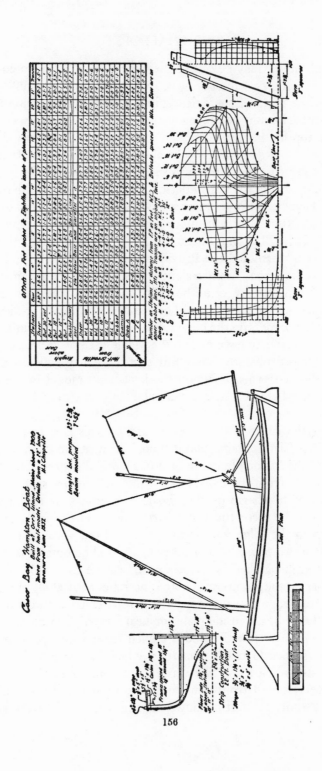

156

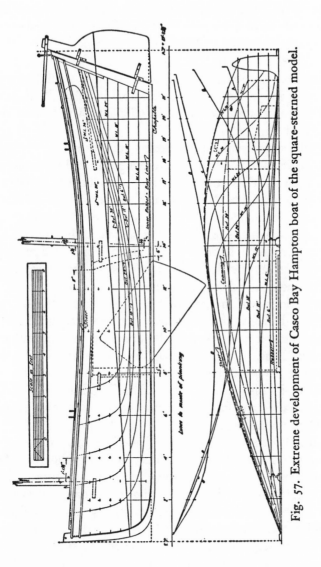

Fig. 57. Extreme development of Casco Bay Hampton boat of the square-sterned model.

times carried in these boats in summer. The rig, otherwise, is about the same as in the double-enders already described.

I experimented with a similar boat built in 1938 as a pleasure boat, and found her to be a smart sailer, though somewhat undercanvased in light summer weather. The boats should be sailed at moderate angles of heel, as in any boat having narrow side decks only, but otherwise they are readily understood. Weight should be kept out of the ends and concentrated amidships. If an auxiliary engine is desired, its power must be low to be efficient; these boats drive very easily indeed.

The two-masted, half-decked boats—most of which were spritsail-rigged—were also very popular among Massachusetts fishermen. A type used in Massachusetts Bay was commonly known as the "Kingston lobster boat," "Plymouth lobster boat," "Hull lobster boat," or "North Shore boat." These were originally skeg-built, square-sterned, lap-strake or caravel-plank centerboarders. They had a wet-well amidships, smack-fashion, and had outboard rudders. The rig was the usual one: loose-footed foresail overlapping the main, the latter boomed and smaller than the foresail, with no jib. These boats were in use in the late 1850's, but after the Civil War they went through many changes. Being used in waters where yachts were common, it was not long before they felt the influence of the pleasure boat. In 1871, Nathan Watson began to build the lobster boats at Kingston; he is reputed to have built the first caravel-planked one in this town, in 1874. Edward A. Ransom began building there in 1879 and introduced the counter into these boats about 1885, when racing began.

The first boat so built is said to have been named *Solitaire*, and local tradition states she also introduced hollow garboards. The boats were originally 16 to 18 feet long; when the counter was added they ran up to 20 feet in length. The introduction of the counter and the hollow garboards, the latter bringing the planked-up dead-wood with them, led to increased cost, and the advantages of the original boat were entirely lost. However, the type survived until power craft took over the fishery, and a few boats existed in Plymouth Harbor as late as 1939, though rerigged as sloops and used as pleasure boats. In the 1880's, a Kingston boat cost about $250 complete; the last boats cost double this. The Kingston boats, as

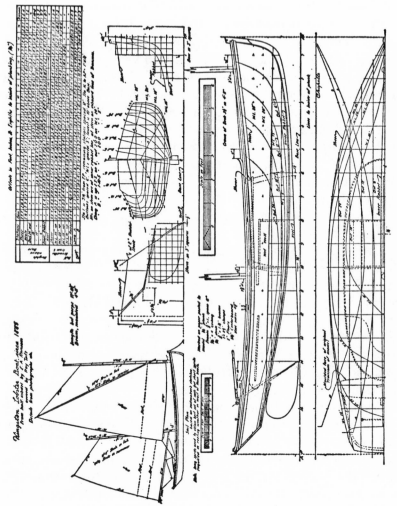

Fig. 58. A working Kingston lobster boat, before racing had affected the model

well as Hull's, were considered very fast sailers and this led to
much racing, which in turn produced boats that were really yachts
rather than working craft. The changes can be traced in plans and
half-models of Kingston boats.

Figure 58 shows the lines of a Ransom half-model in the possession of Mr. Ray Taft; the drawing shows the rig as reconstructed
by Charleton Smith and has been checked with other sources, including plans of a later boat by Martin C. Erismann. The model
is said to have been made before 1885; originally it was for a boat
having a flat transom and outboard rudder. To this a block had
been added and a counter formed on the model. The drawing shows
both the shape of the original transom and of the counter. Figure
59 shows a later boat, measured at Duxbury in 1937. This plan
shows the "improved" model, having a fishing schooner's counter
and the altered run in which the deadwood is planked and hollow
garboards are used. The model was now more like that of the sloop-
yacht of the late 1880's.

The boats were usually planked with ¾" white pine or cedar;
the frames were steam-bent of oak, ⅞" by 1", or 1" by 1⅛" on the
flat and spaced about 6" on centers. There was a ⅜" white pine
ceiling inside; the sheer clamps were 1" thick and 2½" or 3" deep.
Decks were ¾" thick, usually laid in narrow strips. Deck beams,
sided 1" and molded 1½", were of oak. Fastenings were originally
wrought iron; later, copper was used. Originally, plank keels were
used with the skeg, but the later boats had the molded scantling keel
of the modern yacht.

When picking up lobster pots, these boats usually worked under
foresail alone, the main being furled, as on Casco Bay, with sprit
and boom against the mast. The fishermen usually beat up from
leeward, picking up each pot while luffing, but the more active
picked them up on the run if the wind was not too strong. The
boats were very seaworthy under short sail, and in the late fall the
mainsail was often shifted to the foremast and the boats worked
under the single small sail. They rowed easily and were very
handsome little craft. Old fishermen said they were spoiled if given
any than their original rig, but many yachtsmen would not agree.

The boats built in other towns than Kingston usually had skegs
and many were strip-planked; the Hull boats had very tall rigs. It

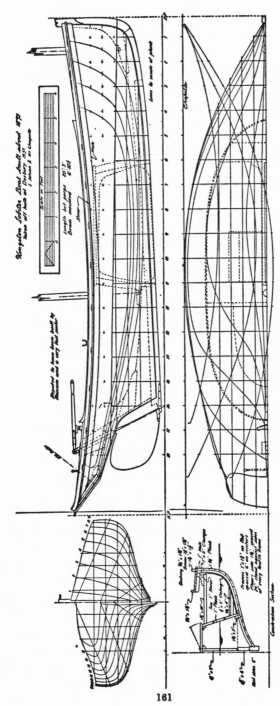

Fig. 59. Last model used in the Kingston lobster boats, in which racing had shown its effects in form and fittings, as well as in greater cost.

161

was the opinion of some that the boats having skegs were inclined to gripe and that the planked-up deadwood produced the better boat. This was probably true if both boats were rather deep; usually, the skeg-built hull is very shallow, and in such a model the skeg seems to have no great disadvantage and its use makes a cheaper boat to build. A few of the Kingston boats had some outside ballast; the *Vixen*, a Ransom-built boat, whose lines were taken off by Erismann, was one of these. The quantity of weight carried in the ballast shoe seems small, and it is very doubtful if any marked advantage was obtained.

The Tancook Whaler

The half-decked boats on the Atlantic seaboard were not all small, and some types reached nearly 50 feet in length. One of the finest of the larger boats was the double-ended Tancook whalers of Nova Scotia. These boats were apparently introduced about 1860–70; local claims at Tancook Island indicate that the first boat was built in that period at Lunenburg, on the mainland. This boat was so well liked that copies were built on the island.

It is possible that the Tancook boat was originally based on the New England boat or Hampton boat, as it too was a lap-strake keel boat and was schooner-rigged. The Tancook model is reputed to have had a bald clipper bow from the first, like that of the New England fishing boat, and seems to have had more rake in the ends than the New Hampshire model. The length of the early Tancook boats was about 24 to 28 feet. No contemporary model has been found of one of these, and there are only recollections of the islanders and a few photographs of the harbors of nearby towns in Mahone Bay to indicate what the boats were like.

The requirements for the Tancook Island boats were severe. This large island is in the mouth of Mahone Bay, some thirty miles southwest of Halifax. It had no natural harbor and became a settlement only because it was conveniently close to the fishing grounds. The boats were required to be moored off the island without shelter, and they also had to face severe weather offshore. The prolonged morning calms in the summer made it often necessary to row the boats out to the fishing grounds. The distance the boats were re-

quired to go to sea in fishing, and their value in transportation to
and from the island, made it desirable that they be craft of some
capacity.

The Stevenses, Masons, and Langilles were the Tancook Island
builders of the whalers and were responsible for the evolution of
the design. By 1900 the boats had reached their final form—they
were built in lengths up to nearly 50 feet and were caravel-planked.
They had very raking sternposts and bald clipper bows in which
the rabbet followed the stem profile. They were fitted with boiler-
plate centerboards and drew about 4 feet with the board up; stone

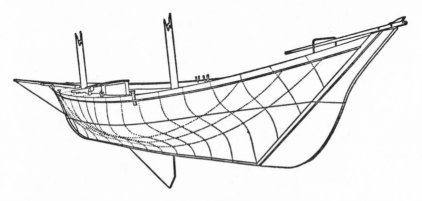

Tancook Whaler

ballast was also carried. They usually had a flush deck forward,
under which was a cabin with two platform berths and a stove.
Abaft the cabin was a large oval cockpit. The side decks were
quite narrow, and the deck at the stern was quite short. The cockpit was divided by bulkheads or "parting boards" into standing
rooms and fish holds; one of the parting boards was located at the
main thwart, which served to support the mainmast. A low finger
rail ran around the deck at the sheer; in some of the boats this rail
was substantial and was extended abaft the rudderhead, as in the
pink stern. The ends of this projection were joined by a bolt passing through a length of pipe, which acted as a spacer to fix the ends
of the projecting rail pieces at the proper distance apart. The pipe
served as a main-sheet horse. This may have been an adaptation of
the New Hampshire boat's stern outrigger under the influence of

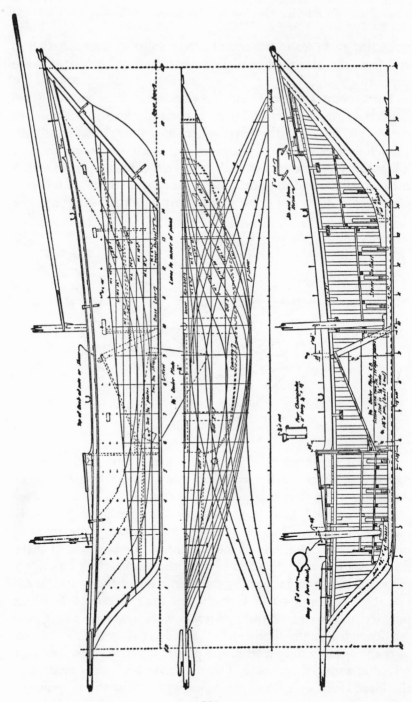

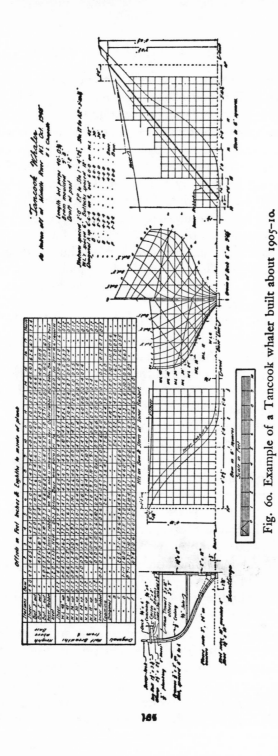

Fig. 60. Example of a Tancook whaler built about 1905-10.

the pinky; the latter was a very well-known type in Nova Scotia.

The lines of the Tancook whalers were remarkably sharp; the midsection showed a very hollow garboard and hard bilge; the wide plank keel was another feature. The boats sat low in the water and had a very graceful sheer. Altogether the Tancook whaler was one of the most handsome of the double-enders used on the Atlantic Coast, as may be seen by Figure 60. This drawing was made from a boat found at Middle River, on Mahone Bay, in 1948. Though the hull had been ruined by ice and snow, enough remained to enable an accurate set of lines to be made. This boat, noted as a good sailer, is about average in size, and was built somewhere between 1905 and 1910. The lines require little additional comment; it would probably be very difficult to make the hull finer without losing power to carry sail.

The noted sailing qualities of the Tancook whaler have led to some attempts to copy the hull, but in nearly all cases great departures were made which have usually rendered the new boats tender and uncomfortable. It is to be noted that the usual proportions of the Tancook whalers were close to a beam-to-length ratio of four, with the draft at the post a little less than one-half the beam.

The construction of the boat is well worth study. She was built entirely of local species of timber, many of which are held in disrepute in yacht building, yet the wreck of the boat showed that she had withstood the elements very well indeed. She was said to have been on the beach nearly twenty years, and so must have been in service around fifteen years. There were not above seven bolts in the entire hull structure, excepting the small ones used to secure the ironwork. Spikes had been used in the floor timbers and part of the deadwood; the remaining fastenings were boat nails. The plans show the mode of structure; there is no rabbet on the keel. The posts were formed out of the lower trunk and a root of larch trees; the keel appeared to be birch. The outer shoe was elm or beech, I am not certain which. The frames were wide and thin, and many seem to have been put in without steaming, probably in a green state. One of the notable features of the structure is that the floor knees have no direct connection with the light frames; these members are tied together only by their common fastening to the keel and lower hull planking. The floors were spruce knees with rather long arms amidships and aft. The planking was a local "pine," which was harder than any white pine I have seen, and seemed to be an eastern fir with which I am unacquainted. The ironwork used in the boat is shown on the plans; the ring on the foremast was used to moor the boat; the end of the mooring line often had a hook that

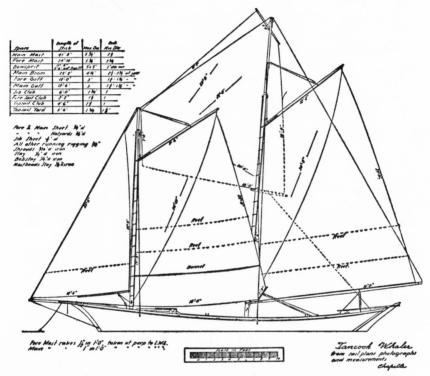

Fig. 61. Sail plan and rigging of Tancook whaler in Figure 60.

engaged the ring to secure. There were two wooden chocks on the bowsprit; the portside chock had an iron sheave and was used for the manila anchor cable. The starboard chock was "dumb" (having no sheave) and was used to hold the hemp mooring cable. A short lanyard passed through a hole in the bowsprit, between the chocks, and this was used to lash the mooring line into the chock, by passing the lanyard around all. This prevented the mooring cable from chafing or jumping out of its chock when the boat pitched heavily. The boiler-plate centerboard is of a rather poor shape, for when lowered there is little of it remaining in the case, which would strain the latter; the board would have been better had it been rectangular in shape. The case shows very little clearance on either side of the centerboard. The lanyard was missing, but was reported to have been wire rope with a manila tail; a chain was sometimes used instead of the wire rope.

The rig of the boat is shown in Figure 61 and is reconstructed from the sailmaker's description and photographs. The rig was the old pilot-schooner with a long pole mainmast head in lieu of a main topmast. The whole rig was simple and powerful; the boat was worked in strong winds under foresail alone, or under full mainsail and jib. If these changes in area showed too much sail, in either case, she was reefed. The rig was supplemented in light weather by the powerful pilot-boat main staysail, now called the "fisherman staysail." The working rig was not a small one, by modern standards, and this gave sufficient sail for work in moderate weather, without necessitating use of light sails. By keeping the height of the rig moderate it could be carried longer without reducing sail. In spite of the present prejudice against the schooner-rig, it was a very flexible and powerful one when properly designed. The only objection to the whaler rig that I ever heard of on Tancook Island was that the foresail sheet was hard to flatten in a breeze without luffing, owing to the powerful lug-foresail.

No Man's Land Boat

Beach boats have been mentioned as being of the New England boat model; these were the small, two-masted double-enders once used on the south side of Cape Cod, in the immediate vicinity of Vineyard Sound. The type-name usually applied to these craft was "No Man's Land boats," as many were once employed at a fishing camp on that island. Properly, perhaps, the boats might better be called "Vineyard Sound boats," as they were used on Martha's Vineyard, on Nantucket Island, and on the cape shore of the Sound.

The history of the type is unknown, but there are the usual statements that the boats were descendants of whaleboats—statements which are unsupported by any argument or evidence. The type was in use as early as 1856 at least. The boats were small as a rule; the

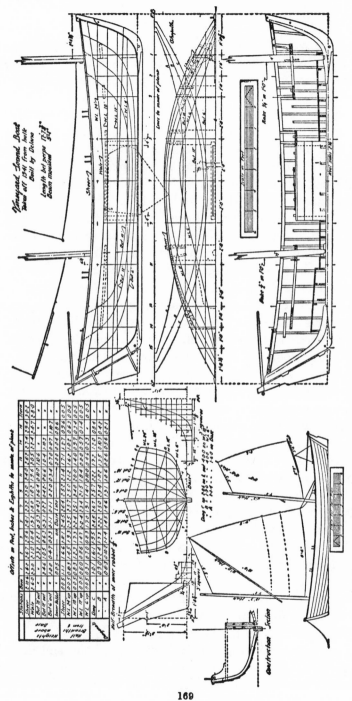

Fig. 62. Old No Man's Land boat, showing typical rig and construction of the type.

169

popular size was about 17 or 18 feet long. In the last years of the type, the boats were built up to 24 feet in length, and it is said at Martha's Vineyard that this was accomplished by changing the scale on the half-models used in laying down the boats.

The boats were all originally keel craft, and a model of one in the Watercraft Collection is of this design. About 1886, the centerboard came into use; this seems to have been brought about by the necessity of the boats going farther away from home to fish, which was also responsible, no doubt, for the increase in size mentioned. The evidence regarding the centerboard boats is based on a number of half-models and three hulks that have been measured, as well as descriptions from various sources. It appears that the boats were commonly built at Martha's Vineyard, New Bedford, Fairhaven, and along the cape shore of Vineyard Sound. The boats were also built at Providence, Rhode Island. The models used were varied to some extent, and the boats became stock-models with such builders as the Delanos and Beetles in the New Bedford-Fairhaven section. They were all open and were lightly built of cedar and oak. Some builders used bent frames, but others preferred single sawn-frames of cedar root; all the boats were lap-strake and copper-fastened. An iron strap protected the keel in beaching.

Figure 62 is a drawing of an old boat, found on Martha's Vineyard, which was said to have been built by Delano and to be one of two surviving boats by this builder, in 1941. The hull somewhat resembles the rigged model in the Watercraft Collection, and the rig shown here is taken from that model. The hull is of conventional lap-strake construction, which requires no comment. The rig is two loose-footed spritsails of small area with light spars, readily unshipped and stowed in the boat. The foresail is the larger of the two; the mainsail has a club on its foot, as in the Cape Ann dory and the Matinicus boat. In the 1890's, when the beach boats were going out of use, other rigs were used—for example, gaff foresail or gaff mainsail, with the mainsail sometimes fitted with a boom. At this period, some of the larger boats were half-decked, but these were not used on the beaches, of course.

The beach boats were particularly designed, built, and fitted to be launched from an open beach and to beach on return. They usually worked from a fixed location, and it was common for a number of boats to work together, so that the crews could help one another in the beach work. One of the important requisites of a beach boat is lightness; another is ability to work under oars. Sailing qualities were desired in the No Man's Land boats because they had to sail some distance to the fishing grounds. The result of conflicting requirements can be seen in the plans. The double-ended boats were thought best in this section for beach work, but the opinion was not universal. The ballast employed in the No Man's Land boats was in the form of sandbags which could be filled or emptied as conditions required.

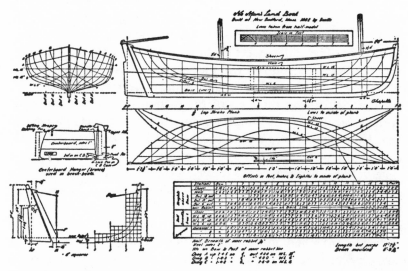

Fig. 63. No Man's Land boat of the more powerful type designed to sail well.

Figure 63 shows the lines of a Beetle-built boat, somewhat more powerful than the Delano boat. This drawing also shows a common method of hanging the centerboard in these beach boats; this permitted rapid removal of the board from its case when ready to beach. There were a number of methods of accomplishing this, most of which used what were called "patent hangers," and the American surfboats were often fitted with these when sail was employed in such craft. The No Man's Land boats commonly had the centerboard slot in one of the garboards rather than on the centerline of the hull and through the keel. The offside position was used because this avoided the slot becoming jammed with small stones or dirt through contact with the beach in landing.

The No Man's Land boats had an excellent reputation for safety and were very good sailers. They were never as large and powerful as the regular surfboats, such as those of the Monomoy and Cape Race types. Beach work, as carried on by the fishermen, was an art and could be learned only by long experience under trained supervision. It was never a singlehanded operation, of course.

The beach gear used with these boats should be described, as it would be useful for many other purposes. The boats were hauled and launched on "ladders." These were made in short sections, hooked together end to end. Each section consisted of two timbers, laid parallel, joined together by a series of wooden rollers, like rungs of a ladder. The rollers were often only a foot or so long. Two or three spreaders of iron rod and pipe were also used in each section to prevent the side timbers from binding the rollers. Iron hooks and strap stirrups at the ends of the sections served to join them. Sleepers secured to the underside of the side timbers prevented them from sinking into a sand beach. The sections were often laid out into the water and staked there when the boats were ready to come in. The "ladders" thus formed a simple marine railway. The boats were moved by placing their keels on the rollers and then, with the beach crew holding them upright by the gunwales, the boats were easily launched or hauled. The fall of the beach to the water was a help in launching, of course. Holes at each end of the keel were used for hauling lines. A turntable was sometimes used; this was a plank platform on which was a pivoted block shaped to take the keel of a boat. The boat was worked off the rollers on to this, turned end for end, and then worked back on to the "ladder." Capstans were not used, but at Block Island, where large beach boats were once used, horses and oxen aided in the beach work. The launching cart, used by lifesaving stations, does not appear to have been employed by fishermen.

The Block Island Cowhorn

Perhaps the best known of all American beach boats was the Block Island boat, or cowhorn. A number of drawings of these boats have been published: the *Lena M*, in *Rudder* magazine April, 1912; the *Dauntless*, in *Forest & Stream* magazine, February 9, 1907 (both by the late Martin Coryell Erismann); and the *Island Belle* in Dixon Kemp's *Manual of Yacht and Boat Sailing*, 4th edition, 1884 (taken off by J. Hyslop). In other sources, extensive descriptions of the boats supplement the published plans. However, the boats represented in these plans and in most of the other sources are the larger ones, so it is desirable to show what the small boats of this type were like.

The cowhorns have had a very fine reputation for safety and, according to local records, only one has ever "gone missing." The name of the type apparently came from a fancied resemblance of the profile of the boats to a pair of horns. The traditional history of the type is that they were originated by Trustrum Dodge, the only one of the sixteen original settlers of Block Island in 1661 who was a boatman. It is also said that the boats were built during the Revolution by John Rose, who was followed by Lemuel Rose, both Block Island boatbuilders. From 1850 to about 1870, the prominent builder was Deacon Sylvester D. Mitchell, who is credited with the *Dauntless* and other noted boats. The claims for Dodge and the other early builders appear unsupported by any evidence, and it is by no means certain that the type actually existed in a recognizable form before 1840. It is often supposed that the boats developed from whaleboats; a standard assumption, apparently, for the origin of nearly every American double-ender.

The cowhorns ranged in length from 17 or 18 feet, over the gunwales, to about 40. The boats over 30 or 32 feet in length appear to have become very common after a breakwater was constructed at "Old Harbor," which allowed boats to remain afloat rather than having to be beached. The maximum draft of the large boats was between 6 and 7 feet, and the greatest beam was about 14 feet. The older boats, built for beach work, were small; the most common size appears to have been between 18 and 24 feet length, 7 to 10 feet beam, and 2½ to 4½ feet draft. The model was a peculiar one, having great beam, much sheer, and very raking ends. The midsection was almost a perfect V. The ends were relatively full, and only the after water lines showed much hollow as they approached the rabbet. The boats were not stiff; they were designed to be rowed, and this probably had much to do with the model. The small boats had no decking; beach stones were used for ballast. The larger cowhorns were decked forward (the deck seems to have had no crown), and under this a cuddy was built. The small boats were worked on the beach with the "ladder," as a rule. It seems that the form and size of the Block Island boats must have been much influenced by the fact that they had to travel some distance to fishing grounds by 1850 and that they were also required as transportation between the island and the main.

The construction of the boats varied; some had bent frames, others had sawn frames of a single futtock made of cedar root. All were lap-strake, planked with cedar. The keel and posts were larch or oak. When bent frames were used, the floor timbers were also of bent stock, and these were placed between the side frames and clear of them; the ends of the floor timbers amidships were carried well up the sides nearly to the water line. The strength of the hulls depended to a great extent on the flexible frame and also upon the substantial thwarts, of which there were three to five, depending upon the size of the boat.

The rig was that of the old shallop, with but slight modification. There were two masts, set with some rake, the foremast well forward in the boat and the main about amidships. The masts were of about the same height; on these were sails having very short gaffs hoisted by single halyards. The foresail was loose-footed and overlapped the main. The mainsail was loose-footed but was fitted with a boom. No light sails or jibs were carried. The sail area was respectable, and so each sail had many reef bands; the main commonly had four, the foresail five.

Figure 64 shows the lines, rig, and construction of a small cowhorn of a once popular size. This drawing is copied from ones made from an old hulk by Paule Loring and Commander George Cunha, U. S. N., which was used by Mr. Loring to build a replica named *Glory Ann*. Some modifications in the arrangement of the boat were made in the replica; the drawings here have the inboard arrangement as shown in photographs of a very similar boat contained in Paul C. Nicholson's article in the *Rhode Island Historical Society Collection*, 1923. The drawings show the washboards, called "leeboards," that were set up along the rail cap in bad weather to

Port Isabel, Texas, scow sloop.

A small Tancook Whaler from Nova Scotia. Stern altered for auxiliary power.

Photo U.S. National Museum

Scow sloop *Target* of Portland, Maine, used in fyke fishing for flounder. Boats of the Whitehall type carrying single spritsail are shown in the foreground.

'yster sharpies hauled up for winter at New Haven, Connecticut, 1891. One-man sharpie in ckground immediately in front of sloop, another in extreme foreground. Square-stern racing arpie second back.

Seine boats from the Higgins and Gifford boat shop.

Sailing dories and two-masted lobster boats at Rockport, Massachusetts, about 1891.

A small-class Eastport "Pinky" or "carry-away" boat under sail.

Model of the cowhorn *Island Belle*, made by Alfred S. Brownell.

Photo U.S. National Mus

This is the only known photograph of the type of New Hampshire "Hampton whaler" once s to Novia Scotia and Newfoundland. The picture appears to have been taken at St. Joh Newfoundland.

Photo U.S. National Mus

An old Fish Commission photograph of a fully rigged boat variously called a "North Caroli shad boat," an "Albemarle Sound seine boat," or a "Croatan Island boat."

Photo J. P. Shaw

...an fishermen and hauled-out fishing boats at Monterey, California, 1889. The boats were built ...San Francisco.

Model of a Monhegan fishing boat, 1883.

raise the low freeboard. These leeboards were in short lengths for
stowage and were stepped by means of stanchions inside each section whose heels socketed into holes in the rail caps. The great flare
of the sides of the hull produced the well-known phenomenon of

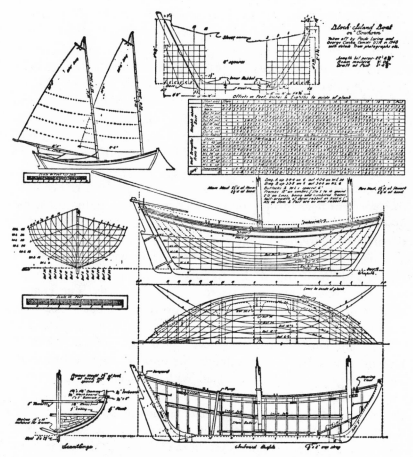

Fig. 64. Typical small Block Island boat.

the gunwale appearing to be below the level of the sea, when the
boat was heeled and moving fast, without water being shipped. The
washboards merely kept out the dollops thrown off by a cresting
sea in a strong wind.

The Block Island boats are so well known to American yachtsmen that it would not be necessary to discuss the type further, were it not that many of the copies of the cowhorns, built as yachts, illustrate the dangers of attempting to cure imaginary ills in a working-boat type, or to make a type into something it was not intended to be originally.

The cowhorn was originally designed to be worked by two men, or a man and boy, in fishing in open waters in all weathers. This controlled the hull and rig design to some extent; the additional factors were the necessity of working on the beach and of being rowed in calm weather. Quick tacking was not necessary, but certainty in staying in heavy seas was very important. This meant, in a small boat, the need of having full control of the boat every instant, and so the boat was intended to be sailed around, in staying, by handling the foresail, as would be done with a jib in a heavy sloop. Thus, if a sea hit the boat in stays she was not stopped and put into irons, as would be the case with a small and rather light-displacement boat turning on helm alone and depending upon momentum to come around. Now, this has not been understood by yachtsmen interested in the type, and so, the boats being "slow in stays," the replicas were fitted with jibs or were completely re-rigged and "modernized" by rigging the hull as a cutter or ketch with the popular high and narrow jib-headed sails. The result is disappointing, for the hull profile still prevents the boats from spinning around when the helm is shoved over, as in a short-keel hull.

It is common to find the replica, rigged in a modern fashion, to be tender under sail. This is due to the high center of effort in the modern rigs, of course, combined with the slack-bilged cowhorn model. So outside ballast is often added in the hope of overcoming this difficulty. The result is usually again disappointing, for the depth is insufficient to allow the outside ballast to be very effective. The process of improvement has, in the meantime, raised the building and rigging cost of the original to yachting standards and has produced only an inferior yacht. The rather short run, great beam, and full bow do not permit the cowhorn to be a very fast sailer on all points, and so she cannot benefit from a large and "more efficient" rig.

The cowhorn has no qualities that make it suitable for all waters and every use. It has great value for individual use in open water where it may meet heavy weather. The fishermen could not drive a small, open boat to windward in a gale by carrying sail, because they would soon become exhausted, and this would lead to some fatal mistake in handling; it is this that makes the cowhorn what she is and not a racer, ocean or otherwise. In short, the cowhorn was a boat that must work under short sail in heavy weather; hence the numerous reefs, so that the crews could take it as easy as possible in a small, open boat in a winter gale. In its original form and rig, the cowhorn makes a splendid family boat, or small cruiser, for use in exposed waters, and she would be a relatively

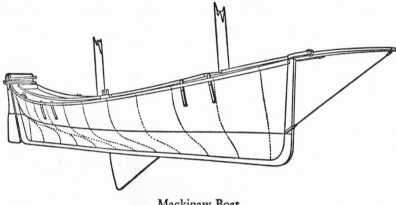

Mackinaw Boat

cheap boat to build and maintain. She can be made into a racing yacht or "fast cruiser" only by being completely redesigned into something having none of the qualities that made the cowhorn so noted.

Three types of half-decked boats, or ones having washboards, with two-masted rigs were used on the Great Lakes, aside from the pound-net sharpies and some of the stake boats. These were the square-sterned boats built at Erie, Pennsylvania, which carried the Lake sharpie rig and were called "Erie boats." Another type of square-sterned boat of slightly different model and rig was built on both the American and Canadian sides of Lake Huron and was called the "Huron boat." The third was a double-ender of similar rig to the latter, built on Lakes Huron, Michigan, and Superior, and known as the "Mackinaw boat." The models of hull used in the Huron boat and the Mackinaw were not standardized, and there was some variation in proportions and lines within each type. This was also true of rigs, the greatest variation being in the Huron boats. The latter were sometimes known as "Carver," "Wheeler," and "Hayward" boats, named for prominent builders who turned out satisfactory stock boats in this general type. The Mackinaw boat was also known as the "Collingwood skiff," and the name "Mackinaw" was also applied to all the two-masted lake boats in the western lakes area without distinction of type of hull.

The history of these types is uncertain; the double-enders appear to have originated from a small, double-ended, open rowing and sailing boat and may have been developed from the St. Lawrence skiffs, which became very well known to eastern sportsmen in the 1870's and 80's. Paul James Barry, writing on the Mackinaw, Collingwood, and Huron boats in *Yachting* (November, 1940, and April, 1942) traces the Collingwood skiff built on the Canadian side of Lake Huron from a small boat built on Lake Ontario, about 1854, by William Watts. This man moved to Collingwood, on Georgian Bay, about four years later and there developed the Collingwood skiff. The models and the photographs of the Collingwood skiff in the *Yachting* articles show some similarity in appearance to the old St. Lawrence skiff, but there is no historical proof of descent.

The name "Mackinaw" comes from a corruption of "Mackinac"; the straits of this name were known locally as "Machinaw" or "Mackinaw." The double-enders were most popular in the vicinity of the straits. The name "Mackinaw" was also applied to large bateaux used there in the fur trade in early days; there is no reason to suppose that these were the forerunners of the later fishing type. The Erie and Huron boats appear to have been developments of the early ships' boats, such as the yawl, employed on the Lakes, if one may judge by their appearance and construction.

The Erie Boat

The Erie boat apparently was the product of two or three builders at Erie and was built nowhere else. The boat has long been

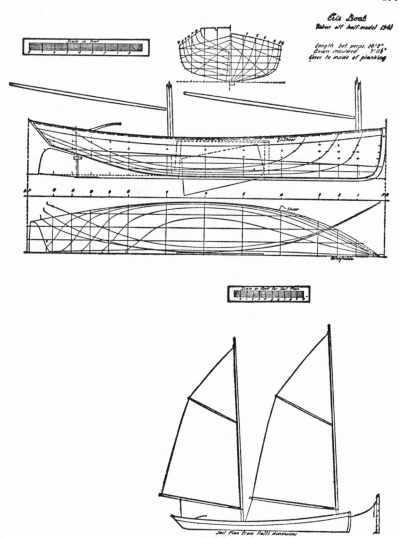

Fig. 65. Lake Erie fishing boat, arranged like the sharpies used on the lake.

extinct and is recorded only in a couple of known half-models and by a few descriptions. Hall's description, in his report on shipbuilding for the Tenth U.S. Census, is the most complete.

Figure 65 shows the lines of one of the known half-models. The boats were skeg-built with a short and rather heavy counter; the rudderpost was inboard, and its head was supported by a high and strong sternsheet on which the fishing net was stowed when working. The model shows good lines, and the boats are said to have been both fast and seaworthy. They were built almost entirely of oak, and in many boats oak was used for planking. Sawn frames were used in some of the boats, making them very heavy, and consequently they sat low in the water.

The rig shown is reconstructed from Hall's description, which states that the rig came originally from New York. Hall also mentions in his field notes that, in 1881, Loomis, who built boats with skegs, intended to omit these in his new boats. This indicates that some of the boats may have been built with balance-rudders, like sharpies. The half-models and Hall's description lead to the conclusion that the Erie boat was built to a very narrow range in dimensions; the boats were apparently all about 28 feet length and 8 feet beam, which shows they were practically stock boats.

The Mackinaw Boat

The Mackinaw boat may be said to have been built in three distinct models; one was the rather straight-sheered Collingwood skiff, as built on both the American and Canadian shores of Huron. Such a boat is shown in Figure 66. This drawing, made from a half-model with details reconstructed from local information and photographs, shows finer ends than some others seen and is, perhaps, somewhat less burdensome than usual. This type had very little drag to the keel. The boats were usually planked lap-strake over bent frames and were quite light in construction. They ranged from 26 to 35 feet in length, and some of the larger craft had a cuddy forward. The Canadian builders employed boiler-plate centerboards at one time, but wooden boards were standard in the last years of the type. The boats were often fast and powerful. However, it is doubtful that such shoal hulls, with so little drag to the keels, would be as good performers in rough water as some of the double-enders used on the eastern seaboard.

The rig of the boats built on Lake Huron was never standardized; the American-built boats usually were ketch-masted and gaff- or sprit-rigged. Up until about 1882 the boats did not carry jibs and

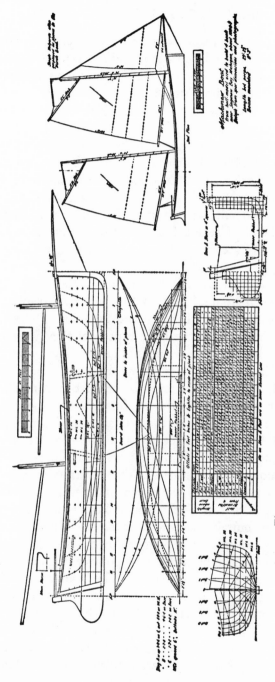

Fig. 66. Lake Huron Mackinaw boat or "Collingwood skiff" type.

181

bowsprits; these were made popular by the Georgian Bay builders, and by 1885 the additional spar and sail were in common use.
In many of the boats, the masts were almost of the same length, and
the two sails were of about the same area. A few of the early boats
appear to have had boomed foresails, which became standard by
the time the jibs were added.

The type shown, the Collingwood skiff model, reached its highest
popularity about 1885–86. Boats of this model were sent to British
Columbia for the Fraser River salmon fishery, and one was used
for survey work on James Bay. The boats were also taken to Lake
Winnipeg for commercial fishing. The decline of the Huron
fishery was the chief reason for the disappearance of this style of
boat, though a few employed as yachts have survived until very
recently.

Another variant of the Mackinaw boat is shown in Figure 67.
This plan is taken from a half-model for a caravel-planked boat of
the style built on Lakes Michigan and Superior. These were unquestionably the finest of the Lake types, for they were not only
fast but were also very fine seaboats. The drawing shows the characteristics of these boats; a very strong sheer and a high, bold bow;
almost plumb stem; marked rake to the post; and much drag to
the keel. The beam is carried well forward and the run is long
and fine. The midsection of these boats varied somewhat from
boat to boat. The models inspected and various descriptions show
that some boats were built with straight, rising floors, while others
had some hollow at the garboards. The construction was conventional; bent or sawn frames were used, and a plank keel was standard. The rig was that of a schooner or ketch—with the masts the
same height in some boats—and a jib seems to have always been
used. The bowsprit was much hogged downward. The rig shown in
the plan seems to have been the most popular; the lug foresail was
sometimes replaced by a boomed sail. The boats are not described
as ever having spritsails, nor are such sails shown in any of the early
photographs that have been seen. Clench-built boats of this type
usually had very raking bows and also had very hollow garboards.
A drawing of one of the lap-strake boats, among the plans in the
Historic American Merchant Marine Survey collection, in the National Museum (Smithsonian Institution), shows much fuller ends

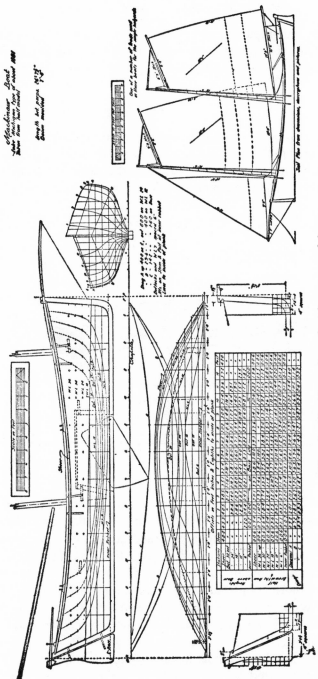

Fig. 67. Mackinaw boat for the western lakes.

than in the half-models seen and so may not be wholly typical. So far as is known there are now no boats of either build now in use on the Lakes.

The Huron Boat

The Huron boat was usually more burdensome than the double-enders used on the same lake, yet the square-sterned boats were considered to be generally the faster of the two. The Huron boat shown in Figure 68 was built on the American side about 1888. These

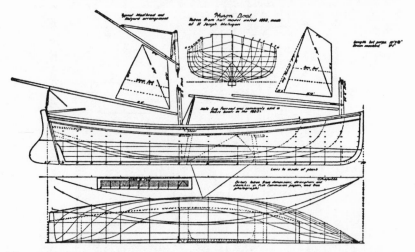

Fig. 68. Lap-strake square-sterned Huron boat of a once popular type for gill netting.

boats usually had no jib and were ketch-masted. Both gaff and sprit-sail rigs were used; some boats had the lug foresail. On the Canadian side, the boats usually had bowsprits and many were schooner-rigged. At least one was three-masted. The boats were commonly lap-strake, and some of the boats, particularly the Canadian-built craft, had short counters. Some were built with "chicken-beak" clipper bows, like those of some American steamships of the 1840's. This style of bow was introduced by a schooner builder who turned to boatbuilding.

The drawing shows a boat having a short, but well-formed, run which was required by the weight of the nets carried aft. This weight also necessitated a wide transom. This combination, with the very slight drag to the keel, accounts for one great fault in those boats: when running hard in a heavy sea and wind they were inclined to broach. The Huron boats ranged in length between 30 and 40 feet generally, but in some localities the type was constructed as small as 24 feet. Among the smaller examples were the Carver boats, which were 24 to 26 feet long, schooner-rigged with jib and bowsprit, and said to have carried gaff topsails. This boat was going out of fashion in 1881, according to Goode. The Hayward boats were 32 feet long, schooner-rigged, and rather flat-floored. The Carver and the Hayward were caravel-planked. The Wheeler boat was lap-strake and schooner-rigged, and is said to have been a very good model. As early as 1882, the two-masted Ohio sharpie began to replace the Huron boats in many localities on the lake.

The Delaware Sturgeon Skiff

A craft slightly similar to the Huron boat was used in eastern waters; this was the sturgeon boat, or sturgeon skiff, employed on the lower Delaware. These boats, between 30 and 34 feet in length, were square-sterned, two-masted centerboarders and were used to handle nets. Like the Huron boat, they had a short run. The eastern boats were powerful craft, as they had to be to face the rough, current-ridden waters of Delaware Bay. The boats were built in both the lap-strake and caravel methods; they were rigged with two spritsails, both loose-footed, but otherwise much like the two-masted garveys. Some boats carried two leg-of-muttons with sprit booms, sharpie fashion, with the mainmast as tall as or taller than the fore. This was a late-comer on Delaware Bay; the older boats seem to have all been spritsail-rigged, with a very large foresail and a small main. The boats had very large centerboards and are reported to have been exceptionally weatherly.

Figure 69 shows an example of the Delaware boats. This plan was made from an old boat at Bivalve, New Jersey, in 1940, and is somewhat similar to boats shown in the collection of plans in the Historic American Merchant Marine Survey in the Smithsonian Institution. No rigged boat has been found, and the mast positions of the Bivalve boat do not agree with those of the Smithsonian's plans. The reconstruction of the rig is therefore based upon local information, which seems reliable.

The Delaware boats were built with bent frames as a rule and had cedar planking. They had wide rail caps, with a low coaming from about amidships forward. At the stern there was about three feet of decking, which was used in working nets and gear. In heavy weather they worked under foresail alone; the mainmast and sail were struck and stowed. The mainmast was stepped to aid in this.

Some of the boats inspected had been altered by the addition of a false keel, deeper aft than forward, which indicates that more drag had been found desirable. The boats carried sandbag ballast and were fitted for rowing. The history of the type is uncertain; it is usually said they were developments of local yawl-boats—which, indeed, they do resemble. The sturgeon boat was in existence as early as 1870, at least. The type was a very able, powerful sailing boat, and a few have been converted into small auxiliary cruising yachts, sloop- or schooner-rigged.

Columbia River Salmon Boat

The Pacific Coast has produced some remarkable types, though most of the types used there originated in the east. One type, however, whose development was wholly western was the double-ended Columbia River salmon boat, or gill-net boat. As its use was not wholly confined to the Columbia River, the type varied somewhat, but generally it was a powerful, seaworthy rowing and sailing boat. It is said to have originated at San Francisco, where, in 1868, J. J. Griffin built the first of the type for a fisherman called "Greek Joe," according to field reports of the Fish Commission in 1885. The boat was for use on the Sacramento River, where fishing was then being done in Whitehall boats and skiffs. The new boat was followed by a sister that was sold the next year to George and Robert Hume for use on the lower Columbia. The two boats proved wholly satisfactory, and the type was extensively built, not only in the San Francisco area but also on the Columbia.

The early boats were 22 to 23 feet long, but the length was increased, and in the late 80's was about 28 feet, which seems to have become standard. By that time the boats had been introduced into

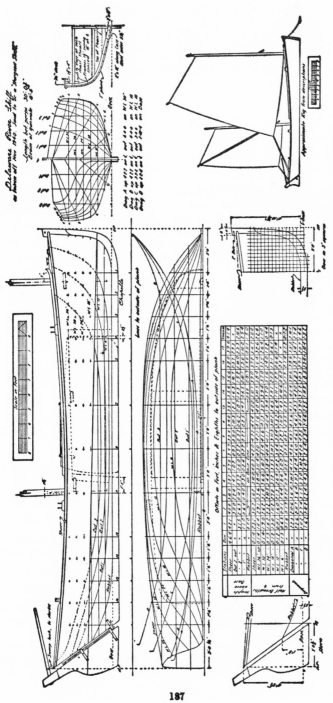

187

Fig. 69. Delaware River sturgeon skiff developed after the Civil War for sturgeon fishing.

Alaskan waters. The rig was usually a single spritsail; some boats carried a jib tacked to the stemhead. The model was rather full-ended; the run was slightly finer than the entrance. The dead rise was moderate, and the boats could carry a great deal of weight for their length and draft. The original boats had been entirely open, but, by 1876, washboards and short end-decks were in use. In early years a few boats on the Sacramento had leg-of-mutton sails in place of the spritsail, but the latter became the standard sail in the type.

The boats were often required to stay out over a few days, and the crew of two or three then used the sail and a spar to make a cockpit tent and cooked on an oilstove. Most of the boats were owned by the fish canners, who rented the boats to the men who worked them. This led to the purchase of the boats in large numbers, thus creating a reason for making the boats a "stock" model and mass-producing them. As a result, the cost was low—in 1872, an undecked boat cost but $220 at San Francisco; in 1880, one with washboards cost $240; and, in 1886, $400.

The design of the boat was controlled by the need to carry a great load, yet it had to be of such size that it could be rowed. The strong winds met on the Pacific Coast dictated a small, handy rig. The simple rig, as shown in Figure 71, was reduced in a squall by unshipping the sprit and tying the peak to the mast hoops to form a small triangular sail. The boom could also be unshipped easily. Figure 70 shows the lines and construction of a typical boat of this type. This was a stock design built in 1925–26 for use in Alaska.

The boats were built with steam-bent frames, which were first bent over molds and later placed in the boat, cold. Planking was Oregon fir (Douglas fir, Oregon pine), and larch was sometimes used for the keel and the posts. The boats were built in a sound manner without frills. In spite of the hard usage inherent in their employment—which included abuse and neglect by crews who had no economic responsibility for the welfare of the boats—they are said to have had an average working life of from ten to fourteen years. The construction was quite conventional in all respects and was moderately heavy.

The Columbia River salmon boats were not intended to be

very fast sailers, yet in fresh winds and with a load they showed a good turn of speed. The type is hardly one that would appeal to the usual pleasure sailor, but there may be individual require-

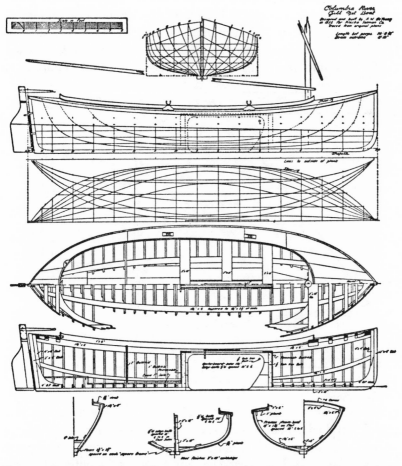

Fig. 70. An example of excellent construction in a "stock" model work-boat, the Columbia River type of salmon boat.

ments that would make it serviceable. These boats show the strength and lasting qualities possible in the old standard building methods and prove that the "stock boat" may be well built under mass-production methods if the builder desires. Poor construction, or jerry-building, is not inherent in the mass production of boats, if emphasis is placed on quality and not upon fancy finish or some other unimportant detail.

The mass-produced stock boat used for commercial fishing has never been recognized by writers for what it really was: a successful design that had been proven by trial and that had achieved sufficient recognition of this to permit repeat sales. Of course, the

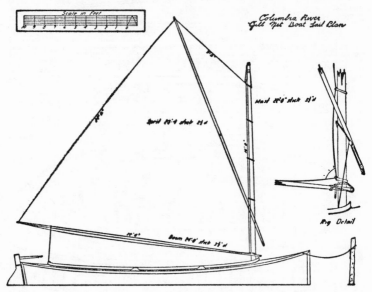

Fig. 71. Rig of West Coast salmon or gill-net boat.

application of "mass-produced" to small-boat construction is a little farfetched, since in only a few cases were there large yearly outputs of a single model. Among the types which were built in very large numbers in a single year, the Banks dory is the outstanding example. The rest, with a few exceptions, would be more properly classed as stock boats which were repeated without major changes over and over again, for a period of years. The yearly production of one of these boats, in a single boatshop, may range from two to a hundred, as was the case of the Gloucester seine boat, the New Bedford whaleboat, the New Haven sharpie, the Columbia River salmon boat, and others.

Many local types of small working boats were produced by a very small number of professional boatbuilders, with additional boats being built by amateurs, fishermen, and others. The professionals trended toward the stock boat, for they knew that any new design was, to a great extent, an experiment. Once a successful and outstanding model had been produced, it was well to repeat it when possible. This would not only avoid the uncertainties of a new design, but would also allow the use of existing molds and patterns and of the experience obtained in building the first boat. This would lead, normally, to a freezing of the designs and to a lack of improvement—the usual complaint against standardization. However, in the boatshops this difficulty was rather academic for a number of reasons. In early days, mass production was not a fetish, and the builders did not begin business by obtaining a design and then tooling up to produce it in huge numbers. They began business as "custom" builders, constructing boats to order. When one was found that appeared to be in demand, it was repeated as long as sales were possible. As a result, the stock boat in a shop came into being very gradually and usually without extensive and speculative "stocking-up" of boats in advance of sales. The lack of expensive jigs and special equipment enabled the shift to be made from one design to another, when such a change was evident in the demand for boats. Therefore, the effect of competitive design in these small craft was constantly met and the possible braking effect of mass production was rarely felt.

In a few small craft, such as the dory, this gradual rise from "custom" to "mass" production did not occur, and a few builders are known to have set up shop for mass production. But in such cases they had the advantage of being able to copy successful boats, which, individually, were neither complicated nor expensive. The sales of these boats, in addition, were seasonal and local, so it was not extremely difficult to estimate the required inventory of finished boats in advance of the seasonal sales. The costs of advertising and sales organizations were not required. It will be seen, therefore, that the builders of the dory and similar mass-produced craft were not faced with great administrative or technical difficulties if a shift in product was required. The basic advantages of mass production are not modern discoveries; early boatbuilders in America apparently employed quantity production of small boats for military purposes in the Revolution and afterwards. Commercially, however, mass production in boatshops seems to have begun about New York in the 1830's and 40's, in the construction of the Whitehall boat and similar small craft. The idea slowly took hold and quantity production of dories, yawls, whaleboats, and seine boats began at various towns along the coasts; by 1880 the practice was very widespread all over the United States. This resulted in a great spread in some types; the government surveys of the Treasury Department and the Fish Commission show that boats built at Kittery, Cundy's Harbor, and Bremen, Maine, at Saybrook and New Haven, Connecticut, and at New York were being sold in the South and in Canada. In nearly all such cases the boats were "stock" models.

CHAPTER 4

THE Skiff AND Yawl-Boat

A LARGE NUMBER of rowing boats, of varying models, were used by American fishermen and watermen in the days of sail. These working-boats ranged from small gunning skiffs, 12 to 16 feet long, used by the commercial market-hunters, to combination rowing-and-sailing craft up to 24 feet in length, used by some fishermen. It would be impossible to separate the larger boats of this class from those previously referred to as successors to the colonial shallop. However, in the classification under discussion, the rowing, or rowing-and-sailing, craft will be limited to open boats in the largest sizes. In the smaller boats, particularly the gunning skiffs, decking was used in some types. In the rowing work-boat, the square transom stern was most common, but there were a few types that were double-ended. In nearly all of the latter the hulls were exactly alike in both ends.

The rowing work-boat was rarely very short, nor was it always a light craft. With very rare exceptions, the fisherman's or waterman's rowing boat had no relation, in model or proportions, to the yachtsman's dinghy of today. The rowing work-boats had to be rowed relatively great distances against sea and wind, as well as in protected waters and good weather. Therefore, they were likely to be long, fine-ended craft of rather heavy construction. A very

193

light boat does not row easily against wind and sea, as anyone knows who has rowed a light yacht-dinghy any great distance under such conditions. A short, wide boat is equally unhandy and tiring. The reason is that momentum between strokes must be maintained to make easy progress against wind and sea in a rowboat. The light boat loses momentum owing to lack of weight and the short, wide boat to the constant change in fore-and-aft trim caused by the shifting weight of the oarsman. Hence, rowing work-boats were rarely built under 14 feet in length or weighing less than 250 to 300 pounds stripped. The exceptions were the hunting skiffs, some of which were light enough for portaging from lake to lake or for hauling over a marsh or a mud flat.

Rowing boats were expected to require little care and attention to keep them in serviceable condition, so they were substantially built of lasting materials as far as was practical. The rowboat fisherman was not necessarily a poor man who could afford nothing more pretentious; he used the rowboat because it was the best type for the intended work. In some cases the rowboat, with or without sail, was to be employed in shoal or obstructed waters, where the ordinary sailing boat would not work with safety or precision. Sometimes, the work done produced only a moderate and seasonal return, which warranted only a small investment in boat and gear. In all cases, the rowboat worked relatively close to home. Only in very rare instances were long runs attempted in these craft, since such voyages were not in line with the boats' regular employments. In the majority of instances, the users of rowing boats or open rowing-and-sailing boats also employed larger craft over part of the year in other fisheries, each being seasonal.

The lack of reliable records makes the histories of the small, open rowing or rowing-and-sailing work-boats highly speculative. While it is undoubtedly true that many types were descendants of some older form of boat, there are very few cases, indeed, where it would be safe to assume these were direct descendants of some local form of hull of the colonial period. There were many cases where it is apparent that the types were the product of much more recent influences and, indeed, it seems obvious that some boats were adaptations of some standard style of hull that had become established through the stock boat, such as the hunting skiffs and the old yawl-boats. It should also be noted that many small-boat fisheries did not exist continuously from colonial times, and this fact influenced the rise of types in relatively recent times.

The Whitehall Boat

Perhaps the most noted of American rowing work-boats was the Whitehall. This type is mentioned in all literature relating to the lives of seamen in the days of the clipper ships and of the "down-Easters" that followed them. It was the Whitehall that brought out the "crimps," or boarding-house runners, to meet new arrivals and entice men into their ruthless hands. The use of the Whitehall was not confined to crimps, however, for it was used by such respectable people as ship chandlers, newspaper reporters, insurance adjusters and agents, pilots, and all others having business with shipping. The Whitehall was also used by the "Battery Boatmen," who ran the equivalent of the modern "water taxi." In addition, the boat was used for pleasure and was the successor to the colonial gentleman's wherry. The Whitehall was not intended as a ship's boat and was not used as such, except in very rare instances where it served as a gig.

The Whitehall was noted for its fine qualities; it rowed easily and moved fast in smooth or choppy water; it was safe, carried a heavy load easily, and was dry. The boat was not for use in the open sea, but was designed for large bays and harbor work, where a heavy chop might be met. The boats ranged from 14 to 22 feet in length, or thereabouts, to fit the use intended. The small boats, used as for-hire craft and for the transport of one or two passengers, were rowed by one or two oarsmen. A ship chandler would require a slightly larger model, 16 to 18 feet, to carry samples or take out gear in an emergency. The largest boats were those of the crimps, who had to carry out a gang of henchmen to help in handling and bringing back drunken seamen; these rowed with three to five pairs of oars. Each oarsman handled a pair of oars; only in the largest boats, when heavily loaded, were single-banked oars used. Boats which covered great distances, such as ship-chandlers' boats, often were fitted to sail, and had a small centerboard and a low spritsail. In the 1870's and 80's a patented metal folding board, operating on the fan principle, was sometimes used, as its low case was convenient in rowing boats.

The original Whitehall first appeared at New York City and took its name from Whitehall Street, where the boats seem to have first been built. The late W. P. Stephens, who had known the boats in his youth and who was interested in the type, believed that they came into existence sometime around 1820–28 and that they had been built at first by former Navy Yard apprentices. The craft did resemble the naval gig in many ways, it is true.

The Whitehall represents a refinement in an old type rather than a distinct and local innovation. The boat was on the same general model that was used in fast, pulling boats, the wherry, cutter, and gig, from 1690, or earlier, on to the end of the nineteenth century. The New York Whitehall was apparently an accepted and recognizable type, or class, by the end of the 1830's, and by 1855 was in use in practically every large port in the United States. There were local departures from the New York model, but, on the whole, the Whitehalls all followed a standard pattern if not a fixed form.

Figure 72 shows a standard New York Whitehall of the period between 1860 and 1895; the boat represented was built at the Brooklyn Navy Yard in 1890. It is very much the same as a partial set of molds, owned by the late W. P. Stephens, which were made before 1862. The New York boats usually had plank keels, skegs, rising floors, slack bilges, and flaring sides. The after sections were slightly hollow at the garboards, and the transom was heart-shaped. The bow was long and sharp; the run was rather short and full in pulling boats, but longer and flatter in those using sail.

Originally, the Whitehall was lap-strake, but caravel had become common in the New York boats by 1850. The construction was conventional: steam-bent frames, white cedar planking, and oak keel and posts. The sheer strakes and rail caps were often finished bright and were of mahogany in some "fancy" boats. The Whitehall was usually painted white and, when used commercially, had a broad band of color at the gunwale to aid in recognition. By 1840, the New York Whitehall was being built in quantity production, on a stock-boat basis.

The New England Whitehall was commonly built with a scantling keel; lap-strake remained popular at Boston much longer than

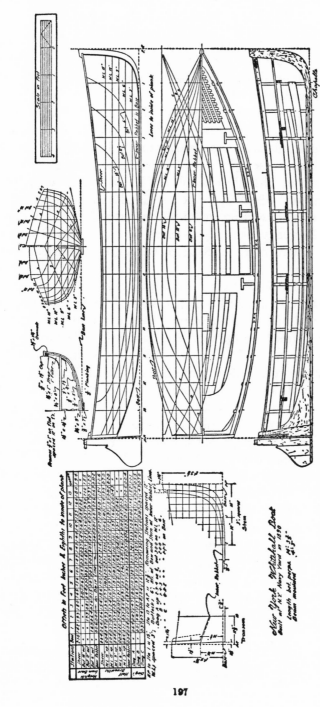

Fig. 72. Popular style of Whitehall boat showing a widely used keel construction in American small boats.

at New York. Figure 73 shows the plans of a Boston ship-chandler's boat used there before 1876. The plan, made by Albert Green, a Navy Yard draftsman, and probably taken off the boat by him, appears to have been used to design a pulling Whitehall at the Portsmouth Navy Yard about this time. Another plan of a Boston Whitehall, in the Historic American Merchant Marine collection in the Smithsonian Institution, was drawn from a large model that had been used to advertise Winde and Clinkard's boatshop in the 1840's. It shows less sheer than the example and is more burdensome. When the scantling keel was used, the skeg was reduced to a minimum and the rabbet was brought up round to the bottom of the transom, or tuck. The Boston Whitehall was often fitted to sail and was used by harbor fishermen in the 1840's, as well as by the various professional boatmen.

A very similar boat was used at San Francisco, but with greater proportionate beam. The Pacific Coast model was apparently the most powerful of all and was often fitted to sail. Here the crimps' boats were 22 feet long and usually carried a jib tacked to the stemhead, in addition to the low spritsail. Both the Boston and San Francisco boats usually had their centerboards off center, with the slot in the garboard. The 22-foot boats carried three oarsmen rowing six oars. The smallest Pacific Coast Whitehall was 16 feet long. All Whitehall boats steered with an outboard rudder, controlled by a yoke and rudderlines. A noted San Francisco builder was J. C. Beetle, who came from New Bedford, Massachusetts. The San Francisco boats were built of imported eastern cedar, which had many small "pin" knots, and with imported oak frames, steambent. Some bastard Whitehalls were fitted with washboards but were otherwise about the same as the standard model.

The Whitehall sailed very well with her small rig. Whitehall boats have been mentioned as having been used on the Sacramento for commercial fishing boats. In the 1880's, the Whitehall model was adopted by yachtsmen, without important changes, as a "combination" (row-and-sail) boat, usually with a length of 14 to 17 feet.

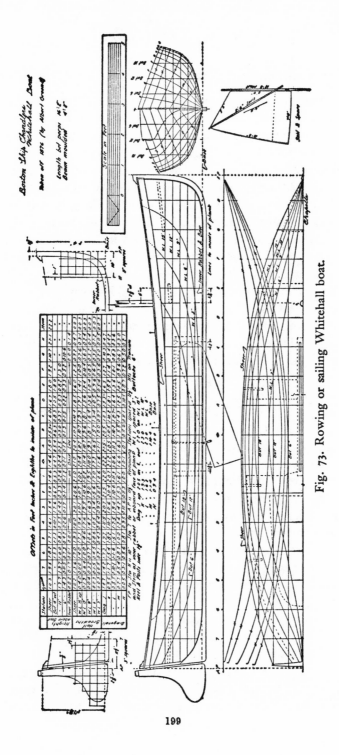

Fig. 73. Rowing or sailing Whitehall boat.

199

The Connecticut River Shad Boat or Drag Boat

The boats used on the lower Connecticut River, in the shad fishery, and in other fisheries on the nearby Connecticut shore, were quite noted for being fast-sailing and handy small boats. They were usually lap-strake built and had wide plank keels with a skeg aft. The hull-model was roughly that of the New York Whitehall but with increased depth and capacity. They were also known as "drag boats," from their method of fishing. These fine craft were half-decked, a short foredeck with the side decks extending clear to the transom. No stern deck was used in the drag boat, as she worked her gear from the stern. A small spritsail, which was readily unshipped, was the usual rig. Some boats were sloop-rigged, however, and a few had a two-masted rig. This was much like that carried in the Casco Bay Hampton, except that the Connecticut boats used a boomed loose-footed mainsail instead of the laced foot seen in the Maine type. A jib was usually carried with its tack on a short plank bowsprit. The boats ranged in length from 15 to about 18 feet if spritsail-rigged. The sloop and two-masted boats were larger, and reached 20 feet in length. In the large size, the drag-boat model shaded off gradually into that of the "Noank" sloop, or its sister, the Narragansett Bay sloop. In these large drag boats, the model differed from that of the sloop only in the stern and in the narrower beam.

Though the Connecticut River shad boat was built in some variety of model, two rather distinct forms were popular. One was a boat of moderate dead rise, of the type shown in Figure 74. These were extensively built around Essex, Connecticut, and were the favorite boats in the Connecticut River fishery. The reputation of the boats became so great that they were built in quantity production, and in 1881 such boats were being shipped to southern states for use in the coastal fisheries. A modern replica, shorter than the boat shown but similar in model, has recently been built and tested on Long Island Sound and was found to be very fast and seaworthy for so small a boat.

The second form was of more depth and had great dead rise for this type of boat. Figure 75 shows one of this model, which was a favorite with some of the fishermen on Long Island Sound near

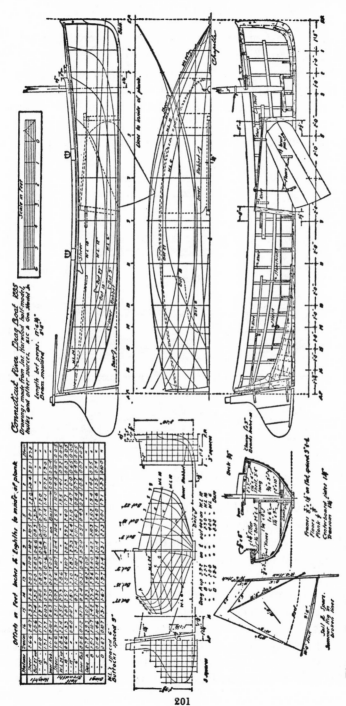

201

Fig. 74. Popular type of Connecticut River drag boat, showing style of construction popular in many small work-boats.

the mouth of the Connecticut. These boats were ballasted with sandbags and were liked because their extra weight made them work under sail with greater certainty in choppy water. They carried somewhat less sail than the first-mentioned model due to their rise in floor and slack bilge, and depended upon ballast for stability to an unusual extent in such craft. The drag boats were built with steam-bent frames. Oak was used for frames, keel plank, and

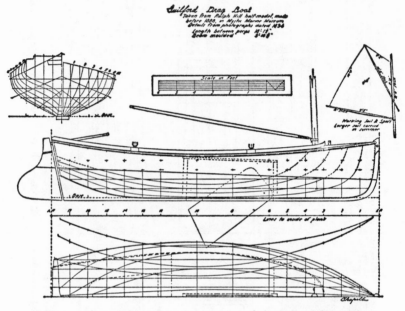

Fig. 75. Long Island Sound drag boat of the ballasted model.

deadwood, and the planking was cedar or white pine. The boats were often steered by a yoke and rudderlines while fishing. A two-man crew was usually employed in the 1880's. The drag boat still exists, though no longer built, and is now used with an outboard engine.

There were a great many similar boats in use elsewhere, some of which did not carry sail. The Cape Roseway wherry is mentioned by Goode as being used on the Eastern Bay of the Penobscot and is described as a lap-strake boat of the Whitehall model with plank keel, 12 to 18 feet in length. This type is now extinct, and no model has been found. The Reach boat used in the 1870's and 80's near Jonesport, Maine, was a similar boat, 14 to 18 feet long. This model was much like a drag boat, but without a centerboard and with a scantling keel, to which a deep false keel was added to enable it to work to windward. The Reach boat carried one or two small spritsails. It took its name from Moose-a-bec Reach near Jonesport. The name "Reach boat" was also applied by some to the double-ended peapods used in this area. Boats very similar to the square-sterned Reach boat are to be seen in old photographs of Portland harbor. Another boat of this class was the Hudson River shad boat, on the New York Whitehall model.

The Delaware Gill-Net Skiff

A combination rowing-and-sailing skiff of this general type was once used by the gill-net fishermen on the lower Delaware. The model was that of the sailing Whitehall, with scantling keel and off-side centerboard. The Delaware boats were large for the class, ranging from 19 to 23 feet in length. Figure 76 shows the plan of one of these boats. They were slack-bilged with flaring sides and had skegs. The usual small spritsail was carried, commonly loose-footed. They had short foredecks, the side decks tapered toward the stern, and the coaming was not carried abaft amidships, as in the sturgeon skiffs, which enabled nets to be hauled from aft. The skiffs were usually caravel-planked over bent frames and were built of cedar plank, with oak frames, keel, deadwood, and stem. They were well finished, copper-fastened, and rather lightly built. Most of them came from the once noted boatshops that lined the Delaware shore from below Philadelphia to Wilmington. It has not been possible to trace these skiffs earlier than 1887; however, the paucity of records does not permit the assumption that the boats were not in use much earlier. The Delaware skiffs were fast sailers in spite of a small sail area and must have rowed very well. They worked with a two-man crew.

Oars, Tholes, and Rowing

The equipment used in rowing work-boats should be mentioned. Many of the work-boats already described used double tholepins.

These were cheap and readily replaced if broken or lost. The double thole pins were placed far enough apart to allow the oar to swing without binding, but caused noise and chafing. The thumping of a Bank dory's oars will be recalled by anyone who has cruised the Maine coast. Single tholepins were used in colonial times but rarely in the nineteenth century in the United States. With these a rope grommet was fastened to the oar and was dropped over the pin. Galvanized-iron oarlocks appear to have become popular in the 1870's and were made in some variety of pattern. The centerline of the oarlocks or tholes was usually somewhere between 8 inches and 12 inches from the after edge of the thwarts, and the bottom of the oarlock or the top of the thole chock was usually between 7 inches and 9 inches above the thwarts, depending upon the height of freeboard and the length of oars. When the double tholepins were used, the after one was sometimes weaker than the fore one, so that it, rather than the oar, should break if the oar became jammed in the pins in coming alongside a boat or wharf. The fore pin, against which rowing was done, was sometimes the higher of the two. When a boat was half-decked, it was usual to mount the oarlocks, or tholepins, on chocks high enough to allow the oars to clear the coamings, though in some cases the coamings themselves were used to mount oarlocks, or tholes.

Rowing boats employed in sea work employed oars having narrow blades, about 4 inches wide in most instances. The blades were often as long as 36 or even 40 inches. Square looms were apparently uncommon in America after 1820 and the round loom was used in all work-boats afterwards, so far as is known. The looms were usually leathered in the way of the tholes or oarlocks. The length of oar used seems to have been decided by handiness rather than by efficiency, in most cases. The average length of oars was about twice the beam of the boat, if used in pairs; some were 6 inches over this. If the boat was rowed one man to the oar, the length might be as much as two and a half times the beam or a little less. Oars longer than 12 feet were avoided when possible, as the longer lengths were unhandy in rough water. Few fishermen row with hands overlapped. However, the famous Battery boatmen at New York are mentioned as using overlapped hands and even the curve-bladed sculls of the racing oarsmen. The sweeps for large boats

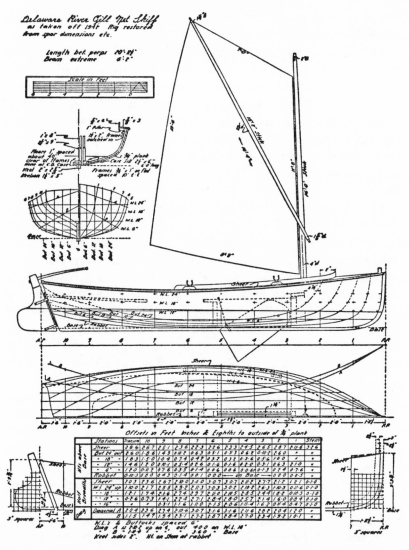

Fig. 76. Burdensome type of skiff on a model much like a Whitehall boat.

were usually under 16 feet long, but steering sweeps in some of these were as long as 18 feet. Sweeps and oars were made of spruce, except the short oars used in open water. which were most commonly of ash. The ends of the blades were sometimes tipped with metal, but, on the whole, this practice was confined to hunting skiffs and some beach boats. Long oars and sweeps often had heavy looms inboard, to allow better balance.

The usual rowing stroke of the fisherman is short and jerky. He commonly stands facing forward when rowing and uses the weight of his body, the recovery taking place long before the arms are extended. Feathering on the recovery is common among all fishermen. Except in the Whitehalls and a few others, rowing was no more than auxiliary propulsion, for the American fishermen have never regarded rowing with much enthusiasm and have used it as seldom as possible.

The plank-keel mode of construction was common from New York to the eastward, and was also much favored in southern New Jersey. The plank keel was employed in two ways: the most common was to make the plank keel straight with the skeg erected on it. The latter would then be a thick knee or plank hewn to the required taper of the plank keel toward the stern. This mode of construction was usually employed in the Whitehall type of hull. A less common method was to spring the plank keel so that it followed the rabbet aft and then to apply the skeg below it. This made a very good construction, but there was sometimes great difficulty in bending the plank keel and holding it in place while building. It was this that made the straight plank keel the most favored in commercial small craft.

The South Jersey Beach Skiff

Unlike the Cape Cod men, the South Jersey beachmen preferred a square-sterned boat for work on the exposed Atlantic shore. The flat-bottomed beach skiff of the north shore of the state was not favored; instead a plank-keel, lap-strake, round-bottomed hull was employed. These skiffs had rather large centerboards and were half-decked. An example is shown in Figure 77. They were modeled with a very raking transom, a handsome curved stem, and a graceful sheer; altogether, they were very attractive craft. The rig was a low sprit-mainsail without a boom, with a jib tacked to the stemhead. The boats were usually copper-fastened and lightly built of the fine local cedar and oak. The frames were

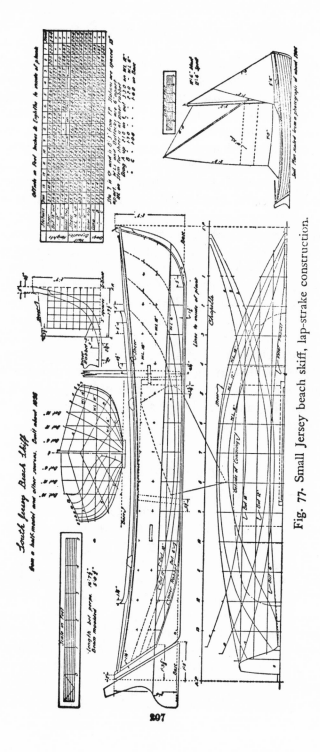

Fig. 77. Small Jersey beach skiff, lap-strake construction.

often sawn futtocks of cedar root. The beach skiffs appear to have been built in a very small range of size—15 to 18 feet long. They were ballasted with sandbags and worked with a crew of two. The boats were very seaworthy and often ventured some distance offshore even in heavy weather. In the days when wrecking was a profitable occupation, the boats were used in salvage work as well as for fishing. When beaching in a heavy surf, the boats came in stern first, the outboard rudder being unshipped before entering the surf. Steering in the surf and in a heavy sea was done with a sweep.

The South Jersey beach skiffs were built all along the ocean shore south of Barnegat, but the center of building and the place of their greatest popularity was in the immediate vicinity of Atlantic City. Boats on this model but with sharp sterns were sometimes built and were called "sharpies," though the use of this name in referring to sharp-bowed flat-bottomed boats is apparently known in this section.

The history of the beach skiff is most uncertain; it is not mentioned with reference to the fishing industry before 1887, and it seems likely that it may have been a descendant of one of the old boats used for lifesaving and wrecking on the coast thereabouts in the 1830's and 40's.

The Melon Seed

A remarkably handsome gunning skiff known as the "melon seed" was once built at Little Egg Harbor, New Jersey. It seems quite apparent that this skiff was intended as an improvement on the Barnegat Bay sneak box, to produce a more seaworthy and drier boat for use in the choppy waters of the Jersey bays. It has much the same rig and arrangement as the sneak box and is completely decked except for a small rectangular cockpit and, sometimes, a small rectangular hatch forward. The melon seed had a dagger board and steered with an outboard rudder operated by a yoke and rudderlines. The rig was a single-boomed spritsail. It was a larger and heavier boat than the sneak box and was intended for use in open water rather than in the marshes and among the mud flats.

Figure 78 is the plan of an old melon seed of 1888; the plan was once in the files of *Forest & Stream* magazine, but was never published. A good rigged model of one of these boats is in the Watercraft Collection. The melon seed, as can be seen, is modeled after the beach skiff but with much less depth in proportion to length. It had fine lines, like its larger sister, and sailed very well indeed,

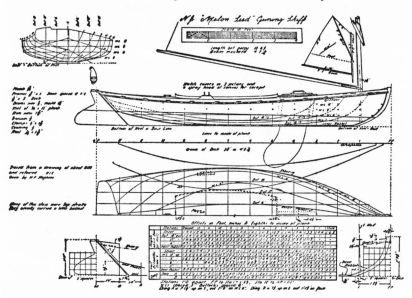

Fig. 78. A very seaworthy type of gunning skiff once popular in New Jersey.

by all accounts. Unlike the beach skiffs, the melon seeds appear to have been caravel-built, though it is reported some were lap-strake in early years. Most gunners think a lap-strake hull is too noisy to be a good gunning type, yet many such boats were planked in this manner, so it must have not caused much real trouble. Reference to the melon seed earlier than 1882 has not been found, and the type is wholly extinct in New Jersey waters as far as could be learned in 1951.

The Barnegat Sneak Box

No discussion of New Jersey's small craft should fail to mention the famous Barnegat sneak box. This was originally a gunning skiff developed for use by the market-hunters of the Barnegat region. The name "box," long applied to gunning skiffs in that region, is probably taken from "sink box," a rectangular pontoon, decked over, with a small rectangular cockpit. The sink box had its decks carried outboard, to overhang the four sides, and was sometimes anchored by poles passed through holes in the overhanging deck into the mud. It was towed to the desired position, anchored, and then ballasted until its deck was nearly awash. The overhanging parts being on the surface of the water, a high coaming around

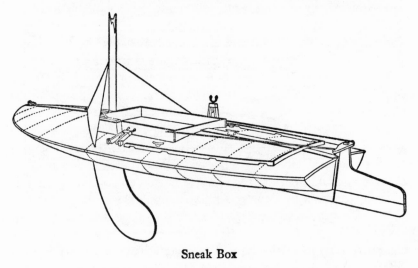

Sneak Box

the cockpit kept the craft from swamping. After the deck was covered with marsh grass or reeds, the sink box became a floating duckblind. The sink box was incapable of movement, of course, and had to be attended by a skiff. The alternate to the stationary sink box was a propelled skiff which could "sneak up" on the birds and be used to shoot from—hence the name "sneak box."

The traditional history of the sneak box states that the original boat was built by Hazelton Seaman, at West Creek, New Jersey, on Barnegat Bay, in 1836. The boat was first known as a "devil's coffin." The second boat was built by M. M. Crammer, and the third by Samuel Perine, each builder adding improvements. There are some who think Seaman's boat may have been the original sink box rather than a sneak box. At any rate, the boat known as the sneak box was fully developed by 1855 and became well known to American sportsmen through *Forest & Stream* magazine, particularly in articles by N. H. Bishop, who took one of the boats from Pittsburgh to the Gulf of Mexico by way of the Ohio and Mississippi rivers, and afterwards wrote a book describing his adventures.* Another *Forest & Stream* writer who did much to popularize the sneak box was one who signed himself "Seneca." The sneak box was eagerly taken over by the then numerous and active canoeists and later by yachtsmen. These latter immediately began improving the gunning skiff into cruisers and racers and finally "improved" it out of existence as a type. In the process, the sneak box became a large, half-decked sailing boat having some of the characteristics of the later racing scows.

The true gunning sneak box was small—nearly all were about 12 feet long and 4 feet wide. They were fitted to be rowed and sailed; their crew was one, the gunner. They were decked, except for a rectangular cockpit, and sat very low in the water so as to be readily hidden. The hull-form was much like a teaspoon, and they deserved the name "melon seed" far more than the Little Egg Harbor skiffs. The early boats are supposed to have had a single leeboard mounted on a high chock, secured to the deck at the gunwale, about opposite the fore end of the cockpit; this was replaced by a dagger board, scimitar-shaped, by 1860 or earlier. The sail seems to have been a small boomed spritsail in early years, and it was not until "Seneca" and others began adapting the boat into something she had not been that the lug, gaff, and leg-of-mutton sail, with or without jib, were applied to the sneak box.

The early boats had some sheer: the transom was nearly plumb; the bow, in plan, was a sharp-pointed spoon-shape. The midsection usually showed some dead rise and a slack but noticeable bilge. At the bow the frame-sections became rather V-shaped, to quiet the boat in a ripple. As early as 1874, some boats had bows which were round or elliptical in plan. Steering was done with an outboard rudder having a yoke. The hull, keel to sheer, was very shallow; the depth inside was much increased, however, by a high-crowned deck. Figure 79 shows a typical market-hunter's sneak box, of about 1880, in which the peculiar model of the boat can be seen.

* *Four Months in a Sneak Box*, N. H. Bishop, Boston.

The construction was very simple; the frames were sawn futtocks and were set up to serve as the molds as well as frames. There
were no longitudinals in the boat, her strength in this direction re-
siding in her plank; the keel was nothing but a centerline bottom
strake. The deck beams were part of each frame and were secured
by knees at the gunwale. Around the bow, along the sheer, there
was a horizontal stem liner to which the hood-ends of both hull and
deck plank were nailed; these were covered by the guard-molding.
A stem block, nailed to the horizontal frame, formed the stem profile. A light ceiling was laid over the frames in way of the cockpit to form a seat for the gunner. The crown of the deck was so
great that washboards were set up on the after deck to hold the
decoys. The hull was built entirely of cedar except for skeg, dagger board, and rudder, which were of oak.

Oarlocks were usually formed of a short length of plank on end,
hinged to fall inboard out of the way. In some boats a light wrought-
iron mounting was used as shown in the plan. The oars were short,
6 to 8 feet long, and a paddle was carried; some boats had a short
punting pole as well. A large-bore gun, a bag of cartridges, blanket,
waterproof sheet, lunch, a pint of whiskey, pipe, tobacco, matches,
windbreak-canvas, and a heavy shooting coat, hat, and mitts, completed the gunner's gear.

The small size of the professional gunner's skiff was fixed by
the necessities of its employment. It was worked by its one-man
crew, who had to row, paddle, pole, or sail the boat, or tow it over
a mud flat, or drag it over a marsh or sandspit, as well as lift it over
a bank in one of the creeks. Therefore, the boat was as small and
as light as the hard usage it must receive would permit. The gunners often spent a couple of days away from home, during which
they lived and slept in their small skiffs. The cockpit had to be
large enough and sufficiently clear of obstruction to permit stretch-
ing out in some comfort; the canvas windbreaker was rigged to the
mast, as shown, to give some shelter from a cold wind, rain, or sleet.

When the dagger board was introduced, it was decided that its
case must not obstruct the cockpit, so it was placed well off center
in the boat—just outboard of the cockpit coaming. Such an unor-
thodox position of a centerboard did not disturb the Jerseyman,
whose artistic regard for symmetry had been blunted by long years

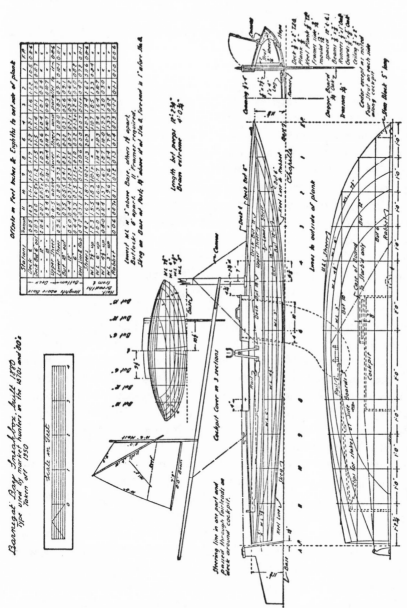

Fig. 79. An old professional gunner's sneak box of a superior model.

of acceptance of the single leeboard. But when the more sensitive and more theoretical canoeist and yachtsman began to adapt the working sneak box to a cruising and racing type of boat, their prejudice against any unsymmetrical arrangement caused the boards to be placed on the centerline. This made the case a great obstruction to the crew, even though the board's case and the mast were moved as far forward as was practical. Hence, where a 12-foot boat had been big enough for the professional gunner, the pleasure-boat sailor required a 14- or 15-foot boat to produce the same usable room inboard. This is a case where "improvements" to meet fashionable standards actually produced a less efficient boat with regard to size and cost—and performance too.

The usual objections to the off-center installations of a centerboard, a mast, or both, are that they must hurt the sailing qualities of a boat on the wind on one tack and that they do not look "right." As to the first no boat should be sailed at very great angles of heel, for when this is done, the sails are not efficient and the boat, whether keel or centerboard, makes increased leeway and carries weather helm. The latter causes the rudder blade to have a braking effect, particularly on a light-displacement boat. The angle of heel at which efficiency starts downward appears to be in the neighborhood of 20 degrees from the perpendicular. At such angles, the off-center board does not lose enough of its effectiveness to be inefficient. The off-center mast is in the same category; there is no scientific reason why the mast in such a position is any less effective than the wing placed off-center in the profile of an airplane's fuselage.

In spite of the rather cheap and simple build of the old sneak box, there have been many attempts to produce an even more inexpensive boat. Figure 80 shows a rather common modification that came into existence in the 1890's. In these, sharpie sides are used; the bottom and deck frames are not true circular arcs as might be supposed. The builder, in this case, had probably discovered that the arc-bottom is a very poor idea for any gunning skiff, as it has always produced a boat too tender to stand in and shoot from with safety. The drawing shows the usual style of wooden oarlock that is both cheap and simple. It is apparently as satisfactory as the more finished wrought-iron mountings. The pivoted centerboard seems too small and rather ineffective; a dagger board would be far better. The board and mast have been placed well forward in this boat to keep the case clear of the cockpit, but the boat is little benefited from a gunner's point of view. It was noticed, in measuring this boat, that she was much heavier than the boat shown in Figure 79.

The sneak box, being practically a small racing scow in model, is a very fast boat under sail when properly modeled, rigged, and fitted. However, it has little bearing forward, and when running

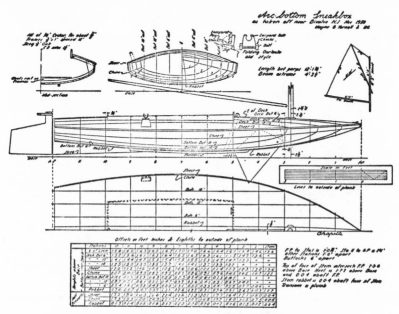

Fig. 80. Common modifications of the sneak-box model.

hard has a tendency to run under, in spite of its overhanging shovel-nose. This is due to its very low bows and, in many modern boats, to having too large a sail placed much too far forward.

Sneak boxes are safest and most satisfactory when they are rigged and masted in the old gunning-skiff fashion. They are not safe boats when heavily canvased, though fast in smooth water with such a rig. Some modern gunning skiffs of the sneak-box model are now rigged as sloops, but the jib seems to be a nuisance in gunning and also presses the boat in strong winds. The sneak box is not a gunning skiff for very rough water, where the melon seed is the better.

The Delaware Ducker

The market-gunners of the lower Delaware employed a very lightly built double-ended skiff—lap-strake, half-decked, and about 16 feet long. These boats closely resembled some of the sailing cruising canoes of the 1880's, or some of the hunting skiffs used in the Adirondacks at this time. The ducker was usually a rowing boat, though some had false keels and a spritsail. When these boats were raced, they very often were rigged as catboats, with a gaff sail of about 112 square feet.

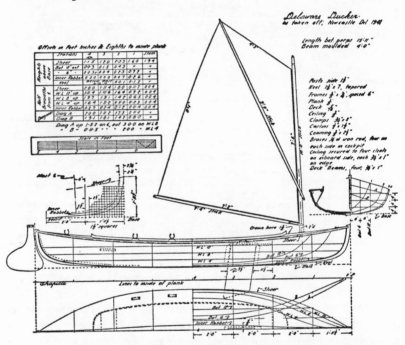

Fig. 81. Common style of American hunting skiff, 1870–95.

Figure 81 shows a ducker, which was one of the relatively rare boats fitted with a dagger board. Like most of the Delaware skiffs, the ducker was the product of the Pennsylvania boatshops, in and below Philadelphia. The model of the boats varied but little; they were exactly alike at both ends and were slack-bilged. It seems probable that this style of hunting skiff was a rather late develop-

ment. It may have been related to the many New York State
Adirondack skiffs, which were manufactured in the 1870's and
which may have spread to the Delaware to be copied with minor
modifications in the ducker. The Delaware ducker was a seaworthy
skiff well suited to her work on the exposed Delaware shore. These
boats worked with a crew of two, a gunner and a man who either
rowed, paddled, or sailed the skiff, as occasion allowed. The boats
were light enough to be handled in the marshes and on the flats by
two men, and they were perhaps the most able of the gunning skiffs
for use in rough water by two men.

The Peapod

One of the noted double-ended rowing and sailing boats used
in the fisheries was the Maine peapod. The peapod appeared in
two basic models; one was a boat best suited to rowing, though able
to sail, and the other was a balanced combination in which sailing
and rowing qualities were equal. The peapod looked somewhat like
a whaleboat in the first model, and somewhat like a No Man's Land
boat in the second. However, the peapods seem to have had no
relationship to either and appeared in the Maine fisheries very late.
Fish Commission investigators working in Maine in the early 1880's
were informed that the peapod originated at North Haven, about
1870. In the 1880's the boats were being built both caravel and lap-
strake. The popular length was about 15 feet; however, the boats
were occasionally built in lengths up to 20 feet.

The peapod was most commonly employed in lobstering, to work
among the ledges where a large boat might not be ventured. In this
employment the boats were worked under oars and the rower stood
facing forward. To make this stance comfortable, the oarlocks had
extensions welded to their shanks so that they stood 4 to 8 inches
above the gunwales. The oars used were short, 8 to 8½ feet long,
so as to work in a confined space. The boats used this way were
rather flat-floored and exactly alike bow and stern. Often, they
had a rather shallow false keel and carried a small spritsail, to help
in getting to and from the fishing ground, but sailing was usually
limited to running and reaching, as the boats were not very weatherly. When under sail, the boat was steered with an oar.

Figure 82 shows a typical peapod of this class and is the design used by lighthouse keepers also. The boats are planked with local cedar, having many small knots, or with white pine. Lap-strake is not seen now, and some boats are strip-planked. The frames are steam-bent oak running if possible in one piece, gunwale to gun-

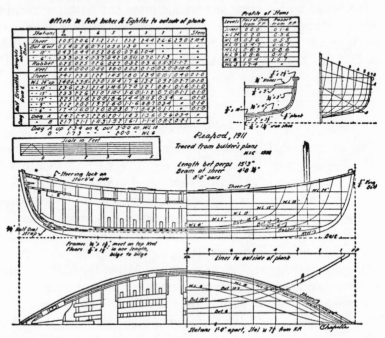

Fig. 82. Lobster fisherman's peapod, often used by lighthouse keepers on the Maine coast.

wale. In the middle half of the boat there are also steam-bent floors between each pair of frames. The model of these boats may have been suggested by the old birch-bark fishing canoes of the Penobscot and Quoddy Indians.

Some builders used a rabbeted stem and stern, but many used an inside stemson and, in finishing off, bent an outside cutwater over it and the ends of the planking. The boats are quite heavy and very strong. They can be rowed long distances at great speed by an experienced oarsman in the standing position. This allows the boat to enter places among the rocks that the rower in the ordinary position could not attempt with safety.

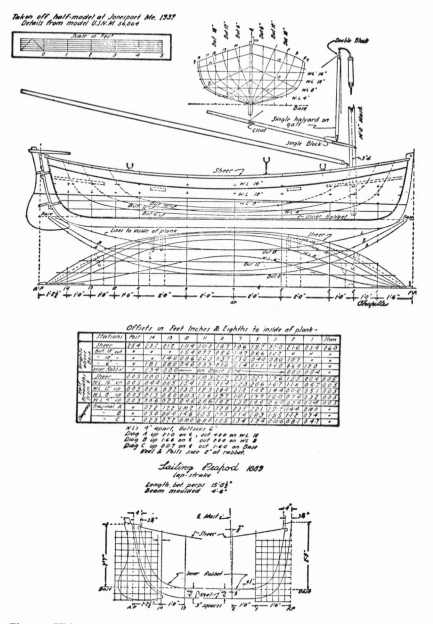

Fig. 83. This peapod was designed and built at Jonesport for the lighthouse service and was gaff-rigged.

219

There was much variety among the sailing peapods. Some had straight sternposts and some had curved, and the amount of dead rise and form of sheer were matters of the builder's preference. The sailing peapods were used extensively by the Lighthouse Service and for utility work in which enough distance was traveled to make rowing laborious. The boats were therefore fitted with deep

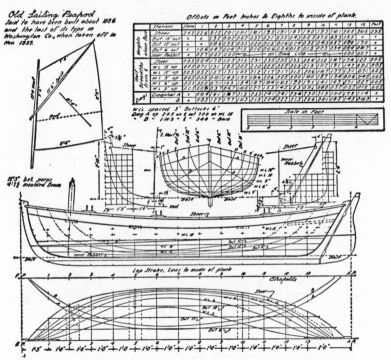

Fig. 84. An old working peapod once used by lobstermen when sailing qualities were desired.

false keels and often had rudders. The bow and stern were unlike and in early years lap-strake predominated.

Figure 83 shows the lines of an old peapod of a type once much in favor among lighthouse keepers. These boats had a good deal of dead rise and much resembled the No Man's Land boats in hull. They were built by contract near Jonesport, and their design may have been affected by plans made by government naval architects. These peapods had a gaff mainsail using a single halyard and with the masthead block on the usual iron crane, such as was described in the Isle of Shoals boats.

Another style is shown in Figure 84; this was an old lobstering "pod" built in the late 1880's. She has very moderate dead rise and a full, round bilge; she would row and sail very well. Boats of this form were in use near Jonesport as late as 1938, but none of this form had been built then for over 30 years.

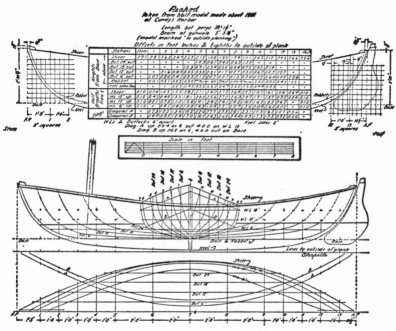

Fig. 85. Large sailing peapod built on Casco Bay.

The lines of a large peapod are shown in Figure 85; the plan was made from a builder's half-model used to build some boats on Casco Bay. The model showed an unusually deep false keel and very raking ends. The powder-horn sheer is evident forward, and it is claimed by some that boats of this particular profile closely resemble the very early "pods," which had the powder-horn sheer fore and aft and thus somewhat resembled peapods. As a rule, the rig of the large peapods was the single spritsail, but a few were rigged with a jib tacked to the stemhead. Jonesport and vicinity has been the center of building of the boats in recent years; the boats were formerly built extensively from Casco Bay to Machias Bay. This type does not appear to have become popular at Eastport.

The peapod is considered by all who know the type to be a very fine pulling boat for use in rough water and to be very stable. Stability is necessary in the "pods" because the rower usually stands with one foot on the gunwale, while hauling a lobster pot over the side. A good peapod will support a 200-pound weight on one gunwale. The great weight of the boats is unquestionably a factor in their stability, and also helps in maintaining momentum when rowing against a head sea. They are too heavy and too long to serve as dinghies, and a boat smaller than 15 feet on the model would probably be lacking in the good qualities of the "pods."

The Yawl-Boat

There seem to be many reasons for believing that some American small-boat types were adaptions of ships' yawl-boats. Throughout the last half of the nineteenth century, nearly every shipbuilding town in the United States had one or more shops that produced a stock yawl-boat and other boats for shipboard use. Such shops soon had a collection of old yawls returned for repair, which were cast aside when not considered worth the expense. These boats drifted into the hands of fishermen, junkies, and other waterfront workers, and many were rigged and so became shore work-boats. Most of the boats were wide models, 16 to 20 feet long, and were of a suitable size for small-boat fishing; while others of the ships' boats were too large. Each large shipbuilding town had its standard model. Some models had skegs, some planked-up deadwood; and there were variations in the amount of dead rise, degree of hardness in the bilge, and width of the stern.

Figure 86 shows a rather typical yawl-boat. These lines are from a builder's model used between 1860 and 1890 at Essex, Massachusetts, to build yawl-boats (or stern boats) for Grand Bankers out of Gloucester. Similar boats were built at Gloucester; while in Maine, and in many southern ports, the yawls were built with planked deadwoods. The yawl-boats were usually fitted to carry a sail; the common spritsail was most popular, though some were gaff-rigged and many had jibs. There are references to the use of these boats in the harbor and shore fisheries in the period just following the Civil War, at Boston, Portland, and Rockport, in New England. Since many of these boats were good sailing models, it seems very probable that they had some influence on the designs of small fishing craft in the East, and, as has been suggested, on the Lakes.

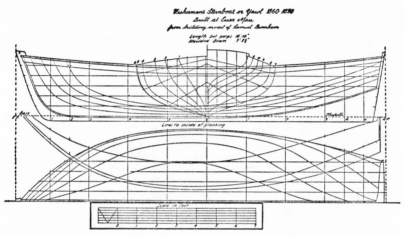

Fig. 86. Yawl-boat once popular on large fishing schooners and carried on stern davits. A very common form of hull is shown.

Newfoundland Boats

The yawl-boat seems to have fathered the only small-boat types, other than Bank dories, built in Newfoundland. One of these types was the old sealing skiff, or Toulinguet boat, introduced from Nova Scotia sometime before 1870. This was a square-sterned, round-bottomed boat, having some dead rise and flaring sides, a strong sheer, and very raking ends. The boats have an exceptionally long fine run for an open boat. A rather deep false keel allowed windward sailing. The rig was the usual jib and low loose-footed spritsail. Figure 87 shows an example of one of these skiffs. They ranged from about 15 to 18 feet long and are considered very sea-worthy and fast sailers. The sealing skiffs were originally lap-strake planked, but in recent years the boats are caravel.

A modification is replacing the old skiffs in a fine open boat be-

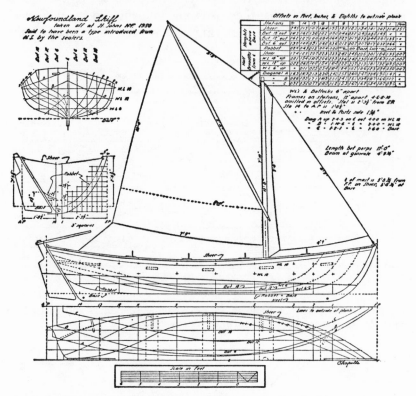

Fig. 87. A fine yawl-boat type from Newfoundland. Model was known as "Toulinguet boat" and originated in Nova Scotia, where similar hulls may still be seen, particularly at Cape Breton Island.

tween 16 and 20 feet in length. Figure 88 is one of the newer models; the boats vary slightly in rake of ends, curve of stem, dead rise, and hardness of bilge—a few of these boats showed rather slack bilges. All have fine ends and a peculiarly shaped stern, which looks like a dory's when viewed from astern. The boats have bold sheers and are seaworthy craft that sail surprisingly well in spite of not having a centerboard.

They row with the single thole in the old fashion. The rig now most used is a two-masted gaff sail—one in which the foresail is the larger. The gaffs are standing with their heels secured aloft by eyebolts. There is a single-part peak halyard. The booms usually have jaws. All blocks are metal awning "pulleys." Furling the sails is done by first dropping the peak, until the gaff hangs up-and-down

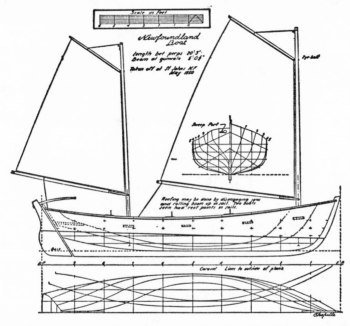

Fig. 88. Common type of boat used in Newfoundland for shore fishing. Most now have motors.

the mast. The boom is then topped vertically and the sail wrapped around all and secured by the peak halyard fall, as in the large boat's spritsail. Few of the boats inspected had reefs. The standing gaff would require the boom to go up in order to reef, which seems somewhat awkward. However, the small masts and sails rarely require reefing, and when the winds are strong many boatmen shift the small mast, sail forward, and stow the foresail in the boat, in preference to reefing. Many of the boats now have a Nova Scotian–made, one- or two-cylinder, heavy-duty gasoline engine, but most of these boats, if above 18 feet long, retain the sailing rig. Stone or scrap-iron ballast was seen in some of the boats; none were decked. They have from three to five thwarts, according to length, and short stern-sheets. There is a sculling port in the transom, which would also permit steering with a sweep in a heavy sea.

The construction of the Newfoundland skiffs and small boats is strong and plain, in fact, somewhat rough. The boats are built almost entirely of spruce and larch and are said to last ten to twelve years. The frames, spaced about 12 inches apart, are sawn from crooks and are single futtocks, lapped when short. The gunwales are capped, and the thwarts are well kneed into the gunwales. These boats make long trips along the rough and thinly populated Newfoundland shore and are locally deemed very seaworthy and handy craft. They are usually painted black or dark green, with copper paint or tar below the waterline, and white, gray, buff, or natural finish inboard.

The Bahama Dinghy

The characteristic small sailing boat of the Bahamas is the dinghy —a heavy keel boat having very raking ends and a heart-shaped transom. The model appears in a number of variations, but all are of the yawl-boat type. These boats are from 13 to 20 feet long. In the sizes above 17 feet in length the dinghies are often seen decked over, with a small cockpit and a hatch under which is a large fish-well. Some have jib and mainsail. Figure 89 shows a good boat of the type. She was built on Great Abaco in 1898, and was an excellent sailer in the strong Trades, and was somewhat better-looking than most boats of her type. Some of the dinghies are slacker in the bilge and have more dead rise; but all are skeg-built, with some hollow in the garboards aft. The rabbet along the keel and skeg often curves its full length, as in the drawing. The boats are roughly built, having sawn frames in single-lapped futtocks of black mangrove or local ironwood (called "horseflesh," as it looks like "salt-horse" when seasoned and weathered). The plank and keel are usually yellow pine. The boats are very heavy and also carry some sand, rock, or scrap-iron ballast. Large boats of this same general type, but with more dead rise and decked, were called "sharp-shooters." Most of the small Bahama boats have straight raking stems.

The Bahama dinghy has a reputation, which is often warranted, for seaworthiness and speed in her home waters. The boats not only make the long jumps from island to island, but a number have crossed the Gulf Stream to Florida. However, as in the case of

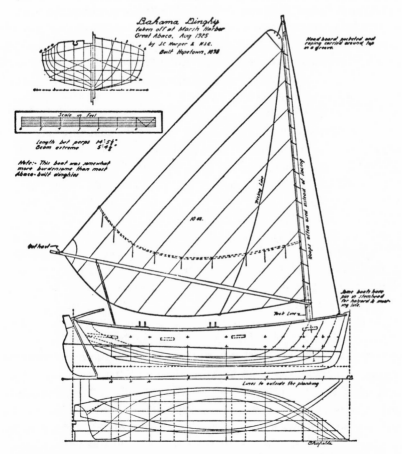

Fig. 89. Bahama dinghy with the old Bahama mainsail.

some modern small craft that have crossed the Atlantic, these voyages were rarely without incident, and the successful conclusion is hardly acceptable evidence that the boats were suitable or even reasonably safe for these ventures. The Bahama boatmen, white and black, are commonly skilled in the handling of these small boats, and it is this, rather than any remarkable qualities in the boats themselves, that accounts for some of the very hazardous passages that the dinghies have made.

The sail used in the Bahama boats, whether dinghy, sharpshooter or sloop, is a distinctive one. It appears to be a modification of the old shoulder-of-mutton sail of colonial times and probably is directly descended from that form of sail. The original short gaff, or properly the club, has been replaced by a large headboard, one cloth in width. The foot of the sail is now cut with an unusual amount of roach, which takes the peculiar form shown in Figure 89. The sail of the dinghy is made from unusually heavy canvas (8 or 10 oz.), and the roping along the foot is usually ¾″ diameter, while ⅜″ is used elsewhere. The cloths are full width in the sail, and bights are never used in making up the sail. In most cases seen, the sails were cut with a good deal of draft. The boom is of the cutter style, fitted with a running outhaul. The tack is usually secured to the boom jaws with a long tail. A single tricing line is used; the standing part is secured aloft and the line is passed under the foot, usually, but not always, through an eye spliced into the foot-roping of the sail. The line is then rove through a block aloft and the fall brought to deck or to the boom. This tricing line is used to raise the foot of the sail, the tack being let go, to reduce or "scandalize" the sail in lieu of reefing. This is also done when working a boat in narrow quarters as the deep roach prevents the helmsman from seeing to leeward or under the sail when broad off. Most boats also have at least one row of reef points; however, these are rarely used in the open boats, as the heavy canvas makes an awkward bunch when reefed and wet.

The sail is not as effective when made of light canvas; the heavy cloth enables the roached foot to stand, and the sail will "sleep" on the wind in light airs, even though there is motion to the sea. The use of the full-width cloths also makes a smooth sail; this would not be possible with light canvas and still have the required strength. However, the sail is rather heavy for a small boat, and therefore the dinghies are not as heavily canvased as, say, their old Bermudian counterparts. The Bahama sail is always made long on the foot and not excessively lofty. This, with the heavy roach at the foot, brings the center of effort low by modern standards for a triangular sail. The heavy canvas gives the sails a very long life.

The dinghies, and the larger craft such as the sharpshooter, are fitted with tholes for rowing, but this is very rarely done, as the Bahama boatmen prefer to scull. This they do standing, and surprising speed is achieved. It is not uncommon to see a large sharpshooter or a sloop being sculled by two men, one on each quarter. The sculling oar is a special one having a slight curve sprung into the loom perpendicular to the flat of the blade. This approaches the form of the Chinese yuloh, but the line, from handle to deck, used by the Chinese, is not known in the Bahamas, and the method used there requires more practice and skill.

It will be seen that the Bahama sail belongs to the leg-of-mutton family, which appeared in but two sections on the North American mainland—in the Chesapeake Bay and on Long Island Sound in the immediate vicinity of New Haven, Connecticut. These two areas employed the true jib-header, in which there was either no head block or, at most, a very small one. The old Bermuda sail seems to have usually had a short club, judging by the few pictures available, but in the nineteenth century the Bermudian sail was often made with a very small head block instead, though the short club remained in use as late as 1880. The Bahama sail, and those used in some of the other islands, retained the club or large head block, and it is rare to see a true jib-header. All West Indian sails were not of this form, of course, and the gaff sail was widely used in small sloops.

As can readily be seen from the descriptions and plans already given, the most common rig in North America over a wide area was the spritsail, at least in boats under 40 feet in length. This remained true until around 1885–95, when some of the spritsail-rigged craft had gone out of use and the gaff sail rose in popularity among small work-boats, under the influence of the yacht. Today it would be difficult to find a boat of any kind rigged with the spritsail, and inexperience with this sail has led to assumptions that it was highly inefficient. This is not true; it was perhaps the best form of sail for a seagoing small boat, open or half-decked, where safety and speed were desired. This being the case, the work-boats adopted this form of sail in preference to the leg-of-mutton in most sections of the country, particularly where boats were required to face heavy weather.

The lack of standing rigging in small work-boats stands out in contrast to modern practice, where even very small boats with solid masts are often to be seen with two shrouds on a side, spreaders and stays. The modern fashion is undoubtedly inspired by the need of such rigging when hollow masts are used in racers and "fast cruisers"; rigging has thus become synonymous with speed in the minds of many. Working-boats omitted rigging as much as possible, for it was far more expensive than an increase in spar diameter would be. Many small boats, particularly open ones or those that were rowed a good deal, required rigs that could be quickly and easily unshipped. Rigging, therefore, was considered undesirable in most small work-boats and was deliberately avoided as far as possible.

Unstayed masts were sometimes looked upon as a safety factor, for it was thought that the bending of lofty masts, as in the New Haven sharpie, for example, spilled the wind out of the sails to some extent in a knockdown. The same idea may be heard on the Chesapeake, where the leg-of-mutton has been used, but not heard in regions where the low spritsail rigs are used. In the Bahamas, the unstayed masts are thought to permit carrying sail longer, before reduction becomes necessary, and it is believed that the unsupported masts do not "press the boat" in strong winds. The same idea existed at Bermuda in the past. In a few cases it was claimed that the masts were intended to break before the boats capsized, as in the New Haven sharpies during the 1870's and 80's when they were rather over-canvased, but it seems very doubtful if this was actually the case. These boats were only over-canvased when light, and it is extremely doubtful if masts could be made to break in this trim and still stand, even with reefed sails, when heavily loaded.

Perhaps the greatest theoretical advantage of the unstayed masts would be less windage owing to the absence of a network of stays and shrouds. But, in the work-boats, low cost was perhaps the true reason for the unstayed rigs. This led to large mast diameters in some types and very careful mast design. Most of the craft using unstayed masts carried the largest diameter from below the partners or thwarts to a point between one-fourth and one-third the mast height. There is some evidence that a few leg-of-mutton-rigged boats had the greatest mast diameter placed a foot or two above the thwarts or partners and a very gradual taper either way. One builder of New Haven sharpies is said to have done this, and it may also have been done at Bermuda. In spritsail-rigged boats, the mast carried its greatest diameter, with only a very slight reduction, well aloft and then a rapid decrease in diameter took place in the head, above the halyard sheave. Unstayed masts were often made of material—such as cedar, white pine, or some of the southern pines when seasoned—that resisted bending even though it might be rather brittle.

CHAPTER 5

Sloops AND Catboats

IN SPITE OF the large number of sloops employed in American waters in the age of sail, there were relatively few distinct types of jib-and-mainsail-rigged small craft in the fisheries, compared with the diversity of types found in two-masted rigs. The limited number of small sloop-rigged types is emphasized when flat-bottomed and V-bottomed hulls are eliminated from consideration. It is noticeable that the majority of small sloop-rigged craft used in the American fisheries show physical evidence of having come into existence comparatively late in the sailing period. Most of them were obviously descended from the New York style of small centerboarder developed in the middle of the nineteenth century; others are keel forms of relatively recent origin. Perhaps the reason for the relative scarcity of small sloop-rigged types is that the sloop rig was expensive compared with the one-masted, one-sail sprit rig that we have seen predominating in the small, working sailboats.

The catboat might be taken as a cheaper form of the sloop rig. While it is common practice to define the cat loosely as a boat having one mast and one fore-and-aft sail, the type is more narrowly defined in our mental picture of the American catboat. This is a centerboard hull, of considerable beam in proportion to length, in which the one mast is in the eyes of the hull, and the boat is rigged, until the last few decades at least, with a single large gaff sail, in which the foot is laced to the boom. This picture of the catboat makes it impossible to consider the type as having descended from any of the older keel, one-masted, one-sail models of earlier times.

The catboat, as we know it today, appeared in two widely separated sections of the Atlantic seaboard—New York Bay and Narragansett Bay—and the two types appear to have had no early relationship. The New York model appears to have developed out of, or with, the small centerboard sloop, at any rate; the history of the Narragansett Bay type is controversial. As we shall see, there had been a one-masted, gaff-sail-rigged keel boat in use in this area in the early nineteenth century.

There have been a few types of sloop-rigged boats that do show possible descent from older forms. The Bermuda sloop and many of the jib-and-mainsail craft of the West Indies have, in some cases, retained the old form of keel hull developed late in the eighteenth century and have also carried sails related to the old forms.

The Bermuda Sloop

One of the last of the sloop types to retain an old hull-form was the famed Bermuda sloop, which survived, in a rather decadent form, until as late as 1908. The craft had a rig that surely descended from the old "shoulder-of-mutton" of the seventeenth century. There had been a class of large sloops, up to nearly 70 feet in length, built at Bermuda from the last half of the seventeenth to the first quarter of the nineteenth century. Schooners had also been built there very extensively between 1785 and 1830, when the building of large vessels at Bermuda had practically ceased. The small sloops at Bermuda seem independent of these in that they had a shoulder-of-mutton mainsail originally, whereas the others were gaff-rigged. The small sloops retained the old sail-form until somewhere around 1840, when it began to be replaced by a jib-headed mainsail. So far as has been found, the small sloops built at Bermuda are first mentioned in 1805. They became known in England as early as 1827, when E. W. Cooke (the noted English marine artist) showed a Bermudian boat sailing in the Portsmouth regatta.

The origin of the small Bermudian sloop is very uncertain; Folkard, writing in the early 1850's, gives an account in his book, *The Sailing Boat*, in which the credit for the origin of this sloop is given to the Honorable H. G. Hunt, who, he states, introduced the rig (date not given) in order to defeat a schooner that had previously beaten his boat for high stakes. Both the sloop rig and the shoulder-of-mutton sail are known to have existed at Bermuda since the early years of the colony; hence, it is difficult to accept this story of an innovation, and the most that can be said of the Folkard account is that it may apply to the reintroduction of the small sloop in Bermudian racing after 1820–25, following the period of the schooner's popularity there.

A large number of full-sized Bermudian sloops and small boats were brought to England between 1826 and 1850 by officers of the Royal Navy and Army who had been stationed at Bermuda. Models and plans were also imported, and one man in particular, William Prattent, of Devonport, England, collected a number of plans of boats of this type. The earliest boat of which much is known is the *Corsair*, a sloop 13½ feet long on the keel, built at Bermuda in 1807. A rigged model of the *Lady Ussher* is next; this sloop was lost in the 1839 hurricane at Bermuda, so the model is earlier than this date.

Figure 90 shows the *Corsair*. The original plan is undated but was obviously drawn much later than the date given for the building of the sloop. The method of fairing and style of draftsmanship indicate plainly that the plans were made in the 1840's; they were probably taken from the boat in England. Some of Prattent's plans were made from measurements taken at Bermuda by dockyard draftsmen, but these are commonly so marked. The drawings of the *Corsair* were very well made and seem to be accurate.

The hull-model of the *Corsair* follows the standard practices used in modeling the fast American schooners of the late eighteenth and early nineteenth centuries. The midsection shows the same steep rise of floor without hollow in the garboards, the same high bilge and low freeboard. Shown are the same great rake at bow and stern and the moderately full bow combined with a long and fine run that are to be seen in plans of early American pilot schooners. The *Corsair*, being a small boat, is much wider and deeper in proportion to length than would be normal in a larger schooner, of course. The plan of the *Corsair*, and of some of the others studied, indicates that the older Bermudian sloops were on the same model

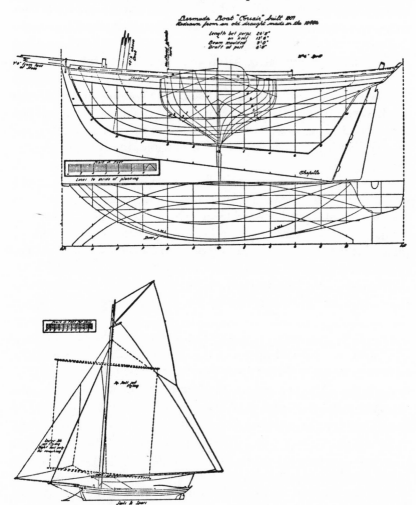

Fig. 90. Plan of old Bermuda sloop showing "Clipper" model of the period and the "Bermudian" rig.

as the type, now called the "Baltimore clipper" in this country, which was also used on the American mainland for small fast-sailing craft, schooner-rigged or sloop-rigged, as well as for large vessels.

The most marked feature in the *Corsair's* design is the enormous amount of external deadwood and false keel outside the rabbets. The common arrangement of the small Bermudian sloop is shown: a single long hatchway divided by a beam and coaming into two hatches. For cooking, the forward contained a charcoal-box and a sheet-iron fireplace with a portable stack. This hatch was covered when not in use. The after hatch was the standing room or cockpit. The size of boat most popular at Bermuda seems to have been between 22 and 28 feet long on deck. The counter of the *Corsair* is what was known as the "square tuck," which was then used extensively in larger craft in both America and Great Britain. It will be seen that it is formed of three flat portions, making a counter in profile.

Instead of a boom these sloops had a sprit, sharpie-fashion, which projected a little forward of the mast. This could be set aft, to flatten the sail, by a heel-tackle, which was secured to an eyehole in the heel of the sprit and to a rawhide-covered strop around the mast. The boats had a working rig of jib and mainsail as shown. The racing rig was much larger, and usually a racing mast and bowsprit were shipped to carry it. When racing, the boats carried a jibboom to which was set a flying jib; when running, a large square sail, set flying, was also carried. A curious topsail was common; this in effect was a small boat's spritsail, complete with a light mast. The latter was hoisted up-and-down at the masthead of the sloop, to form a gunter-pole topmast. The exact mode of reeving its gear is unknown. The sail appears to have been first unfurled and the sprit put in place; then the whole was hoisted aloft to leeward of the mainsail, and when secured the sail was sheeted to the boom end. This gave a very powerful and lofty topsail for light weather. In the early boats, such as the *Corsair*, the mainsheet appears to have been double, as in the large schooners of the time, so no mainsheet horse was used. The headsails seem to have had the usual double sheets also.

These sloops were built entirely of a local cedar, called "pencil cedar," which was very light and lasted extremely well. The construction was orthodox: double-sawn frames to the turn of the bilge and single top-timbers or futtocks above. The hulls were usually ceiled above the cockpit floor. The keel was fitted with a deep hardwood shoe. The spars were commonly of imported white spruce; the favored mast stock was that showing a spiral surface-grain. The small boats had no shrouds, and those above 28 feet on deck had only one shroud on a side. These were not very effective in supporting the mast, however, owing to the small spread at deck level, the mast being too far forward to allow proper staying. As a result, the masts were large in diameter, and some drawings seem to indicate that the largest diameter of the mast was actually a little above the partners, in the neighborhood of the sprit-heel.

It will be noted that the *Corsair* is a heavy-displacement boat; the light weight of the material used in her construction, and her lack of cuddy and furnishings, permitted the use of a great quantity of pig-iron ballast stowed inside, between and over the frames. This weight not only gave stability but also maintained momentum when tacking or shooting up into the eye of the wind. The latter was highly valued in the Bermudas, where a long forereach in stays was often desirable when passing through a channel too narrow for tacking. These boats really sacrificed sailing on other points to obtain the utmost weatherly qualities. Contemporary opinion among English sailors experienced in the Bermudian small sloops seems to have been uniform: that they were extremely fast to windward but less impressive running and reaching. In racing, the Bermudians used a two-legged course—dead to windward and return. The rig and the hull, with its great external deadwood, would certainly hold on well to windward. One noted boat, 6 inches shorter on the keel than the *Corsair*, sailed 3 miles dead to windward, in a very light breeze, in 36 minutes.

While it was racing that made the Bermudian sloop known, the boats were valued for transport between the islands in the group. Some were used for fishing and usually had wet-wells, as in the Bahamas. The boats did not venture far to sea but worked among the islands, where shelter was readily available in case of need. For all her depth and power, the Bermudian sloop was too exaggerated in proportions to be an extremely seaworthy model.

The proclivity of the Bermudian for racing led to constant attempts to improve the model of the sloops, and in the 1850's the true counter was introduced. Nevertheless, modifications of the old square tuck were to be found even in the 1880's, as may be seen in the plans of the *Nameless*, a noted racing sloop, taken off in 1885 by J. Hyslop, a clever amateur designer and the official measurer for the New York Yacht Club. Hyslop, during his visit to Bermuda, measured this boat as well as a few others, including a couple of dinghies. He laid out the rigs of a number of sloops also, so that he had a rather complete record of the type in his time.

The lines of the *Nameless*, Figure 91, show that there had been a marked increase in displacement, in proportion to length, since the time of the *Corsair*. The boats might truthfully be said to have become even more specialized in forereaching ability, with additional sacrifice of sailing qualities when reaching and running. They were becoming decadent, in fact, and were far less practical craft than in earlier times. But speed, under the racing rules in force, was the principal aim, and the boats were developing toward the general form of the English cutter-yacht of the 1880's, though without the serious lack of beam that had come to mark the latter. The working rig as well as the racing jib and mainsail of the *Nameless* is also shown in Figure 91. The jib-headed mainsail had replaced the short club of the "shoulder-of-mutton" in the sloops before 1840, at least.

The sloops gradually died out in the Bermudas, and the last boat of the class to be built, the *Nea*, was modeled on modern lines, having a short fin keel and overhanging bow. She was rather full aft, however, and had much trouble competing with some of the old boats. In her first year, 1899, she raced against one British and two American "raters," and was usually beaten. This brought sloop racing to an end, and the type rapidly went out of existence. The practical uses of the sloops had also disappeared when other craft became available for interisland transportation.

Besides the sloop, the Bermudians have used other types of small craft—an open dinghy somewhat similar to the Bahama type, with Bermudian mainsail and jib, and a schooner-rigged gig. The latter was a long, narrow, open boat much like a naval captain's gig, but with raking or round bow. The transom was very narrow, and the boats had fine lines and some dead rise. The rig was a jib-headed schooner, in which the foresail was lug-footed and overlapped the main. The jib was rather large and was usually set on a long bowsprit. The sailing gig was used extensively by the Bermudian pilots and is now extinct. Both the dinghy and the gig were raced a great

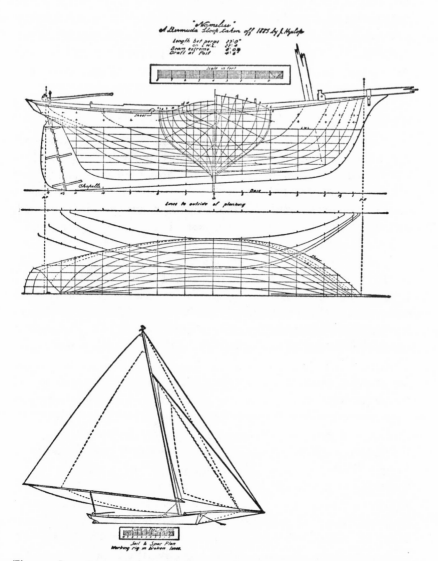

Fig. 91. Late form of Bermuda sloop, at the end of the development of the type, showing the extremely heavy displacement and excessive sail area which resulted from local racing rules and requirements.

deal and, when so engaged, were fitted with deep fins of boiler plate in lieu of centerboards, after about 1880. The "fitted dinghy" is revived periodically for racing but no longer has any utilitarian purpose. It is a very fast boat under some conditions and requires great skill in handling because of the very large rig carried.

The Newport Boat

The Bermuda sloop hull of the early nineteenth century, as seen in the *Corsair*, was also used on the North American mainland. A good example of one of these was the boat built on Narragansett Bay and sometimes known as the "Newport boat." This was a keel boat of great depth, having a raking transom and stem, much drag to the keel, and a strong sheer. The rudder was outboard, and the boats were half-decked; some had a cuddy as well. The mast was stepped on the stem knee and carried a short-gaff sail, which was hoisted by a single halyard. The sail was loose-footed, with the cutter-style boom in use in American schooners in the early 1800's. There was also a short bowsprit, which usually could be unshipped when not wanted, to which a small jib was set flying in light weather. It can be seen that this rig has some resemblance to the later catboat sail plan, except that the mast was not as far forward, because of the rake of the stem in the keel boat and certain differences in the manner of cutting the sail. The Newport boat existed as late as 1850, when it was gradually replaced by the catboat and by small centerboard sloops in the lower Bay.

Only one half-model has yet been found that could be assumed to be a "Newport boat." Figure 92 shows the lines of a very old builder's model which is now in the South County Museum, at Kingston, Rhode Island. The model was made with the lifts fastened together with gun-stock screws and shows the very old style of double wales. The date of the model is not recorded in the papers relating to its acquisition, but judging by the appearance of the model and by some of the features shown, it must be of a date prior to 1840. The name *Corsair* is painted on it, and this appears to be contemporary. The deck is scribed to represent a U-shaped standing room aft; forward of this, there would be room for a small cuddy, placed about amidships. A faint mark forward may

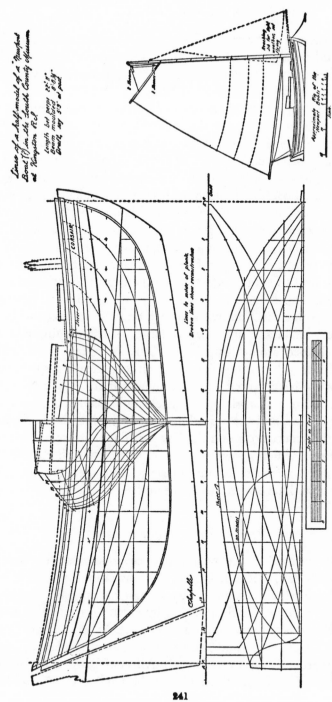

Lines of a half-model of a "Newport Boat"(?) in the Smith County Museum at Kingston R.I.

Length bet. perps. 22'11"
Beam moulded 8'6¼
Draft say 5'6 at post

Approximate rig of the Newport boat
Scale in Feet

Fig. 92. Lines of an old half-model believed to have been a Newport boat of about 1840. The rig, reconstructed from various descriptions, was about the same as that used in the later Quoddy boats of the smaller sizes.

241

be the centerline of the mast. The scale is uncertain; if one inch, the boat would be about 23 feet on deck and about 8 feet 10 inches extreme beam, and would draw about 5 feet 9 inches. This would be about the right size for a Newport boat.

Figure 92 shows the model rigged in this manner, and reconstruction is indicated on the drawing by dotted lines. The hull is even more extreme than that of the Bermudian *Corsair* in dead rise and is less powerful, which indicates a much smaller rig was used; this gives some support to the claim that the model is an old Newport boat. It should have been a fast sailer and an easy-working boat. One-masted, one-sail keel boats have one disadvantage: if they miss stays and get into irons, the sail must be backed to gather sternway; the helm is then put over the opposite way to which the boat should pay off. Such a maneuver takes room and also might lead to a knockdown when the boat pays off, as she has no way on. This is the reason why keel cat-rigged boats have not been very popular in America, and such craft, when used, are commonly very small and light, hardly larger than a dinghy, and can easily be helped around by an oar. Only four keel boats which might be termed "cat-rigged" and which were heavy displacement are known to have existed among commercial craft—the Newport boat, the Bahama sharpshooter, a keel double-ender once used at Eastport, Maine, and the waterboats used at Gloucester and Boston. The Newport boats and the Eastport double-enders often had a bowsprit on which a small jib was set in light weather to help in tacking; the waterboats do not appear to have used the jib, and a bowsprit would have been a nuisance in their work.

Providence River Boat

A small keel cat-rigged boat was once popular at the head of Narragansett Bay, in Rhode Island. This was a dinghy-like hull having a gaff sail which was hoisted by a single halyard. It was a shoal keel boat, lap-strake, and slack-bilged, intended for relatively smooth waters. These boats were built at Newport, Warren, Bristol, and Providence in the 1870's and 80's. Figure 93 shows the plans of one of these boats recently discovered by Mr. Alfred S. Brownell. The lines were taken off by Commander George M. Cunha, U.S.N., and the

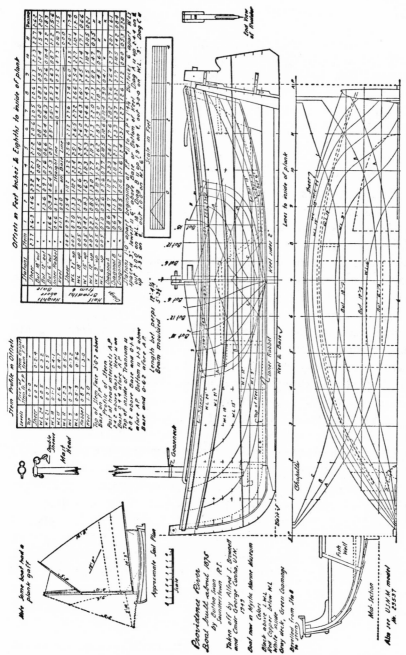

Fig. 93. A small boat once common at the head of Narragansett Bay.

243

drawing has been made from his plans and notes. A rigged model
of a rather similar boat (a builder's exhibition model of great accuracy), is in the Watercraft Collection. The keel of the boat shown
had been deepened aft by the addition of a tapered shoe. This type
of craft is sometimes mistakenly called a "Newport cat"; the latter was actually a centerboarder.

The Waterboats

The waterboats used at Gloucester and Boston were the largest
of the keel hulls that were cat-rigged. These were boats between
32 and 45 feet in length, with moderate dead rise and rather deep
false keels trimmed to a moderate drag. The bilges were rather
hard, and the sterns were usually round, much as in a tugboat, but
with a very low rail instead of the deep bulwarks of the latter.
Water, which they carried in large wooden tanks below deck,
could be supplied to vessels by means of a manually operated force
pump located on deck amidships. The hull was completely decked
except for a couple of small hatches and a standing room for the
helmsman. The boats were fitted with large wooden cleats inside
the log rails for tying up. The rig was rather moderate in area, as
speed was not an important consideration. The gaff was hoisted
by a single halyard. This style of gear seems to have been a characteristic of the keel boats having the one-mast, one-sail rig, cat-
fashion, in the United States in the nineteenth century. It does not
appear in the catboats, however, and this might be accounted for by
the fact that the latter, being centerboarders, required the ability
to drop the peak of the gaff as a safety factor to avoid capsizing in
a squall. The waterboats were handy craft, operating with a crew of
not more than two men, although they had to be worked in
very congested waters, particularly among the wharves of Gloucester in the days of the sailing fishermen. The sailing waterboat hull
may still be seen, but the boats are now unrigged and are motor-
driven.

The New York Sloop

The most important of the sloop-rigged small-boat types used
in the fisheries was the New York sloop, which had a style of hull

and rig that influenced the design of both yachts and work-boats for over thirty years. The New York boats were developed sometime in the 1830's, when the centerboard had been accepted. The boats were built all about New York Bay, particularly on the Jersey shore. The model spread rapidly, and, by the end of the Civil War, the shoal centerboard sloop of the New York style had appeared all along the shores of western Long Island Sound, in northern New Jersey, and from thence southward into Delaware and Chesapeake waters. In the postwar growth of the southern fisheries, during the 1870's and 80's, this class of sloop was adopted all along the coasts of the South Atlantic states and in the Gulf of Mexico; finally, the boats appeared at San Francisco. The model did not become very popular, however, east of Cape Cod.

The New York sloop was a distinctive boat—a wide, shoal centerboarder with a rather wide, square stern and a good deal of dead rise, the midsection being a wide, shallow V with a high bilge. The working sloops usually had a rather hard bilge; but in some it was very slack, and a strongly flaring side was used. Originally, the ends were plumb, and the stem often showed a slight tumble home at the cutwater. V-sterns and short overhanging counters were gradually introduced in the 1850's, particularly in the boats over 25 feet in length on deck. Round sterns were rather popular in large sloops, after 1858. Most of the old boats had sawn frames, single futtocks in the topsides, and plank keels with a short skeg. However, the planked deadwood was not uncommon and appeared in some boats in the 1850's, if not earlier.

The rig was a simple jib and mainsail with a moderately long gaff and a very long boom to which the foot of the sail was laced. A very large jib was set on a long, hogged-down, plank bowsprit. The mast was rather well forward in the early boats, but as time passed it was moved aft somewhat. The early sloops usually had a marked rake in the mast, but this was decreased, and after the Civil War the mast became nearly plumb and the gaffs longer. Most of the boats under 25 feet had no shrouds and only a single headstay.

The emphasis on yacht racing in New York Bay in the late 1840's and in the early 50's attracted attention to the small working-sloops. These boats were very fast sailers and very weatherly. The model was taken in hand by yacht-builders, who gradually evolved a racing model, in which the bilges were high and thin and the sides flared. The lines forward were very sharp and the run rather short and often fine. The boats were given enormous rigs; to keep them on their feet in a fresh breeze required sandbag ballast, which had to be piled on the weather rail. They were out-and-out racing machines and showed great speed in smooth water; they became known as "sandbaggers," and there was much racing for large stakes among them. The largest were about 28 feet long and the smallest of the popular classes were 20 feet. The lines of these boats very closely resembled the modern racing dinghy, except that the sandbaggers usually were beamier in proportion to length and could carry more sail. From this class of racing boat, the New York sloop model spread to larger craft, and by the 1870's it was considered the "national type" of yacht. It retained its popularity until late into the 1880's, when a deeper and heavier model became fashionable for a while.

Work-boats of the New York model were usually between 18 and 36 feet on deck. They were built very extensively on Long Island, in northern New Jersey, and along the lower reaches of the Hudson. When a particularly fast work-boat came out, it was usual for the boat to be purchased by a sportsman and converted to racing. Normally, however, the work-boats were much more burdensome and seaworthy than the "improved" type represented by the fast sandbagger. The work-boats under 26 feet did not carry a sloop rig all the year round; the jib-and-mainsail rig was really a "summer rig" in early days. In the early fall, many boats took out the masts and removed the plank bowsprit, under which, and well up in the eyes of the boat, there was a second mast hole and a step. The mast was placed in this, and using the sloop mainsail, the boat became a cat. This originally produced a smaller spread of canvas and a "winter rig," which was replaced with the jib-and-mainsail rig in the late spring. In some of the smaller hulls, under 20 feet on deck, the cat rig was permanent, the jib never being used. Such boats were in existence before 1845 and were probably a natural development, once the centerboard came into use in small craft in New York Bay. There was really no difference between a

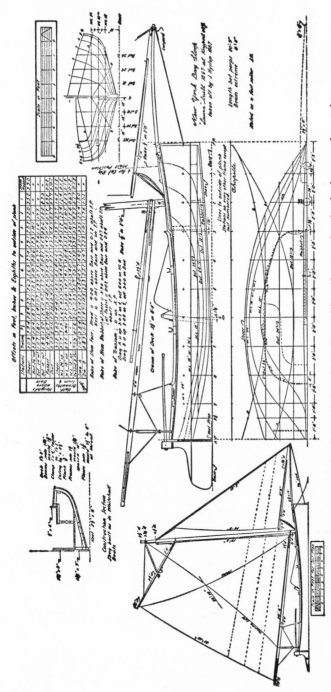

Fig. 94 New York Bay model and rig of small working-sloop, using both sloop and cat rig.

cat-rigged and a sloop-rigged boat in model, and the two must be considered as one type.

Figure 94 shows a good example of the small New York work-boat with the mast-position for the cat rig. This sloop was built in 1868 at Keyport, N.J., for oystering and line fishing. She was a very fast boat, and her lines were taken off by Hyslop when she became a yacht in her old age. The boats of this class usually had more sheer than a sandbagger, particularly forward. The rockered keel had been rather common as early as 1850, though many work-boats and most of the sandbaggers appear to have had straight keels. The boat shown had sawn frames, but by her time steam-bent timbers were in fashion and the construction followed that of the Whitehall in principle. The sloops were built both lap-strake and caravel, the latter build predominating.

The small New York working-sloop was half-decked and had a large cockpit fitted with a U-shaped bench around the sides and across the stern. This, with the boat's relatively great beam, made a roomy hull well suited to work in protected waters and for pleasure sailing. Boats over 28 feet were deep enough to be fitted with a cuddy, and the fashion at New York after the Civil War was to make both the cuddy-sides and the cockpit coamings of vertical tongue-and-groove staving, the whole in an oval shape in plan view. The small working-sloop was an excellent boat for protected waters, and, until "improved" into an unstable racing machine, was a sensible and trustworthy craft.

The New York sloop had a long boom which overhung the counter and would not permit the crew, while standing on deck, to pass the reef earing when the boat was close-hauled on the wind. To accomplish this very necessary chore in working-sloops and cats, the reef-pendants were kept rove off. A line was spliced into each reef cringle in the leech of the sail and each pendant rove through a roller or dumb sheave in a long cleat on the side of the boom and from thence inboard to suitable cleats on the boom within reach from deck or cockpit. In large sails, more power was obtained by having the standing end secured in a cleat on the opposite side of the boom by a stop-knot. From there, the pendant rove through the reef cringle and from thence as before. The outermost reef points could be reached in the work-boats because the rake of the leech was great enough to shorten the foot of the sail a good deal as it was reefed. The experienced sloop sailor tucked in a reef before it blew so hard that he would be in difficulty. If caught in a sudden squall the gaff sail could be reduced very easily and quickly by dropping the peak of the gaff. A light vang to the head of the gaff was a standard piece of gear in working-sloops and cats and gave control of the gaff when the peak had been dropped. The only precaution required was to make the gaff jaws and its jaw rope so that the peak could be dropped without damaging either.

The New York sloop, and the cat-rigged boat of the same model, have come into great disrepute. They are claimed to have been very dangerous craft and prone to capsize. In truth, the model is not as dangerous as many of the modern small centerboarders of the dinghy model, with the present lofty rigs. The New York model was one that suffered from over-canvasing when the type was adapted to yachting, with the sandbagger the most extreme case. The cruising-racer of the 1870's and 80's was almost as bad. Inspection of the sail plans of such craft in *Forest & Stream* magazine and in contemporary yachting books shows the rigs to have been out of all proportion to the requirements of seamanlike design. The limited range of stability in any shoal centerboarder had been wholly disregarded in order to obtain high speed in the smooth water and light winds that mark most summer weather on the Atlantic seaboard. In squalls, or gales, the huge sail areas became uncontrollable and capsizes occurred. The racing sailor has too often forgotten that no small-boat type and no rig can be carried to extremes without danger, once it begins to blow.

The Noank Sloop

An adaptation of the New York sloop model to the requirements of the fisheries in more exposed waters is illustrated in the small sloops once built in the boatshops at Noank, Connecticut, and other towns along the Long Island Sound shores, and in Narragansett Bay. These working-sloops were intended for tonging and dredging oysters, lobstering, and line fishing. In general, they were relatively deeper and heavier than the old New York sloops and the cats.

They carried more ballast and were less heavily rigged, as befitted their employment in waters subject to severe squalls and storms, even in summer. Actually, these sloops had no proper class- or type-name. However, "Noank sloop" was often applied to Long Island Sound boats because the Noank boatshops had become celebrated for the good design, workmanship, and materials that they employed in building small working-sloops, in the 18- to 28-foot lengths. Equally good centerboard sloops were also being built, during the 1870's and 80's, at other towns in Connecticut and Long Island and on Narragansett Bay, in neighboring Rhode Island, on Buzzards Bay, and on the south shore of Cape Cod, in Massachusetts.

Figure 95 shows one of these small sloops, a fine, able, half-decked craft about 23 feet long on deck. Though the small-boat sloops of this class ranged from 18 to 36 feet on deck, the example is about the most popular size. The boats with cuddies—those over 26 feet in length—were often somewhat deeper, in proportion to length, than the example shown.

After 1870 the New England fashion in work-boats was to make the cuddy more or less rectangular and the cockpit oval and somewhat wider than the after end of the trunk in plan view. The sloop shown was built by Saunders, of Wickford, Rhode Island, in 1886 or 1887 for oystering. The V-stern was very popular in Eastern waters, following both yacht and pilot-schooner fashions at the time the boat was built. These sloops, under 36 feet in length, were built with steam-bent frames and had molded keels with a good deal of wood outside, compared with the New York type. Many of these sloops had wet-wells, one on each side of the center-board case, and were employed extensively in the lobster fisheries. A few of the small sloops of this class are reported to have had long pole topmasts and to have sported gaff-topsails in summer weather. The mainsail-and-topsail-in-one, seen on the Lake Erie pound-net sharpies, is said to have been employed in some of the Long Island Sound sloops in the 1870's. The smaller sloops had no shrouds.

Like her New York sister, the Noank sloop was ballasted with sandbags, which could be shifted if necessary—and if men were available. Iron ballast inside was also carried in some of the boats; this was not shifted, of course. The sloops 20 to 25 feet long usually worked with a crew of two. They were planked with cedar, yel-

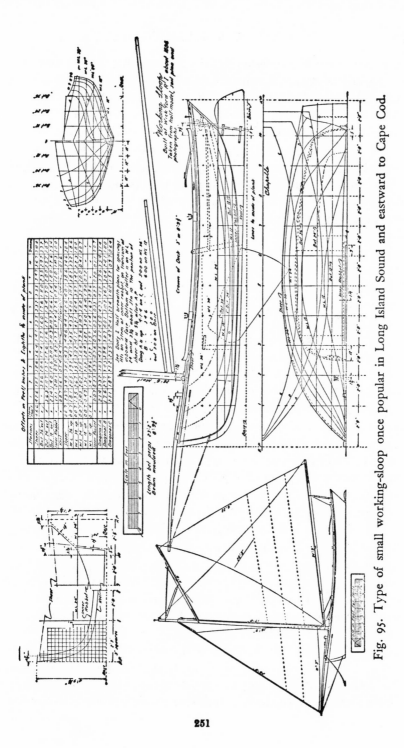

Fig. 95. Type of small working-sloop once popular in Long Island Sound and eastward to Cape Cod.

251

low pine, or white pine, as the owner preferred. Many were lap-
strake, though caravel seems to have been the most common. The
older boats of this type, built before 1880, are described as having flat transoms set at a slight rake. The Noank style of centerboarder illustrates one of the best of the centerboard sloop models
in the fisheries, where rough water and strong winds were to be
met. The lines shown in Figure 95 are much fuller than in the
New York models; the bows in particular do not have the exaggerated fineness seen in nearly all of the drawings and half-models
from the New York Bay area.

Eastern Catboat

As in the New York sloop model, the deeper form of the Noank
style of sloop appeared in catboat dress. There were a number of
local varieties of catboats in use, by 1880, in southern New England
waters. One was the Newport cat on lower Narragansett Bay. Judging by surviving plans and half-models of this local style of cat, it
was marked by a very wide plank keel and a great deal of dead rise
amidships. The ends were plumb and the sheer strong. The sections in the run had some reverse in their shapes, near the rabbet,
and the exposed deadwood, or skeg, was relatively small. The transom was rather Y-shaped, the quarters being unusually high and
very light. These boats were between 18 and 22 feet on deck and
had fine ends. The rig of a 20-foot cat of this type called for a
27½-foot mast, a 24-foot boom, and an 11-foot gaff. The sail area
would thus be about 350 square feet.

The Newport cats had much ballast inside and were considered
very able craft. They appear to have had no physical resemblance,
in hull, to the old Newport boats so far as existing plans and half-
models show; in fact, they appear related to the Whitehall model
or the Connecticut drag boats rather than to a keel type of hull.
So far as can now be determined, the Newport cat is the oldest of
the eastern catboat models.

A somewhat similar boat existed in the 1880's in Buzzards Bay
and along the south shore of Cape Cod; this was the type first
called the "Martha's Vineyard catboat," later the "Cape Cod cat."
These were powerful boats, capable of operating in exposed waters

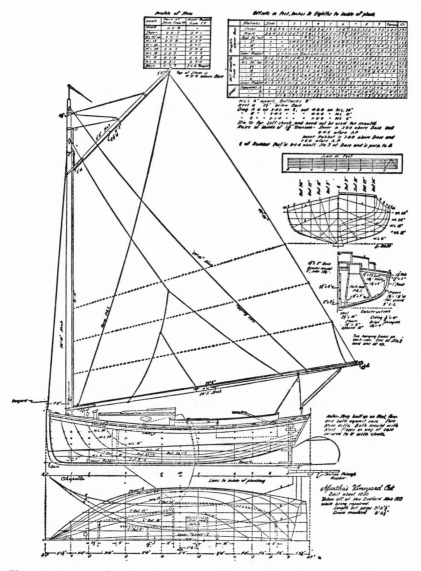

Fig. 96. An example of an Eastern working cat, showing common form of hull and rigging details.

and meeting much heavy weather in careful hands. In working-boats, the range of size was between 18 and 30 feet on deck. Figure 96 shows a Martha's Vineyard catboat of about 1888; the lines show much dead rise and moderate power. The skeg and plank keel follow the more or less standard practices that we have seen in the drag boats and others. The quarters are much deeper and more powerful than in the Newport cat. The boats built at Martha's Vineyard, and on the Cape shore, had a great deal of sheer, and high, bold bows. The Martha's Vineyard cat seems to have been the original Cape cat. These boats often had small standing wells; the rest of the space inside the coaming was decked over much in the fashion followed in the working Friendship sloops of more recent times. Fish-wells were thus under deck, on each side of the center-board. The large cockpit of the traditional Cape cat was used only in boats working in summer weather or as party boats.

There is some question as to whether or not the Martha's Vine-yard and the Cape Cod cats were direct steps in development from the round-bottomed sloop model. The traditions on Cape Cod agree that the catboat first appeared there in the early 1870's, and it has often been stated by older men that these boats were copied from a V-bottomed cat used at Newport. Now, it is known that the so-called skipjack model appeared at Martha's Vineyard in the early 1870's, but all known descriptions of these show them to have been sloops. It is not impossible, of course, that in spite of this some may have been cat-rigged. The Cape Cod style of catboat has been relatively flat-floored since the late 1880's, while the regular Newport cats, and those at Martha's Vineyard in the 1870's, were on models having a great deal of dead rise; it is possible that this may be the cause of the "V-bottomed" tradition rather than the existence of an early chine-built cat in the Narragansett Bay area, to which no other reference has been found.

The model of the Martha's Vineyard catboat, shown in Figure 96, represents quite well the catboats built on the Cape shore and in Massachusetts Bay in the 1880's. Cats with this form of hull were built at Plymouth and Duxbury, and later, in Boston Harbor. These were intended for the lobster fisheries and for summer hand-lining alongshore; many had fish-wells.

The early cats had moderate beam and small rigs, which permitted using a small rudder, and many were built with the style of stern shown in Figure 96, or with that shown earlier in the Narragansett Bay sloop. Some work-boats and the Massachusetts Bay racing cats had the huge "barn-door" outboard rudder that is now considered typical of the Cape cat. The noted Crosby family, of Osterville, on Cape Cod, were the leading builders of catboats on the Cape, and favored the outboard rudder in both working and racing cats. The overhang stern was revived in popularity in the catboat for a short time in the 1890's, but the outboard rudder has remained the favorite in spite of temporary changes in fashion.

The Eastern catboats were originally safe and sane working-boats with the weight and small sail area that made for easy working and stability. Shifting ballast was not used, and the rigs were carefully fitted so that there was the proper gear at hand for reefing or sudden reduction of sail. The cat rig is notoriously close-winded and will lie closer to the wind than a sloop rig, in spite of some modern theories to the contrary. In light airs, however, the old working-cats lacked sail area to make the maximum speed, and the rig did not lend itself to the use of light sails. Hence, when the rig came into popularity in yachts because of its weatherly characteristics, there was an instant demand for greater sail area to give speed in the light summer weather of the Atlantic Coast. The result was that booms, masts, and gaffs were made longer and longer, and to carry the added press of sail, the hulls became more and more flat and the bilges harder, until at last a very powerful, box-like hull was produced; it carried an enormous area of sail and was extraordinarily fast in smooth waters and light winds. In some, the boom was so long that the outermost reef points could be tied in only from another boat or a wharf. Such craft were obviously unsuited for open waters and for practical use, yet, as is usual, the fashions established in racing boats were gradually adopted by cruisers and, to a lesser extent, by some classes of working-cats. The result was heavy loss of life through capsizes and pitchpoling in summer squalls, and so the catboat fell into the disrepute that has continued to this day. Certainly, the cat rig is not an ideal one for a seagoing boat, but when the sail area is reasonable and the hull has some pretensions to seaworthiness, the result is a fine alongshore working or cruising boat, as the Cape cats built as work-boats in hulls and rigs have often shown.

The cat, as has been said, is the least expensive of the gaff-sail rigs and when properly rigged is easily handled in moderate sail areas by one man in average summer conditions. With the centerboard hull of moderate depth at the heel of the rudderpost, getting into irons is not a troublesome accident, for the boat can be paid off on either tack by raising the centerboard and backing the sail. The only danger in this maneuver is a knockdown when paid off, and the mainsheet must be handled to avoid it in a fresh breeze. This is one of the many practical factors involved in the cat which dictate a small sail area in its rig. The relatively shoal working-cat was no more dangerous than the equally shoal sloop, today or in the 1880's, until the inevitable "improvements" took place in the search for higher speed in the light winds of the average summer on the Atlantic Coast.

The catboat, with a moderate spread of sail, was not only a favorite boat of many fishermen in Massachusetts Bay, along the shores of Cape Cod, in Buzzards Bay, and in Narragansett Bay, but also on the south shore of Long Island. The cats used on Great South Bay were good examples of the Long Island boats and were somewhat like the New York boats in model but with a little more depth and with curved, slightly raking stems. The V-stern, set at a sharp rake with the rudderpost inboard, was very popular there in the 1870's and 80's. The boats had the usual cat rig and were very fine working-boats for protected, shoal waters until the fashion for over-canvasing reached the area, late in the 1880's. A somewhat similar catboat was used on Barnegat Bay, New Jersey, for oystering and fishing. The square transom, with rudder outboard, seems to have been favored there. Similar cats were used along the Gulf Coast and in some of the South Atlantic states in the late 80's, and eventually they were tried out in San Francisco Bay in the oyster fishery. There the very strong winds and heavy sea often met with, made the popularity of the catboat of the New York style rather short. The deeper and more able Eastern catboats were rarely transplanted as work-boats and never achieved the popularity of the New York cat and related models.

Albemarle Sound Boat

While there were a number of small American working-boats
fitted with the sprit mainsail and a jib, such as the sailing dory and
the Matinicus Island boat, there was only one that is known to have
carried a topsail, such as was popular in many of the European spritsail craft. This American spritsail-and-jib rig with a topsail was used
in the sounds that line the coast of North Carolina. The sound boats
were employed in the shad fishery, which uses seines. Hence, they

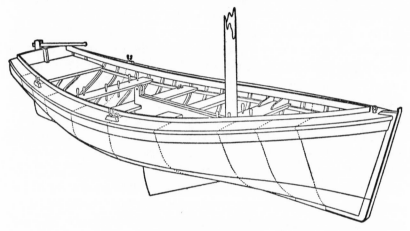

Albemarle Sound Boat

are usually called "North Carolina shad (or seine) boats," and are
also called after the sounds on which they were found—Albemarle,
Pamlico, Currituck Core, and Croatan. Many of the boats were built
on Roanoke Island (the site of the famous "Lost Colony") and on
the western shores of Pamlico Sound. They ranged in size from
about 18 to 30 feet over-all length, and in hull faintly resembled
the New Jersey beach skiff, once used about Atlantic City, but the
Carolina boats were caravel-planked. They usually had plank keels
and skegs; the run was short but well formed; and the sections there
showed some hollow in the garboards. The midsection had straight,
strongly rising floors and well-rounded bilges. The topsides usually
had some flare. The bow was straight and raked strongly. The
transom raked also, and the rudder was outboard, hung on an

outside sternpost. The transoms were rather heart-shaped, and the quarters were quite deep for carrying heavy weights stowed well aft in the boats. The hull was undecked except for side decks, or washboards, which ran from the bow to the transom, and was finished on the inboard side by a low coaming strip. The frames, spaced about 12 inches on centers, were about 1½ inches in siding and molding and were single futtocks cut off on the plank keel and not overlapping there. Floors were cut of plank and were placed between the frames and clear of them with independent fastenings. The washboards were supported by small knees fastened to the frame heads and to the topside planking.

The construction was simple. There was rarely a rabbet on the keel—the outboard edges were beveled at the top to take the garboards. The stem was usually formed by an inside stem liner, apron, or stemson, and the cutwater piece was added after the hull was planked. The skegs were always molded. The mode of construction shows that the boats were usually built over molds and that frames were placed only after the planking was temporarily secured to the molds or to a few mold frames. Local juniper, often called "southern cedar" in boatshops, was used throughout in building these boats, and they have lasted extremely well. Many are still in use, converted to power and fitted with squat boards aft to prevent the stern from settling while underway. The frames are cut from natural crooks, probably root knees. There are four to six thwarts. in addition to sternsheets, in these boats, and the mast thwart is kneed to the gunwales. Figure 97 shows the lines of a typical boat of this type. This model is no longer built, as a number of cheaper models have taken its place.

A dead-rise skiff, commonly called a "skipjack," was built using the same hull profile as the old round-bottomed boat; and a sharpie skiff, about 18 feet long and under 6 feet beam, of similar profile is to be seen. These are said to have been rigged with sprit mainsail and jib only, without the topsail that marked the rig of the older boats. The V-bottomed model is now built only as a powerboat, but three of the sharpie type of sailing skiffs fully rigged were at Roanoke Island in the spring of 1951. The sharpie and V-bottomed boats were all marked by great flare to the sides.

All of the boats in this section of the coast were well built in a

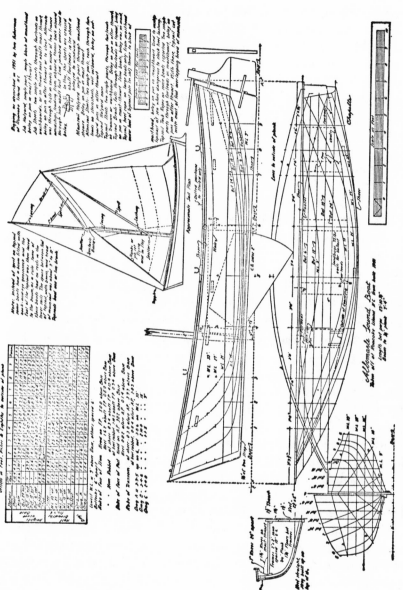

259

Fig. 97. Albemarle Sound sailing seine boat with topmast over a sprit mainsail.

plain, workmanlike fashion. The topsides are usually painted white; some boats have black and red bands in three narrow stripes along the gunwales, which set off the strong sheer very well indeed. No local tradition as to the introduction of the round-bottomed type could be discovered, but it seems very probable that the type was introduced after the Civil War and may owe its origin to the ubiquitous yawl-boat. No example of the type has yet been discovered in the numerous Civil War photographs of the Union naval operations in this area.

The rig, shown in Figure 97, is peculiar in that the topsail is wholly independent of the mainsail and can be used when the latter is not set. The mode of rigging this sail is not very clear, and the available information is conflicting. The lower sails are the usual jib and a sprit mainsail without a boom; the mainsail is laced to the mast and has no halyard. The lacing often passed through a masthead sheave at the head of the sail and then spiraled down the mast and made up on a cleat just below the tack. The large boats are known to have furled the sail by letting go the lacing and partially unreeving it; the sail was then furled tightly while hanging from the sprit, which was topped up by the lacing line leading through the masthead block. The usual method of topping the sprit and furling the sail around it and the mast was also used. Small boats unshipped the sprit and furled the sail to the mast in the usual way. The jib was tacked to the stemhead and was usually set flying; a few large boats had forestays, and the jib was hanked to these. The jibs were cut very low and overlapped the mainsail slightly. The double-sheet arrangement was used and the sheet fairleads were small cleats on the washboards. The mainsheet was usually a single part and belayed to pins in the washboards on either quarter. Some boats had double mainsheets which rove through holes in the washboards and belayed to cavils below.

The topsail looked like a dory's leg-of-mutton on a long, light mast; its setting was slightly like that of the Bermuda topsail described earlier. The sail had a light sprit at its foot as a boom, set as the Bermuda sprit-booms. The mast had a spectacle iron (or a band much like the old jibboom iron at the bowsprit end) placed just below the sprit. The topsail was usually fitted with two light brail lines and was set brailed. The long topmast with the sail was first lifted aloft and the after eye in the spectacle iron was dropped over the short masthead; the heel of the topmast was then lashed to the mast a little above the mast thwart. The brails were then let go, and the sail set. The sheet, which might be double or a single part, was led to pins in the after thwart or in the washboards. In shipping or unshipping the topmast and sail, the head was steadied by a light line to the topmast head, which also served, when set up to the stemhead, as a topmast stay. Setting the topmast was usually a two-man job, particularly if the wind was at all fresh. When unshipping the topmast in a breeze, it was often thrown into the water and then brought aboard. The purpose of the sail was to give high working canvas when sailing along the then heavily forested shores, which would becalm the lower jib and mainsail. The rigged model of one of these boats in the Watercraft Collection has had its rigging incorrectly repaired, and so it does not show the whole rig properly.

The boats, according to their size, were ballasted with from 15 to 30 sandbags, and these were often shifted to windward in blowing weather. Each bag weighed from 50 to 75 pounds and was made of sail canvas. It is said that these boats were once used in oystering; however, they had been replaced in this occupation by the sharpies in the 1880's. The shad boats were very numerous until power craft came into use, and now the old hulls are gradually disappearing. They are being replaced by V-bottomed power boats with round sterns, deeper, but otherwise built like the sterns of the old New Haven sharpie. The bows are fine; the chines die out a little abaft the bow at a straight-sided V-section and so are often unapparent to the casual observer. The fine bow usually makes the water line forward quite hollow, just abaft the stem.

The shad boats had a great reputation for speed and seaworthiness; the latter was an important quality in the larger sounds, where the shoal waters were often dangerous enough, before the present canals were built, to bring southbound yachts to grief in the fall gales.

The Eastport Pinkies

One of the two double-ended sloop-rigged types of fishing boats used in North America was the Eastport pinky. This sloop existed from about the end of the Civil War until the coming of the motor-driven fishermen. The origin of the Eastport pinky can best be described as the result of crossbreeding. The hull was an adaptation of the pinky-schooner model to that of a small boat, and to this was added a sloop rig apparently taken from the old coasting sloops. The boats were built to two classes very early in their existence. A small boat from 20 to 26 feet long, rigged with one mast having a high and rather short-gaff mainsail hoisted by a single halyard, was popular. This boat had its mast much farther aft than in a cat. Like the Newport boats, these keel cat-rigged hulls often used a light bowsprit and a jib set flying which could be shipped in summer weather. The majority of the so-called "pinkies," which formed the larger and second class of boat in this type, had a standing bowsprit and jib, and ranged in size from 28 to about 40 feet on deck.

Figure 98 shows a typical example of one of the larger boats. There are few half-models of this type in existence. These sloops were called "carryaway boats" in the Fish Commission reports, as they were employed in taking fish from the weirs and carrying them away to the sardine-canning factories at Lubec and Eastport and on Passamaquoddy, or "Quoddy," Bay. Some sloops fitted with fish-wells were often employed as lobster smacks, or as carryaway boats for lobster pounds. The smaller boats of the type, which were similarly employed, were primarily intended for tending small weirs or traps.

None of these sloops or one-masted boats had the pink stern of the older pinky-schooner and had merely taken the name "pinky" from the hull-form and local usage. The sloops were usually very smart sailers and were splendid sea boats. The boat shown in Figure 98 is about the average in dead rise and in fineness of run. Some of the more extreme models had some hollow in their sharply rising floors amidships and had extremely fine ends. While such craft were the fastest sailers, they were not as good carriers as the boat shown, nor were they quite as good sea boats. Some of these Quoddy Bay double-enders were rather full-ended with less dead rise amidships than shown. These were the best carriers of the type but at the expense of speed in fresh winds. All of the type used a local iron ore stowed inside for ballast.

The Richardson family, of Deer Island, New Brunswick, and the

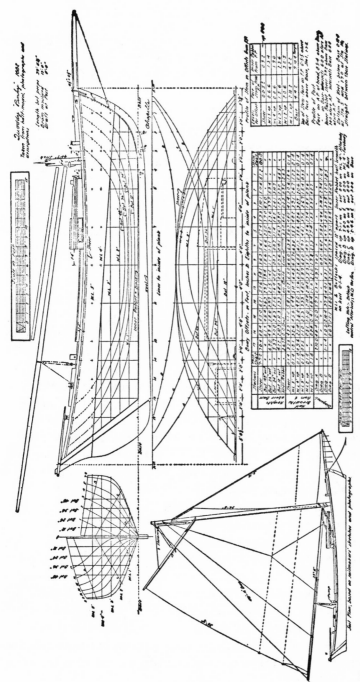

Fig. 98. Large Quoddy sloop, called a "pinky" locally, which was known as a Lubec boat, or (in government reports) as an Eastern Carryaway boat.

Hallets, of Eastport, Maine, were among the prominent builders of the type. This style of boat was built on Quoddy Bay and among the islands near its entrance; in the 1890's a few boats of the type were built in Nova Scotia, on Fundy, but on the whole the small pinky-schooner boat retained its popularity in this area until the end of sail. Unfortunately, the numerous types of small schooner-boats cannot be discussed here for lack of space, but these, with the Eastport pinkies, were equal in seaworthiness and superior in speed to the famed Norwegian sailing double-enders, with which so many American yachtsmen became familiar some years back.

Like most of the small fishing craft in America, the Eastport pinky was built cheaply of local materials, yet the boats appear to have lasted very well, judging by the age of some of the hulks seen. The keel was usually of yellow birch, and no rabbet was cut along it for the garboards until the deadwood was reached; the top corners of the keel were beveled to take the edge of these strakes. The frames were double-sawn of 2-inch plank and were put together as in a large wooden vessel. Local oak, a poor species for boatbuilding, was used, as well as northeastern cedar, birch, or spruce. A keelson was placed on the floors as in large vessels. The deck beams were kneed to the sides, except the short beams. The hull was planked with local pine or cedar, usually 1¼ to 1½ inches thick. The decks were commonly of 6-inch plank, 1 to 1½ inches thick, and the ends ran to the covering board, without nibbing. The hull was ceiled inside with 1-inch plank. In general, the boats were strongly but rather roughly built; for example, the ends of the futtocks were shifted as the stock in hand allowed in the individual frame without regard to the shifts in the neighboring frames.

The rig was marked by a rather high and narrow mainsail with a rather short gaff, which was hoisted by a single halyard in most of the boats. There were usually three reef bands in the mainsail. The jib was loose-footed and without overlap. Most of the boats had no shrouds. There were two practices with regard to placing the mainsheet: most of the boats in the 1880's had the sheet on a horse forward of the steersman's standing room, but later practice was to use an iron horse placed well aft and secured to the outside of the hull. The rig was, in general, a very simple and inexpensive one.

The arrangement of the deck seems to have been quite standardized. A small cuddy was placed forward having two berths and a stove. Abaft this, in the larger boats, was a large fish hold entered through a large hatchway on deck. Next was a short deck in which the two round wooden pump-barrels stood and where the mainsheet horse was placed. Abaft this was a small standing room for the helmsman. The boats steered with a rather long tiller, which was fitted with a comb and lock. Sweep locks were placed abreast the standing room. The smaller boats sometimes had a long cockpit abaft the cuddy, or a short bridge deck and then a large cockpit. Under the bridge deck there was sometimes a fish-well, as in many of the Friendship sloops.

In the last years of building these craft, the model became somewhat decadent: the runs were very full and the dead rise rather extreme. The small boats of the type seem to have departed somewhat from the model used in large sloops in having strongly rounded stems in profile, whereas the latter had rather straight, raking stems. The Fish Commission reports indicate that some of the Eastport sloops were lap-strake built, but this must have gone out very soon after the Civil War, as the oldest builders and fishermen do not remember this construction in the Quoddy pinks.

Somewhat similar sloops, square-sterned and rather low aft and full in the run, were built on Quoddy for shad fishing in the Bay of Fundy. They usually had a straight and rather upright stem and a rather wide, heart-shaped transom with rudder outboard. Some had a small cuddy forward but were otherwise open except for washboards. These boats were less deep than the sardine sloops and had very short bowsprits. American boats were permitted by treaty to engage in shad fishing in Canadian waters. After a gun battle, in which a few men were killed, broke out between Canadian and American fishermen, the shad ceased to run in the customary waters. The fighting and loss of life were blamed for the disappearance of the fish.

Muscongus Bay or Friendship Sloops

The sloops built on Muscongus Bay, in Maine, are best known today as the "Friendship sloops" or "Morse sloops." These names imply a deep keel sloop having a clipper bow, a counter stern, and a strong sheer. The names came from the town of Friendship, where many of the boats were built, and from the Morse family, of this vicinity, whose boats were long noted for their excellent sailing and working qualities. The small sloops were jib-and-mainsail boats; the larger ones, often as long as 36 to 40 feet on deck, had a staysail and jib and often a fidded topmast carrying a gaff topsail and, usually, a jib topsail as well.

This style of keel sloop is not extremely old nor was it built only at Friendship. Other towns on the Bay, notably Bremen, were equally active boatbuilding centers, and, in the early years of the period immediately following the Civil War, Bremen was the most noted of all. The early Fish Commission reports show that the sloop used then was a centerboarder with jib and mainsail and that its hull was commonly lap-strake planked. A rigged model of such a boat is in the Watercraft Collection. A rough sail plan is contained in a sketch in the fifth volume of Vice-Admiral Pâris' *Souvenirs de Marine*. A few half-models of such sloops exist, and until about 1940 the rotting hulk of one of these centerboarders, but caravel-planked, lay near Kennebunk Beach. These sloops had as great a reputation in their time as the later Friendships have had in recent years and should be better known. Figure 99 shows the lines of a half-model of one of these fine boats, with details reconstructed from the hulk just mentioned, photographs, descriptions, and the Watercraft Collection model.

These sloops were deep centerboarders of very moderate power with well-proportioned rigs. The hulls show very rising floors and rather heavy quarters; the run was long and flat. The counter is that of the modern Friendship sloop, which seems to have been copied from the fashionable stern in the Gloucester fishermen of the late 1850's; the whole appearance of the Muscongus Bay sloop types indicates they were developed not earlier than the Civil War period. The centerboard model did not have shrouds, and the gaff was hoisted by a single halyard quite different in reeving than has

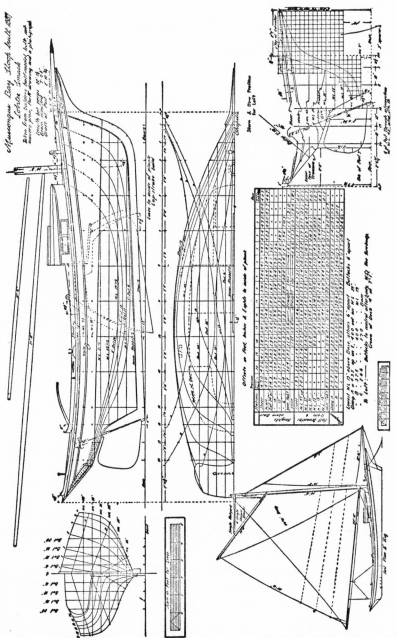

Fig. 99. Centerboard lobster smack once popular in Maine. Some hulls of this type were thirty-five feet long and part of these were schooner-rigged.

267

been seen elsewhere. The rig is shown as pictured by Pâris. The proportions are roughly those of the rigged model and a couple of old sailmakers' drawings. The half-model was made at Bremen, about 1888, for building two sloops. I have shown the double sheer-moldings that appear in the Pâris sketch and on the Watercraft Collection model; old photographs show that this was the fashion in lap-strake sloops, while most of the caravel-planked sloops had a single sheer molding or just a rail cap.

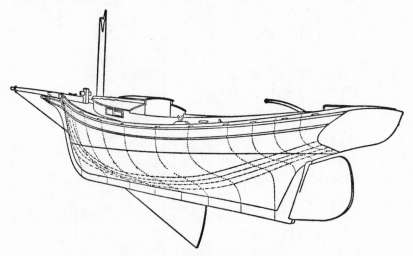

Centerboard Muscongus Bay Sloop

The caravel-built boat at Kennebunk Beach was built in the same manner as the later Friendship sloops, except for having a centerboard and case. Most of these sloops had fish-wells. The deck arrangement of some of the centerboarders followed the keel sloop practice, but others had merely a large open cockpit, sometimes with a small cuddy forward which might or might not have a bulkhead at its after end.

Goode states that at the time of his survey, sometime before 1887, the centerboard Muscongus Bay sloops were between 16 and 26 feet long, 6 to 9 feet beam, and were being built at Bristol, Bremen, and Friendship. This shows that the boats were then, on the average, smaller than in more recent years. The centerboarders were employed extensively in the lobster fishery and did some hand-lining in season. The cockpits were deep and not self-bailing. Hulls on the same general model, lap-strake and schooner-rigged, were also built; such small schooners (complete to fidded topmasts) appear in some old Fish Commission photographs of Provincetown in the late 1880's or early 90's.

The centerboarder remained popular into the early 1890's; by that time it was rapidly being replaced by a keel hull of the same rig and general appearance. The records are not clear as to why this occurred but indicate that the centerboard sloop had been ousting the Casco Bay Hampton boat type in the vicinity of Muscongus Bay. This seems to have begun as early as 1885, and by 1890, or thereabouts, the Monhegan and Matinicus boats were quite out of fashion there. The centerboard sloop had a rather short reign and was soon being replaced by the keel model.

The keel lobster sloop did not represent an innovation, of course. The Muscongus Bay builders had turned out keel fishing sloops as early as 1850, and their craft followed the trend in design that existed in the Gloucester sloop-boats. In the late 1870's and early 80's, the then popular model of fishing schooner, a shoal and very sharp keel boat, came under violent criticism as the cause of much loss of life. As a result, new schooners were built in the early 80's of greater depth in proportion to beam and length; this set up a new trend in design that shortly affected the sloops. It seems very probable that this change in fashion was felt in Muscongus Bay, and the fishermen now wanted a deeper boat in place of the older center-boarder. The keel sloop of the present Friendship sloop style of hull and rig certainly appeared late in the 1880's, and this model was shortly a very popular one among the lobstermen. The sloops also grew in size, and gaff topsails soon appeared. The old "jumbo" headsail of the fishing schooner had just gone out of style, and the double-headsail rig was now the rage. So the lobster sloops had double headsails in the place of the old single jib. These additions and changes did not occur as a result of trial of the comparative merits of the old and the new, but were the result of a fad for a given hull and rig form that was being created by publicity in behalf of a safer fishing schooner.

Figure 100 shows the lines of a good example of a modern Muscongus Bay or Friendship sloop of the keel model. This boat, the

Pemaquid, was built about 1914 at Bremen by A. K. Carter, a builder of sloops of local renown. The *Pemaquid* became a yacht, and once belonged to Andrew Hepburn, Jr., through whose courtesy the lines are shown. These were taken off the sloop in 1935 by the late Charles G. MacGregor, N. A., of Boston. I have shown the hull as she was when a work-boat. The lines of this sloop differ from many of the Morse sloops built at Friendship in having more hollow in the garboards and a flatter run. Her body is shoaler than usual in a sloop of this type, and her counter is partly immersed. This form gave a flatter run and more speed than would a deep body and a high counter, with a steep, rounded run. These sloops carried their ballast inside, using rock extensively, though some of the boats had pig iron, which was more expensive than granite boulders, but much more effective. The *Pemaquid* shows the typical sharpness in bow and the usual sheer of her type.

The construction shown in Figure 101 is approximately that of the *Pemaquid,* though the details were taken from another boat of about the same size. The building methods employed in these sloops were much standardized and so were the scantlings. These boats were not really inexpensive to build because of their model; for example, not only was the schooner stern quite difficult to build but it also took excess hours of labor compared with the flat stern or usual square transom. The hollow in the garboards also added to the time required in construction. Yet the sloops were quite cheap: in the late 1890's, a 25-foot sloop cost $675; in 1899, a 28-foot boat, complete for sea, was built for $780. The low prices were the result of low-cost labor and the use of local materials, and of short cuts in construction.

The general framing arrangement can be seen in Figure 101, which shows the usual proportions of scantlings used in the sloops. The frames were of local red oak as a rule—this is known as "gray" or "blue" oak but is of the red species. The frames were steam-bent —in theory at least—but in practice they were often put in green or after a soaking in cold water. Hence, it was not uncommon to have some broken frames in the tuck, where the reverse curves in the frames were hard and short. The keels were usually of oak in these sloops; the early boats had keel and the posts all of the same siding, but in the late 1890's some builders began to mold the keel

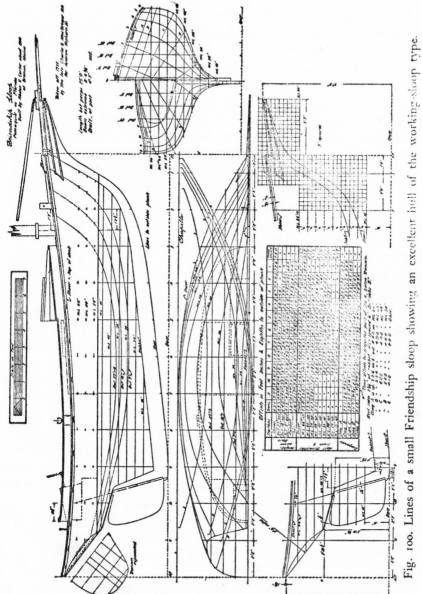

Fig. 100. Lines of a small Friendship sloop showing an excellent hull of the working-sloop type.

271

even though no outside ballast was fitted. It was said, by one builder, that molded keels were used because it was thought the wider keel amidships made it possible to carry a greater part of the ballast lower than was possible with the straight-sided keel, when the iron was available for ballast.

The frames were usually thin and bent on the flat; their heels were toenailed to the keel. The heads were brought up to a sheer timber that was characteristic of these sloops and that accounted for their surprising strength and life. The sheer timber ran the full length of the boat; it was made of heavy plank scarphed end-to-end and shaped to the side of the hull and also to the sheer. In order to accomplish this, the sheer timber was in short lengths, as shown in the construction drawing. This timber had its top at the underside of the decking, at plank-sheer; its outer edge might come to the inside of the sheer strake, and then the frame heads were notched in, or, in the cheapest build, the sheer timber's outer edge was at the inside of the frames. The deck beams had their outboard ends halved into the sheer timber and nailed. The decking, of narrow plank, covered the deck-beam ends and helped tie the beam ends and sheer timber together. If the deck did not leak, this was a very lasting and strong construction; the sheer timber was nearly as strong as the keel structure, and was usually of oak 2 inches or more in thickness. The planking was sometimes of oak or yellow pine, while white pine and northeastern cedar were very popular with experienced owners.

The sloops rarely had many floors or knees; they usually appear to have had a pair of hanging knees at one of the mast partners and another pair at the "great beam" amidships. Often this beam was a double one, as shown in the construction drawing. Five floors were the most used, and many boats had none. The floors, if used, were of plank and were placed on top of the frames rather than beside them or were located clear of the frames and fastened to keel and planking. The transom plank was usually sprung over the transom frame, in the manner customary in a transom curved athwartships. Some builders built up the transom of thick plank, edge-fastened, and then dubbed it to the desired curve, using only a small frame as a nailing piece for the side planks. In general, the construction was conventional except for the sheer timbers, as can be seen. The fastenings were iron, usually galvanized.

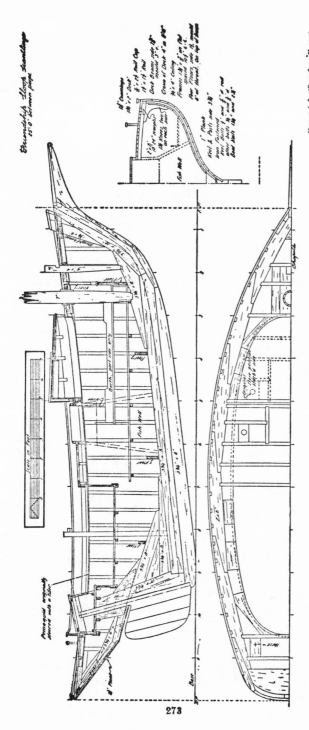

Fig. 101. Construction drawing of a Friendship sloop of the better class, showing fairly typical scantling proportions.

In order to save labor, these sloops were often rather slightly fastened, and the quality of timber used was not first class. In spite of this, the boats have lasted very well indeed. A number of reasons account for the relatively long life. One is that the sheer timbers and the keel structure were much stronger than was necessary. Another is that most of the boats were ceiled inside with 1-inch plank carried the full length of the hull as far as was practical, from near the keel to the underside of the sheer timber; sometimes a small air space was left here or holes were bored for this purpose in the uppermost strake of the ceiling. Thus, the boat had almost a double skin. The third, and most important, reason is the apparent neglect with which most fishermen treat their boats. The boats when laid up are not covered, and their cockpits and cuddies are left open to the elements. Though snow, ice, and rain may enter them, so does plenty of air, and this ventilation prolongs their lives. In a number of cases, where Friendship sloops have been treated as yachts, rotting occurred very rapidly. The fishermen's treatment of these sloops places a limitation on the kind of finish that a boat can have and also upon the style of furniture and cabin fittings that are built into her—but it is a cheap way to avoid rot.

The rig of the *Pemaquid* is shown in Figure 102 and is typical of these sloops. Many of the small sloops had no topmast and gaff topsail; three lowers constituted their sails. The boomed staysail was universal and was either sheeted to a horse or was fitted with double sheets; the horse is the most common lead. The old working-sloops had at least three rows of reef points in the mainsail and two in the staysail. Some boats carried a small jib-headed riding sail, set above a furled mainsail. Many of the sloops would work under a triple-reefed mainsail alone, without a headsail, but usually the latter was carried if the boat had to tack often or was in narrow, dangerous waters. The keel boats usually had shrouds and at least two headstays. The working sails were rather low, and the base of the sail plan was long; this gave a good deal of sail with a low center of effort, though the boom overhung the counter a good deal and the bowsprit was often very long. The low sails, the great beam, weight of ballast, and the deep draft, part of which was the flat-sided false keel, made these boats very weatherly in blowing weather, and they could beat off a lee shore when a less stiff and powerful boat would be knocked down and driven to leeward. This was their great quality—they would bring you home as well as they took you out. Their ability to sail in heavy weather has given them a great reputation and this has led many of the boats to be converted into cruising yachts.

When a Muscongus Bay sloop becomes a yacht, it is usual to dock her main boom and shorten the bowsprit a bit—"to bring the

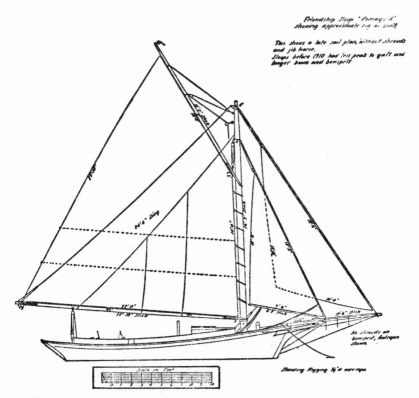

Fig. 102. Working Friendship sloop in its last stage of development.

sails inboard as much as possible." The result is that sail area is lost, and the boat neither sails as fast nor tacks as readily as before. Many of the converted sloops become slugs and unhandy brutes. The boats do not stand up as well when the height of their rig is greatly increased, and the hull-form is not one well suited to the modern high and narrow sail plans, nor is it a good one for the ketch rig. In fact, it is one that requires the sail plan it originally had, no matter how hard such a rig is to handle. It is a great pity that so many of these fine, powerful sloops have been spoiled in an effort to make them "easy-working" cruisers.

There are a number of other sloop types—such as the jib-headed keel sloop once used on the Florida coast, the double-enders used at Portland, Oregon, and the centerboard spongers and oyster sloops —that must be left for some future investigation. Altogether, there were about eighteen local sloop types used in North America in the last half of the nineteenth century that were under 40 feet on deck; only two were double-enders. About half of these sloops were really distinctive in hull or rig, or both.

Before leaving the sloop types, there is one feature to be seen in many of them that deserves attention. This is the very long mainsheet horse seen in many working-sloops, particularly in wide centerboarders. Such mainsheet horses as these would be considered objectionable by many yachtsmen on the ground that the mainsail could not be sheeted hard down so that the boom stands close to the centerline of the boat. However, there are a few boats that are capable of sailing well, even in very smooth water, with the mainboom pinned down in this fashion—and certainly the number of cruisers that can be sailed in this manner is extremely small. If photographs of many modern cruisers are examined, it will be seen that many, when on the wind, lift their booms and by this throw a twist into the sail that the jib-headed mainsail is supposed not to have. The same trouble existed in the gaff rig—nowadays it would be said it was because of the gaff. The old boat sailors did not know of this "fact," so they cured it by the simple expedient of having a long horse, which allowed the sheet to aid in holding the boom down. While the boom could be pinned down by proper sheeting of the fall, it could also be held from lifting by the long horse when the sheets were slightly started, aided by shifting the belay of the fall. That is why many working-sloops had long mainsheet horses, and long jib horses when the jib was boomed, and why there were usually a number of belaying cleats for the sheet falls. Sheeting of boomed sails is as important as the sheeting of loose-footed sails, to obtain proper results. It is common, today, to find sheets set up to very short horses or even ringbolts, or to lead blocks on a mast in two-masters, and so the modern jib-headed sail may be seen with a marked twist in it.

CHAPTER 6

Foreigners AND A Native

IN A COUNTRY whose population is predominately European in ancestry one would expect to find many evidences of foreign influence in the hull-designs and rigs of small American fishing craft. Yet such influence is difficult to identify with any degree of certainty, except in certain areas where immigrants were sufficiently numerous to establish their culture and customs, temporarily at least, in the economic life of the new country. Such areas were not numerous, and not all immigrant nationalities were so well established. The heavy influx of immigrants, in large national groups, did not begin until the 1830's and 40's, and hence foreign types of small craft did not appear as distinct models and rigs until after this date.

Of the four known cases where foreign small craft, obviously of European origin in rig and hull, appear in this country, one surely was of North European extraction. Though there were a large number of Scotch, English, Dutch, German, and Scandinavian fishermen who came to America and pursued their trade here, they did not settle extensively in a single community, and so they readily adopted the existing American small craft instead of introducing the craft they had been accustomed to in their homeland. They also

277

found that American hull-forms and rigs did not depart widely from those with which they had sailed in Europe.

The Boston Hooker

The one great exception to the foregoing was the Irish who settled at Boston, Massachusetts, in great numbers during the mass emigrations from Ireland in the 1840's and 50's. A very large number were fishermen and waterfront workers. Those who had been fishermen in the old country were trained in small-boat fishing and naturally trended toward a similar occupation in America. The intense concentration of Irish at Boston soon led to a self-contained small-boat fishery there, wholly independent of Yankee influence or economic control. As a result, in the late 1850's, an Irish type of fishing boat appeared in Massachusetts Bay fisheries; this has been called the "Irish cutter" in government reports, but the type was really a modification, very minor in extent, of the Galway hooker.

This type of Irish fishing cutter had been used on the west coast of Ireland in the early nineteenth century and probably was descended from the English cutters of the last half of the eighteenth century. The Galway hooker was a weatherly and fast-sailing boat, and plans of the Irish model may be found in Dixon Kemp's *Manual of Yacht and Boat Sailing*, 4th edition, 1884. According to the reports of the Fish Commission, the first of the hookers to be built in America came out in 1857 and was built by Patrick Gannon, who had been a Galway County builder. With the passing years the hooker went through a series of modifications which consisted of adding a straight and slightly raking stem and in fining the entrance. The old Irish model had been rather full forward and very fine aft; the Boston Irish retained the old form of run unchanged. The rig was also modified somewhat by the addition of a longer gaff and by lacing the foot of the mainsail to the boom.

Figure 103 shows the lines of one of the Boston hookers drawn from measurements taken off an old boat by the late Charleton Smith and appears to be fairly representative of the type. The earlier boats retained the extreme tumble home amidships that had marked the old Irish hooker, but in the 1880's the Boston Irish had begun to dispense with this feature. About this time, the mast was moved

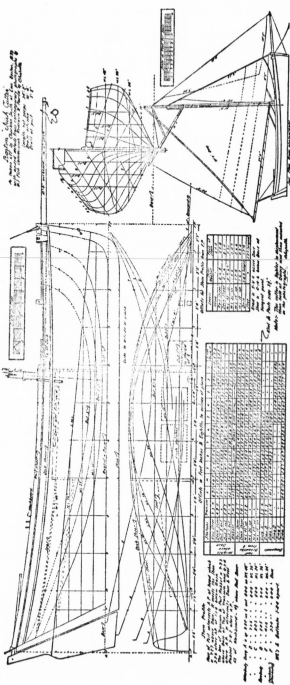

Fig. 103. These cutters, sometimes called "Dundavoes" by the Boston Irish fishermen, were able boats though commonly less sharp than this example. The boats were roughly built and had tarred sides.

forward somewhat, judging by the rigged model of an improved hooker in the Watercraft Collection.

The Boston hooker was usually between 30 and 38 feet long; she had a cuddy under a short deck forward, and abaft this, a fish hold or, in some, a large fish-well. There was a large cockpit at the stern. There was no side decks abaft the cuddy and, in most of the boats shown in old Fish Commission photographs, the freeboard in the way of the fish hold and cockpit was increased by a monkey rail as shown in the plans. The hookers were caravel-built and had sawn frames. They were cheaply and rather roughly built, judging by old photographs. There was some variety in the models used—some boats were quite full-ended, while others were very sharp. Some of the latter, like the boat shown in Figure 103, were sold and converted to yachts. Captain J. W. Collins, in his efforts to improve the model of the Gloucester fishing schooners in the early 1880's, referred to the hookers as examples of safe and fast models. He designed some small fishing cutters which were inspired by this type and tried to have the model adopted on the Pacific Coast, without much success, however. The hooker had her rudder outboard; the counter was not employed in the type. The Irish type went out of fashion in the 1890's and was replaced by the Gloucester sloop-boat and by the small schooner-boat, 36 to 54 feet long.

The rig of the Boston hooker was that of a bald-headed cutter; the mast was placed a little forward of amidships and the long pole bowsprit was fitted to run in, or reef, in heavy weather or in a crowded slip. To allow this, the bowsprit was placed to port of the stemhead, which stood high above the rail, and the heel bitts were set farther from the centerline to allow the bowsprit to come in past the mast. This arrangement brought the nose of the bowsprit to the centerline of the boat when it was run out. A heel tackle, cutter fashion, was used to force the stick out into place. The bobstay was fitted with a tackle at its outer end, in place of the usual lanyard, to allow it to be set up hard when the bowsprit had been run out.

The hooker had three sails: a gaff mainsail, a fore staysail, and a jib; light sails were not carried. The mast was supported by a single shroud on each side and by a heavy forestay which set up with a thimble and lanyard to the stemhead. The jib was set flying with its tack hooked into an iron ring which traveled over the bowsprit. This ring could be hauled in or out by a line made fast to it and rove through a sheave in the outer end of the bowsprit. The hookers seem to have been without bowsprit shrouds. The fore staysail was hanked to its stay. The mainsail had three or four reefs; the staysail, two. The jib was the first sail taken in when it came to blow hard. In many of the boats there were no mainsheet horses; the sheet was shifted in going about and was belayed to a suitable timberhead or cavil aft. In the early 80's the horse became more popular and the old shifting sheet eventually disappeared.

One characteristic of the Boston hookers was a peculiar anchorline chock or hawse timber. This was a short piece of hardwood, with a chock cut into its top, bolted to the outside of the bulwark just to starboard of the stemhead. In some boats it appears to curve slightly outboard; in the rigged model in the Watercraft Collection this timber is placed far aft (apparently, the model builder thought it was a cathead because of its outward curve). None of the photographs of the hookers show a cathead or any anchor windlass, but they do show that many of the boats had low, heavy guards to protect their sides in the crowded slips, such as at T-Wharf in sailing days.

These fine Irish cutters became extinct early in the present century. I inspected one of the last of the hulks of this type at Quincy, Massachusetts, in 1936, and took off the lines, but this example was not so fine a model as that shown in Figure 103. The decline in popularity of this type in the 1890's is not the sole instance in which a boat type passed out of favor in the years just preceding the appearance of the motorboat in the fisheries. It is impossible to say, now, just what reasons existed in each case in which a type lost its popular acceptance, but it is apparent that one contributing factor was the practice of many of the leading newspapers, in the large seaports, of printing long articles on the leading yachts of the day, complete with pictures, sketches, and a discussion concerning features of design. This information thus reached the hands of fishermen and boatbuilders who would not otherwise have been aware of what was going on in the yachting field. As a result some work-boats appeared that at least looked like yachts, if not always built on their lines and with all the features of their rigs.

The rise of the famous "forty-foot class" in New England waters attracted much attention to a fine type of yacht, and there is some evidence that the design of this class of yacht, at least, had some influence on that of the Gloucester sloop-boats. But, of greater importance, the yachting news and ideas led many fishermen to want the "latest thing," and so a number of less impressive, but very useful and economical, small-craft types gradually disappeared. The then prosperous condition of the fisheries hastened this change to a more expensive style of work-boat, as it has done in more recent times, when economic considerations no longer were the decisive factor in the selection of a small work-boat.

The New Orleans Lugger

In the vicinity of the Mississippi Delta a lug-rigged boat was in wide use during the last half of the nineteenth century. The history of this type is speculative; "luggers" are mentioned in the first decade of the nineteenth century at New Orleans, before the centerboard that later marked the New Orleans lugger was in use. The evidence indicates that the early luggers were keel yawl-boats in model and that the centerboarder developed from these. The keel hulls were in use as late as 1880–85, though by then the centerboard lugger was very common. The dipping lug used is that of northern France and of the Channel side of the British Isles. The same sail was employed in such craft as the Deal galley punts on the English side and in some of the small French boats on the opposite shore.

In the 1880's and later, these luggers were built and manned to a very great extent by Italian immigrants or their descendants, but it should not be inferred from this that the type was an Italian one. The rig is not popular in Italian waters, where the standing lug and lateen predominate; rather it came from northern Europe and may have been introduced into Louisiana by early French colonists from the Channel coast of France. The hull developed to carry this single dipping lug had become very similar to that of the New York centerboard sloop, except that the lugger carried her beam well forward, which gave her a rather straight side. Nevertheless, the hull resembled very strongly a burdensome centerboard sloop of the 1860's or 70's.

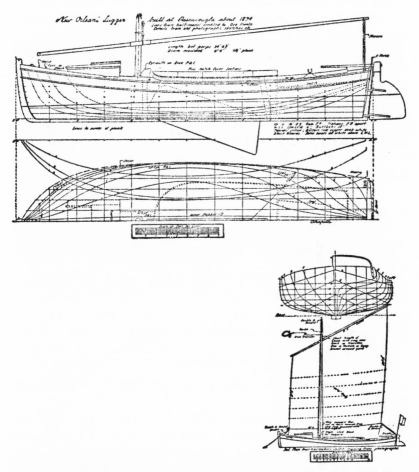

Fig. 104. New Orleans lugger, once a popular style of work-boat on the Gulf Coast, now extinct.

Figure 104 is a drawing of a New Orleans lugger built in 1894; the general appearance of the hull, the deck arrangement, and the rigging details are typical. Some of the models used had more dead rise and were sharper forward, but the lines shown were apparently the most common form used in the Gulf fisheries. Boats of this

type were once employed in oystering and shrimp fishing from
Texas to the west coast of Florida, but they have been replaced by
powerboats, which are still called "luggers" in Louisiana.

The construction of the boats was conventional: sawn frames,
caravel planking, and the usual plank keel of the centerboarder.
The timbering and plank were often local longleaf pine and cypress.
The boats usually had a long and well-formed run and trimmed by
the stern, which reduced the bluntness of the rather full bow. These
luggers sailed very fast, were powerful boats, and were reputed very
close-winded. The deck arrangement was almost standardized: there
was a large U-shaped cockpit, the forward portion of which was
bulkheaded off and covered with four to six hatch covers. The open
part aft was fitted with a U-shaped bench and was the steering well.
At the extreme bow, in the larger boats, was a small trunk cabin
containing the cuddy with two berths. The centerboard case divided
the hatch-covered hold longitudinally; the boards were very large
in these boats. The luggers ranged in size from about 18 to 45 feet
in length, and it is claimed that it was the practice of many builders
to construct all of their boats on one model, varying the scale to
suit the owner's requirements and pocketbook. Most of the luggers
had a good deal of crown in the decks. The rudder was always hung
outboard, and the ends of the hulls had very little rake. The curve
of the stem below the water line was very slight, which made the
lower forebody very fine; the hollow in the forefoot was often
very marked. This was supposed to help the boats to hold on close-
hauled in shallow water where the board could not be lowered very
much.

The rig is of interest chiefly in that it is the only dipping lugsail
to be used in an American work-boat type in the late nineteenth
century. The shape of the sail closely resembled the one used in the
Deal galley punts, but there were some differences in fitting, owing
to the different methods of handling the sail. The dipping lug has
long been recognized as a very powerful and highly efficient sail
but with one great drawback—it has to be lowered wholly or partially each time the boat tacks, to place it to leeward of the mast.
For this reason it has been used almost entirely in boats operated
in the open sea, where there is room to allow the sail to be dipped;

thus, the American example, used in narrow waters, is a departure from the usual in the use of the dipping lug.

Actually, the luggers at New Orleans dipped their lugsail only when there was room and when a tack was stood on for a long time. They were fitted with long horses for both tack and sheet, both powerful tackles. When on a tack that would have had the fore part of the sail aback against the mast, the tack of the sail was hauled out to windward on its long horse and held there by the fall, which was belayed to a cleat inside the weather-bow chock. A snatch block hooked into eyebolts on the bow chocks was often used as a lead block for the fall to help in this. The powerful main-sheet was then utilized to flatten the foot of the sail as much as was possible, and this created a very flat sail, standing almost entirely to windward of the mast and with none of the sail aback except for a very slight amount at the yard, which did no appreciable harm. The relatively great beam of the hull, with its fullness at the bow on deck, permitted such long horses to be employed so that this setting was practical.

A single shroud on each side supported the mast; each shroud was set up on tackles or runners so that it could be slacked off and gotten out of the way when it interfered with the sail. In strong winds these luggers were very dangerous when caught aback, and their handling required great skill and a knowledge of the characteristics of the boats and rig.

A fine rigged model of one of these luggers, as well as a half-model of a larger lugger than that shown in Figure 104, by the same builder, is in the Watercraft Collection. The half-model appears to be fuller in the run and more burdensome than the boat in the drawing. Many of the boats were rather wall-sided, judging by old photographs. The New Orleans lugger is not a type that would appeal to a modern yachtsman, but the dipping lug is still referred to with great respect by many Europeans and therefore there may be some who would like to experiment with a boat so rigged. There is no question as to the speed and weatherliness of the New Orleans lugger; whether it would be a handy and safe boat would be a matter of opinion, and, perhaps, of experience.

The San Francisco Dago Boat

The lateen sail was used in at least three types of American work-boats in the last half of the nineteenth century. One of these is, perhaps, questionable when placed in this category—the Piscataqua River gundalow, of New Hampshire. This craft has already been mentioned; its rig was, fundamentally, a loose-footed leg-of-mutton set on a mast fitted to allow easy raising and lowering of the rig when passing under low bridges. The gundalow's sail was bent to a yardlike mast slung on a low stump or post, and this gave the rig a somewhat lateenlike appearance.

A more well-defined example of the lateen rig occurred in the seine boats once used near Apalachicola, Florida, on the bay of that name, and on St. George's Sound. Goode describes these craft as having been much like the sponge dinghies (a boat on the same model as the Bahama dinghies), 20 to 22 feet long, 6 to 7 feet beam, and decked at the bow with washboards running along the sides to the transom. These, at the time (1887 or earlier), had a single-masted lateen rig. The boats worked in rather protected waters, but have been extinct for at least forty years, if not longer, and no information on the origin of the rig has yet been discovered.

The third example of the lateen rig was the San Francisco felucca, a name given by governmental publications, including the catalogue of the Watercraft Collection, to a type of San Francisco fishing boat used extensively by Italian fishermen there. It appears, however, that this name was unknown on the San Francisco waterfront, where, Mr. J. P. Shaw assures me, the name "Italian fishing boat" or, far more commonly, "Dago fishing boat" was the actual type name.

The origin of the type is obviously southern European, from the Mediterranean coast. The boats were almost all built by Italians, which suggests that they originated in some similar Neapolitan type. However, the San Francisco boat also shows strong resemblance to other Mediterranean craft of the south of France and the Spanish coast. If the Dago boat existed before the arrival of the Italian immigrants, it would then be possible to assume that it may have had a Spanish or French origin; this seems extremely doubtful at present. I have been unable to find any reference to the type before 1881, but the sources are not complete enough to determine when the type first appeared.

The hull-form was that of a shallow keel boat, double-ended, with rather upright stem and sternposts. Some of the boats showed a slight curve in the bow profile and some a straight stem with a

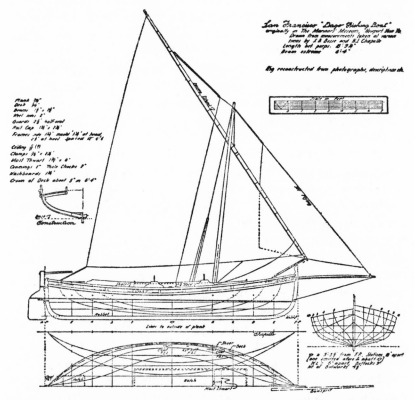

Fig. 105. Plan of a small example of the now extinct San Francisco fishing boat politely called "felucca" in the U. S. Government reports.

slight tumble home above water. The midsections seem to have followed no standard form. Some showed a very rounded shape, in which the rise of floor was moderate, the bilges slack, and the sides flaring. Others appear to have had strong dead rise and a midsection not unlike that of the old New York sloop but without a centerboard. Drawings of larger craft of the type and a rigged model indicate many of these had a rising floor, hard bilge, and a slight flare in the sides. The water lines fore and aft were more or less hollow; the degree of sharpness appears to have varied also. The deck was crowned strongly and the usual deck plan had a large hatch amidships with a small standing room aft; there were low bulwarks around the deck upon which thole pins for sweeping were chocked.

The rig was a single large lateen sail set on a mast, which raked forward and was not supported by shrouds or stays. The jib was set to a bowsprit which came through the bulwarks to starboard of the stemhead; the latter reached well above the rail. The bowsprits appear to have been hogged downward by a bobstay. On the bowsprit the jib was set flying, as in an old cutter, to an iron ring traveling on the stick. The bowsprits could be run inboard. The masthead was usually swelled at the halyard sheave and followed the old galley style.

Figure 105 shows the plan of a small boat of this type; the smallest, in fact, since they were built from 18 to about 36 feet in length. The greatest number are reported to have been somewhere between 26 and 32 feet long. The boat shown here was preserved for some years at the Mariners' Museum, Newport News, Virginia, but was so infected with rot that the hull has disintegrated. The lines were taken off by S. B. Besse, of the museum staff, when the boat was first brought to the museum; the details are drawn from the remaining portions of the hull and from photographs. The sail plan shown in Figure 105 is reconstructed from dimensions and from numerous photographs of the boats and so is as correct as possible with the means at hand. The lines of another small boat of the type are to be seen in Figure 106, which shows the boat restored after the bulwarks had been removed. These lines were taken off at Sacramento, California, in 1941 by Henry Rusk.

The construction was plain and neat. The frames were sawn, single futtocks of natural oak crooks. The caravel-planking was cedar and was protected by two rather heavy, half-round, oak guards, one at each side at plank-sheer level, and by projecting rail caps, or half-rounds applied to them, at sheer. Between these, some of the boats had a number of small vertical guards spaced about 30 inches apart. The boats were ceiled except in the smallest sizes. The hatch was fitted with covers made in small sections. Parting boards could also be fitted in the hatchway. Single thole pins in high chocks on the rail cap were used, and rowing was done standing and facing forward. Stone ballast from about 400 to 1,500 pounds, according to the size of the boat, was carried. The reputation of these boats was very great, and they were said to have been very fast and seaworthy. In the 1880's, the Italian fishermen were considered remarkable for the manner in which they carried sail in the strong winds that are so common in and about San Francisco Bay. The lateen rig was a very dangerous one in unskilled hands; nevertheless these boats suffered very few accidents, as the crews were generally very skillful in handling the rig. Like most

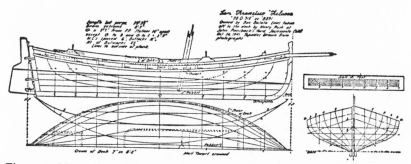

Fig. 106. Lines of a medium-sized "Dago fishing boat" showing a hull-form that appears to have been popular in a large number of this type.

of the Mediterranean small craft, the San Francisco boats were designed to row easily, and this appears to have been resorted to very often, when working in narrow waters as well as in calms. The Italian fishermen used another source of auxiliary power whenever possible. An important piece of gear was an iron hook on a length of chain. This was used to hook on to the rudder chains of any steamer going in the desired direction. The ferries were particularly favored, for their overhangs prevented the ferry crew from getting at the hook. To express their dislike of the practice, the ferry crews threw coal and any other "suitable" object, along with the proper insults, at the Italians, who replied with offal, fish, and the expressive and well-understood Italian epithets and gestures. The search for cheap auxiliary power in those days took some interesting turns.

The boats were usually painted white, and in the 1880's and somewhat later, many of them had wide bands of bright colors along the topsides, from the rail cap to one strake below the plank-sheer. Some boats were varnished instead of painted, but this was not a common practice. The decks were painted yellow, green, or with the hard unpleasant blue used in some Mediterranean boats. The planking usually ran the length of the hull without butts and was so carefully fitted that caulking could be dispensed with, since the cedar used would swell tight. The outboard rudders were worked with a tiller—the whole unshipped in the slips. The Fish Commission reported the boats to last on the average of from 12 to 15 years in good condition.

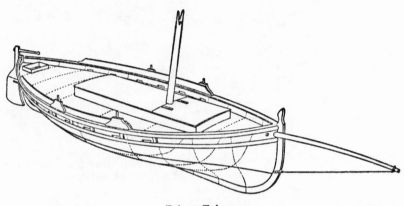

Frisco Felucca

When it was necessary to remain out overnight, the crew slept in the main hatchway, partly under deck, with some of the hatch covers laid on. This gave dry, though cramped, quarters. In protected waters an awning was sometimes rigged over the partially lowered yard, to give shelter at night. The mast was stepped in the large hatch, where there was a mast thwart fitted with the common mast clamp. A heavy wooden beam fitted across the bows, which, with the high stemhead, was used as a means of securing the tack tackle at any desired position. The beam also supported the heel of the bowsprit, which could be run in when desired. The small boats often had washboards on their rails, which extended from a little abaft amidships to about the fore side of the steering well or hatch. Some of the small boats rowed only one pair of sweeps, but two pair were the most common; the crews were usually two or three men. The rather small size of the type was due to the necessity of rowing during the frequent calms, and large boats were not built until motors became available. The model then developed into what is now commonly called the "Monterey boat," a canoe-sterned, double-ended powerboat usually built with a bald clipper bow, or "chicken beak."

Greek Sponging Boat

Another type that appeared in the United States, with little or no variation from the original European model, was a sponging boat used by Greek immigrants who settled on the lower west coast of Florida. This type became common in the early years of the present century. The hull was a caravel-planked double-ender, with very great sheer, well-raked ends, and the bow profile more or less curved, and a slightly rounded V-midsection, remarkable for its entire lack of bilge. The freeboard was very low amidships, and the boat was well suited for rowing but was not able to carry much sail. The rig was a sprit mainsail with a forestaysail set up to the stemhead and a jib set on a bowsprit. This rig was soon replaced by a gaff mainsail. Both the rig and hull-model followed that of the old Greek "Sacoleve" in nearly all respects. Appearing so late in the period of sail, it had a short existence as a sailing boat and soon was modified in model, to allow the use of power. The changes included a square-stern modification in the hull. Lines of the Greek sponging boats have been published in *Motor Boat* magazine, and there is a rigged model now in the Watercraft Collection, but no satisfactory plans of the type, showing the original hull arrangement and rig, have yet been obtained that could be used here. As a sailing boat, this type was perhaps an inferior one and of only historical interest.

The Chesapeake Bay Log Canoes

The antithesis of these late importations was the Chesapeake Bay log canoe, which included three distinct types of rig and hull-form, as well as two subtypes. All but one were descended from the most primitive of all colonial small craft, the Indian dugout canoe. The three basic types of log canoe were the Poquoson, the Nanticoke or Pocomoke, and the Tilghman's Island.

The Poquoson was developed in the vicinity of the village of this name on York River, in Virginia. The double-ended hull, variously rigged, usually had straight stem and stern posts set at moderate rake. In the late 1850's, the boats were often two-masted leg-of-mutton-rigged, without a bowsprit or jib, but later most were one-masted and many had jibs. Sometime in the late 90's, these canoes were built with a peculiar ram bow or "swan's bow," which is said to have been the result of pictures of men-of-war in contemporary illustrated magazines at the outbreak of the Spanish-American War. Still later, the "chicken-beak" clipper bow became popular. The hull-form of this type, in the last ninety years, was that of a shoal centerboarder, and the midsection usually showed moderate dead rise and rather hard bilges. The topsides usually flared a little amidships. The beam was often forward of amidships, and the bow was commonly fuller than the run. The mast was sharply raked aft and unsupported by shrouds. The boats had been fitted with centerboards since sometime soon after the Civil War, if not earlier.

In Maryland and on the Eastern Shore of Virginia, a different style of canoe was used. This was a low-sided and usually narrow double-ender with a curved, raking stem; the hull was made distinctive also by the use of a lap-strake sheer strake, or rising strake, which forms most of the topsides above the water line, and by the use of remarkably high and prominent coamings, running nearly the length of the boat. The rig was striking, consisting of two leg-of-muttons, the fore the larger, set on masts that raked rather sharply aft. These had sprits instead of booms. There was a short mast in the extreme bow, which raked sharply forward like an "artimon" in the Roman ships; on this was set a small leg-of-mutton sheeted to the foremast, or to a span between temporary shrouds set up for the purpose on the foremast, or to fair-leads in the cockpit coamings. This sail plan was called the "stick-up rig" and seems to have stemmed from the "periagua" rig of earlier times. It was a far more efficient rig than has been recognized by the writers who have referred to it in the past. They have considered the stick-up sail no more than an assistance in steering. Actually, it was a most efficient jib, for its luff was always straight, and, when properly sheeted, it stood very well indeed. The sheeting was not difficult, for the sail was fitted with a sprit in the same manner as the other two sails.

The stick-up rig was employed from the Eastern Shore of Virginia northward into Maryland, at least as far as the Choptank River. The hulls used in this area were not uniform, for those north of the Nanticoke River were commonly built without the rising strake and had straight stems. This style and rig of canoe had a number of local names; it is known most generally as either the "Pocomoke Canoe" or the "Nanticoke Canoe" after the rivers on the Eastern Shore, where building was centered.

The third model and rig of canoe was built in the area from the Choptank River northward to Kent Island, with building centered on Tilghman's Island. This was a two-masted canoe; it had the usual sprit leg-of-muttons, with the fore the larger. These canoes commonly had a bowsprit and jib, and, in boats prior to about 1885, the stem was straight and almost vertical, while the post had a very marked rake. In the early 80's the "long head" of the bugeye became common in these canoes; this had become a fashion in the Bay schooners sometime before 1845 and had been used in the bugeyes when they appeared after the Civil War. In these the head rails of the "long head" were useful to the men working on the bowsprit, since they were a more stable platform than footropes. But the "long head" does not seem to have had any practical value in the canoes and may have been the result of fashion only.

The various styles or models of canoes were not strictly confined to given areas, for the boats were sold all around the Bay, and thus a Tilghman's Island canoe might be found on the Western Shore or below the Choptank. The improved sailing canoe appears to have come into existence in the 1850's, and the first craft of the type were probably the Poquoson boats built on York River, in Virginia. By the time the Civil War began, a well-defined sailing canoe with the modern two-masted rig and a jib was in existence, though the jib was often omitted in both the Poquoson and Tilghman's Island canoes until later. Except for the Virginia model, no distinctive model or rig of log canoe seems to have been produced on the Western Shore nor at the head of the Bay.

The early log canoes were small, 20 to 30 feet in length, and were built of a single large log; when large timber became scarce, the boats were built of two or three logs fitted together side by side. Once the art of building the multiple-log hull was accepted, the canoe type was built to greater sizes than before and a large canoe type, 38 to 50 feet in length, came into use. This class was known as the "standing-rig" canoe, as the spars could not be unshipped as in the smaller boats. In the process of developing the large canoe, a type called the "brogan" existed in the Tilghman's Island area. In the brogan the bottom was made of a single log, which formed the keel and floors of the boat, the rest of the hull being framed and planked. These were otherwise standing-rig canoes. The latter were sometimes called "coasting canoes" or "coastin' canoes"; this may be a corruption of "Poquoson," which on the Bay is usually pronounced "Po-co-sin." The large canoes were but a step in the production of the log bugeye and, from this, the same model framed and planked. In spite of its primitive construction, the bugeye is not a very old type; it grew out of the multiple-log canoe through the requirements for larger craft, soon after the Civil War.

The centerboard seems to have appeared rather late in the canoes. It is evident that the early boats were fitted with false keels—a rather deep plank on edge running the full length of the bottom. In the rising-strake and stick-up rigged canoes, the false keel was deepest a little abaft a point one-fourth the water-line length from the stem, and the taper in depth was somewhat greater aft than forward.

In the Tilghman's Island type the keel is said to have been of constant depth, or slightly deeper aft than forward, and straight along the bottom. These canoes were usually trimmed so that the keel had some drag in any case. According to the testimony of Robert D. Lambdin, a builder of St. Michaels, Talbot County, Maryland, given in *The Maryland Historical Magazine*, June, 1941 (Vol. 36, No. 2), he introduced the centerboard in canoes, in this district at least, in the year 1872. The evidence of the late introduction of the board is supported by Fish Commission reports in the early 80's which show that the keel was still in wide use in canoes at that time, particularly in the stick-up rigged craft. No information has been obtained as to when the centerboard was installed in the Poquoson canoes; Civil War photographs taken during the Peninsular Campaign show a number of canoes, and one of them has something amidships that may be a centerboard case. However, the centerboard was in use in the canoes at Norfolk by 1881.

Racing of sailing canoes began at St. Michaels as early as 1859. Lambdin states in this connection that the first two-log canoe was built there in 1858 and that a little later a three-log, 30-foot boat was built there. Racing continued, except for a break during the Civil War, well into the present century and has been revived since the last war. This competition led to the development of the racing canoe, a special type with an enormous rig which requires the use of springboards to out-rig the weight of the crew to windward, in the same manner as in the racing sharpies at New Haven. These canoes have evolved into extremely fast boats of the "racing-machine" class, in which speeds approaching twenty statute miles are not uncommon. Owing to hull-form used and the sharp stern, the boats cannot plane successfully and so are not capable of the highest possible sailing speed in fresh winds, but in a moderate breeze, or in light airs, they are extraordinarily fast and far superior to any of the planing types.

The log construction has been described in articles and books and so requires only general explanation here. The multiple-log construction has now been in use since the Civil War and is therefore the important mode of building. Most of the canoes are built of three or more logs of old-growth pine (virgin loblolly pine) of large dimensions. A large amount of heartwood is required, so the trees are bored before felling to ascertain if they have enough of this to warrant selection. The first log to be shaped is the center one; this forms the keel and at least part of the floor of the boat. The outside is first shaped, and the thickness of the sides, during the hewing, is controlled by dark-colored or scorched wood pegs driven into holes bored in the log. The centerboard slot is cut in the center log, where it is from 3 to 6 inches thicker than elsewhere, to form the bed for the case.

The thickness of the bottom varies with the size of the canoe; the smallest boats usually have bottoms about 3 or 3½ inches thick, and a 35-foot canoe may have the bottom as thick as 7 inches along the centerline of the hull. From the centerline of the keel log, the bottom is reduced in thickness until the edges are about half as thick as at the centerline. The edges are then dressed straight and smooth, and the next two logs are prepared. These, in a three-log canoe, form part of the floor and reach just above the turn of the bilge. They are shaped by hewing and adzing, until the desired outside form is obtained, then hollowed out with an adze and gouges to the required thickness, which is the same as the outer edges of the center log at the lower faces of the side timbers. At the edges above the turn of the bilge, the logs will be reduced in thickness to about 1 inch. When the edges have been dressed, the logs are pinned together with iron dowels, usually about ½ inch in diameter, on about 6-inch centers. Locust treenails are also used: these are fox-tailed at the point so that when the pin is driven against the bottom of its hole, the wedge in the point will be driven home. Iron staples, or "dogs," are also used where it would be difficult to edge-pin the timbers; the dogs are usually on the inside of the boat. Wooden dovetails or "butterfly plates," secured in mortices by wooden pins, are also seen in some canoes. These cross the seams at right angles and are of locust or oak. Most of the canoes have a few heavy rod bolts driven athwartships, through-and-through, at bow and stern; the heads are upset over clench rings well countersunk. The logs are usually forced together in pinning by the use of chains and wedges.

Finishing the topsides varies among the builders and sections. The Poquoson canoe is built up of one or two tiers of short pieces edge-bolted to the bilge logs, and capped with two timbers, one on each side, having enough natural crook to allow them to be shaped to the deck line of the hull and run from end to end. The rising-strake canoe has its topsides framed up with short natural crook top-timbers and the lap-strake topside is bent around these in a single wide strake. In a well-built canoe, the short frames are usually carried down inside until they pass around the bilge. The practice in the Tilghman's Island type is either to piece up the topsides with short "chunks" or to plank up caravel on short frames; the latter system was used in the most recent canoes.

In all canoes, the objective was to get a heavy, strong, and lasting bottom, and for this purpose the log construction was ideal. Though the more advanced builders tried to hold to a half-model, the construction methods made the use of templates rather difficult, and actually few or none of the canoes were ever built accurately to their half-models. Yet the builders, "working by eye," were able to get the sides pretty much alike and fair. The log bottom has been known to last at least ninety years and to outwear four topsides.

The log canoes were half-decked; all types had washboards running the full length of the hull with the fore and aft decks formed by the joining of the side decks. The washboards are usually supported by a series of natural crook knees along each side; racing canoes sometimes have iron-rod brackets and tie-rods as well. In some canoes, particularly the racing boats, the decking may be laid in strips and a foredeck of some length has been used.

The five-log bottom is built in the same general manner as the three-log, but the second set of logs will be in the rise of floor in the five-log build. In the log bugeyes, as many as seven or even nine logs were used. The heavy bottoms and light topsides made much ballast unnecessary, and the canoes were unsinkable. Repairs to the bottom were made by cutting out a damaged or rotten spot and graving in a dutchman, or short "chunk," as required. Except for a few racing canoes, sail has been dispensed with, and gasoline motors have been installed. This requires the case to be removed and the slot plugged; the stern is bored for the shaft, and an aperture is cut into the deadwood aft, out of the center log. This necessitates dressing the stern at the aperture, so that its fore side will not be excessively wide.

The mast steps, particularly for the foremast, were tumbling blocks in which the step was hinged, or pivoted laterally, at its after end, so that it raised at the fore end when the mast was lowered. This kept the mast tenon in the step at all times. The masts were of pine and, on working canoes, were often very heavy. The step was either secured by a U-shaped timber, in which it fitted and pivoted, or was held between two fore-and-aft beds, or "runners," which gave lateral support and took the ends of the pivot bolt. The clamps were formed, in most canoes, so that the rake of the masts could be altered quickly and easily. These clamps were U-shaped plank secured to the top of the mast thwarts, the arms of the U being quite long. Blocks fitted the U, forward and abaft the mast, and were held in place by pins athwartships, through arms and blocks. Iron clamps of various types were also used.

The large canoes often had a cuddy forward; most of these fitted outside the coamings and rested on deck. The cuddies were secured by hooks and eyes inside and were unshipped in summer. The centerboards were usually large and were raised and lowered in the older boats by the popular iron handles.

There was a great variety in detail in the log canoes because the models used in any one area were never wholly standardized. Most of the working canoes had a straight rise of floor and very hard bilges, sometimes so hard as to resemble rounded chines. Usually the sides flared slightly above the water line amidships. Only the racing canoes were slack-bilged, and the midsection of some of these resembled that of the racing "sandbagger" sloop.

In most of the log canoes, the greatest beam is slightly forward of amidships; the deck line is carried full at the ends, so the side is rather straight in the middle third of the length. The amount of hollow in the ends varies a great deal; in some, the after sections in particular show a marked Y-form, while others show a V-shape there. Rocker in the keel line is relatively common in the old boats, and some hollow in the rising floors is also to be seen. The use of the long head has been confined to the Tilghman's Island type, and the cutwater is often very long and beaked, following the profile of the beak of the old Mediterranean galley.

The rig of the canoes has been the sprit leg-of-mutton rather consistently since the 1850's. A few of the large canoes experimented with gaff sails, particularly on the foremast where the gaff could be used in handling the deep-water tongs once employed. A few of the very large canoes tried the gaff-sail schooner-rig. The canoes using the gaff rig in any way were called "square-rigged," as opposed to the "sharp rig," which the leg-of-mutton is often called on the Bay. The sails are jib-headed and have no head blocks or clubs as a rule. Many of the canoes did use a sort of gunter pole at the

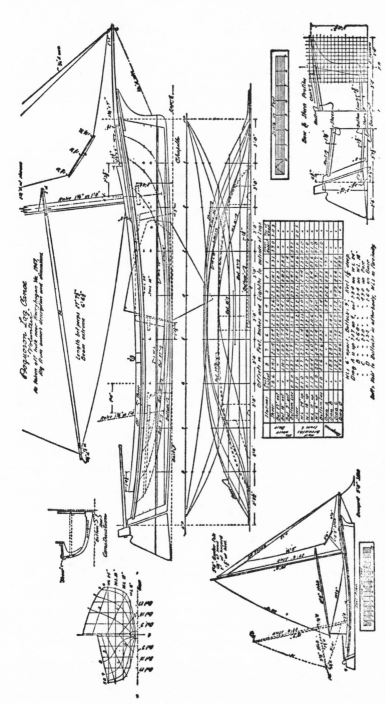

Fig. 107. Virginian log canoe, showing highly developed hull and rig. The mainmast shown in dotted lines in sail plan was only used on a long reach, according to the owner.

head of the sail. This was a short staff standing up-and-down the luff at the head, to allow the head of the sail to reach the masthead or above it without regard to the masthead sheave of the halyard. The end of the halyard was shifted on the staff as the sail stretched, and it has not been uncommon to see the head of the sail a foot or more above the masthead, as a result. The sails were cut in the same fashion as in the New Haven sharpies—the tack low and the clew high. Racing canoes used the vertical club at the clew, and some had two sprits as in racing sharpies.

The evidence is too scant to allow final conclusions to be drawn, but what can be offered so far indicates that the vertical clubs in the canoes appeared on the Bay long after they had been used in the sharpies. The canoes often have what is known as a "balanced jib"; this is a jib which is set flying and has a club the whole length of its foot. Instead of the tack being secured to the bowsprit end, the club is "balanced" by a line from the end of the bowsprit to the club so that the latter projects forward of the nose of the bowsprit as much as one-third the total length of the club. The balanced jib has continued in use in racing canoes, though many sailors are doubtful that it is a good sail; it had a very short popularity in working canoes. The balanced jib was apparently copied from the "sandbaggers" and appeared on the Bay in the late 1880's. The heel tackle of the sprits was often a simple tail in small canoes; in the larger ones the tackle set up to a rope grommet around the mast. In racing canoes, the sprit tackle is set up to an iron bail mounted on the mast; this is the usual mainsheet boom iron. The masts do not revolve as in the sharpie; in fact, the canoe masts are commonly square at the partners or clamps.

Figure 107 shows the lines and sail plan of a Poquoson canoe of a superior design; other plans are preserved in the Historic American Merchant Marine Survey collection in the United States National Museum. Figure 108 is the drawing of an example of the Nanticoke style with its striking stick-up rig.

Figure 109 is the plan of one of the most famous of the racing canoes, the *Jay Dee* or, as she appears to have been originally named, the *John D.* This was one of the only two known square-sterned log canoes and was built in 1931 by the late John B. Harrison, of Tilghman's Island, for John D. Williams, of Oxford, for whom the boat

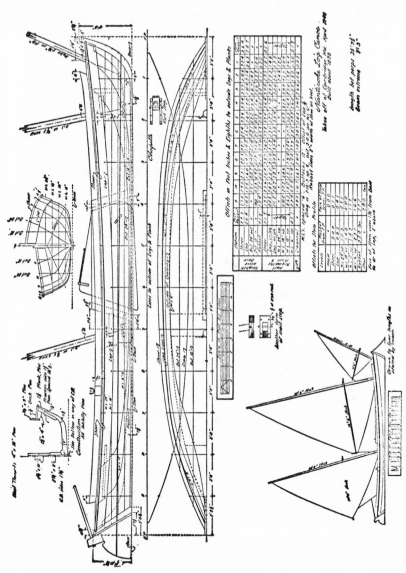

Fig. 108. A style of Chesapeake log canoe once very popular in the southern part of the Eastern Shore, called variously "Nanticoke," "Pocomoke," or "rising strake" canoe.

was named. The next year, the second square-sterned canoe was built by Harrison, the *Flying Cloud*. This canoe was soon altered to a sharp stern. These boats were built from a half-model, but neither followed it very closely. The *Flying Cloud* was deeper than the *Jay Dee* and had more flaring topsides, which make her the wider on deck of the two. Both canoes are less powerful than the half-model indicates. Though the *Cloud* was intended to beat the *Jay Dee*, she was not wholly successful, and if she had any superiority it was in a fresh breeze, when her greater beam and depth paid dividends. The *Jay Dee* cannot be said to be typical of the Tilghman's Island type in model, as she is a highly refined design. She is a very handsome boat and an extremely fast one, so her plans are well worth recording. The bottom is made of five logs and the topsides are planked; the middle log is about 7 inches thick alongside the false keel. The *Jay Dee* is probably the fastest log canoe ever built, and only by a remarkable method of handicapping can she be prevented from killing canoe racing on the Bay. She and the *Cloud* were large craft for racing canoes, and this has permitted an over-all length measurement to be employed in setting up the handicap, making it practically impossible for either boat to win races today.

The racing log-canoe is another example of over-sparring and over-canvasing, along with the racing sharpie, the sandbagger sloop, and the Bermuda dinghy. Most of the canoe builders apparently felt that the great rigs which had come into use had overpowered the boats, and that many of the boats, particularly the smaller canoes that had been working craft, would be faster all round with smaller rigs. This is probably true, but the big rigs were persisted in and have had an unexpected result. Where the working canoe with a normal rig had been a rather inexpensive boat to race and maintain, the huge racing rigs of such boats as the *Jay Dee* were found very costly, and so log-canoe racing became a spectacular sport for wealthy men alone. Attempts to revive log-canoe racing have proven very difficult as a result, but the basic cause of this does not seem to have been recognized in recent years by the sponsors of log-canoe racing.

The construction of the log canoe is now a thing of the past, for there are very few men who have the knowledge and manual

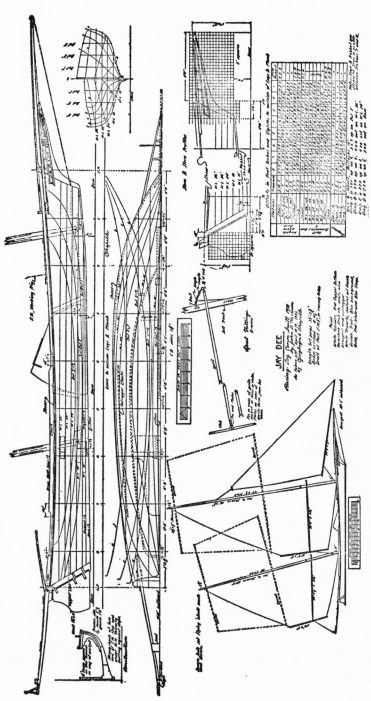

Fig. 109. Plan of one of the fastest and finest of the Chesapeake Bay racing log canoes and the first built with a transom stern. The profile above LWL represents a Tilghman Island canoe in most respects, but the lines are very different from those of the working canoe of this type. This canoe is an out-and-out racing machine when sailing with the rig shown here.

skill to build such craft. There have been discussions as to the practical possibilities of building these craft on the strip-planking system. So far, nothing has actually been attempted in the way of such construction, and the existing racing rules bar any but log-built canoes. It seems reasonable to suppose, however, that strip-built canoes employing the same lines and the heavy bottom of the log boats would be a practical solution for continuing the type as a racing class in the future.

The sprit booms and clubs of the racing canoes are often awkwardly handled today when making sail. It is common to see the mainsail hoisted and followed by a struggle to ship the sprit, while the vertical club thrashes about in a fresh breeze. The old practice at New Haven and on the Bay was first to stretch the foot of the sail and lay the club on deck athwartship the hull. The sprit was then shipped, but not set up, as this would prevent hoisting the sail. Many of the old boatmen had a short tail, or lanyard, secured to the outboard end of the sprit—usually it passed through a hole in the stick and was made fast there with stop-knots—which was used to lash the club securely to the end of the sprit. This made it impossible for the club to leave the sprit in hoisting sail. The sail was now hoisted, and finally the sprit tackle was set up very hard.

Tracks are often employed on the masts in racing canoes, but these may be damaged by the sprit when the sail is broad off; lacing or mast hoops are safer and more practical with this form of sail. The double sprit is now out of use, and only single sprits are used. The huge balanced jib is still used, and its pull usually causes the masts to bend a great deal, which spoils the set of the racing sails to windward in a fresh breeze. It would appear that some of the canoes would work better to windward were the jib not used, and the additional sail placed in the leg-of-muttons, if area must be maintained.

The Chesapeake Bay log canoes are, as a class, thoroughbred sailing craft, and it is a great pity that the expensive and impractical racing machine has been allowed to dominate the type for pleasure sailing. As has been proven in the alteration made in the *Flying Cloud* to make her an afternoon sailer and week-ender, these boats are much faster on most points of sailing than similar yachts and are, in addition, great beauties.

CHAPTER 7

THE Newcomer, THE V-bottom

T HE RISE of the V-bottomed hull-form in America came late in the nineteenth century, yet there is little information on its origin and evolution. The earliest known use in America of a V-bottom (in which a straight rise of floor is combined with straight sides, so that an angular bilge, or chine, is formed) occurred on Lake Champlain and on the St. Lawrence during the Revolution. Some of the "gondolas" built as gunboats by the Americans appear to have had this form, for Arnold's specifications show this feature. Also a *radeau*, or scow, built by the British, had the same rise in floors and chine construction. The rise in the floors was very slight in each case, and, in Arnold's design, it appears that the same angle of rise was carried the whole length of the bottom, so that rabbet and chines came to the same point at the heel of the stem—and since Arnold's specifications called for a double-ender —at the sternpost as well. For the lack of an exact type name for such a bottom, it will be referred to hereafter as a "modified sharpie" hull-form.

No other use of a V-bottom in America has been discovered, with the exception of one reference which suggests that the V-bottom appeared at New York, or in the vicinity, around the year 1860. There is little to support an assumption that the V-bottom, or "skipjack," as it came to be called, was an outgrowth of the sharpie, logical though this may appear. It is true that such a development could be traced in the career of one builder, Clapham, but neither he (nor anyone contemporary with him) ever claimed that he originated the V-bottom. His activities in the support of his "Nonpareil" sharpies did lead to one piece of evidence that has been referred to above. A letter addressed by a member of a noted family of yachtsmen to the editor of *Forest & Stream*, published in October, 1880, says that "the type was tried twenty years ago" and that it "has been condemned through practical experience." The quotation not only suggests that the V-bottom reappeared about 1860 but also how wrong the judgment of a yachtsman can be.

In 1877, the same magazine published a description of a skipjack to help amateur builders, and the editor, Kunhardt, later reprinted this in his book *Small Yachts*. Though the description went into much detail about the construction, a complete set of plans was not published. It has been found that the source of this description was a contributor to *Forest & Stream* and that a plan was sent in. Figure 110, which is a redrawing of the original, shows that the boat originated somewhere on Long Island Sound. The boat is a modification of the New York model of sloop, in which the chine is substituted for the round bilge. As can be seen in the plan, the construction resembles that used today in small yachts, the bottom being planked fore and aft over regular frames; but the old boat had no chine logs.

Clapham, writing in 1880, refers to the skipjacks as being very wide, with sharp rise of floor the full length of the bottom, jib-and-mainsail rigged, heavily canvased, and with a reputation for being fast and weatherly. He seems to have known the type very well and to have adapted its features, to some extent, in a deliberate attempt to improve the sharpie as a cruising yacht of large accommodation. The *Forest & Stream* correspondents also show that the skipjack was being built on the Gulf of Mexico before 1886, where the Creole builders were turning out V-bottomed cats and luggers.

The Fish Commission papers are silent on this form of hull until the late 1880's, when reference is made to V-bottomed sloops being built at Martha's Vineyard. There is a half-model of one of these, built in 1885, in the Watercraft Collection. The lines of the half-

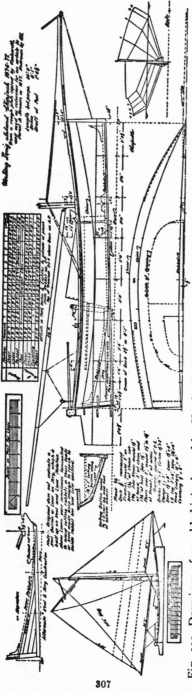

Fig. 110. Drawings of an old skipjack used by Kunhardt for his instructions on building this type in *Forest & Stream* magazine in 1877, showing hull-form, construction, and rig then in use.

model are shown in Figure 111. This was also for a jib-and-mainsail boat, and the drawing shows reconstruction based upon descriptions of these craft. The catalogue of the Watercraft Collection states that these V-bottoms were called "corner boats" at Provincetown, where the type was also used. The lines of the sole example available show that this design, at least, was round-bilged forward and V-bottomed aft. The chine dies out just forward of amidships and this would indicate the boat to have been built with sawn frames. From other sources of a fragmentary nature it is evident that boats

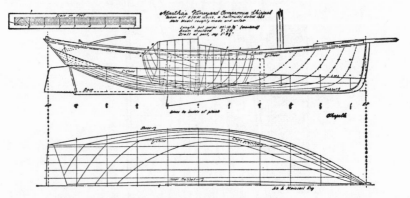

Fig. 111. Combination V-bottomed and round-bottomed sloop, once used in the vicinity of Vineyard Sound for fishing.

much like that shown in Figure 110 were built at Martha's Vineyard, before 1881. Whether or not this form of hull originated there cannot yet be established, but such sources of information as have come to light point toward this area as the place of origin of the skipjack. The name "skipjack" has long been applied to bluefish, and some other fish that leap on the surface, and has often been used as the name of an individual boat. It seems very probable therefore that the use of "skipjack" as a type-name for V-bottomed craft originated in some early boat of this name on the V-bottomed model. Certainly, the name is of northern origin. The V-bottomed hull-form did not win widespread approval in New England and New York waters in the 1880's.

Sometime late in the 1880's, the skipjack was taken up by the Chesapeake Bay boatbuilders, and, from this time on, the Bay became the acknowledged home of the V-bottom. The name "skipjack" is known on the Bay, but is used most commonly as a rig-name, meaning a jib-headed mainsail and a jib such as is now carried by the one-masted oyster dredges there. Thus, the boatmen speak of a round-bottomed sloop with this style of sail plan as a "skipjack," but if she is V-bottomed she is a "bateau" or a "two-sail bateau." A V-bottomed hull rigged as a bugeye was a "three-sail bateau." A skiff, V-bottomed and with a single leg-of-mutton, is sometimes called a "one-sail bateau." It seems probable that the use of the name "two-sail bateau" is now corrupt and that it originally was applied to a two-masted leg-of-mutton rig without a headsail.

Though the true V-bottom does not appear to have developed on the Chesapeake until late in the 1880's, the sharpie type existed there at least as early as the 1870's, and perhaps as early as 1860. These flat-bottomed sailing craft may have arisen from modifications of the common flat-bottomed rowing skiff. But there is also a possibility that the New Haven sharpie, in its drift southward in the 1870's, may have lodged there temporarily. A V-bottomed skiff, once built at Tangier Island, showed strong resemblance to the Connecticut type in having a straight stem and the vertically staved, round stern. The Tangier boat, in fact, looked very much like the sharpie and could be distinguished only by her V-bottom and slightly raking masts. In the early 1880's a square-sterned, two-masted, flat-bottomed sharpie was in use at Cambridge; some old photographs of oystermen at work in the Choptank show these boats very clearly. They were apparently between 20 and 26 feet long and had wide washboards reaching to the transom. The stem was raking and curved in profile, and the transom also raked rather sharply. Center-boards are shown; the rig is that of a two-masted log canoe without a headsail and with sharply raking masts.

The Flattie

Another style of boat hull that appeared in the Chesapeake was the flattie, a sloop-rigged sharpie hull having some dead rise aft, in the run. This form of boat was used originally for carrying produce on the Maryland and Virginia tidewater streams and, to a limited extent, in oystering, crabbing, and duck-hunting. The flattie cannot be traced back very far, but something of the kind seems to have existed in Virginia waters before the Civil War. "Flattie" has usually been used in America to designate a wide sharpie hull with a jib-and-mainsail rig; this type of boat was in use in the Carolinas in the early 1880's and was appearing in Florida and Gulf waters at about this time. The Chesapeake flattie was also called the "Hampton flattie," which suggests the possibility that its first use on the Bay occurred in the vicinity of Hampton, Virginia, near Newport News. Hall's notes show that such craft were much used by Negro boatmen. Kunhardt, in his account of his cruise to the Carolina Sounds in the catboat *Coot* in 1882–83, gives sketches of the flatties, and he states they were used then in the Carolinas, as well as in the Chesapeake area, for shoal-water fishing and gunning.

Kunhardt's articles in *Forest & Stream* show only that the type existed, and his sketch indicates a half-decked boat. But later, in the enlarged edition of his *Small Yachts*, published in 1891, he gave a full description, accompanied by a complete set of plans, of a boat of this type. His example appears to have been drawn with suitable modifications in arrangement to make the boat useful as a yacht, but he does refer at some length to the working-boats of the type. He shows that most of the latter had no bowsprit and had the jib tacked to the stemhead; this rig was a forerunner of the "knockabout" rig that later became so popular. Kunhardt stated that the flattie was usually between 16 and 30 feet in length.

The flattie went out of popularity on the Bay in the 1890's, but in exploring the Eastern Shore in 1940–41 I found that this type had remained in use well into the present century on the eastern side of Bishop's Head, on Fishing Bay, and on the Nanticoke River. Not only were the older watermen acquainted with the type, but I was directed to the remains of a number of the boats, mostly of the skiff size. However, one hulk near Elliot, a small and rather isolated village on the eastern side of Fishing Bay, not only represented a larger class of the flattie but also was in such shape that a fairly satisfactory plan could be made. The result of this discovery is shown in Figure 112; the hull is as measured from the remains, and the rig is restored from Kunhardt's description, sketch, and plans.

The Elliot boat differs from Kunhardt's in a few important particulars—she has a great deal more sheer and fore-and-aft rocker, a much deeper skeg, and a work-boat deck plan. She is also cross-planked forward and herringboned aft, whereas Kunhardt shows his boat planked fore and aft the whole length of the bottom, with a complete framing system. He also shows a plank keelson, whereas the

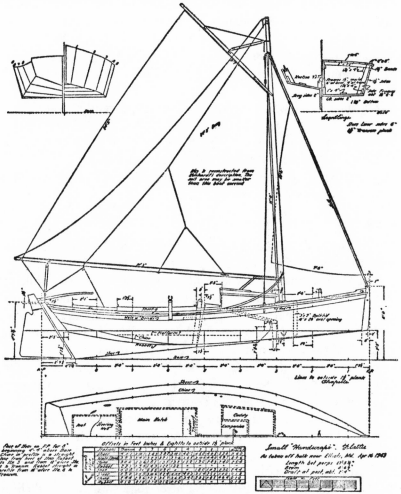

Fig. 112. An old Chesapeake "flattie" sloop, forerunner of the bateau or skipjack on Chesapeake Bay.

Elliot boat had a hewn keelson, about 7 inches square, running from the fore end of the centerboard case to the transom.

No history of the Elliot boat could be obtained; local men said similar boats were used at Bishop's Head for oystering and crabbing as late as 1910, or perhaps later, and that some were fitted with bow-sprits. As far as one may judge the age of a boat by her appearance and condition, the hull shown in Figure 112 must have been built in the late 1880's or early 90's. The arrangement and fittings showed that she had been used as an oyster dredge in the classification known as a "handscraper." This name was applied to dredge boats using manually operated "winders," or winches, to haul the dredge, and so the handscraper was a small boat, in most cases under 40 feet in length.

The model of the Chesapeake flattie was apparently created in an effort to produce a wide sharpie that would sail well. A wide, flat-bottomed hull is often slow when loaded, and, when paying off on a new tack, the boat falls off badly before gathering headway. This may lead to a knockdown or capsize in a fresh breeze, if the handling is careless or slow. Someone had made the discovery that dead rise aft helped such craft, and so the cheap but efficient flattie model developed.

The use of dead rise in the flattie seems to have been confined to the Bay and to the boats turned out by one northern builder, Clapham. The latter had used dead rise at bow and stern, while re-taining a flat bottom amidships, in the early stages of development of his Nonpareil sharpies. Clapham had published his ideas in *Forest & Stream* in the early 1880's but did not claim to have originated the use of dead rise in this manner. There can be, as yet, no statement of where and when the flattie of the Chesapeake model originated. The flattie sloops in New York Bay and in the Carolinas were en-tirely flat-bottomed, as far as is known.

The construction of the flattie was that of a sharpie forward. The run was formed by a heavy keelson sawn to profile, which also formed the centerboard case logs. The herringboned planking of the bottom began at the after end of the centerboard slot, where there was a very wide plank, whose after edge was cut to a shallow V with its apex facing forward and on the centerline of the hull. In the Elliot hulk this plank was 23 inches wide. From this strake, the herringbone began with four tapered strakes which allowed the required angle in the bottom planking to be reached quickly, and after these the strakes were parallel-sided, with edges parallel to the lines formed by the bottom edge of the transom.

Transverse strength in the hull was obtained by a heavy bulkhead just forward of the mast; this was made up of 3-inch stuff edge-bolted. An oval opening allowed egress to the forepeak. A heavy tie-rod was placed between the mast and the bulkhead. The boat was heavily and roughly built of loblolly pine and was iron-fastened. The side planking was not spiled, and the sheer was finished off by a narrow walepiece which had some edge-bolts in the upper strakes of the sides. The boat had been repaired, and it was impossible to decide whether or not there had ever been any great changes in her appearance from the time she was launched.

The Bishop's Head fishermen stated that some of the flatties were given jib-headed mainsails, but that the gaff sail had been much used there. Kunhardt shows that some of the flatties in his time had a diamond-shaped panel painted on their transoms and these had no outside sternpost. The flatties were usually rather short-canvased and were not as fast as the later bateaux. Their worst point of sailing was to windward in a short sea; Kunhardt blames this on the great beam, but it is probable that most of the flatties were too full forward, just as were some of the early bateaux which showed similar weaknesses. The flatties represent a more burdensome type than the true sharpie and stand about halfway in cost between the latter and the skipjack. They have proven to be swift sailers when properly canvased.

A number of examples of skiffs built to the flattie model were found in the vicinity of Bishop's Head in 1941–43, but most were in too advanced a state of disintegration to allow plans to be made. However, two were found that could be used, and the plans of one of these are given in Figure 113, which shows a half-decked skiff with the stick-up rig favored in this class of small boat. The model and construction of the hull have already been described for the large flattie, and the rig has been treated in the discussion of the log canoe. These stick-up rigged flattie skiffs were highly regarded and did not go wholly out of use until the motorboat drove sail out. The skiffs were particularly approved of for weatherliness in a fresh wind, and some were said to be able to go to windward in strong winds under the stick-up sail alone, which seems impossible theoretically.

The V-bottomed hull appears to have had intense development in the southern counties of Maryland's Eastern Shore and ranged in size from skiffs to huge sloops about 60 feet between perpendiculars. Some bateaux have been built on the western side of the Bay and at its head, but these are relatively few in number and were, in addition, usually built by "shoremen." In relatively recent times,

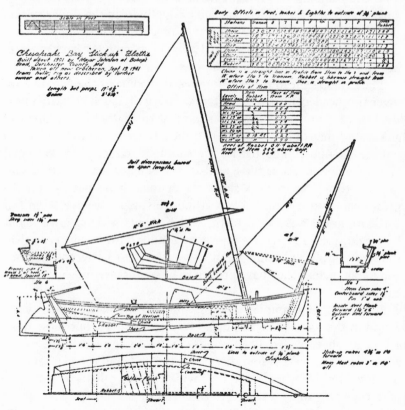

Fig. 113. Eastern Shore stick-up skiff, flattie model.

such craft have been built in great numbers in Accomac County, the northernmost of the Virginia counties on the Eastern Shore. The building centers for these craft were at Bishop's Head and neighboring islands in Dorchester County, on the east side of the Nanticoke and at the mouth of the Wicomico in Wicomico County, and at Deal Island, Oriole, and Chance in Somerset County, Maryland. Only one distinct type was produced on the Western Shore in Virginia—the Potomac dory boat, which was built extensively on the peninsula between the Potomac and the Rappahannock. This was a two-masted boat on the model of the sloop shown in Figure 113; a canoe rig was carried which rarely had a bowsprit.

The northern method of building the V-bottom was used in only a few of the Chesapeake Bay V-bottomed craft. The northern system required a complete frame system, and the bottom plank was put on fore and aft, as is still done in many small yachts of this hull-form. To allow this build, the hull must adhere to certain fundamental rules, and the chine must have quite a sweep in profile forward so that it reaches high on the stem. This feature, which is well shown in Figure 110, allows the plank to reach the stempost without a great twist being formed in the lower strakes. The alternate model is the modified sharpie in which there is no forefoot below the chines and the keel meets the latter at the stem. The Potomac dory boat was on the first model; the skiffs and half-decked, one-masted boats built at Smith's Island, in the vicinity of Crisfield and in Accomac County, often were on the latter model. The rest of the boats were cross-planked on the bottom and employed logs or chunks at the bow, in two methods, which could be dubbed to form the V-forefoot. The logs were later discontinued, and in recent times the forefoot is planked with thick, tapered, vertical staving, which is dubbed fair and smooth after being secured. The vertical staving has been made possible by the deeper forefoot used in the modern V-bottomed, powered work-boats of the Bay, and in some of the sailing bateaux, particularly those built in Accomac County.

The small bateaux and skiffs, which concern us here, show that the earlier boats had the forefoot formed of short balks of timber laid athwartships at the bow. These were thick enough to reach from the heel of the stem to the chines. They were edge-bolted together and then hewn to the required dead rise at the bow, and, finally, the ends were fastened to the chine logs. The keelson employed in these boats was a selected timber whose shape permitted it to be hewn to the rabbet profile of the bottom, fore and aft. This was shaped deep enough, forward, to notch over the bow "chunks" inboard in most cases. The log bow timbers were carried aft far enough to allow plank to be used on the bottom, say from 30 inches in a small boat to 4 or more feet in a large one. The last "chunk" was usually rabbeted to take the edge of the first bottom plank. This was a tapered plank, as were the next few, so that the remaining bottom planks could be put on parallel-sided, with their edges paralleling the bottom line of the transom. In practice, the lowest strakes of the sides were selected, and these were bent over molds upside down. The chine log was fitted, the transom serving as the aftermost mold. The keelson was then set in place and the bottom planked, beginning at the stern. When the change in dead rise forward showed that a twist would soon be required in the cross planks, the log forefoot was placed and hewn. Next, the bottom was closed in by means of the tapered planks just mentioned and the whole dressed smooth. Then the hull was righted and the rest of the building followed.

The keelson is sometimes rabbeted for the bottom plank, or may be merely beveled, with the bottom plank butted against the skeg and foregripe shoe. The bottom planks are fitted with great care so that the bottom does not need caulking; at the chines wicking or hemp marline is laid on the chine plank edges and on the chine log before the bottom planks are put on. The side planking is not spiled but is put on sharpie fashion, allowing the ends to run off at the wales if necessary and piecing up the sheer at the bow and stern by short "stealers," whose inboard ends are notched into the strakes below. The side frames are put in after the side plank is in place; in large boats the side plank is often edge-bolted as well as framed. The frames are short, as in a sharpie, but most Bay builders set the frames on edge and notch each one over the chine log, so the heel reaches the inside of the bottom plank. The deck beams are supported by the usual clamps placed inside the frames near the heads.

The skeg, foregripe shoe, and centerboard slot are all the same siding, so the shoe does not reach abaft the fore end of the centerboard slot, while the skeg stops at the after end of the slot. Many boats have side pieces fitted along the slot to give a smooth keel line; these are placed in finishing the bottom. The stem is formed of an apron and the cutwater is applied after the planking is completed. Loblolly pine is employed throughout. The long-head, if used, is made up of plank and knees, edge-bolted. The transom is edge-bolted and usually has nailing pieces at the sides in place of a transom frame.

The strength of the bottom is obtained by two or more heavy timbers laid over the keelson inside, athwartships, the ends are kneed into the sides of the hull, and the cross-timber is bolted or drifted to the keelson. These are called "strongbacks," and one is placed near the mast, at one of the partners, and another is just abaft the centerboard case in most boats. In large bateaux, a third one may be located farther aft. At the strongback at the mast, a tie-rod, set up by a turnbuckle link at the hull centerline, is often used; this is run athwartships through the sheer strake, the knees of the strong-back, and, sometimes, through the clamps. The outboard ends are upset over clench rings countersunk into the sheer strake or "wale." Most of the large bateaux have a thick sheer strake, or wale plank, which, locally, is called the "bends." The details of construction can be seen in the drawings and require no more description.

Whether or not the log bow construction was a local develop-ment is uncertain. This much can be said, however: Clapham had publicized this form of bow in *Forest & Stream* in the early 1880's, as it was a feature of his first Nonpareil sharpies. It is possible, there-fore, that the log bow was copied on the Bay and did not originate there. On the other hand, it is not proved that the construction of the log bow of the Nonpareil sharpie was original with Clapham. The log bow would be a normal and logical step in the addition of dead rise in a sharpie hull in any case.

The second variation in the use of balk timber in the forefoot in Bay V-bottomed craft was to carry the deep keelson to the stem and to place short, squared timbers on each side of it, running fore-and-aft, edge-bolting these to the keelson, and then dubbing the whole to the desired form. This method gradually replaced the cross-logs in Maryland and remained in use as long as the forefoot was shallow enough to permit it.

The Maryland bateaux held consistently to a general model in which the dead rise was very moderate and the forefoot, below the chines, was quite shallow. The chine profile followed New Haven sharpie practice in being straight, or almost straight, for some dis-tance abaft the stem. The greater number of builders modeled the hull so that the chine was immersed forward and did not curve up-ward in the modern yacht fashion. This appears to be useful in ob-taining speed in a sailing boat of the V-bottomed form, but it can be taken advantage of only when the Maryland method of bottom construction is used. In many of the early Maryland-built bateaux, the bottom was practically flat amidships; dead rise was soon used here, and the difference in rise of the floor abaft the midsection became less marked about 1895. This seems to indicate that the bateaux developed out of the flattie on the Chesapeake at least.

Bay Skiffs

About fourteen distinct types of V-bottomed sailing skiffs were produced on the Chesapeake Bay between 1890 and 1920. Each locality had its popular model and rig. I have shown some of these types in an article in *Yachting*, June and October 1943, and so there is no need to explore the whole range of the type here. In addition to the flattie skiff, there were three types of double-enders having the V-bottom, three two-masted skiffs, one jib-and-mainsail skiff, and the rest were one-mast, one-sail boats having square sterns. There were also at least four flat-bottomed types.

Figure 114 shows one of the Bay skiffs of the larger class. This was a style of hull and rig that shared popularity with the flattie at Bishop's Head, and a number of this type of boat still exist in rotting hulks. The model was one of the best for open-water work. Local tradition has it that these boats were introduced by William Reeves, a ship carpenter born in Nova Scotia, who settled at Wingate and built both skiffs and bateaux of a superior class. He also built some framed bugeyes and a few sloops. His skiffs show he was a skillful carpenter with an excellent eye for design.

The boat shown in Figure 114 is very similar to one by this builder included in the *Yachting* article, but the latter boat has a shorter and steeper run. Like nearly all of the Bay skiffs, the construction is heavy, almost massive, and so these boats have lasted very well. The one-sail skiffs were single-handers and were commonly very smart sailers, though not heavily canvased.

Figure 115 shows another skiff, which is a modified sharpie hull-form that has been very popular about Crisfield and at Smith Island as well as in the Virginia Eastern Shore waters. The example shown is not typical of the larger boats of this model, which are often very low-sided and have very little flare in the sides, particularly those

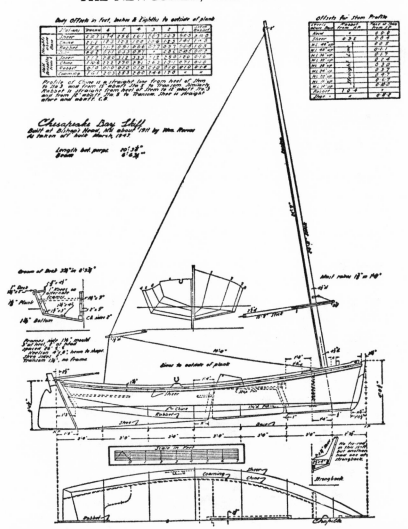

Fig. 114. Tonging skiff of a size and type once popular on the Eastern Shore of Maryland.

built near Crisfield. The small skiffs are on the model shown, and this form has become popular all around the Bay. Though the hull is one that could be planked fore and aft, most builders are using herringbone cross-planking. A similar skiff, in which the sides tumbled home, was built at Smith's Island. This style of boat was al-

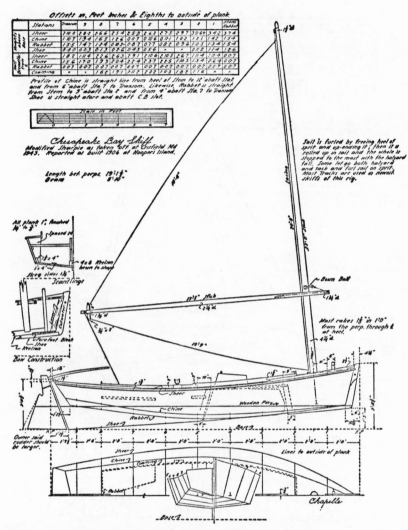

Fig. 115. Modified sharpie skiff, the last sailing model to be very popular on the Chesapeake.

ways planked fore and aft on the bottom like the northern skip-jacks, and, as was the case in most boats built in this manner, there were no chine logs employed.

This modified sharpie model is one that can be traced back to the time of the American Revolution, as has been stated earlier, yet there is no evidence that suggests the build has had continuous existence since that time. Some of the Bay skiff builders are enthusiastic about this form and have interesting theories of how it should be formed. When a very fast boat is desired for pleasure sailing and racing, the stern is made deep and an attempt is made to maintain a constant angle of dead rise from amidships to the stern. The bow chines are, as usual in sharpie hulls, quite straight in profile. When fitted with a jib, these skiffs often have a deep foregripe, or bow fin. The working skiffs usually had a transom formed so that the chines were high; this allowed a load to be carried without excessive drag or change in fore-and-aft trim. The example in Figure 115 is without the very high chines aft, but her stern is not as deep as in a racing skiff.

The construction of this form of hull is far easier than the usual skipjack, since there is no forefoot to be staved or hewn from logs, or that requires steaming of garboards to plank. The majority of the Bay builders employing the herringbone system in this model do use a thick plank at the forefoot; this is flat on top from chine to chine, and the keelson is lapped over it on the inside. When the boat is planked, this thick plank is dressed to the dead rise formed at the bow. In some skiffs the keelson does not reach the stem, the forefoot block or plank serving to join the two. The latter, sometimes as long as 24 inches in a 20-foot boat, is made of two pieces, though the common practice is to make the piece of a single plank about 12 to 14 inches wide, with the grain athwartship. In former years, some skiffs of this model, and some with the usual deep forefoot, had their entire bottom made of thick stuff laid athwartships and dubbed to dead rise. This gave a flat bottom inside and a V outside; the advantage was a very strong and lasting bottom whose weight served as ballast, as in the log canoes. The bottom was edge-fastened, but otherwise put on as in a sharpie. This form of bottom has now gone out of use.

Some of these skiffs employ an unusual method of making the garboard seams and the chines tight which has been used again in recent years, in Bay motorboats. In this method, a length of soldering or lead wire is placed along the keelson, or garboard rabbet, and also along the chines, in place of the usual marline or wicking. The plank is then nailed in place, and, after being secured, the bottom plank is seated on the wire by pounding it with a maul and an oak block; the latter is used to protect the bottom from the maul. Then the nails are set with a nail-set. This method is said to give a tight seam that lasts indefinitely, but it is practical only when the bottom is of cedar or juniper or other rather soft wood. Recently, some builders have been substituting strips of flat lead for soldering wire in an effort to form seams that would be tight for a very long time.

The rig of the modified sharpie model of skiff is commonly a single leg-of-mutton as in Figure 115; only a few skiffs built for racing have jibs. Many of the boats have little or no rake in the masts. They employ a short plank club at the clew and the sprit-end is often lashed to this club. The sail is furled by unreeving the heel rope and up-ending the sprit so its heel is aloft, then the sail is rolled around the sprit until all is against the mast, where the halyard is spiraled around mast and sail to secure the latter. The halyard usually leads through a dumb sheave at the masthead, and the sail is laced to the mast. The whole rig may be easily unshipped if the boat is laid up for any length of time. The sails are of drill. The usual reeving of the heel rope of the sprit is shown in the drawing.

No fixed proportion of beam to length exists in the modified sharpie model; it varies with the builder and locality. In the vicinity of Crisfield and in Accomac County, Virginia, the boats are often very beamy with very low sides that have little or no flare amidships. The Smith Island skiffs are commonly under one-third the length in beam. The skiffs under 20 feet in length are generally much like Figure 115 in model and proportion, while the larger skiffs follow the Crisfield style in these matters. The latter often have the characteristic open rail formed of a log rail and a cap separated by short iron-pipe spacers, through which the rail bolts are driven. The older skiffs, such as the one shown, often had their greatest beam amidships, or even a little afore, but in recent times the beam has been moved farther aft, and the bows are often unpleasantly wedge-shaped and without flare. Since some of these newer skiffs also lack sheer, they are sometimes very ugly craft.

The Skipjack

The types of boat most commonly connected with the Chesapeake, in the minds of yachtsmen, are the bugeye and the skipjack. The latter, under the name of "bateau," ranged in size from boats between 22 and 28 feet over the deck to huge sloops, as has been mentioned, of about 60 feet tonnage length. Most of these were jib-and-mainsail rigged with the jib-headed mainsail laced to the boom and a very short club on the foot of the jib. A few—the "three-sail bateaux"—were bugeye-rigged. The rake of the masts, in all of these craft, was usually very great. All were fitted with the long

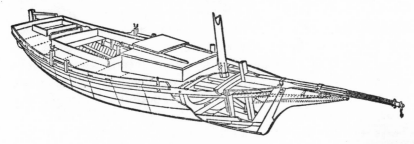

Bateau *Messenger*

head of the bugeye and the Chesapeake Bay schooner. The large craft were decked and were like the large coasting sloops of the middle nineteenth century in that they had a trunk aft and a forecastle hatch forward, with the large cargo hatch amidships. The smaller boats, at the turn of the present century, were decked with a small trunk forward, a cargo hatch amidships, and a large standing-well, extending from a foot or two abaft the cargo hatch to within a few feet of the transom. In the larger boats, the standing-well had a watertight floor above the load water line, which allowed lead-pipe scuppers to be used to make the well self-bailing. In those days the "winders" or dredge-winches were manually operated and were mounted on the deck just abaft the cargo, or main, hatch. The operator stood in the well and the lower level brought his head below the main boom, and placed him at a better height to use the winders. When power-driven winders came into use, most of the boats were raised in freeboard to allow for carrying the additional weight of the massive engines required. All were then decked flush fore and aft, and some had trunk cabins placed aft instead of the old standing-wells, which were removed. The bateaux of this class were between 36 and 45 feet on deck.

The smallest bateaux, not exceeding 32 feet in hull-length, were half-decked; these had a short foredeck and wide washboards, or covering boards, running to the stern along the sides. Some had the canoe's trunk cabin, which could be unshipped and left ashore in summer. These small craft were used for tonging, or even dredging, oysters and for crabbing. They had long-heads and were miniatures of the large bateaux in hull and rig.

In another class were the "oyster pirates." These were fast bateaux that dredged on oyster beds reserved by law for tonging. The poachers often operated at night and were sometimes called "night scrapers." Speed was required to evade the police vessels, which were sloops, schooners, and bugeyes manned by State conservation inspectors with police powers. The poachers used any fast boat available, just as they do today, but some whose pleasure it was to pursue the business regularly had special fast bateaux built. These were usually rather small, from 32 to 36 feet in length, and were often less beamy, in proportion to length, than the honest handscraper.

Figure 116 shows an example of a boat built near Oriole, Maryland, about 1900, for a poacher. In this work she was renamed whenever she came under enough suspicion to be notorious. On the death of the owner she was sold and was used as a pleasure boat —named the *Messenger*—for some years until she was blown up by a gasoline explosion in 1942. The drawings show the common form of fast bateaux and the characteristics in arrangement and rig of most of the poachers, and of the honest handscrapers as well.

The lines follow the general rules for the model of the Maryland bateaux, except in being sharper forward and with a longer run than would be used in most of the type. The beam is under one-third the length, whereas most of the boats would have at least this proportion of beam. The low sides were desired, as it made handling the dredge much easier and faster than if the freeboard were greater. The long-head is detailed on the plans to show just how it was constructed; this is now an almost forgotten art even on the

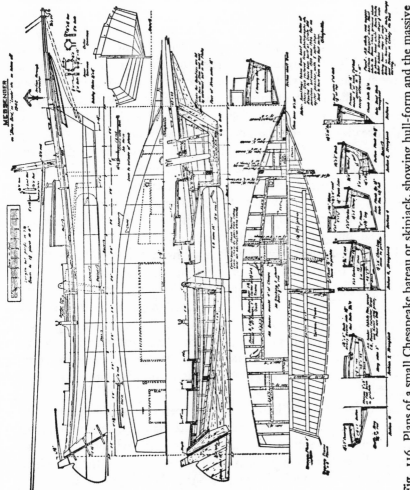

Fig. 116. Plans of a small Chesapeake bateau or skipjack, showing hull-form and the massive construction that has enabled many of these boats to last fifty years or more of hard service. (See Appendix for offsets and dimensions.)

Eastern Shore. It will be noted that the bowsprit does not follow the rise of sheer but comes in almost parallel to the water line. This was a characteristic of the old Bay craft; in later years it has been the practice to stive the bowsprit, and most bateaux now follow the newer fashion.

The construction shown is that already described and is typical of the old Maryland Eastern Shore practice, using the herringbone system with log-forefoot in putting on the bottom plank. Some of the bateaux, particularly the large craft, have counter sterns but these served no useful purpose and added greatly to the cost of construction. A few were built with round sterns like a sharpie or built bread-and-butter fashion, out of edge-bolted timbers hewn to shape. The boats were usually built throughout of the heart-wood of old-growth, or virgin loblolly, pine, except that white oak was used for the centerboard, skeg, and rudder, and, in a few, for the stem apron and cutwater. The head rails of the long-head were also of white oak. Juniper was sometimes used for deck plank and was liked, but was considered expensive.

The boats were massively built to withstand the enormous strains of hauling the dredge and of carrying the heavy rig in winter weather. The sides were edge-bolted along the sheer, where the "bends," or thick wale pieces, were secured to the strakes below. The last plank of the bottom at the transom projected aft and was rounded; the extreme rake of the stern often requires this, because beveling the plank with the face of the stern would make fastening weak, by cutting away too much of the plank edge under the transom.

The rig is very well known and has been discussed in print many times. It is large in area to give power to haul the dredge over the bottom, and so reefing is necessary as soon as the wind becomes very strong. The jib is usually taken in, in heavy winds, as the boats haul their dredge best with a strong weather helm. The boats can be capsized and so the crews do not hesitate to tuck in a reef when the rail begins to go under. It is very necessary that the boats hold on well when close-hauled. They usually dredge on a reach and must be able to retrace their course very closely each time they cross the oyster "rocks" so that they make a clean sweep. If a boat drifts to leeward, a competitor would not hesitate to cut in on her.

The boats, therefore, have well-cut sails and a very large center-board. The sails are fitted with lazy jacks so that they may be lowered quickly, without furling. Figure 117 shows the details of the rig that are quite typical.

The centerboards of the dredging bateaux are fitted so that, when hauled up, they extend some distance below the keel but, if an

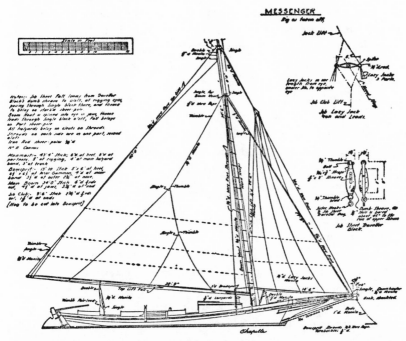

Fig. 117. Sail plan of the Chesapeake Bay bateau *Messenger*, showing typical rigging characteristics of the type.

obstruction is hit, the board can rise in the case. The purpose of this is to enable the boat to sail on the wind in water so shoal that the normal methods of hinging the board would not give enough area below the keel to allow sailing close-hauled. To permit the board to take the required position, the lower fore corner is well rounded, and, instead of a hole for the pivot bolt, there is a slanting slot; the board is somewhat shorter than the slot and case inside. Thus, the board can move up and down and fore and aft a slight amount, when it is hauled up. The boards are not ballasted and for submerging depend upon the weight of their edge-bolting and on being water-soaked. Hence, when the boats are being hauled, for painting and repairs, the board is dropped out of the case afloat and kept in the water, except for the short time necessary to paint it.

The case is so built that a forward section of the cap is removable. Here there is an eye-bolt on the top of the board for a line to be attached. The pivot pin is knocked out, the holes are quickly plugged, and then the board may be dropped out of the case by use of the line to the fore end and the centerboard lanyard. The board is pulled out from underneath the boat by a boat hook, or pike pole, and the lines made fast to the outside of the boat after being removed from the board. The latter is usually secured alongside a pier or float, and the boat is placed on the railway. When painting and repairs are done and the boat is afloat, the centerboard is brought alongside, and the lanyard and fore-end line are secured. The board is then dropped underneath the boat. When the board sinks, it is held only by the two lines. With these, patience, and some profanity, the board is brought up into the case and adjusted so that the pivot pin can be quickly driven. The operation is easier and quicker than the description indicates. The pivot-bolt is often of oak or locust in preference to iron.

The bateaux are surprisingly seaworthy craft and withstand extremely well the steep and dangerous seas met with on the Chesapeake, in the stormy months of the dredging season. Most of them are very fast sailers and work with remarkable certainty. They usually carry some ballast, which, with their great structural weight, helps in working. Their large area of sail, in a rather low rig, makes them move well in light weather, yet not lie over excessively in a breeze. Boats that sail on their sides would be useless as work-boats in the oyster business. The boats require intelligent handling, of course, and in spite of the usual explanation of the advantage of the V-bottom, they pound when upright as most boats will when shallow forward. Heeled, as in the sharpies, they do not pound much. The type, in the small sizes of hull, will not allow much headroom in the cuddy, and the boats are as sensitive to windage as are the sharpies. Attempts to make a working bateau into a roomy yacht have resulted in some shocking failures and have spoiled many good boats of the type.

The bateaux have continued in use as work-boats in Maryland waters because of a law there that permits dredging to be done only under sail. This was intended to prevent depletion of the beds by power-dredging and to keep the business in the hands of small, independent operators. In the last the law has been successful, but the beds are being depleted because of the number of boats employed and the size of the dredges now permitted. It seems probable that, in a relatively short time, the law may be repealed in favor of private ownership of beds and power-dredging. This will have the usual result of bringing about the extinction of the sailing dredge and of the individual operator, in favor of companies and power craft.

The V-bottomed hull was used on the Atlantic Coast side of the Virginian Eastern Shore in a small sailing skiff of distinctive form and rig. The boats built at Chincoteague Island were half-decked, V-bottomed skiffs marked by very great flare in the sides, light construction, and an unusual rig. Figures 118 and 119 show these boats and their rigs. Most of them were square-sterned, but a few had the round, vertically staved stern of the New Haven sharpie and the Tangier Island skiffs. The boats sailed very well and were used for tonging and crabbing, and, in more recent times, for taking out fishing parties.

The hull is rather wide in proportion to length, and the midsection shows a good deal of rise to the floors, with very marked flare in the topsides. The flare is so great that the sheer strake does not reach the stem but runs out on the sheer-line in some boats. The model is a good one for speed and seaworthiness, and the Chincoteague skiffs had a fine reputation. The construction is that used on the Chesapeake except that no hewn keelson is provided; instead, a plank serves the purpose, and there is a molded keel running the full length of the bottom with the centerboard slot cut through it. The strongbacks of the Bay bateaux were not used, and the whole structure is much lighter in the Chincoteague boats.

The rig is two-masted, with a large foresail, which is a leg-of-mutton, fitted with a sprit and short clew club and with a short gunter-staff at the head. The mast for this sail stands nearly plumb and is well forward in the boat. The mainmast, or more properly, perhaps, the mizzen, is much shorter and stands with a rake aft. It has a simple leg-of-mutton sail sheeted to a V-outrigger over the stern. The rig was obviously designed for single-handed sailing and is a very good one.

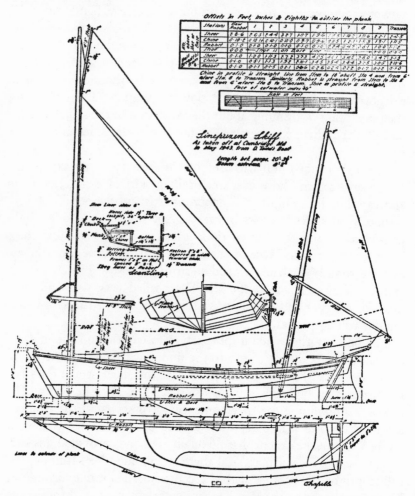

Fig. 118. Type of V-bottomed skiff built at Chincoteague Island, Virginia, for fishing. Only two boats were alive in 1951.

The boats were rarely very large, and the majority ranged in size between 16 and 26 feet on deck. A few were built larger— up to 40 feet, it is claimed—at Chincoteague Island. None of the boats in recent years have had cuddies. The model seems to have developed from a flat-bottomed skiff, and sailing skiffs having the characteristic sheer, raking bow, and stern of the Chincoteague V-bottom may still be seen occasionally. The latter skiff is apparently a rather late development, and I was told that it appeared in the present century, about 1905. Three builders, John Richardson, Jake Dunning, and William Wimbrough, are said to have built all of the V-bottomed skiffs on Sinepuxent Bay. In 1951, two or three of the Chincoteague V-bottomed skiffs were still in use at Ocean City, Maryland. The power-garvey has almost completely replaced the old V-bottomed Chincoteague boats on Sinepuxent Bay.

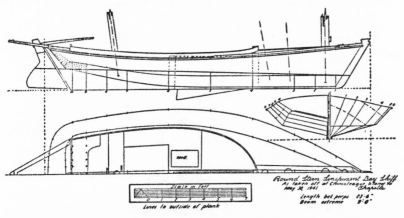

Fig. 119. Chincoteague skiff with a round stern of a form once used by some Chesapeake Bay bateaux.

The V-bottomed sailing hull spread southward from the Chesapeake, and skiffs were built at Beaufort, North Carolina, on the same construction methods as used at Smith Island in the Chesapeake. The Beaufort skiffs are open and are rigged with a spritsail and, sometimes, a jib. These skiffs are narrow and undecked; they have a shallow block forefoot, as they carry their dead rise into the extreme bow.

In Florida, V-bottomed sailing craft were used near Jacksonville; these had hulls like the Potomac River dory boat or northern skipjacks. They had the same high chines and were planked fore and aft over a complete set of frames; the bow was straight and plumb; and the transom usually had some rake. These boats were very heavily and roughly built of cypress and local yellow pine and do not appear to have been a type that had been developed locally. A number of these boats were actually built in Virginia, and it is probable that these were used as models by the Florida builders. The gaff sloop-rig was preferred in Florida waters to the two-masted, leg-of-mutton rig of the Potomac River dory boat. Toward the end of the sailing period, the V-bottomed hull form was employed in the sponging dinghies used at Key West and in the Florida Keys; these were planked fore and aft on the bottom and were modeled on the northern skipjack. A few were fitted to carry sail—usually the Bahama rig with the foot of the sail laced to a boom. These had no centerboard and depended upon a deep false keel to hold on in windward work.

Little has yet been found about the construction and model of the V-bottomed cats and luggers built by the Gulf Coast builders in the early 1880's. What is available suggests very strongly that the hulls were on the northern skipjack type, with a complete frame-system. The few photographs of the early craft are too indistinct to be satisfactory as evidence; they do show that the boats had a good deal of dead rise in the ends at least, and that they were nearly plumb-ended, like the New York sloop. Cat-rigged, V-bottomed work-boats were in use on the Louisiana coast as late as 1921, but these had obviously been influenced by the yacht model of skipjack that had become very popular between 1895 and 1915.

Gulf Scow Schooners

On the western Gulf Coast, the scow had been used for both coastal and river work since the first settlement of the Texas coast by Americans. These craft were either sloops or schooners, and it is apparent that, in the flat-bottomed scows, there had been no striking local development. The scow had been used in Southern rivers since the early nineteenth century; a sloop of this form was employed by the Carolina rice planters and both scow sloops and schooners were used to haul cotton and tobacco to market. These were centerboarders, and this indicates that the type became popular after 1840, approximately, as a sailing carrier.

The Gulf Coast builders soon developed a V-bottomed scow. This may have been either an adaption of the V-bottomed scow

sloops once used by the Carolina rice planters or purely a local
innovation, growing out of the skipjack. It is evident that the
V-bottomed scow model was not extremely old in this section of
the coast, even though the use of dead rise in the scow form existed as far back as the American Revolution. The idea may have
been preserved in large sailing scows, but in the small ones the
V-bottom seems to have come into use as late as 1890–95.

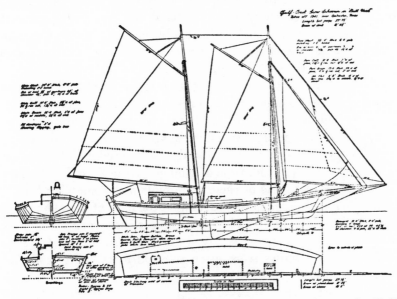

Fig. 120. V-bottomed scow schooner of a type once popular on the Gulf
Coast. (See Appendix for offsets and dimensions.)

Whereas the V-bottomed garvey was cross-planked, the majority of the southern V-bottomed scows have been framed and planked
lengthwise on the bottom. Therefore, the sledlike profile of many
of the northern scows is rarely seen in the south, where most of the
scows have deep transoms at bow and stern, with the bow transom
set at a great rake. In the south the lack of suitable timber
for steaming made for moderate fore-and-aft rocker and very
gently formed curves, to avoid breaking the planking of the bottom.

The area of greatest popularity of the V-bottomed scow seems
to have been westward of New Orleans and extended as far as

the Mexican border. The model most generally seen is flat-bottomed, or nearly so, amidships with increasing dead rise worked in as the bow and stern are approached. The schooner scows were between 32 and 50 feet long and often had a long-head.

Figure 120 shows the lines, sail plan, and construction sections of a good scow schooner of the Gulf Coast type. (The boat illustrated is rather more graceful than many of her sisters.) These craft sail very well and are often extraordinarily fast when light or partly loaded. They are cheap boats to build and can withstand very heavy going for they are very strongly built and are buoyant and lively in a sea. The model of these scows may still be seen in some powerboats on the Gulf today.

The schooner rig of these scows is conventional. They were heavily canvased, though not excessively lofty. A few scow schooners were built with round bilges, but these were comparatively rare —indeed, economically and practically, no excuse existed for the round-bilged scow unless high speed was required in light weather. There were a few of this type of sailing scow built in Texas, and it may well be that some of these were built with some illegal use in mind, such as smuggling or poaching in the days of sail. The scows have had various local nicknames; those sloops once used in the stone trade in Massachusetts Bay were called "square-toe frigates," while the Gulf scows were often referred to as "butt-heads," or "butt-headers."

Port Isabel Scow Sloops

There was a very numerous type of scow sloop used in fishing at Port Isabel, Texas, that remained in use until quite recently. These sloops were from about 26 to 32 feet in length and 10 to 12 feet beam. They were decked and had a trunk aft, if used in fishing. As the boats did not have accommodation for the fishing gang, some boats were fitted with a removable trunk cabin forward and were used as camp-boats, to take care of the additional men. When built as camp-boats, the scow sloops were often beamier than when intended primarily as fishing boats. The sloops were often very smart sailers and, though rough in build and finish, were not ugly craft as were some scow sloops in northern waters.

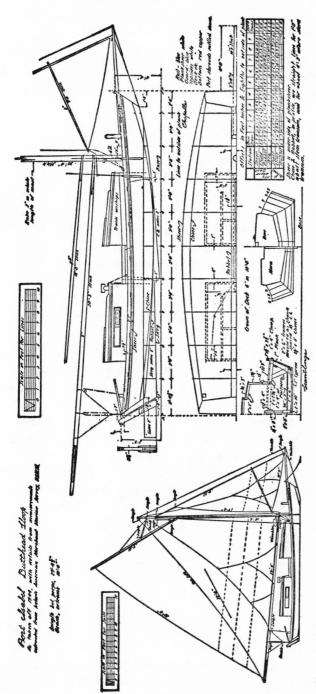

Fig. 121. Texas scow sloop fitted as a camp boat, used in fishing near the Mexican border on the Gulf Coast. Some of these scows are without dead rise. The boats range from 26 to 35 feet in length, 10 to 12 feet beam. The mast is usually stayed with the head sprung forward.

Figure 121 shows the plan of one of the Port Isabel butt-head sloops built for fishing. She has a removable fore-trunk so that she could be used as a camp-boat. The rig is the gaff-mainsail-and-jib, with the mast stepped plumb, or even with a slight rake forward. The use of a sprit on the jib, in place of the common club or boom, gives the advantage of having the sail stand properly without much attention being given to the location of the sheet leads. The sails are fitted with a complete and rather complicated system of lazy-jacks, reminiscent of the Chesapeake Bay bateau rig. The crews of these scows were commonly of Mexican nationality or descent, and the boats were not always kept in a shipshape fashion, but they seem to have been very well handled. The drop-blade rudder appears to have been a most effective fitting, though crudely made. The scows worked in very shallow waters at times, and so the skegs were not as deep as in most V-bottomed types; the Port Isabel sloops have, therefore, the very long centerboards seen in sharpies of equally shoal draft.

The Gulf scows were built of the local yellow pine and cypress, and near the Mexican border mesquite knees were used instead of cypress crooks. The scows were usually built upside-down, using a few feanes and the end-transoms as molds, as in the garveys. The moderate dead rise and absence of twist in the bottom made the boats easy to build. The majority of Gulf Coast scows retained the chine logs in construction; this may have been a feature remaining from earlier scows, which were cross-planked on the bottom, for, as has been noted, most of the southern skipjacks were built without chine logs. The V-bottomed scow came into existence for the same reasons that created the Chesapeake flattie.

The V-bottomed Garvey

The New Jersey garvey is another scow-type employing dead rise. It is uncertain when the V-bottom came into popularity in this type, but it was apparently quite late, perhaps after 1900. A V-bottomed sailing garvey is shown in Figure 122; this boat had been converted to power, and so her rigging details are drawn from her owner's notes and statements. The boat was built in New Jersey about 1906 and was brought to Chincoteague in 1921. She was con-

verted to a powerboat in 1927. The boat is rather yachtlike and is
somewhat similar to a large hulk of the same type seen at Tuckerton, New Jersey, in 1950.

The construction is shown in the plan; the bottom was planked
square across, except at the bow. The garveys on this build were

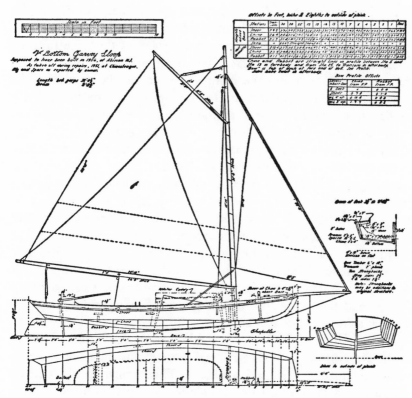

Fig. 122. A yachtlike V-bottomed garvey, the most developed model of the
type, now almost extinct.

noted for speed under sail and most of them were sloop-rigged as
shown. The same model, with a deeper transom, is now popular
as a motorboat. The greater part of the power garveys in southern
New Jersey, Delaware, Maryland, and at Chincoteague are now
V-bottomed to some degree, and this type seems to be slowly spreading to the southward. In most of these the bow retains the shallow
V-form, as shown in Figure 122, but some are square across at

deck. In some the bottom is flat, except in the vicinity of the fore
end of the load waterline. Here the bottom is made of thick plank
dubbed into a shallow V-shape and faired each way, fore and aft,
into the flat bottom; the whole is usually confined to three or four
feet of bottom.

In discussing the V-bottom, reference has been made to the
"northern skipjack," a term intended to indicate craft similar to
the Long Island V-bottomed sloops and those of the same form to
the eastward, the "corner boats." The apparent relationship in structure between these and the colonial bateau can be seen: the absence of the chine log and the fashioning of the side timbers out
of knees, which are secured to the bottom futtocks at the chine.
The appearance of the V-bottom in the Revolution and in some
Canadian lumber bateaux, in the modified sharpie style of hull, suggests that the V-bottom was produced step by step from the
colonial type. Yet this attractive and orderly development cannot
be supported by available evidence, and it seems very certain that
the development of the V-bottom in American work-boats did
not take place in a single area or section of the coast alone and that
there was much local evolution that did not occur through copying of a "master invention." The rise of the V-bottom in the South
can be attributed to the lack of good timber for steam-bending
locally and the gradually increasing cost of sawn-frame construction, in some sections at least.

One variation of the V-bottomed hull-form that is now common
is the arc-bottom. It is seen in small-boat sailing types of the Star
Class and many other racing classes. This form is really that of
the modified sharpie, with the moderate V replaced by an arclike
rounded bottom. The bottom is usually formed over curved floor
timbers, and the form has been shown in one of the sneak boxes
presented earlier. Another mode of construction made use of a
sawn keelson and rather deep sister-keelsons, about half-way between the centerline of the hull and the chines. Over these, the bottom plank was sprung athwartships. This could only be done when
the curve athwartships in the bottom was very slight. The purpose
of the arc-bottom was to obtain speed in light airs, but it seems
doubtful if this bottom is any more effective than the common
V-bottom of the modified sharpie form. The arc-bottom was in-

troduced in small racing classes by Huntington and Clapham (the latter should perhaps receive credit for the innovation) on Long Island Sound about 1890–92. A few boats were built on the arc-bottom style as working craft. Clapham built one with a straight, plumb stem and very raking and narrow transom. The boat, as designed, was rigged with Clapham's yawl-rig, which employed a gunter mainsail. Huntington built two arc-bottomed, working sharpies, which were like the New Haven square-sterned sharpie in rig and hull, except for a slight arc athwartships in the bottom and somewhat more beam in proportion to length than in the old flat-bottomed type. A few scattered craft were reported to have been built by others, but the model had only a short-lived popularity for it was more expensive than the modified sharpie and the flat-bottomed hulls; furthermore, it appeared only a short time before the gasoline motor began to drive out sail in working craft.

Whether or not Long Island Sound and the Cape Cod shore deserve the credit for the "reinvention" of the V-bottomed sailing hull is open to a difference in opinion, but it is certain that these sections of the coast had a great deal to do with the sudden rise in popularity of this hull-form. In any event, the rise of the various V-bottomed forms appears to have taken place nearly simultaneously in work-boats and yachts, beginning in the early 1890's. But in the work-boat models, the trend was toward cross-planking and low-cost build in most cases, while yachting practice held to the more costly and more difficult-to-build northern-skipjack construction. Hence, the yacht V-bottom is not looked upon by professional boatbuilders as being a "cheap type" in spite of that very common assumption to the contrary, by many yacht designers and writers. Even when the work-boat builder felt moved to use the longitudinally planked bottom of the northern skipjack, he successfully omitted the costly and troublesome details that so often plague the yacht builder. For example, V-bottomed sailing yacht designs often require a massive molded and rabbeted keel, whereas the work-boat had either a plank keel or a heavy squared keelson without a rabbet. The yacht often has a shallow forefoot and a strongly cutaway and curved stem. This creates a great twist forward in the garboard, and the difficulty is made greater by the feather-thin forward end of the strake. The work-boat, planked fore and aft on the bottom, retained the straight stem and angular forefoot and also used a great deal of dead rise as the bow was approached. When the shallow forefoot was used, as on the Chesapeake, the work-boat builder resorted to "chunk" construction or vertical staving. The modified sharpie form was much neglected in yachts since Clapham's day and has only recently been revived. Work-boat builders have used it in some sections at least since the 1890's.

CHAPTER 8

ON Building Boats

LOCAL ideas on boat construction often affect the choice of model and building method when an amateur undertakes to build a boat. The modern professional boat carpenter is often narrow in his experience and views. The "chunk" forefoot of Maryland would be objected to very strongly by most New England carpenters, usually on highly imaginary grounds; on the other hand, the Marylander would object equally to the thin, bent frames and the schooner stern of the Friendship sloop. It is desirable, therefore, to take local advice with some caution.

It is unnecessary to detail the modes of construction to be followed in all of the designs that have been shown; a number of books on boatbuilding give all desirable information on each step in building a boat of any specific model. It may be well to emphasize again, however, the fact that "good construction" is not adherence to a narrow selection of material and building methods; it is, rather, the use of the materials and methods best suited to the boat's model and to the pocketbook, with a realistic view of the requirements of its use and life that are to be expected.

The selection of rig and fittings follows the same rule as the hull; and in this matter it should be borne in mind that it is foolish to build a cheap hull and then spend a very large sum on the rig if a low-cost boat is the aim. Yet this practice is seen time and again and grows out of the urge to "improve" a basic design as well as from a slavish acquiescence to yachting fashion without respect to actual use requirements and economic common sense. But even in a very low-cost boat, the builder does well to loft the hull carefully and set up his molds correctly and securely, for then a boat goes together without trouble and annoyance.

The time to change one's ideas about a boat's form, rig, and fittings is in the planning stage, not after construction is started. It is necessary, then, not only to choose the right plans but to figure out each building step in advance and to have the required tools in hand and to carry out the plans properly without needless improvisations.

In building any boat it is particularly important to have proper clamps and other means of twisting the plank so that it bears on the molds, as well as for holding each strake in place while fastenings are being driven. The twist in a plank must be made as it is bent around the molds, and some twist will exist in almost any design, even in the flat-bottomed hulls.

The reader must decide for himself whether or not it is necessary for his own requirements to follow yachting fashion and pay the concomitant price; but at least the alternatives have been suggested here in the variety of working-boats that have been discussed and represented in plans. There is a boat for almost any pocketbook if a realistic view is taken of practical pleasure sailing. Only in racing is there a justified acceptance of high costs, for experience has shown, time and again, that there can be no racing class, even in low-cost hulls, that does not eventually become relatively costly through "tolerances" and the constant pressure for rig and fitting "improvements." It seems to follow, then, that racing is an inherently expensive pastime and that its fashions are prime factors, when applied to cruisers and day sailers, in the increased cost of small boats. If this is understood, the first step has been made in obtaining an inexpensive boat, other than the racer. But this should not lead to an acceptance of "any old thing" in the way of a boat; one may still have a strong, long-lived craft that will sail well and satisfy reasonable needs, as the small working-craft of the past have shown.

Tuning Up

The need of making adjustments in the rig of a sailing boat in tuning up is well known to all practical boat sailors, but is often overlooked by a builder. It is often desirable to alter the rake of a mast during trial sailing. The best and most common way to allow this to be done easily is to fit the mast-heel tenon into a slot in the mast step. The heel may be fixed here by blocks fitted afore and abaft the mast heel in the slot, and these blocks may be nailed to the step if the mast is to be unshipped. By altering the blocks, the rake may be changed very quickly. A few boats are built so that the rake may be altered by shifting the mast at the partners or thwarts. These usually have a large mast hole in which the rake is established by use of the required size of mast wedges. A variant in small craft is to have a wooden plank, with the mast passed through it, which is bolted over the mast hole in a thwart. This plank, or "plate," is through-bolted on the top of the thwart. Often, a series of holes are bored in the thwart, so that the plate may be quickly shifted. Movable mast steps are least common; the best way of fitting these is to place the step between two longitudinal sleepers or beds and to bolt through-all athwartships. By having a number of holes in the beds, the step may be shifted and refastened. In passing, lag bolts should not be used to secure mast steps in any boat, for they lose holding power very rapidly with age.

The rig of a boat may require some changes as a result of trials. Before making changes, however, it is well to stretch the sails first. When this is accomplished, it is often necessary to shift the position of sheet blocks on deck. No rule that will meet all conditions can be given for placing these, so the blocks should first be placed with the temporary fastenings. After the proper position is found, they may be placed permanently, though, if it can be arranged, the deck blocks should be fitted so that they can be shifted to alternate positions at any time. Loose-footed sails require the greatest attention in this matter. However, in recent times poorly sheeted boomed sails are to be seen in most yachting centers. In these, the usual fault is the use of too short a horse or the placement of a sheet block too near the centerline of the hull on deck rather than in the fore-and-aft position of deck leads. With the sheet too near the centerline of the hull, the sail will usually show quite a twist in its leech on the wind, and the boom will lift. On the wind, close-hauled, this lead of sheet will back-wind the sail abaft the foresail in a two-masted boat, or the jib in a single-sticker. It seems very probable that there should be some experimenting with the fore-and-aft position of the sheet on boomed sails as well, though here the problem may only appear when the boom is quite short and the hoist great.

Alteration in the quantity and position of ballast is often very useful in tuning up. By ballasting a boat by the stern or, in reverse, nearer to an even-keel position, it is sometimes possible to change steering characteristics somewhat. Stability may also be affected by such changes. Some V-bottomed craft require a great deal of trimming ballast forward, where it is not advantageous for stability. Boats with full ends are usually ballasted so that the weight is well spread out fore and aft, but in a boat having very fine ends, as in a Tancook whaler for example, the weight should be well concentrated about amidships or slightly aft of this. In very shoal boats, such as the sharpies, the ballast should be spread out athwartships in most cases, to avoid piling it up and thus raising its center of gravity.

Boats that are uncertain in stays in choppy water may be benefited by additional ballast, but this may cause them to be slightly slower in light weather. Weight of gear aboard must be treated as ballast weight. Poor staying may be caused by a number of things: for example, improper sheeting (particularly of the head sails), or incorrect helmsmanship (through putting the helm over too fast, or, less commonly, too slowly). Few boats of the working types will "spin" on their heel, and so they must be sailed around. The New Haven sharpie, without a skeg, is an important exception. But her large balance rudder makes her sensitive to her helm, which should not usually be put down too quickly, particularly in a fresh breeze.

Staying qualities may be affected, in some craft, by fore-and-aft trim. Boats having long, rather straight keels are usually insensitive to trim and sail balance and are often slow in stays and turn in a rather large circle. Centerboarders are more sensitive as a rule and so require careful adjustment in trial sailing. In tuning up, make only one change at a time—*never more than one*. Know your type of boat as well as possible, so as to know what to expect in proper trim and balance.

If a boat carries very strong weather helm, it is a sign that her sail area is centered too far aft, or that her after sails are not standing properly. In the first case, try changing the rake of the mast or trim the boat by the stern. In the second, see if you can alter the set of the sail—if not, take it to the sailmaker. If a boat is light-headed, increase the rake or trim more by the bow and also watch the set of the foresail or jib. If she does not point up well, it is usually faulty sheeting in one or more sails. Make sailing trials in moderate weather, because you cannot tune up a boat well in very light winds nor in reefing breezes.

Some boats balance well when nearly upright but carry a strong helm when sharply heeled. This may be corrected sometimes by adding ballast and by reducing rake in the mast if the weather helm becomes very strong, as is commonly the case. In some craft this increase in helm appears to be inherent owing to hull-shape or rig proportions; if this is the case, the rule is to sail the boat without heeling excessively. V-bottomed craft often show a marked increase in weather helm when sharply heeled owing to chine form and other causes. Narrow, deep boats with lofty rigs have much the same characteristics.

A great deal has been written on the art of tuning up a boat; the foregoing is merely the bare outline of the fundamental problems and those of particular interest when building. Foreseeing while building what alterations may be required in the trials will save troublesome alterations in tuning up. Changes in rudder area are rarely required but may occur in extreme cases. In a centerboard boat be sure both sides of board and skeg are equally smooth, as this will affect pointing in light winds.

Seaworthiness

Since there are many American types of small sailing work-boats that were noted for seaworthiness, it is possible that some craft, influenced by these, will be built for open-water use or for long voyages. What is a seaworthy small boat? It is supposed here that such a boat is one that in all reasonable weather can keep to sea, without failure of the hull, rig, and gear, and without unduly endangering a competent crew; in short, a safe boat in skilled hands. Two points must be emphasized in the very beginning of a discussion of seaworthiness in boats under 40 feet on deck. The first is that no known type of boat can be considered *wholly* safe in heavy weather, for there are conditions of sea and wind that will overwhelm even the best surfboats and lifeboats. Fortunately, such conditions are relatively rare and, with forethought, can usually be avoided by small-boat sailors. The second is that a good boat is no more seaworthy than her crew—in other words, skill of handling is part of seaworthiness in small craft.

For a beginner, or a relatively inexperienced sailor, to venture out into a heavy sea and wind in any small boat is folly and invites disaster. To be reasonably safe under such conditions requires exact knowledge of handling small craft, and this can be gained only by gradually learning how to handle a boat, beginning in smooth water and working up to the more extreme conditions. There are many treatises on small-boat seamanship which will aid the beginner, but "book learning" must be supplemented by practical experience.

The owner of a seaworthy type of small boat sometimes suffers from overconfidence; disaster may result. Too much sail should not be carried in blowing weather. In spite of romantic ideas that "driving" a sailing boat in heavy weather is evidence of skill, the truth is that it is more commonly evidence of ignorance or foolhardiness. Not only may this practice lead to the boat being finally overpowered or placed in a position where she is likely to be, but it also exhausts the crew—and it is when a small boat's hands are very tired that accidents happen. There are rare occasions when it is necessary to carry a good deal of sail in heavy weather, but this is usually for a very short period. For instance, when caught on a lee shore, it may be very necessary to carry sail to beat off.

This brings up a well-known misconception about hull-form. Many think that a boat must have deep draft to be weatherly in heavy weather and so insist upon deep and relatively narrow hulls. Actually, weatherliness in heavy weather exists only when a boat can carry the necessary quantity of sail in blowing weather and remain in sailing trim, that is, at moderate angle of heel. A deep and very narrow hull will heel sharply when pressed with sail, even though she is in no danger of capsizing, and in this position her sails are not developing the required driving power and she is sliding off to leeward, owing to the inefficiency of her lateral plane when at excessive heel. Initial stability is therefore very necessary if a boat is to carry sail on the wind in a blow.

Self-righting qualities in a small boat are created by a combination of hull-form and weight distribution. In simple language this means that weights such as anchor, chain, tanks, stores, stove, engine, and structural weight—not just the ballast—must be low in the hull. If this requirement is met, and if the hull-form is of a suitable nature, a decked boat should be self-righting up to great extremes of heel. However, it must be remembered that a boat knocked down to a great angle of heel may be fatal to her crew, whether or not she capsizes. The crew may be washed out of her or she may swamp. Carelessness or ignorance may lead to such a disaster even in the most heavily ballasted and deep boat. Some well-known disasters in cruising yachts can be traced to such an occurrence.

Swamping in heavy weather is the most common cause of fatalities in small craft, power or sail. In an open boat this may happen because the crew have been careless for a moment, owing to weariness, ignorance, or overconfidence; or the boat may have been taken into a condition of sea and wind too great for her capabilities.

In decked craft, swamping may be traced to a number of causes, which, primarily, stem from overlarge deck openings or weak deck structures. Large hull openings such as hatches, skylights, ventilators, ports, or cabin windows, and the "half-house," or "shelter cabin" (usually called the "doghouse") into which a sea may pour, are common causes of such accidents. Large cockpits invite swamping, for they cannot clear themselves of water before the boat is swept by another sea, and finally the boat sinks through leakage in and about the cockpit itself, or through failure of the deck structures.

Weak deck structures have been all too common in cruising craft in recent years; the causes of this are the demands for comfort and convenience in normal summer cruising. So large doghouses, more or less open at the after end, large cockpits, large hatches or skylights, and large ports or cabin windows are used, even in craft supposedly suitable for exposed waters. Under very severe conditions, these large structures and openings may lead to swamping due to the inability to make them reasonably watertight or through damage to them from the blows of heavy seas. It would be improper to attempt to make large deck structures strong in a small boat by mere massive construction, for the top weight soon becomes prohibitive in its effect upon stability. Therefore, it is necessary to design all deck structures properly, and if it is found that strong, very tight structures cannot be obtained, they must then be suppressed.

Rig is a factor in seaworthiness. Mere small area is not evidence of sea-keeping ability. Many short-rigged cruisers and boats cannot sail well enough to be safe without the use of a motor in working in narrow waters. It does not appear to make any great difference what rig is used—if it is properly designed for heavy weather and is well understood by the boat's crew. Sloops, schooners, yawls, ketches, cats, and the less-known rig forms are to be found among the world's small working sailing boats that must face heavy weather. The one common characteristic in these is simplicity in gear and fitting. No matter how fetching the theoretical arguments in favor of a gadgety rig may be, the fact is that a complicated and highly mechanized sailing rig is inherently dangerous in heavy weather. No small boat, venturing far from shore and dependent on a sailing rig, is safe if her rig will not stand up under prolonged stress without constant attention and if it cannot be readily repaired at sea when relatively minor failures occur. Hence, there is need for excess strength, far and above what is required theoretically to meet sailing strains, for in a prolonged period of heavy weather it is impractical to expect the crew to maintain constant attention to the tension of stays and shrouds and the state of rigging aloft.

Deterioration occurs, and this must be liberally allowed for in determining rigging and rigging methods. All rigs have inherent faults and advantages, in theory at least, but all but the extremely light and complicated can be made to work well if they can be made strong, simple, and well understood by their users, and if they are of the proper sail area for the boat for which they are intended.

Above all, skillful handling is a major factor in the safety of small craft at sea or in rough water. Even bays, sounds, and lakes can often make up a very dangerous sea for a small boat if she is not properly built, fitted, rigged, and handled.

Appendix

Offsets in Feet, Inches & Eighths
to inside of all plank

	Stations	Bow	Cant A	1	2	3	4	5	6	7	Cant B	Transom
Height above Base	Sheer	4·8·0	4·1·1	3·9·2	3·5·3	3·2·5	3·0·6	3·0·0	3·0·2	3·1·3	3·3·4	3·7·6
	Chine	1·4·3	1·4·2	1·2·3	0·1·0	0·0·3	0·9·2	0·9·4	10·7	1·1·0	1·3·3	1·4·4
	Bottom of Skeg & Fin	1·0·4	1·0·4	0·11·4	*	*	*	*	0·4·6	0·3·3	*	0·1·4
Half-Breadth from Base	Sheer	0·0·3	1·5·6	2·2·4	2·10·6	3·2·6	3·5·4	3·4·6	3·1·4	2·7·6	2·0·2	1·0·1
	Chine	0·0·3	0·2·3	0·9·2	1·5·4	1·11·3	2·1·3	2·0·2	1·8·2	1·1·4	0·6·6	0·1·0
	Inside of Coaming	*	*	2·2·4	2·9·0	2·11·0	2·10·0	2·10·1	2·6·6	2·1·0	1·5·6	*

See Lines for shape of
top of Transom.
Sheer is underside of
deck
Chine is inside of bottom
plank

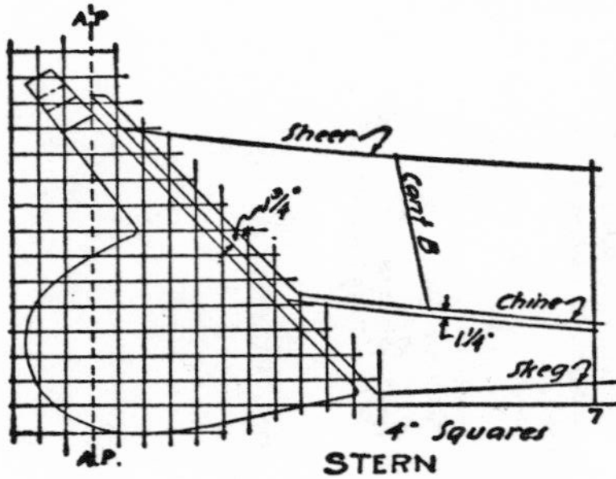

Stations spaced 2·6·0 except F.P. to 1·5·4·0 and 7 to A.P.= 6·5·4.
Cant A is 3·00 from F.P. at Sheer, 3·6·4 at Chine.
Cant B is 3·10·4 from A.P. at Sheer 4·3·4 at Chine.
Sheer intersects face of stem-liner (Hood-ends) 0·1·7 abaft F.P. and
4·8·0 above Base. Chine intersects face of stem-liner 3·2·4 abaft F.P.
and 1·4·5 above Base. Inside face of 1½ Transom is 0·2·0 afore
A.P. at 4·1·2 above Base; at chine it is 2·7·2 afore A.P. and
1·4·5 above Base.
℄ of Fore-mast crosses Sheer 4·1·0 from F.P; Chine 4·0·0
℄ of Main mast " " 1·5·4 abaft Sta 5 Chine 1·4·6
Fore end of Trunk is 6·2·4 from F.P. Trunk 5·8·0 long.

Sailing Dory (Two-masted)
Built at Gloucester in 1891

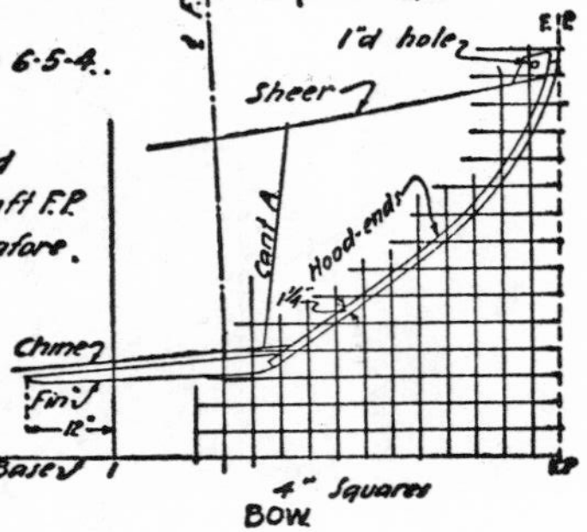

Frames are on Stations
Crown of Fore Deck 3" in 50"
Note:- Cant A is curved
and should be made
and fitted after hull
is planked.

STERN

Fig. 32A. Offsets and dimensions for two-masted sailing dory, Figure 32, page 93.

351

Offsets in Feet, Inches and Eighths
to outside of plank.

	Stations	Bow	1	2	3	4	5	6	7	8	9	10	℄ Stern
Heights above Base Line	Sheer	3·7·3	3·4·1	2·11·6	3·8·0	2·4·6	2·2·2	2·0·4	1·11·4	1·11·2	1·11·6	2·1·1	2·3·2
	Wale	3·4·2	3·0·5	2·8·0	3·4·1	2·0·6	1·10·1	1·8·3	1·7·3	1·7·2	1·7·7	1·9·5	2·0·0
	Chine	1·1·6	1·0·2	0·10·1	0·7·5	0·5·3	0·3·5	0·2·6	0·3·3	0·6·2	0·11·2	1·5·2	1·10·2
Half Breadths from ℄	Sheer	0·0·3	0·10·1	1·6·2	2·4·2	2·9·4	3·0·2	3·0·6	2·11·3	2·8·6	2·5·1	2·0·4	x
	Chine	0·0·3	0·5·7	1·2·1	1·8·6	2·1·6	2·4·2	2·4·5	2·3·6	2·1·6	1·11·2	1·8·1	x
	Coaming (at Face of Stem)	x	+	x	1·10·1	2·0·5	2·1·2	2·0·4	1·10·1	1·6·4	x	x	x

Stations spaced 2·6·0, F.P. to Sta 1 is 1·10·0. Hull is 26·10" bet. perps.
℄ of Foremast is 1·8·0 abaft F.P. at Sheer; 1·7·7 at Chine. Fore end of C.B slot is 8·2·4 abaft F.P. at Chine; after end is 16·9·2 abaft F.P. at Chine. ℄ of Mainmast is 17·3·2 abaft F.P. at Sheer; 17·2·7 at Chine. ℄ of Rudder Stock is 1·4·4 afore A.P. Fore-end of Hatch is 5·4·0 abaft F.P. at Deck. Hatch is 16"x16" inside. Fore end of Coaming is at Sta 3 and after end is 3·6·0 afore A.P. ℄ of 2nd Mast Position is 7·5·0 abaft F.P. at Sheer and 7·4·5 at Chine
Top of Stem is 3·10·0 above Base and 0·0·2 abaft F.P. Heel of Stem is 1·1·6 above Base and 0·4·1 abaft F.P. Stem Plates are 2⅜" wide at Sheer, 3¼" at Chine, of ⅜" Brass Plate. Stemband is ¼"x¾" Brass Bar
Stem sides 5¼ at head, 3" at heel. Top of Rail is 1¾" above Sheer and parallel to it.
℄ of Stern intersects A.P. 2·3·2 above Base and rounds at 1·11·0 radius along Sheer
℄ of Stern at bottom is 1·10·2 above Base and is 0·3·2 afore A.P. - rounds on 1·6·6 radius along Chine.
Chine in profile is a straight line from heel of Stem to Sta 3 (bulkhead) and from a point 4" afore Sta 9 to the Stern; the rest of the Chine fairs into these lines. Crown of Deck is 4" in 6·2.
Center of C.B pin is 9·1·2 abaft F.P. and 1·2·4 above Base. Top of C.B case is 1·8·0 above Base at fore-end, ℄ 6·0 at after end and the case is 8·0" long between head-ledges, along top.

Old One-man Tonging Sharpie of the 1870's from "B"

Fig. 38A. Offsets and dimensions for one-man tonging sharpie, Figure 38, page 106.

Offsets in Feet, Inches and Eighths
to outside of plank

	Stations	Bow	1	2	3	4	5	6	7	8	9	10	11	12	Stern ℄
Height above Base	Sheer	4·6·2	4·2·2	3·10·7	3·6·2	3·2·2	2·11·2	2·8·6	2·7·2	2·6·4	2·6·4	2·7·2	2·8·7	2·10·2	2·11·4
	False Wale	Bottom of Wale is 3 inches below Sheer and parallel to it in the profile —													
	Chine	1·9·4	1·7·2	1·5·3	1·2·5	0·11·0	0·9·3	0·8·0	0·7·7	0·8·6	0·11·4	1·4·2	1·10·1	2·2·0	2·4·4
Half Breadth from ℄ Base	Sheer	0·0·3	0·10·1	1·6·1	2·4·3	2·11·3	3·4·3	3·6·2	3·6·0	3·4·2	3·1·2	2·9·2	2·4·2	2·0·0	x
	Chine	0·0·3	0·7·3	1·1·2	1·9·5	2·4·5	2·9·1	2·11·0	2·11·6	2·9·2	2·6·5	2·3·3	1·11·5	1·8·1	x
	Inside of Coaming				1·6·1	2·2·5	2·5·2	2·5·5	2·4·4	2·1·7	1·7·6				x

Ht. of Chine at Bow is 0·1·0 afore F.P.   Ht. of Chine at Stern is 0·3·5 afore A.P.

Stations, beginning at F.P., are spaced:- F.P. to 1 = 2·3"; 1 to 2 = 2·0"; 2 to 3 = 3·0" and rest spaced 3·0, except 11 to 12 = 2·0" and 12 to A.P. = 1·7". The L.W.L is not parallel to Base and is up 174 on F.P. 1·6·6 on A.P.
Top of Stemband is 4·10·2 above Base, intersecting F.P. here. {Stemband is ⅜" fore-and-aft, ¾" wide and covers
Heel of Stemband is 1·9·0 above Base and is 0·1·1 afore F.P. here {stemhead; extending 4·2" under the bottom.
Top of Stern ℄ is 2·11·4 above Base, intersecting A.P. here. Top of Stern rounds on 2·1 radius.
Bottom of Stern ℄ is 2·4·4 above Base and is 0·3·5 afore A.P. here. Bottom of Stern rounds on 1·8¾" radius.
Side Plates of Stern after-edge is 3¼ abaft F.P. and parallel to it. Rail is 1⅜" above Sheer and parallel to it.
Note Chine is a straight line in profile from Heel of Stem to Sta 4 and from Sta 10 to Stern.
The rest of the Chine in profile must fair into these lines.
Moulds required for each Station.   34·10" bet. perps.

New Haven Sharpie, 35 Ft Class
Built before 1870 by Lester Rowe
Taken off by W.B. Yarnall + H.I. Chapelle 1949.

Fig. 40A. Offsets and dimensions for New Haven sharpie, 35-foot class, Figure 40, page 111.

Offsets in Feet Inches & Eighths
to outside of 1¼" Plank

	Stations	Bow	1	2	3	4	5	6	7	8	9	10	11	12	13	14	Stern ℄
Height above Base	Sheer	3·9·4	3·8·6	3·5·5	3·2·3	2·10·6	2·7·6	2·5·3	2·3·2	2·1·3	2·0·3	1·11·6	1·11·5	1·11·5	2·0·3	2·1·6	2·3·6
	Wale	3·7·2	3·5·4	3·2·4	2·10·7	2·7·1	2·4·0	2·1·3	1·11·2	1·9·3	1·8·3	1·7·6	1·7·3	1·7·6	1·8·4	1·10·2	2·0·4
	Chine	1·2·3	1·1·3	0·11·5	0·10·0	0·7·7	0·5·7	0·4·2	0·3·0	0·1·7	0·1·4	0·2·1	0·3·7	0·7·1	0·11·3	1·4·7	1·9·2
Half-Breadth from ℄	Sheer	0·0·4	0·7·0	1·4·2	1·11·7	2·7·3	3·1·0	3·4·5	3·6·5	3·7·0	3·6·4	3·5·2	3·3·3	3·0·5	2·9·0	2·5·0	x
	Chine	0·0·4	0·4·6	0·11·3	1·5·6	2·0·3	2·5·6	2·9·2	2·11·2	2·11·6	2·11·8	2·10·1	2·8·3	2·6·0	2·3·0	1·11·5	x
	Coaming	x	x	x	x	x	x	x	2·3·7	2·6·0	2·6·5	2·6·3	2·5·0	2·2·7	2·0·1	x	x

Ht. of Chine at Bow is 0·1·0 abaft F.P.   Ht. of Chine at Stern is 0·3·4 afore A.P.

Stations, beginning at F.P. spaced thus, 1 to F.P. is 1·2; 1 to 2 is 2·0; 2 to 3 is 2·0; 3 to 4, and others, all spaced 2·6.
Top of Stem Band is 4·2·6 above Base.; and intersects F.P. at this point. } Stem Band is ⅞ x ⅞, covers stem-
Heel of Stem Band is 1·1·7 above Base ; and is 0·0·6 abaft F.P at this height } head and runs 6·0 all on bottom.
Top of ℄ Stern is 2·3·6 above Base; and intersects A.P. at this point.   Top of stern rounds on 2·4·2 radius
Bottom of ℄ Stern is 1·9·2 above Base; and is 0·3·4 for'd of A.P. at this height.   Bottom of stern rounds on 1·0·4 radius
Side Plates of Stem are 2⅞ fore and aft at sheer and 3¼ at chine.
Note:- Chine in profile must be a straight line from heel of stem to 9·0" abaft F.P.
and from bottom of ℄ of stern to 6·9" for'd of A.P. The chine in profile must
fair into these lines.
Moulds to be made and correctly placed on stocks for each Station given here,

New Haven Sharpie built about 1900   35'2" bet. perps
as taken off at Fairhaven Sept 25 1928
by Chapelle

Fig. 41A. Offsets and dimensions for New Haven sharpie, Figure 41, page 115.

Offsets in Feet, Inches & Eighths
to outside of plank

	Stations	Bow	1	2	3	4	5	6	7	8	9	10	11	12	13	Stern	Stations
Ht above Base	Sheer	3·11·3	3·8·5	3·5·3	3·2·3	2·11·5	2·9·2	2·7·1	2·5·3	2·4·1	2·3·3	2·3·2	2·3·6	2·4·6	2·6·4	2·9·2	4 th above Base
	Chine	1·4·5	1·2·6	1·0·5	0·10·1	1·7·6	0·6·0	0·4·2	0·3·0	0·2·3	0·3·2	0·5·2	0·8·7	1·1·2	1·6·2	1·9·2	Base
Half-Breadths from ℄	Sheer	0·2·4	1·3·3	2·4·5	3·2·3	3·9·3	4·1·7	4·4·2	4·5·0	4·6·1	4·2·2	3·6·0	3·8·4	3·6·1	3·0·4	2·7·4	Half-Breadths from ℄
	Chine	0·2·0	0·11·2	1·9·1	2·5·2	2·11·6	3·4·1	3·6·2	3·6·7	3·5·3	3·6·4	3·4·4	3·2·2	2·11·6	3·4·5	2·5·3	2·3·2
	Inside of Coaming	x	x	x	x	3·1·3	3·4·3	3·5·3	3·7·2	3·2·4	2·11·3	2·8·0	x	x	x	x	x

Note: Offsets for Bow are at Rabbet

Stations spaced 2·6·0 apart. F.P. to Sta 1 is 2·5·3 and Sta 13 to A.P is 2·10·0. Boat is 35·3·3 bet. perps.
Top of Stem band is 3·3·2 above Base and 0·2·0 abaft F.P. here.} Stemband is ⅜ x 1" half-oval iron
Heel of Stemband is 1·4·4 above Base and intersects F.P here.}
Rabbet of Stem is 0·5·0 abaft F.P on Sheer and 0·4·6 on Chine.
Stern intersects A.P. 3·0·2 above Base, Bottom is 1·9·2 above Base and 1·4·0 afore A.P
Chine in profile is a straight line from heel of Stem to Sta 4 and from Sta 12 to Stern; the rest of the
Chine fairs into these lines
Built of Juniper plank, Y. Pine and Oak. Stem-liner & Cutwater used
Scantlings about the same as in a 35' New Haven Sharpie
Sand-bag ballast, estimated at 800 lbs.

North Carolina Sharpie, built about 1890
as taken off at Beaufort N.C. in 1927
by L. Huntington for H.I. Chapelle

Fig. 44A. Offsets and dimensions for North Carolina sharpie, Figure 44,
page 123.

353

Offsets in Feet, Inches & Eighths to outside of all Plank

	Stations	Bow	1	2	3	4	5	6	7	8	9	10	11	Transom
Height from Base	Gunwale	5·0·4	4·7·0	4·2·5	3·10·5	3·6·7	3·4·3	3·2·3	3·1·1	3·0·5	3·1·0	3·2·3	3·4·5	3·7·7
	Sheer of side	4·7·2	4·2·3	3·9·6	3·5·6	3·2·0	2·11·5	2·9·6	2·8·3	2·8·2	2·8·6	2·10·5	3·1·2	3·4·4
	Chine	1·8·2	1·6·0	1·2·6	0·11·4	0·8·4	0·5·5	0·3·6	0·3·3	0·4·4	0·8·0	1·2·2	1·9·4	2·1·6
Half-Breadth from ℄	Gunwale	0·2·4	1·6·7	2·10·0	3·10·4	4·6·0	4·10·7	5·0·7	5·0·2	4·10·1	4·6·5	4·2·0	3·8·3	3·2·4
	Chine	0·2·4	0·9·6	1·10·5	2·9·0	3·4·2	3·8·3	3·10·2	3·10·0	3·8·4	3·6·1	3·2·6	2·11·2	2·9·0
	Inside of Covering Brd	—	0·9·3	1·11·6	2·11·3	3·7·3	4·0·4	4·2·4	4·2·4	4·0·6	3·9·6	3·5·2	3·0·0	2·6·4

Face of Stem 0·0·5

Stations are spaced 3·0·0, except from F.P. to Sta. 1 which is 3·0·4. L.W.L. is 1·6·0 above Base.
Top of Stem band intersects F.P. 5·1·0 above Base (Stem band is ⅜" fore and aft, 1¼" athwart) and comes in over Stem 8½"
Bottom of Stem band is 1·7·9 above Base and 0·11·2 abaft F.P. Stem band extends 31" aft, under bottom.
Face of Stem is 1¼". False Rabbet is 3¼ abaft F.P. at Gunwale, 1·5·0 at Chine. This is rake of stem-liner, on fore edge.
Top of Transom intersects A.P. 4·0·0 above Base. Bottom of Transom is 2·1·6 above Base and 1·4·0 for'd of A.P.
Inside of Covering Board in profile is ¾" above Gunwale. Top of Centerboard Case is 3·10·0 above Base at fore end, 3·8·2 at after end.
Note: Chine in profile must be a straight line from heel of Stem to Sta 3 and from Sta 10 to bottom of the Transom. The rest of the chine must fair into these lines.
Moulds to be made and properly placed on stocks at each Station given here.

Ohio Pound Net Boat,
1888
36·0½" bet. perps.

Fig. 47A. Offsets and dimensions for Ohio pound net boat, Figure 47, page 129.

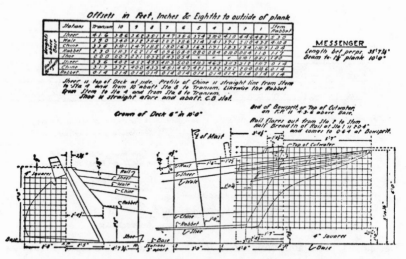

Offsets in Feet, Inches & Eighths to outside of plank

	Stations	Transom	10	9	8	7	6	5	4	3	2	1	Stem Rabbet
Height above Base	Sheer	4·1·6	3·8·6	3·8·2	3·8·1	3·4·7	3·5·6	3·7·4	3·9·0	4·1·3	4·4·6	4·8·7	5·3·0
	Wale	3·9·0	3·4·0	3·1·8	2·8·4	2·11·2	3·1·6	3·1·4	3·4·1	3·7·1	3·11·0	4·3·5	4·10·0
	Chine	2·6	2·10·1	2·4·7	1·11·5	1·8·0	1·6·3	1·6·3	1·7·1	1·8·3	1·9·4	1·10·7	1·11·8
	Rabbet	2·3·0	1·11·3	1·6·2	1·1·4	0·9·6	0·6·0	0·8·0	0·10·0	1·0·0	1·0·4	1·1·0	1·1·7
Half-Breadth from ℄	Shoe	0·0·0	0·0·7	0·2·1	0·3·2	0·4·3	0·5·4	0·0	0·10·1	0·8·1	1·0	
	Sheer	3·3·6	4·0·2	4·5·2	4·9·3	4·11·3	5·0·0	4·10·3	4·6·3	4·1·2	3·7·1	3·0·1	0·1·4
	Chine	3·1·7	3·7·2	4·0·0	4·3·3	4·5·1	4·4·7	4·2·1	3·8·2	3·2·0	2·6·0	1·9·6	0·1·4
	Rabbet	0·1·4	0·1·4	0·1·4	0·1·4	0·1·4	0·1·4	0·1·4	0·1·4	0·1·4	0·1·4	0·1·4	0·1·4

MESSENGER
Length bet. perps. 35'7¼"
Beam to 1¼ plank 10'0"

Sheer is top of Deck at side. Profile of Chine is straight line from Stem
to Sta 4 and from 10 abaft Sta 6 to Transom. Likewise the Rabbet
from Stem to Sta 4 and from Sta 6 to Transom.
Shoe is straight afore and abaft. C.B. slot.

Crown of Deck 6" in 10'·0"

Bed of Bowsprit, or Top of Cutwater
on F.P. is 4·3·6 above Base.
Rail flares out from Sta 9 to Stem
Half Breadth of Rail at Sta 11 is 0·0·4
and comes to 0·6·4 at Bowsprit.

Fig. 116A. Offsets for Chesapeake Bay bateau *Messenger*.

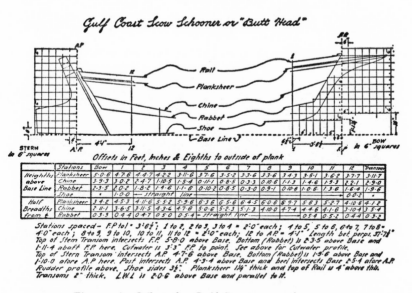

Gulf Coast Scow Schooner or "Butt Head"

Offsets in Feet, Inches & Eighths to outside of plank

	Stations	Bow	1	2	3	4	5	6	7	8	9	10	11	12	Transom
Heights above Base Line	Planksheer	5·0·6	4·7·6	4·4·7	4·2·2	3·11·6	3·7·6	3·5·2	3·3·6	3·3·6	3·4·3	3·5·1	3·6·2	3·7·7	3·11·7
	Chine	3·9·3	3·0·2	2·4·7	1·10·5	1·5·4	0·11·1	0·8·5	0·3·3	0·10·6	1·1·3	1·4·6	1·9·3	2·2·1	2·9·0
	Rabbet	2·3·5	2·0·2	1·8·2	1·4·6	1·1·6	0·10·2	0·8·5	0·3·0	0·9·1	0·10·6	1·0·6	1·3·6	1·6·4	1·9·6
	Shoe	·	1·0·0	→ straight	line		·					·	0·0·2		·
Half Breadths from ₵	Planksheer	3·4·2	4·5·3	4·11·6	5·5·2	5·9·6	6·3·6	6·5·6	6·4·5	6·0·6	5·9·7	5·6·3	5·2·7	4·10·6	4·1·2
	Chine	2·11·1	3·6·5	3·11·5	4·3·6	4·7·6	5·0·6	5·2·3	5·1·3	4·10·0	4·7·4	4·4·6	4·1·6	3·10·4	3·5·4
	Rabbet	0·3·3	0·4·4	0·4·7	0·5·0	0·5·4	→ straight	line				0·5·4	0·5·2	0·4·4	0·3·2

Stations spaced — F.P to 1 = 3'·8⅞"; 1 to 2, 2 to 3, 3 to 4 = 2'·0" each; 4 to 5, 5 to 6, 6 to 7, 7 to 8 = 4'·0" each; 8 to 9, 9 to 10, 10 to 11, 11 to 12 = 2'·0" each; 12 to A.P = 4·1" Length bet. perps. 51'·7½"
Top of Stem Transom intersects F.P. 5·8·0 above Base. Bottom (Rabbet) is 2·3·5 above Base and 1·11·4 abaft F.P. here. Cutwater is 3'·3" F.P. to point. See above for Cutwater profile.
Top of Stern Transom intersects A.P. 4·7·6 above Base. Bottom (Rabbet) is 1·9·6 above Base and 1·10·0 afore A.P here. Post intersects A.P. 4·3·4 above Base and heel intersects Base 2·5·4 afore A.P.
Rudder profile above. Shoe sides 3½". Planksheer 1¼" thick and top of Rail is 4" above this. Transoms 2" thick. L.W.L is 2·0·6 above Base and parallel to it.

Fig. 120A. Offsets for Gulf Coast scow schooner.

Index

Abaco (Bahamas), 226
Accomac County, Va., 314
Adirondack skiff, 216-217
"Adirondak Murray," 126
Admiralty, plans, 11, 20, 27, 35
Alaska, 188
Albemarle Sound boat, 257-261
Albemarle Sound rig, 260-261
Alice, 142
Amesbury, Mass., 87, 145
Anderson, R. C., 20
Apalachicola, Fla., 286
Arc bottom, 338, 339
Armed sharpie, 125-126
Atlantic Coast, 45, 65, 122, 131

Bahama dinghy, 226-229
Bahama sail, 228-229, 332
Bailey's Island, Me., 137
Baker, Mathew, *Fragments of English Shipwrightry, circa* 1584, 11-14
Balance jib, 103, 300
Ballast, 92, 101, 130, 136, 162, 171, 174, 202, 208, 226, 246, 250, 252, 261, 289, 344, 345
Bank dory, 85-90
Barge, 9, 11, 17, 22, 23
Barnegat Bay, N.J., 53, 61, 96, 208, 209, 256
Barry, Paul James, 178
Bateau, 17, 33-38, 45-47, 50, 80-82, 85, 102, 309, 323-324, 328-329, 338
Bath, Me., 72-74
Bay of Fundy, 71
Beach gear, 172
Beach operations, 172, 208

Beach skiff, 46, 94-97, 206-209, 257
Beaufort, N.C., 122-133, 331
Beetle, boatbuilders, 191, 198
Bell, Fred, 97
Bermuda, 16, 78, 231-240
Bermuda dory, 78
Bermuda rig, 236
Bermuda sloop, 233-240
Bermudian sail, 229
Bêtes, 85
Beverly, Mass., 86
Birch-bark canoe, construction, 12, 17, 37, 218
Bishop, N. H., 211
Bivalve, N.J., 185
Black Pinnesse, 12
Block Island boats (cowhorns), 172-176
Boatbuilding, 10, 11, 16, 341-342
Boat-canoe, 13, 17
Boat timber, 36, 57, 58, 89, 94, 101, 104, 114, 128, 145, 149, 160, 166, 167, 179, 186, 188, 196, 198, 202, 203, 212, 218, 226, 236, 237, 252, 258, 264, 270, 272, 284, 288, 295, 326, 331-333, 336
Boom, 14, 19, 20, 92, 126
Boothbay, Me., 152
Boston, Mass., 17, 18, 20, 28, 29, 70, 92, 198, 223, 242, 278, 280, 282
Boston hooker, 278, 280, 281, 282
Bremen, Me., 86, 154, 155, 192, 266, 270
Bristol, R.I., 242
British Navy, 11, 18, 24, 37, 40, 234
Brownell, Alfred S., 242
Burlington, Vt., 126
Butthead, 334
Buzzards Bay, Mass., 252

Caïque, 516
Cambridge, Md., 309
Canada, 33, 34, 45, 131, 192
Cannow, 9
Canoe, 8, 9, 12, 15, 17, 36, 37, 38
Canot, 17, 37
Cape Ann, Mass., 90, 91, 92, 152, 170
Cape Cod, 67, 96, 252-256, 339
Cape Cod cat, 252-256
Cape Roseway wherry, 203
Caravel-built, 47, 80, 93, 136, 158, 185, 257, 268, 280
Carter, A. K., 270
Carrie V., 117, 118, 121
Carver boat, 178-185
Casco Bay, Me., 75, 137-140, 145, 148-150, 160, 200, 221, 222, 269
Cat boat, 232-233
Cathcart, James L., 41
Cat ketch, 65
Cat rig, 67, 68, 104, 155, 242-249, 255-262
Cedar Keys, Fla., 102, 124, 126
Centerboard, 50, 59-60, 69, 75, 90-93, 110, 113, 114, 137, 141, 149, 154, 167-171, 180, 185, 195-198, 206, 214, 245, 249-252, 266-269, 282, 284, 294, 295, 327, 328
Centerboard lifts, 59, 60, 113, 114
Chapman, F. R., Architectura Navalis, 1768, 11, 19, 22-28, 54, 78
Charnock, History of Naval Architecture, 12
Charnock collection, 20-22
Chase, Enoch, 137, 138
Chebacco boat, 20, 29, 38
Chesapeake, 13, 16, 17, 34, 37, 104, 133, 229, 291, 304, 308, 309, 329
Chesapeake Bay log canoes, 291-304
Chincoteague, 67, 329, 330, 331, 336, 337
Chine, 33, 34, 47, 49, 51, 52, 57, 75, 78, 100, 135, 261
Chinese, 39
Clapham, Thomas, 105, 122, 306, 312, 317, 339, 340
Clench-built (see Lap-strake)
Clipper dory, 92
Coast and Geodetic Survey, 117
Collingwood skiff, 178-180
Collins, Capt. J. W., 280
Colonial trade, 13-16
Columbia River, Ore., salmon boat, 186, 188, 189
Connecticut, 46, 76, 126, 200, 202
Construction, 10 et passim
Cooke, E. W., 233
Corsair, 234-236, 240, 242

Cost of boats, 66, 121, 136, 158, 188, 270
Counter, 136, 140, 152, 154, 158, 184, 266, 270, 326
Cowhorn, 172-176
Cradle, 29
Crammer, M. M., 210
Creole builders, 306
Crimps, 195, 198
Crisfield, Md., 103, 318, 319
Cross-plank, 36, 46, 47, 48, 52, 53, 78, 81, 82, 100, 133-134, 310
Crotch Island, 139, 145, 150
Cuddy, 20, 21, 67, 92, 240, 248, 265, 328
Cundy's Harbor, Me., 86, 139, 192
Cunha, Commander George, U.S.N., 174, 242
Cutter, 9, 13, 17, 18, 24, 25, 196
Cutter-model, 13

Dagger board, 39, 40, 64, 212, 214, 216
Dauntless, 173
Deadrise, 22, 23, 222, 223
Deal galley or cutter, 24, 282
Deal Island, Md., 103
Deck construction, 54, 58, 59, 64, 91
Deer Island, N.B., 262
Delano, boatbuilder, 170-171
Delaware, 22, 53, 67, 185, 203, 216, 337
Delaware ducker, 216-217
Dinghy, 12, 238, 240
Dodge, Trustrum, 173
Dogbody, 20
Dorchester County, Md., 314
Dory, 15, 17, 35, 36, 46, 47, 90-94, 170, 191, 223, 224
    sailing, 90-94, 152, 257
    weight of, 90
Dory-built, 47
Dory lap, 82, 87
Double end, 13, 27, 33, 46, 80, 81, 85, 102, 103, 104, 136, 138, 171, 173, 216, 287
Double moses boat, 29
Double shallop, 13, 29, 136
Doughty, David, 137
Dover Bay, Ohio, 128
Drag boat, 200, 202, 203, 252
Drop-keels, 40
Dudley, Sir Robert, 12
Dugout, 12, 18, 19, 36, 37
Dunning, Jake, 331
Durgan, P. A., 138-140
Dutch influence, 16

Eastport, Me., 222, 242, 261-265
Eastport pinkies, 261-265

Egret, 124
Elliot, Md., 310, 311
Elm bark, 12
End logs, 54
England, 8, 11, 14, 15, 29, 33, 34, 40
Erie, Penna., 131, 177
Erie boat, 177-178
Erismann, Martin C., 160, 162
Essex, Conn., 200
Essex, Mass., 20, 86, 90, 222

Fairhaven, Mass., 170
Ferry, 19, 29, 32, 289
Fish Commission (U.S. Commision of
  Fish & Fisheries), 126-128, 152, 217,
  265-266, 269, 280, 290, 306
Flare of sides, 25, 51, 54, 59, 128, 223, 329
Flat, 17, 29, 32., 33
Flat bottom, 12, 15, 16, 32, 33, 45-52, 80,
  82, 85, 86, 100, 133-135
Flat-iron skiff, 46, 100-102, 133
Flattie, 309-314
Florida, 117, 227, 276, 331, 332
Flying Cloud, 302, 304
Folding centerboard, 90, 195, 196
Folkard, H. C., sailing boat, 234
Forest & Stream magazine, 104, 105, 122,
  126, 140, 173, 209, 211, 249, 306, 310,
  317
Formosans, 39
Frames, 46, 47, 52, 58, 59, 78, 80, 87, 160,
  166, 218
Friendship, Me., 266, 270
Friendship sloop, 265-275, 341
Fundy, Bay of, 72
Fyke net scow, 76

Gaff, 14-19, 28, 42, 54, 55, 68, 76, 104, 117,
  126, 131, 144, 154, 211, 225
Galley, 9, 17, 25
Galley-frigates, 12
Galley-ship, 11
Galway hooker, 278
Gannon, Patrick, 278
Garvey, 38, 51-67, 78, 94, 122, 336-338
Gig, 25, 42, 196, 238, 240
Glory Ann, 174
Gloucester, Mass., 85, 86, 90, 92, 145, 222,
  242
Gondola, gondalow, gondolo, 32
Goode, 140, 185, 268, 286
Grand canots, 17, 37
Graves, New Haven boatbuilder, 114
Great Lakes, 45, 67, 68, 76, 177
Great shallop, 13

Greek Joe, 186
Greek sponge boat, 291
Green, Albert, 198
Green Bay, Ohio, 128
Greenland whaleboat, 23
Griffin, J. J., 186
Gulf Coast scows, 332, 333, 334, 336
Gunning skiff, 54, 64, 102, 133, 134, 193,
  194, 210, 215-217

Hall, *Tenth Census of the United States,
  Note Books,* 86, 126, 128, 152, 179, 180
Hallets, boatbuilders, 264
Halyards, 18, 56, 107, 131
Hampton boat, 137-141, 145, 150, 152,
  155, 162, 200, 269
Harpswell, Me., 137, 140
Harrison, John B., 300
Hayward boat, 178, 185
Hepburn, Andrew, Jr., 270
Herringbone plank, 311, 312, 326
Higgins and Gifford, 86, 87
Hillhouse plans, 29
Hiram Lowell, 87
Historic American Merchant Marine
  Survey, 182, 185, 198, 300
Hooper Island, Md., 103
Houari, 41
Hoy, 13, 15
Hudson River, 78, 203, 246
Hull, Mass., 158
Hull proportions, 56, 61, 62, 102, 116,
  128, 246, 324, 326
Hume, George and Robert, 186
Hunt, Hon. H. G., 234
Huntington, Larry, 118, 122, 124, 339
Huron, Ohio, 128
Huron boat, 177, 178, 184, 185
Hyslop, J., 173, 238, 248

Irish cutter, 278, 280, 281
Island Belle, 173
Isle of Shoals boat, 141-145
Italian fishermen, 92
Ives, George C., 122

Jangada, 40
Jay Dee, 300, 302
Jib, 14, 15, 54, 55, 90, 137
John boat, 33, 78
Jonesport, Me., 203, 220, 221

Keel, 10, 23, 25, 39, 48, 52, 53, 155
Kemp-Dixon, *Manual of Yacht & Boat
  Sailing,* 50, 105, 106, 173, 278

Kennebec River, Me., 74
Ketch, 22, 104, 137, 149, 182, 184
Keyport, N.J., 248
Kingston (Mass.), lobster boat, 158, 160, 162
Kittery, Me., 142, 145, 192
Kunhardt, C. P., *Small Yachts, Their Design and Construction*, 105, 117, 306, 310, 313

Labrador boat, 138
Lacing, 57
Lady Ussher, 234
Lake Champlain, 35, 45, 76, 118, 126, 305
Lake Erie, 68, 69, 70, 126, 131, 132
Lake Huron, 177, 178
Lake Michigan, 177
Lake Ontario, 178
Lake Superior, 177
Lant, T., *Celebritas et Pompa Funeris*, 1587, 12
Lap-strake, 25, 46, 47, 80, 82, 141, 154, 158, 180, 182, 185, 196, 200, 203, 206, 216
Lateen, 12-17, 22, 76, 286, 288
Launch, 10, 17, 20
Launcha (Spanish), 20
Leeboards, 16, 39, 40, 48-50, 72-74, 174-175
Leg-of-mutton, 14, 16, 17, 22, 41, 64, 76, 92, 98, 102, 104, 107, 117, 126, 132, 185, 211, 228, 229, 230, 231, 322
  unpopularity, 132, 133
Lena M., 173
Le Yacht, 106, 126
Lighter, 13, 29
Littleton, George, 126
Log canoe, 47, 50, 104, 121, 291-304
Longboat, 10, 17, 18, 20, 28, 29
Long Island Sound, 200, 229, 249, 250, 306, 339
Loomis, boatbuilder, 180
Loring, Paule, 174
Louisiana, 332
Lowell, Hiram, 87
Lucky, sharpie sloop, 104-105
Lug, 14, 15, 25, 42, 131, 211, 282, 284, 285

MacGregor, Chas. G., 270
Machias Bay, Me., 222
Mackinaw boat, 178, 180, 182
Maine, 12, 35, 37, 67, 72, 74, 75, 137, 138, 155, 204, 217, 222
Mainsheet horse, 276
Maître canot, 17

Mariners' Museum, Newport News, Va., 78, 110
Maritime Provinces, 45
Martha's Vineyard, Mass., 170, 252, 254, 306
Martha's Vineyard cat, 252, 254
Martha's Vineyard corner boat or skip-jack, 308
Maryland, 14, 78, 292-294, 337, 341
Maryland Historical Society, 14
Mass production, 86-89, 190-192
Mast rake, 343, 344, 345
"Masts and Yards," 15
Matinicus Island, Me., 140, 152, 170
Medieval craft, 33-34
Melon seed, 208-211
Messenger, 323, 324
Mexico, 45
Miami, Fla., 124
Mississippi River, 33, 97
Mitchell, Deacon Sylvester D., 173
Molds, 10, 36
Monhegan Island, 9, 152, 154
Monterey boat, 291
More, L., 125
Morris, E. P., *Fore & Aft Rig in America*, 9, 128, 144
Morse sloop, 266, 270
Moses boat, 17, 29
Motorboat magazine, 291
Munroe, R. M., 124
Murray, Rev. W. H. H., 126
Muscongus Bay, Me., 138, 152, 266, 268, 269, 275
Mystic, Conn., 37
Mystic Marine Museum, Mystic, Conn., 114

Nameless, 238
Nanticoke canoe, 292, 293, 300
Nantucket, Mass., 168
Narragansett Bay, R.I., 17, 240, 249, 250, 252
Narragansett sloop, 200
National Maritime Museum, 20
Nea, 238
New Amsterdam, 16
New Bedford, Mass., 170, 198
New Brunswick, 72, 74, 262
Newburyport, Mass., 86, 137, 144
New England, 11-14, 35, 76, 85, 102, 155, 162, 196, 223, 252, 282, 341
Newfoundland, 9, 138, 223, 226
"Newfoundland boat," 138, 223-226
New Hampshire, 137-142, 162

New Haven, Conn., 16, 17, 36, 46, 50, 104-107, 110, 116-118, 121-124, 128, 131-132, 192, 229-231, 300, 309, 317, 329, 339

New Jersey, 38, 51-53, 67, 94, 96, 206-212, 245-248, 256, 257, 336, 337

New Orleans lugger, 255, 282, 283, 284

Newport, R.I., 240, 242

Newport boat, 240, 242, 252, 262

Newport cat, 244, 252, 254

Newspaper advertisements, 17, 20, 21, 25

New York, 18, 19, 29, 32, 35, 96, 152, 192, 196, 198, 204, 244-252, 256, 282, 305, 306

New York sloop, 244-252

New York Yacht Club, 104, 238

Nicholson, Paul C., 174

Noank, Conn., sloop, 200, 249-252

No Man's Land boat, 168-172, 217, 220

Nonpareil sharpies, 306, 312, 317

North Carolina, 122-124, 257, 260

North Haven, Me., 138, 217

Nova Scotia, 93, 155, 223, 318

Oars, 204-206, 217

Oar ports, 25, 32

Ohio, 126, 128, 185

Ohio River, 33, 97

Orr's Island, Me., 155

Outrigger, 118, 142, 162, 330

Oversparring, 249, 255, 302

Oyster pirates, 324

Ozarks, 33

Pacific Coast, 45, 76, 85, 186, 198, 280

Painting, 21, 67, 113, 117, 196, 226, 260, 289, 290

Pamlico Sound, N.C., 257

Pâris, Vice Admiral, Souvenirs de Marine, 266

Passamaquoddy Bay, Me., 262

Peabody Marine Museum, Salem, 85

Peapod, 217-222

Pemaquid, 270, 274

Penn, William, 22

Periagua, 17-19, 32, 36

Perine, Samuel, 210

Philadelphia, Penna., 203, 216

Pink-sterned, 22, 137, 139, 150, 262

Pinnace, 9-14, 17, 22

Piscataqua River, N.H., 37, 76, 133

Pivot, centerboard, 59, 327, 328
  leeboard, 60, 73

Plank, 15, 19, 34

Plank keel, 155, 182, 196, 202, 206, 245, 252

Plat, 15, 34

Plymouth, Mass., 158

Poquoson canoe, 292-295, 300

Port Isabel, Tex., 334, 336

Portland, Me., 16, 76, 223

Portland, Ore., 276

Portsmouth, N.H., 37, 76, 133, 198

Potomac dory boat, 315, 331, 332

Powder-horn sheer, 152, 221

Prams, 34

Prattent, William, 234

Preble, Edward, Capt., U.S.N., 41

Proportions, hull, 56, 61, 62, 102, 116, 128, 246, 324, 326

Providence, R.I., 155, 170, 242

Providence river boat, 242, 244

Provincetown, Mass., 68, 70

Pump, 68-69

Punt, 19, 29, 32, 33, 36, 37, 54, 78, 79

Quebec, 81

Quincy, Mass., 78, 281

Racine, Ohio, 97

Radeau, 32, 305

Rafts, 39

Raising strake, 19

Rålamb, Åke Classon, Skeps Byggerij eller Adelig Offnings Tionde Tom, 1691, 10, 11, 25

Rambargo, 12

Ransom, Edward A., 158, 161

Reach boat, 137, 138, 202, 203

Reeves, William, 318

Rhode Island Historical Society, 174

Richardson, boatbuilders, 262

Richardson, John, 331

Rig, 9 et passim

River yawl, 97, 98, 100

Rocker of bottom, 25, 54, 80, 81, 89

Rockland, Me., 152

Rockport, Mass., 92, 223

Rose, John, 173

Rother (River), 34

Round stern, 112, 121, 245, 261, 309, 326

Rowboats, 193-195, 202-204, 218

Rowe, Lester, 114

Rowing, 61, 62, 81, 203-206

Royal Navy (see British Navy)

Rudder, 60, 61, 69, 72, 113, 128, 130, 131, 160, 255, 256, 336

Rudder magazine, 173

"Sacoleve," 291

Sacramento, Calif., 186, 198

St. Lawrence River, 15, 33, 34, 35, 76, 81, 102
St. Lawrence skiff, 178
Salisbury, Mass., 86
Sandbagger, 118
Sandusky, Ohio, 126, 128
San Francisco, Calif., 70, 188, 198, 256, 286
San Francisco Dago boat, 286-291
Saunders, boatbuilder, 250
Saybrook, Conn., 192
Schanck, Lt., 40
Schooner, 19, 35, 40, 41, 104, 162, 167, 168, 262
Schouw, 33
Scows, 13, 15, 19, 29, 32, 33, 38, 40, 45-48, 52, 53, 67-80, 305, 332-336
Scow schooner, 332, 333, 334
Sculling, 133, 229
Seabright skiff, 94-97
Seabrook, N.H., 86, 137
Seaman, Hazelton, 210
Searsport Marine Museum, Searsport, Me., 126
Seaworthiness, 135, 180, 226, 227, 261, 274, 275, 289, 328, 345, 346, 347, 348
Seine boat, 257
"Seneca," 211
Sennet, David Perry, 137, 139
Settee rig, 42
Shad boat, 200, 202, 203, 257, 265
Shallop, 9, 10, 13, 17-22, 38, 136, 193
Shallop rig, 22, 28
Sharpie, 36, 45-50, 104-118, 121-126, 185, 208, 215, 230, 231, 258, 261, 300, 317, 328, 338
Sharpie rig, 107, 108, 116, 117, 118, 177
Sharpshooter, 226, 228, 242
Shaw, J. P., 286
Shay, 140
Sheets, 55-57, 92, 107, 150, 264, 276
Shin-cracker, 76
Ship chandlers, 195
Ship's boats, 8-12, 17, 18, 22, 24, 41, 195
Shoulder of mutton, 14, 17, 228, 233
Sides, 58
Single halyard, 220, 240, 242, 244, 264, 266
Single leeboard, 48-50, 60
Sinepuxent Bay, 331
Sink box, 210
Skeg, 28, 29, 72, 75, 97, 158, 162, 179, 180, 196, 203, 245, 252, 258
Skiff, 9, 12, 15, 36, 45-49, 80, 81, 82, 85, 96, 102, 103, 223, 224, 226

Skipjack, 254, 258, 306, 308, 309, 323, 338
Sliding gunter rig, 41
Sloop, 9, 13, 16-18, 40, 41, 54, 68-70, 78, 102, 104, 117, 131, 152, 154, 158, 200, 232-240, 244-252, 276
Smith, Charleton, 160, 278
Smith, George, 97
Smith Island, Md., 103, 318
Smithsonian Institution, 123, 185
Sneak box, 54, 64, 209-215
Snotter, 56, 149
Solitaire, 158
Somerset County, Md., 314
Spanker, 14
Spars, 116, 118, 145, 231
Speed, 25, 62, 64, 69-72, 91, 92, 122, 130, 134, 135, 176, 180, 188, 189, 200, 203, 215, 237, 238, 246, 261, 289
Spencer shipyard, 14
Springboards, 117
Sprit, 41, 56, 107, 108, 116, 118, 149, 150
Sprit boom, 304
Spritsail, 14, 16, 22, 29, 55, 56, 57, 89, 90, 92, 95, 98, 101, 149, 150, 154, 158, 185, 195, 200, 203, 216, 217, 223, 229-231, 257, 260, 331
Spy, 117
Square sail, 14-16
Stability, 274, 275, 347
Stake boats, 68, 70
Stem, 10, 18, 22, 25, 48, 81, 87, 97, 128, 155, 218
Stephens, W. P., 105, 196
Stevens, John R., 40
Stickup rig, 293, 300
Stock boats, 188-192, 200
Stockless rudder, 70, 72, 73
Strip planking, 137, 155, 160, 218
Sturgeonhead, 78
Sturgeon skiff (Delaware), 185
Surf boats, 172
Swain, centerboard patent, 40
Swampscott, Mass., 91, 92

Taft, Ray, 160
Tancook (N.S.) boats, 162, 163, 166, 168
Texas, 332, 334
Tholes, 81, 203, 204, 225
Thwarts, 59, 81, 204
Tie rod, 112
Tilghman's Island canoe, 292, 293, 294, 295, 298, 300, 302
Tombstone, 87
Tools, 10, 11, 342
Topsail, 42, 126, 131, 184, 185, 260, 261

Toulinguet boat, 223
Transit, 117
Transom, 10, 18, 27, 28, 87, 89, 100, 101, 152, 160, 196, 258
Tuckerton, N.J., 53, 58, 64, 66
Tuning up, 343, 344, 345
Turkish caïque, 25
Two-mast boat, 20, 21, 22
Two-masted rig, 14, 17, 20-22, 28, 92, 102, 104, 107, 108, 126, 131, 177, 200
Types, 10, 16, 17, 37, 38, 42, 43

U.S. Army Engineer Corps, 97
Unstayed mast, 229-231, 250, 266
Upside-down construction, 57-58

Vargord, 15
V-bottom, 34, 46, 52-55, 78-80, 103, 135, 254, 258, 261, 305-309, 313-317, 329-333, 336-339
V-bottom construction, 315, 316, 317, 321, 322, 326, 328
Vineyard Sound, Mass., 168, 170
Virginia, 16, 21, 67, 292, 293, 294, 332
Vixen, 162

Walker, John, 150
Warren, R. F., 242
Waterboats, 242, 244
Watercraft Collection, Smithsonian In-
stitution, 128, 140, 152, 154, 170, 244, 266, 268, 281, 285, 286, 291, 306, 308
Watson, Nathan, 158
Watts, William, 178
Weaver, J. W., Sr., 97
Well, 158
West Creek, N.J., 210
West Indies, 13, 18, 19, 27, 78, 229, 233
Whaleboat, 17, 23, 41, 42, 137, 138, 173
Wheeler boat, 178, 185
Wherry, 17, 25, 26, 32, 195, 196, 202, 203
Whitehall boat, 192, 195, 196, 198, 200, 202, 203, 206
Whole molding, 11
Wickford, R.I., 250
Wicomico County, Md., 314
Williams, John D., 300
Wilmington, Del., 203
Wimbrough, William, 331
Winde & Clinkard, 198
Wingate, Md., 318
Woolwich, Me., 74

Yacht, Le, 106, 126
Yacht construction, 339, 340
Yachting magazine, 178, 318
Yarmouth, Me., 145, 150
Yawl, 17, 27-29, 104, 139, 186, 193, 222-224
Yoke, 92, 202, 208, 211
York, Me., 141

Books That Live

THE NORTON IMPRINT ON A BOOK
MEANS THAT IN THE PUBLISHER'S
ESTIMATION IT IS A BOOK NOT FOR A
SINGLE SEASON BUT FOR THE YEARS

W · W · NORTON & COMPANY · INC ·